T0369118

JESUS HEALS
TODAY!

JESUS HEALS
TODAY!

*Biblical Exposition and Contemporary
Testimonies of the Healing Power of
Jesus the Christ*

TOM CALDWELL

WESTBOW
PRESS®
A DIVISION OF THOMAS NELSON
& ZONDERVAN

WestBow Press books may be ordered through booksellers or by contacting:

WestBow Press
A Division of Thomas Nelson & Zondervan
1663 Liberty Drive
Bloomington, IN 47403
www.westbowpress.com
1 (866) 928-1240

ISBN: 978-1-4908-0347-0 (sc)

Library of Congress Control Number: 2013913779

Print information available on the last page.

WestBow Press rev. date: 10/24/2018

Contents

About the Author

Tom Caldwell graduated from the Southern Baptist Theological Seminary (M. Div., 1995) and was ordained as a Southern Baptist minister in 1994. He served as pastor of a small church in Louisville from 1994-2000. Tom later changed denominations and was ordained by the Assemblies of God in 2003. In 2001, Tom was introduced to Kim at a prison ministry function, and they married in December 2001. Tom and Kim have two daughters, Emma and Anna, whom they homeschool. Since 1998, Tom has served as a full-time chaplain in various prisons in Kentucky. He has seen many incarcerated men and women, in their brokenness, turn to faith in Jesus Christ and discover for themselves that Christ is the all-sufficient Supplier of every good and perfect gift. Tom has a passion to proliferate God's holy Word through his personal preaching, teaching, writing, and praying for others. Tom has also written a book on marriage: *Love, the Bond of Perfection.*

Acknowledgments

I want to take a moment to acknowledge my lovely wife, Kim, to whom I have been blessed to be married since 2001. God has given you to me as my helpmate, and best friend. Thank you, Kim, for your continual support of the ministry to which God has called me. I love you.

God has blessed Kim and me with two children so far, Emma (born in 2005) and Anna (born in 2007). Emma and Anna, Mom and I are so thankful to God to have you as our beautiful daughters. God's gracious work in your hearts is obvious, and I am truly grateful for your love for Him, for each other, and for us. I am proud of both of you.

I want to acknowledge my mother and father, Janet and Tom Caldwell, and my brother, Tim Caldwell, his wife, Sara, and their children, for being such a great blessing to Kim, the girls, and me. I thank Mom and Tim for editing a few of these chapters.

I want to acknowledge a close friend of mine, James Grant. Through the years, James, you have shared with me, at my request, many insights pertaining to the Word of God, and many of your insights are reflected in this book. Thank you, James, for your immeasurable contribution to my spiritual growth over the years, and especially for your valued friendship.

After I published the first edition of this book, I began to dig deeply into an excellent book, *Christ the Healer*, by an eminent evangelist, F. F. Bosworth (1877 – 1958). I was thoroughly enriched by what I read. So in this second edition, I have included quotes and insights from his book. I have truly been blessed by this very honorable servant of God.

I thank the Lord Jesus Christ, who died on the cross for the sins of the world and was bodily raised from the dead three days later. I thank my heavenly Father for graciously showing me of my infinite need of Jesus and for drawing me to Him when I was twenty-four years old. I thank the Holy Spirit for convicting me, comforting me, empowering me, and leading me every day. May You work in the body of Christ, in my family, and in me both to will and to do Your good pleasure. I ask this in Jesus' name. Amen.

Chapter 1

Proclamation and Demonstration

**"And they went out and preached
everywhere, the Lord working with them
and confirming the word through the
accompanying signs. Amen." (Mark 16:20)**

Testimony—God Heals a Man with Leukemia!

In April 1980, Jack, a friend of mine, was diagnosed with an aggressive type of leukemia and was given only six months to live. The doctors said if he took chemotherapy he may live up to two years. Jack exceeded those expectations, and in April 1984 he underwent a bone marrow transplant. Jack did relatively well until June 2002 when his leukemia returned. Jack was told that when a relapse occurs after a bone marrow transplant, one usually dies within a year. In November 2002, ninety-six percent of Jack's bone marrow was cancerous and he was feeling terrible. The doctor told Jack he would not live to see Christmas. Within a few days, Jack came across a Christian friend. When he told her about his grim prognosis, she asked Jack if he believed in James 5 and the practice of anointing the sick with oil. Jack, who also was a Christian, replied that he did. She said that if Jack would come to her house on Friday, she would arrange for some believers to come anoint Jack with oil and pray for him. When Jack arrived, eight people were present, including two pastors. One pastor poured an entire bottle of oil on Jack, and the group prayed for Jack to be healed. Jack said he didn't feel anything as they prayed, but he simply believed what the Word of God says: "Is anyone among you sick? Let him call for the elders of the church, and let them pray over him, anointing him with oil in the name of the Lord, and the prayer of faith will save the sick, and the Lord will raise him up. And if he has committed sins, he will be forgiven" (Jas. 5:14-15). Within days, Jack began feeling better. The following Friday, Jack's blood test produced amazing results: even though his red blood cell count was still low, his white blood cell count, which the week before was extremely low, was now at the normal level. The following week, another blood test revealed that all his blood cell counts were normal! In December, Jack was given a bone marrow test (bone marrow is extracted from the hip). The results revealed there was no trace of cancer in Jack! In June 2003, Jack went to the Markey Cancer Center at the University of Kentucky where another bone marrow test was performed. Again, no trace of cancer was found. Jack said he has had a blood test about every two months since 2003 (at least up until March 2008), and his blood has appeared completely healthy every time. Two doctors told Jack they had never seen anything like what they had witnessed in him. To God be all glory!

The Biblical Model for Evangelism

When one seeks a Biblical model for evangelism, one should begin by looking at the Bible's premier evangelist, Jesus. When Jesus began His public ministry as recorded in Matthew 4:23-25, His fame immediately spread and great multitudes followed Him. In fact, throughout Jesus' public ministry, the multitudes would often flock to wherever He was, so that at times He and the disciples could not even find time to eat or rest (Mk. 6:31-33), and so that at one point the Pharisees exclaimed, "Look, the whole world has gone after Him!" (Jn. 12:19). Jesus' attraction of people models what all evangelists should aspire to do: to preach and demonstrate the gospel with such power and effectiveness so as to appeal to the greatest multitudes possible (obviously without compromising the Word of God such as the requirement that people repent, Lk. 13:5). Therefore, let us examine Jesus' ministry as the model for evangelism.

I consider Matthew 4:23 to be the mission statement for Jesus' evangelistic ministry: "And Jesus went about all Galilee, teaching in their synagogues, preaching the gospel of the kingdom, and healing all kinds of sickness and all kinds of disease among the people." (This mission statement is reiterated in Matthew 9:35, likely for emphasis). I propose that Jesus proliferated the gospel through four main methods: *1) teaching, 2) preaching, 3) healing, and 4) casting out demons.* (Casting out demons is not mentioned in Matthew 4:23 or 9:35, but it is mentioned in the surrounding verses: Matthew 4:24 and Matthew 9:32-34. As demons and disease are closely related in Scripture, casting out demons is often an aspect of healing the sick. See Acts 10:38 and Luke 13:11.) Teaching and preaching constitute *proclamation* of the gospel; divine healing and casting out demons constitute *demonstration* of the gospel. I define *demonstration* in this sense as a *manifestation of God's power for the purpose (in part) of verifying the message proclaimed* (also known as "miracles, wonders, and signs," Acts 2:22). In addition to His healings and casting out of demons, the various miracles that Jesus performed such as changing water to wine, walking on water, and feeding five thousand men from five loaves and two fish are also considered demonstrations of the gospel. However, I propose that divine healing is the premier sign (demonstration) in the New Testament due to its high frequency, its being specifically mentioned in the Matthew 4:23 and 9:35 mission statements, and its being specified in Acts 4:29-30 in the disciple's prayer for boldness in gospel proclamation. John Wimber, founder and first pastor of the Vineyard Christian Fellowship, and co-author Kevin Springer, state: "Of the 1,257 narrative verses in the Gospels, 484 verses—38.5 percent!—are devoted to describing Jesus' healing miracles."[1] I count twenty-six separate healing accounts in Matthew, nineteen in Mark, twenty-five in Luke, and five in John. That adds up to seventy-five passages pertaining to divine healing found in the four Gospels. And John's Gospel suggests that Jesus performed many more healings: "And there are also many other things that Jesus did, which if they were written one by one, I suppose that even the world itself could not contain the books that would be written. Amen" (Jn. 21:25).

As we will see in the verses below, any thorough evangelistic model should include proclamation and demonstration of the gospel;[2] they go hand-in-hand. When signs and wonders (demonstration) manifest in conjunction with the Word being preached (proclamation), *then great evangelistic results often occur.*

Each passage below pertains to evangelism: Jesus' evangelistic mission statement, His commissioning of the twelve, of the seventy, and of the church (in Mark's gospel), as well as the evangelistic work of Philip in the city of Samaria. Notice how proclamation and demonstration of the gospel work together. Notice also that demonstration is comprised of either healing or casting out demons, or both, in each passage.

Matthew 4:23-25 And Jesus went about all Galilee, *teaching* in their synagogues, *preaching* the gospel of the kingdom (*proclamation*), and *healing* all kinds of sickness and all kinds of disease among the people (*demonstration*). (24) Then His fame went throughout all Syria; and they brought to Him all sick people who were afflicted with various diseases and torments, and those who were *demon-possessed*, epileptics, and paralytics; and He *healed* them (*demonstration*). (25) Great multitudes followed Him—from Galilee, and from Decapolis, Jerusalem, Judea, and beyond the Jordan.

Matthew 10:1, 7-8 And when He had called His twelve disciples to Him, He gave them power over unclean spirits, *to cast them out*, and *to heal* all kinds of sickness and all kinds of disease (*demonstration*)...(7) "And as you go, *preach,* saying, 'The kingdom of heaven is at hand' (*proclamation*). (8) *Heal* the sick, *cleanse* the lepers, *raise* the dead, *cast out* demons" (*demonstration*).

Mark 3:14-15 Then He appointed twelve, that they might be with Him and that He might send them out *to preach* (*proclamation*), (15) and to have power *to heal* sicknesses and *to cast out* demons (*demonstration*).

Mark 6:7, 12-13 And He called the twelve to Himself, and began to send them out two by two, and gave them power over unclean spirits...(12) So they went out and *preached* that people should repent (*proclamation*). (13) And they *cast out* many demons, and anointed with oil many who were sick, and *healed* them (*demonstration*).

Mark 16:15-20 And He said to them, "Go into all the world and *preach* the gospel to every creature (*proclamation*). (16) He who believes and is baptized will be saved; but he who does not believe will be condemned. (17) And these signs (*demonstration*) will follow those who believe: In My name they will *cast out* demons; they will speak with new tongues; (18) they will take up serpents; and if they drink anything deadly, it will by no means hurt them; they will *lay hands on the sick, and they will recover*" (*demonstration*). (19) So then, after the Lord had spoken to them, He was received up into heaven, and sat down at the right hand of God. (20) And they went out and *preached* everywhere (*proclamation*), the Lord working with them and confirming the word through the accompanying signs (*demonstration*). Amen.

Luke 9:1-2, 6 Then He called His twelve disciples together and gave them power and authority over all demons, and *to cure* diseases (*demonstration*). (2) He sent them *to preach* the kingdom of God (*proclamation*) and *to heal* the sick...(*demonstration*) (6) So they departed and went through the towns, *preaching* the gospel (*proclamation*) and *healing* everywhere (*demonstration*).

Luke 10:1, 9, 17-19 After these things the Lord appointed seventy others also, and sent them two by two before His face into every city and place where He Himself was about to go. (2) Then He said to them, "...(9) And *heal* the sick there (*demonstration*), and *say* to them, 'The kingdom of God has come near to you'" (*proclamation*). (17) Then the seventy returned with joy, saying, "Lord, even the demons are subject to us in Your name" (*demonstration*). (18) And He said to them, "I saw Satan fall like lightning from heaven. (19) Behold, I give you the authority to trample on serpents and scorpions, and over all the power of the enemy (*demonstration*), and nothing shall be any means hurt you."

Acts 8:5-7 Then Philip went down to the city of Samaria and *preached* Christ to them (*proclamation*). (6) And the multitudes with one accord heeded the things *spoken* by Philip (*proclamation*), hearing and seeing the *miracles which he did* (*demonstration*). (7) For *unclean spirits*, crying with a loud voice, *came out* of many who were possessed (*demonstration*); and many who were paralyzed and lame *were healed* (*demonstration*).

I want to include one more passage, Matthew 11:2-5, where Jesus affirmed to John the Baptist that He was (and is) the Messiah, when John, during his incarceration, developed doubt about Jesus' identity.

Matthew 11:2-5 And when John had heard in prison about the works of Christ, he sent two of his disciples (3) and said to Him, "Are You the Coming One, or do we look for another?" (4) Jesus answered and said to them, "Go and tell John the things which you hear (*proclamation*) and see (*demonstration*): (5) The blind see and the lame walk; the lepers are cleansed and the deaf hear; the dead are raised up (*demonstration*) and the poor have the gospel preached to them (*proclamation*).

The above passages overwhelmingly affirm that the Biblical model for evangelism includes not only *proclamation* of the gospel but also *demonstration* of God's power, especially through divine healing and casting out demons. Any person who is called to the office of the evangelist should seek to be equipped with the spiritual gift of healing (1 Cor. 12:9) and should pursue the faith and the anointing of the Holy Spirit to heal the sick and to cast out demons. Philip, who healed the sick and cast out demons in Acts 8:4-8, is called "Philip the evangelist" in Acts 21:8. Notice in Acts 8:6 that as the multitudes in the city of Samaria "heeded the things spoken by Philip (*proclamation*), hearing and seeing the miracles which he did (*demonstration*)," the miracles captured the attention of the people, overriding any doubts and deception, so that they were willing to hear and believe the gospel message.

Please note some of the other appearances of signs and wonders in the New Testament.

Acts 2:22 Jesus of Nazareth, a Man attested by God to you by *miracles, wonders, and signs* which God did through Him in your midst....

Acts 4:29-30 Now, Lord, look on their threats, and grant to Your servants that with all boldness they may speak Your word (*proclamation*), (30) by stretching out Your hand *to heal*, and that *signs and wonders* (*demonstration*) may be done through the name of Your holy Servant Jesus.

Acts 14:3 Therefore they stayed there a long time, speaking boldly in the Lord (*proclamation*), who was bearing witness to the word of His grace, granting *signs and wonders* (*demonstration*) to be done by their hands.

Romans 15:18-19 For I will not dare to speak of any of those things which Christ has not accomplished through me, in word and deed, to make the Gentiles obedient—(19) in *mighty signs and wonders* (*demonstration*), by the power of the Spirit of God, so that from Jerusalem and round about to Illyricum I have fully preached the gospel of Christ (*proclamation*).

Hebrews 2:4 God also bearing witness both with *signs and wonders*, with various miracles, and gifts of the Holy Spirit (*demonstration*), according to His own will?

Cessationists are those who say that God ceased using signs, wonders, and the spiritual gifts after the apostles died or when the canon of Scripture was completed. In light of their claim, I must ask why God would remove spiritual gifts, miracles, signs, and wonders (demonstration) from the church when He used them frequently in the Old and New Testaments, when His use of them was extremely effective for instilling faith and the fear of the Lord in many of those who witnessed them (e.g., 1 Kgs. 18; Josh. 3-4; though not always—Acts 14:8-20), and when the high majority of the world's population has demonstrated, century after century, that they are not following Christ. Scripture gives no reason to believe that God ceased using signs and wonders after the days of the early church.

For today's church to maximize our effectiveness in evangelizing the lost, the ministry of divine healing (the premier New Testament sign) needs to be raised to the level of prominence that it held in the first century church. Today's church should: 1) seek to walk blamelessly before God; 2) boldly and consistently preach and teach the Word of God showing that Jesus is Savior, Healer, Baptizer in the Holy Spirit, and Supplier of every need (Phil. 4:19); 3) boldly and consistently preach and teach that bodily healing is a benefit of Christ's atonement; thus it is a privilege of all believers, and is appropriated by faith (the all-important doctrine of justification by faith must be embraced and preached by the church); and 4) pray for the sick in Jesus' name, utilizing the methods of the laying on of hands (Mk. 16:18) and anointing the sick with oil (Jas. 5:14; Mk. 6:13). The results will include the church's cultivation of faith and an anointing to heal the sick. We should anticipate that this anointing will grow stronger and stronger upon the church so that we can do the works of Jesus and even greater works! (Note John 14:12.) When this occurs, church growth will explode as in Acts where "the Lord *added* to the church daily those who were being saved" (Acts 2:47), and "walking in the fear of the Lord and in the comfort of the Holy Spirit, they were *multiplied*" (Acts 9:31b). F. F. Bosworth, an eminent American evangelist of the early 1900s, wrote in his excellent book, *Christ the Healer*:

> We preached for thirteen years before the Lord led us to preach this part of the gospel (bodily healing is in the Atonement) in a bolder and more public way.... We have seen more happy conversions in a single week than we ever saw in a whole year of evangelistic work before. As soon as our revivals get under way, hundreds nightly crowd forward to give their hearts and lives to God. Whole cities begin talking about Jesus.... [During the Ottawa, Canada meetings, which lasted seven weeks, attendance was as high as 10,000 in a single service.] Six thousand came for healing and about 12,000 for salvation. I doubt if there would have been more than 1,000 for salvation had it not been for the miracles of healing....One Baptist evangelist...has written... 'healing is the greatest evangelizing agency that the Lord ever used.'[3]

Let us not set our sights too low. Let us expect no less than what was experienced by the evangelists and missionaries in Acts: when the city of Samaria turned from Simon's sorcery to Christ's salvation and its associated joy because of the proclamation and demonstration of the gospel through Philip; when two entire towns, Lydda and Sharon, turned to the Lord as a result of Jesus the Christ healing Aeneas through the faith and words of Peter (Acts 9:32-35); and when the Lord healed every sick person on the pagan Island of Malta through the Lord's bondservant, Paul (Acts 28:7-10). God desires that divine healing be an integral part of the church's ministry today.

Have a Regular Healing Service

The purpose of this book is to expose the body of Christ to many Biblical passages pertaining to divine healing, to insights from myself and others about these passages, and to healing testimonies from church history and from the ministry of famous healing evangelists. (To God's glory, I have many healing testimonies from my position as a prison chaplain to share, but I will not do so before my retirement.) I love to study the healing passages in the Bible, in part because they illustrate that what Jesus did so graciously for people physically—setting them free from sicknesses, He can also do for us spiritually—setting us free from sin (that is the penalty and power of sin, and once we get to heaven the presence of sin). I strongly emphasize that attaining this latter freedom—freedom from sin through faith in the blood of Christ—is the top priority. For what does it profit a man to be physically healed, but die and go to hell?

A major key to having a healing ministry is to consistently teach and preach the healing passages of the Bible. For a good part of seven years, I have held a one hour weekly healing class called "Breakthrough," often at two locations. I have also held healing services in various churches. In the Breakthrough class or a healing service, I teach or preach from God's Word. Then I invite those who would like some of our leaders and/or me to pray for them to come forward. We anoint each of them with oil, lay hands on them, and pray for healing in Jesus' name.

In preparation for Breakthrough or for a healing service, I often spend a lot of time worshipping the Lord and meditating on His Word. I sometimes watch videos of other ministers as they operate in the gift of healing. I want to be filled with the Holy Spirit before I come to such services because only the Holy Spirit can break through any oppression caused by the devil, disease, and doubt. My main goals in having

Breakthrough and the healing services are to preach the Word, and for all in attendance to experience the presence and ministry of the Holy Spirit as well as the Lord's answering our prayers. Many testimonies of answered prayers, healings, people receiving the baptism in the Holy Spirit, and people being refreshed by His presence have come from these services.

Your church can have a healing ministry. Through bold and consistent proclamation of Scriptures pertaining to Jesus as Healer, faith can be cultivated and healings can begin to manifest. Galatians 6:7b says, "…for whatever a man sows, that he will also reap." If the church consistently, and with expectation, sows God's Word that Jesus is Savior, Healer, Deliverer, and Baptizer in the Holy Spirit, then in due season the church will reap the sick being healed by Jesus before our very eyes and believers being filled with the Holy Spirit. Do not give up during the season of sowing, for this season could take several months. Instead, stand steadfast on the promises of God, such as: "by whose (Jesus') stripes you were healed" (1 Pet. 2:24b), God "heals all your diseases" (Ps. 103:3b), "all things are possible to him who believes" (Mk. 9:23b), and through faith in Jesus' name "they will lay hands on the sick, and they will recover" (Mk. 16:17-18). God bless you as you sow to the prospect of having a dynamic healing and deliverance ministry so that scores of people today will realize that "…my God shall supply all your need according to His riches in glory by Christ Jesus" (Phil. 4:19).

Chapter 2

Divine Healing and Health in the Old Testament

"...who heals all your diseases" Psalm 103:3b

Let's look at some Old Testament passages which contain verses about divine healing and health.

Exodus 15:26-27 If you diligently heed the voice of the Lord your God and do what is right in His sight, give ear to His commandments and keep all His statutes, I will put *none of the diseases* on you which I have brought on the Egyptians. For I am the Lord who *heals* you. (27) Then they came to Elim, where there were twelve wells of water and seventy palm trees; so they camped there by the water.

God gave the Israelites, who had just crossed the Red Sea, a covenantal promise of which they could lay hold from that time forth. Covenant means: "1) an agreement...; 2) the conditional promises made to humanity by God, as revealed in Scripture."[4] Covenantal promises are often phrased as *if...then statements*—*if* Israel would obey God, *then* God would keep His end of the agreement and bestow prescribed blessings upon Israel. Here, the agreement was that if the Israelites would fully obey God, then God would give them divine health. Thus, one of the names of God is revealed here—*Jehovah Rapha*, the LORD our Healer.

Though each of us should seek to wholeheartedly obey God, even as Exodus 15:26 stipulates, we must realize that none of us have perfectly obeyed God. On the contrary, each of us has sinned against God (Rom. 3:23). But Jesus Christ has fully obeyed His heavenly Father; thus through one's having faith in Christ as the Savior and Risen King, one can fully lay claim to all the promises of God, including divine healing.

The twelve wells of water and seventy palm trees (verse 27)—an oasis, or place of abundance—could prophetically point to a time in the future when the healing ministry of *Jehovah Rapha* would be realized in a greater capacity. We see this in Luke 9-10, where Jesus commissioned the twelve and the seventy to go throughout Israel to preach the gospel and heal the sick. Indeed, the twelve preached and healed "everywhere" (Lk. 9:6), and the seventy likely had similar results as they returned saying, "Lord, even the demons are subject to us in Your name" (Lk. 10:17).

Exodus 23:25-26 So you shall serve the LORD your God, and He will bless your bread and your water. And *I will take sickness away* from the midst of you. (26) No one shall suffer miscarriage or be barren in your land; I will fulfill the number of your days.

This covenantal promise for healing includes God's removal of sickness, His causing women to become pregnant and go full-term, and His bestowal of longevity upon His people. [The Hebrew word for "sickness" in verse 25 is *machaleh*, which means "disease; infirmity."[5] It is the same word used for "diseases" in Exodus 15:26. *Machaleh* also appears as "sickness" during Solomon's prayer in the temple dedication in 1 Kings 8:37.] Such wonderful promises were contingent upon the Israelites' faithfully serving God (verse 25). In verse 21, God warned His people to obey the voice of the Angel whom God was sending before them; otherwise the Angel would not pardon their transgressions. God continued by saying, "do all that I speak, then I will be an enemy to your enemies" (verse 22). Indeed, "if God is for us, who can be against us?" (Rom. 8:31b).

Deuteronomy 7:9, 11-15 Therefore know that the LORD your God, He is God, the faithful God who *keeps covenant and mercy for a thousand generations* with those who love Him and keep His commandments... (11) Therefore you shall keep the commandments, the statutes, and the judgments which I command you today, to observe them. (12) Then it shall come to pass, because you listen to these judgments, and keep and do them, that the LORD your God will keep with you the covenant and the mercy which He swore to your fathers (13) And He will love you and bless you and multiply you; He will also bless the fruit of your womb and the fruit of your land, your grain and your new wine and your oil, the increase of your cattle and the offspring of your flock, in the land of which He swore to your fathers to give you. (14) You shall be blessed above all peoples; there shall not be a male or female barren among you or among your livestock. (15) *And the Lord will take away from you all sickness*, and will afflict you with *none of the terrible diseases* of Egypt, which you have known; but will lay them on all those who hate you.

Verse 9 tells us the length of time that God keeps His Old Testament covenant. This length of time is also shown in Exodus 20:5b-6: "For I, the LORD your God, am a jealous God, visiting the iniquity of the fathers upon the children to the third and fourth *generations* of those who hate me, but *showing mercy to thousands*, to those who love Me and keep My commandments." Generally speaking, a Biblical generation is twenty to twenty-five years long. Twenty multiplied by 1000 is 20,000—this is at least the number of years that the Old Testament covenantal promises, such as divine physical healing and health, are in effect. Timelines show that the giving of the Old Testament laws at Mt Sinai occurred less than 4,000 years ago, well within 20,000 years. Since we live within 1,000 generations (20,000 years) of the giving of the Old Testament covenantal promises, those promises are still in effect for us today! Actually, I don't believe the Old Testament covenantal promises will run out at the end of 1,000 generations. This is comparable to when Jesus said the number of times we are to forgive our neighbor is seventy times seven (Mt. 18:22). Jesus didn't mean that once we have forgiven someone 490 times, we don't have to forgive anymore. I believe these statements refer to never-ending covenantal promises and the never-ending obligation to forgive.

In verse 9, we see that the Old Testament believer's ability to lay hold of the listed covenantal promises is contingent upon the believer's loving God and keeping His commandments. Both of these conditions flow from a heart of faith, and faith is the spiritual quality that the New Testament emphasizes as the means to access the promises of God. Verse 10 conversely offers a stern warning—those who live in disobedience to God actually hate God; God will repay those who hate Him and He will destroy them. But verse 13 points out that if one loves God, then

God will likewise love that person. And with His love comes many practical blessings, including the blessings listed in verses 13-14. Finally, verse 15 contains the wonderful promise that God would be the Healer of all their sicknesses. God would make sure that any sicknesses they knew in Egypt would be upon their enemies, but not upon them. In other words, God would fight for them.

Deuteronomy 8:4 Your garments did not wear out on you, *nor did your foot swell* these forty years.

For the forty years Israel wandered in the wilderness, God supernaturally sustained their clothing and kept their feet from swelling. This would be a good verse for basketball players to remember since they are prone to ankles injuries!

Deuteronomy 32:39 Now see that I, even I, am He, and there is no God besides Me; I kill and *I make alive*; I wound and *I heal*; nor is there any who can deliver from My hand.

This verse refers to the sovereignty of God; He is in absolute control. God is the One who afflicts, even fatally. God killed Nadab and Abihu, sons of Aaron the High Priest, because they offered profane fire before the LORD, and did not respect His holiness (Lev. 10:1-3). Also, "the LORD desired to kill" (1 Sam. 2:25) the two sons of Eli because they caused the people to abhor the offering of the LORD. He did kill them with the sword of the Philistines. God also redeems one from affliction through making one alive (this can refer to regeneration as well as resurrection from the dead) and through healing. Jesus raised Lazarus from the dead (he had been dead four days), which inspired many to believe in Jesus (Jn. 11). We should always be mindful that we are in God's hands. Therefore, we should walk in His favor by walking in humility and fully obeying Him at all times.

Psalm 103:2-4a Bless the Lord, O my soul, and forget not all *his benefits*: (3) who forgives all your iniquities, who *heals all your diseases*, (4) who redeems your life from destruction....

To whom does the possessive adjective "your" in this passage refer? It refers to *anyone* who is willing to receive God's forgiveness and healing, and these benefits come by faith in Christ. Many churches rightfully preach that God forgives His people of their sins through faith in Christ, but far fewer churches preach that God also heals the sick through faith in Christ. Yet in this passage, forgiveness and healing are side by side; they are two sides of the same coin; they are joint benefits of Christ's atonement. Thus both of these benefits should receive significant attention from the pulpit. Notice from this passage that God wants to forgive you of every iniquity you have ever committed and heal you of any disease you could possibly have. Also, we see in this passage that forgiveness of sins precedes healing of diseases. What does it profit a man if he is physically healed, but then he dies and goes to hell? Nothing. Receiving God's forgiveness of our sins is infinitely more important. But, thanks be to God, we do not have to choose between the two; we can be divinely forgiven and healed! Jesus granted both forgiveness and healing to the paralytic in Matthew 9:2-7, and "God is no respector of persons" (Acts 10:34, KJV). Evangelist T. L. Osborn said of Psalm 103:3:

> As long as He is a sin-forgiver, He will be a sickness-healer....He was, is, and always will be as willing to heal all who are sick as to save all who are sinful....His promises to heal all reveal His will to heal all.[6]

These wonderful benefits and many more are available to all who have faith in Christ. We should not live in a spiritually backslidden condition and expect God to heal us. We need to be repentant (embracing the cross) and believe God's Word. We need to walk as those who are vitally united to Christ by faith in order that we may confidently lay hold of all His benefits.

Psalm 105:37 He also led them out with silver and gold, and there was *none feeble* among their tribes.

The context of this verse is the exodus of God's people from Egypt. Exodus 12:37 reveals that the multitude that came out of Egypt totaled 600,000 men, not counting women or children. As Exodus 12:35-36 indicate, this huge multitude came out of Egypt with God's provision of great riches and physical strength. Third John 2 also testifies of the prosperity and divinely blessed health which can be rightly claimed by those who put God first: "Beloved, I pray that you may prosper in all things and be in health, just as your soul prospers."

Psalm 107:20 He sent *His word* and *healed them*, and *delivered them* from their destructions.

This verse relates closely to Proverbs 4:20-22, which says that the words of God are life and health to one's flesh. It also relates to Matthew 8:8, where the Centurion says, "Lord, I am not worthy that You should come under my roof. But only *speak a word*, and my servant will be *healed.*" Faith in the Word of God brings healing and deliverance. Therefore, we should make the Word of God the basis for our thoughts and speech continuously (Josh. 1:8; Ps. 119:97).

Proverbs 3:7-8 Do not be wise in your own eyes; fear the LORD and depart from evil. It will be *health to your flesh, and strength to your bones.*

Eradicating sin from your life, which comes from the fear of the LORD (Prov. 16:6b), the goodness of God (Rom. 2:4), and the Word dwelling within (Ps. 119:11), will have a positive effect on your physical health. This includes physical health externally—"flesh," as well as physical health for the internal foundation—"bones." God's covenantal provision through faith in Christ includes complete physical health, internally and externally.

Proverbs 4:20-22 My son, give attention to my *words*; incline your ear to my *sayings.* (21) Do not let them depart from your eyes; keep them in the midst of your heart; (22) for they are *life* to those who find them, and *health to all their flesh.*

Attention to God's words (with the eyes, ears, and heart) is what brings *life and health to the flesh.* The Word of God in one's heart, and obedience to that Word, is a major key to having divinely blessed health, and it is mandatory for living in victory over sin. "Do not let them (the words of God) depart from your eyes" (verse 21) is similar to God's commandment to Joshua: "This Book of the Law shall not depart from your mouth... (Josh. 1:8). God's Word should not depart from your eyes or mouth. It is to be the basis for your continual confession, focus, and meditation. As Evangelist F. F. Bosworth stated, you are not to merely glance at God's Word; you are to stare at it.

Proverbs 14:30 A sound heart is *life* to the *body*, but envy is rottenness to the bones.

Your heart, which is the core of your being and from which come your desires and motives, ought to always be kept pure before God (Mt. 5:8). What happens in your heart often, if not always, manifests in the natural realm, as Proverbs 4:23 testifies: "Keep your heart with all diligence, for out of it spring the issues of life." Notice that Proverbs 14:30 specifies the body as that to which a sound heart gives life, and this is in addition to the spirit and soul of a person which are also affected by the quality of a person's heart. First Thessalonians 5:23b says, "may your whole spirit, soul, and body be preserved blameless at the coming of our Lord Jesus Christ." Hallelujah! Also notice that, conversely, sin, such as envy, brings a sickly manifestation to the physical body—the bones.

According To The Original Language, What Does "To Heal" Mean?

The original language of the Old Testament is Hebrew. The Hebrew word *rapha* is used every time the word "heal," "healed," and "healeth" appears in the King James Version of the Old Testament. *Rapha* is defined as: "to mend (by stitching), to cure, to (cause to) heal, physician, repair, and thoroughly make whole."[7] Some say that the word "healing" in the Bible does not mean physical healing, but rather spiritual or emotional healing only. James Grant (a doctoral student in Church History and good friend of mine) says such an interpretation of healing is:

> a result of the Enlightenment and the modern, scientifically-oriented critics. They try to separate our spiritual well-being from our physical well-being. It is an attempt to push the spiritual realm as far away from our daily concerns as possible so they don't have to feel accountable to spiritual authority. It's an artificial device and really has no part in the Biblical scheme of things.[8]

Rapha is used in several of the Old Testament covenantal verses that I listed earlier in this chapter: Exodus 15:26, Deuteronomy 32:39, Psalm 103:3, and Psalm 107:20. Therefore, physical healing is included in the meaning of these verses. The next three passages of which I write contain a form of the word "heal," from *rapha*, and the context shows that the healings spoken of are physical in nature:

Genesis 20:17-18 So Abraham prayed to God; and God *healed* Abimelech, his wife, and his female servants. Then they bore children; (18) for the LORD had closed up all the wombs of the house of Abimelech because of Sarah, Abraham's wife.

Abimelech, king of Gerar, had taken Abraham's wife, Sarah, into his home, likely with the intention of sleeping with her and / or marrying her, though God had so far prevented him from touching her. Taking the wife of another man is sin (adultery), and sin necessarily brings a negative consequence. (In this case, however, such sin would be unintentional because Sarah and Abraham had told Abimelech they were siblings rather than husband and wife.) Because of Abimelech's having taken Sarah, God closed the wombs of all the women of Abimelech's household so that they were barren. When Abimelech heeded God's warning and returned Sarah to Abraham, and when Abraham prayed to God on behalf of Abimelech and his household, then God physically healed (*rapha*) Abimelech of some unmentioned ailment as well as the wombs of these women. In summary, sin caused physical debilities (including barrenness), while repentance and intercessory prayer by one accepted by God caused physical healing. As Abraham stood in the gap for Abimelech's household, so Christ, our High Priest and Intercessor, stands in the gap for us. As Abraham was accepted by God, so Christ's atoning sacrifice was accepted by God. And we also are accepted by God as we identify with Christ by faith.

2 Kings 20:1-11 In those days *Hezekiah was sick and near death.* And Isaiah the prophet, the son of Amoz, went to him and said to him, "Thus says the LORD: 'Set your house in order, for *you shall die*, and not live.'" (2) Then he turned his face toward the wall, and prayed to the LORD, saying, (3) "Remember now, O LORD, I pray, how I have walked before You in truth and with a loyal heart, and have done what was good in Your sight." And Hezekiah wept bitterly. (4) And it happened, before Isaiah had gone out into the middle court, that the word of the LORD came to him, saying, (5) "Return and tell Hezekiah the leader of My people, 'Thus says the LORD, the God of David your father: "I have heard your prayer, I have seen your tears; surely *I will heal you*...(6) And *I will add to your days fifteen years.*"'

King Hezekiah, confronted with a word from God that he was about to die, prayed unto God with bitter tears—casting his cares upon God, as the Bible exhorts us to do, since God cares for us (1 Pet. 5:7). Hezekiah asked God to "remember" Hezekiah's life of loyalty unto God, reminding God that he had "walked before (God)...in truth and with a loyal heart, and (had)...done what was good in (God's)... sight." Other Scripture passages attest to Hezekiah's loyalty to God; for example, 2 Kings 18:3 says: "And he did what was right in the sight of the LORD, according to all that his father David had done";

2 Chronicles 31:20 says: "Thus Hezekiah...did what was good and right and true before the LORD his God." Had Hezekiah lived a life of unfaithfulness to God, then God would likely not have listened to his prayer. Psalm 66:18 supports this, saying: "If I regard iniquity in my heart, the LORD will not hear." In other words, God is under no obligation to listen to prayers offered from an unrepentant heart. Conversely, as Psalm 84:11 says: "No good thing will He withhold from those who walk uprightly"; God's good things include "length of days and long life and peace" (Prov. 3:2). Also a New Testament version of God's promise to answer the prayers of those who obey Him is found in 1 John 3:22: "And whatever we ask we receive from Him, because we keep His commandments and do those things that are pleasing in His sight." "Whatever" would include divine healing. [Jesus the Christ is the only One who has perfectly kept God's commandments, so ultimately it is through faith in Him that one may claim such wonderful promises. Those who have received Christ are to "walk in Him" (Col 2:6) and "walk just as He walked" (1 Jn. 2:6).] Though Hezekiah had walked before God with a loyal heart, had Hezekiah not prayed to God to heal him, Hezekiah likely would have soon died. James 4:2b says "you do not have because you do not ask."

When God heard the prayer of His servant Hezekiah, God quickly spoke to Isaiah to go back and tell Hezekiah the wonderful news that God would heal (*rapha*) him and grant him fifteen more years of life! And God promised to do even more that that—He would deliver Jerusalem from their attackers, the Assyrians; God committed Himself to being Jerusalem's defense! The righteousness of King Hezekiah certainly contributed to God's willingness to defend Jerusalem from their enemies. Proverbs 29:2 says: "When the righteous are in authority, the people rejoice; but when a wicked man rules, the people groan." (See also Proverbs 12:13, 21, 28 for other benefits of righteousness.) The method of healing was to place a lump of figs on Hezekiah's boil; when this occurred "he recovered" (2 Kings 20:7). Furthermore, Hezekiah, wanting to bolster his faith in God's promise to heal him, asked Isaiah for a sign. Likely, it was because God was pleased with Hezekiah's heart that God granted him a sign. This stands in contrast to the "evil and adulterous generation" of Jesus' day who asked Him for a sign but was denied (Mt. 12:39). The sign granted to Hezekiah would allow him to choose whether the shadow on the sundial would supernaturally move forward or backward ten degrees. Hezekiah chose for the shadow to "go backward ten degrees." Isaiah presented Hezekiah's request unto God by crying out unto God, and God performed the miracle that Hezekiah had requested. Thus Hezekiah grew in confidence that indeed he would be granted fifteen more years of life! God is certainly good!

Numbers 12:10-13 And when the cloud departed from above the tabernacle, suddenly Miriam became leprous, as white as snow. Then Aaron turned toward Miriam, and there she was, a leper. (11) So Aaron said to Moses, "Oh, my lord! Please do not lay this sin on us, in which we have done foolishly and in which we have sinned. (12) Please do not let her be as one dead, whose flesh is half consumed when he comes out of his mother's womb!" (13) So Moses cried out to the LORD, saying, "Please *heal* her, O God, I pray!"

In reading all of Numbers 12, you will see that Miriam and Aaron displayed a bigoted attitude when they spoke against Moses because he had married a woman outside of Israel, an Ethiopian. God warns against slanderous speech in Psalm 101:5: "Whoever secretly slanders his neighbor, Him I will destroy." Miriam and Aaron did not slander just any person, but their earthly leader, the one whom God considered to be the most humble man on earth (verse 3). God said that Moses is "faithful in all (God's)...house...to whom God speaks face to face, even plainly...(who) sees the form of the LORD" (verses 7-8). Again, warnings against such evil speech about one's leader occur in Acts 23:5: "You shall not speak evil of a ruler of your people," and Psalm 105:15: "Do not touch My anointed ones, and do My prophets no harm." God rebuked Aaron and Miriam to their face and in the presence of Moses. When God ascended from them, "Miriam became leprous, as white as snow" (verse 10). This reminds us of another aspect of God—not only does God graciously heal, but He also brings judgment upon each and every sin one commits (2 Cor. 5:10; Col. 3:25; Heb. 2:2), and sometimes God does so by afflicting with sickness. Deuteronomy 28 (the entire chapter) testifies that God greatly rewards those who are obedient, but God brings curses upon those who persist in disobedience, and some of those curses include physical infirmity.

We are not told why Miriam rather than Aaron received the penalty of leprosy; perhaps she instigated the slander, or her slander of Moses had been more severe. In any case, Aaron confessed their sin to Moses (verse 11), and then asked Moses, the man whom they sinned against, to intercede for them since God would listen to Moses' prayer. Moses, displaying a heart of forgiveness toward Aaron and Miriam, cried out to the LORD and asked Him to heal (*rapha*) Miriam. This is in accordance with Jesus' words: "pray for those who spitefully use you and persecute you" (Mt. 5:44). God answered Moses' prayer: even though Miriam would be shut out of the camp for seven days, she would be received back into the camp, healed. This reminds us that one's sin is costly, not only to the one who commits the sin, but often to many others: Miriam's sin delayed the traveling progress of the entire nation for a week.

More on Old Testament Healing

As we have seen, divine health and healing are included in the Old Testament covenantal promises. Any Israelite who was obedient to all the laws and commands of God could stand on God's promises and expect to experience divine healing and walk in blessed health. And since in the Old Testament—the comparably inferior covenant—such were the benefits, how much more precious and powerful are the benefits which are available to participants of the new covenant, which we today have through faith in Christ? We shall observe this in the following passage.

Numbers 21:4-9 Then they journeyed from Mount Hor by the Way of the Red Sea, to go around the land of Edom; and the soul of the people became very discouraged on the way. (5) And the people spoke against God and against Moses: "Why have you brought us up out of Egypt to die in the wilderness? For there is no food and no water, and our soul loathes this worthless bread." (6) So the LORD sent fiery serpents among the people, and they bit the people; and many of the people of Israel died. (7) Therefore the people came to Moses, and said, "We have sinned, for we have spoken against the LORD and against you; pray to the LORD that He take away the serpents from us." So Moses prayed for the people. (8) Then the LORD said to Moses, "Make a fiery serpent, and set it on a pole; and it shall be that everyone who is bitten, when he looks at it, shall live." (9) So Moses made a bronze serpent, and put it on a pole; and so it was, if a serpent had bitten anyone, when he looked at the bronze serpent, he lived.

This event occurred during Israel's wandering in the wilderness for forty years after their exodus from Egypt. Their lengthy wandering was a result of their sin (Num. 14). They became discouraged in their journey which led to transgression: they spoke rebellious words against

Moses and God. This transgression could have been avoided had they kept their minds renewed by the testimonies, promises, and commands of God. Instead, they grumbled about God's provision of manna, calling it "worthless." Philippians 2:14 says: "Do all things *without complaining and disputing....*" The Israelites would rather have returned to Egypt and live as slaves under Pharoah than live under the lordship of their Creator. Such sin (rejection of God as well as of His gracious provision of manna, or angel's food) by the Israelites brought God's judgment upon them in the form of deadly snake bites. Galatians 6:7 says: "Do not be deceived, God is not mocked; for *whatever a man sows, that he will also reap.*" You reap a negative consequence or consequences for each sin you commit. Once God's judgment manifested and the people began dying of snake bites, they confessed their sins to Moses and pleaded with Moses to pray to God to take away the serpents (this is similar to the Numbers 12:10-13 account). Again Moses prayed to God on behalf of the people even though they had sinned against God and Moses, and his prayer played a vital role in the healing of the people. (See Exodus 32:9-14 and James 5:16 as other examples of intercessory prayer.) God responded to Moses' prayer by instructing him to make a bronze serpent and lift it up on a pole, and that anyone who looked to the exalted bronze serpent would survive the snake bites. Moses did so, and the people who looked upon the bronze serpent were healed.

That provision by God for the healing of the people foreshadowed Jesus' being lifted up on the cross for the salvation and healing of the world. John 3:14-15 says, "And as Moses lifted up the serpent in the wilderness, even so must the Son of Man be lifted up, that whoever believes in Him should not perish but have everlasting life." The bronze serpent was a type of Calvary. (Calvary represents Christ crucified, Lk. 23:33.) As everyone who looked at the bronze serpent was healed and forgiven, so everyone who, in faith, looks to Calvary—unto Jesus who died on the cross for our sins and rose again—can be forgiven and healed today. Evangelist F. F. Bosworth corroborates this, saying of this passage:

> If bodily healing is not provided in the Atonement, why were these dying Israelites required to look at the type of the Atonement for bodily healing? As their curse was removed by lifting up the type of Christ, so ours is removed by the lifting up of Christ, the Antitype.... None were to receive healing except on this condition: "Everyone

that *looketh.*" *Looking* means to be occupied and influenced….(It) means attention…expectation. *Looketh* is in the continuous present tense. It is not a mere glance, but a continuous stare until you are well…. They could not look at the brass snake and their symptoms at the same time[9]

Since the new covenant and its promises are far superior to the old covenant and its promises, any old covenant benefit is accessible by any new covenant believer (2 Cor. 1:20).

The Resurrection of a Widow's Son

First Kings 17 contains the account of the resurrection of a dead boy in Zarephath. Because of a three and a half year drought in the Palestinian area (which was put into effect through the Word of God pronounced by Elijah, the prophet of God, due to Israel's sin), God sent Elijah to Zarephath where God would continue to supernaturally provide food for Elijah as He had done for him at the Brook Cherith. When Elijah arrived in Zarephath and first met the widow through whom God's provision would come, he immediately asked her for "a little water" and "a morsel of bread" (verses 10-11). The woman replied that the only food she had was "a handful of flour in a bin, and a little oil in a jar" (verse 12). She was in the process of making what she assumed would be the final meal she and her son would eat before they would die of starvation. Elijah told the woman to make him a small cake first and then make some for her and her boy, "for thus says the LORD God of Israel: 'The bin of flour shall not be used up, nor shall the jar of oil run dry, until the day the LORD sends rain on the earth'" (verse 14). The woman obeyed "the word of the LORD which He spoke by Elijah" (verse 16); indeed the flour and oil did not run out, so they "ate for many days" (verse 15). God's provision was just in time, not only for His prophet, but also for this widow and her son. Psalm 33:18-19 say: "Behold, the eye of the LORD is on those who fear Him, on those who hope in His mercy, to deliver their soul from death, and to keep them alive in famine."

Later on, the son of the woman became sick and died. So Elijah laid the son on Elijah's bed. Verses 20-24 say:

Then he (Elijah) cried out to the LORD and said, "O LORD my God, have You also brought tragedy on the widow with whom I lodge, by killing her son?" (21) And he stretched himself out on the child three times, and cried out to the LORD and said, "O LORD my God, I pray, let this child's soul come back to him." (22) Then the LORD heard the voice of Elijah; and the soul of the child came back to him, and he revived. (23) And Elijah took the child and brought him down from the upper room into the house, and gave him to his mother. And Elijah said, "See, your son lives!" (24) Then the woman said to Elijah, "Now by this I know that you are a man of God, and that the word of the LORD in your mouth is the truth."

Elijah's prayer was one of strong passion and fervency, for he desperately wanted this boy to be brought back to life. Elijah did not include in his prayer "if it be Your will." Instead, Elijah discerned that raising the boy from the dead was God's will, so he prayed boldly to that end. Also, Elijah went beyond the laying-on-of-hands method of praying for the sick to the laying of his entire body upon the boy. Apparently, Elijah wanted as much of his physical being as possible, which was anointed of the Spirit of God, to be in contact with the lifeless body of the boy so as to provide the best exposure of the boy to the life-giving Spirit of God. Elijah was *persistent* in his pursuit of the healing of the boy in that he lay upon the boy three times. As Psalm 34:15 says, "The eyes of the LORD are on the righteous, and His ears are open to their cry," so "the LORD heard the voice of Elijah" (verse 22), and the LORD raised the boy from the dead! Consequently, the woman gained a much stronger faith in God, as well as a greater confidence in Elijah as a man of God and that "the word of the LORD" in his mouth was "the truth" (verse 24). Likewise, miracles performed through the hands of Christians today will often bolster faith in the gospel message to many of those who hear and see them.

The Resurrection of the Shunammite's Son

Second Kings 4 contains the account of the resurrection of a dead boy in Shunem. Elisha, the successor to Elijah and the one who had asked for and received "a double portion" of Elijah's spirit (2 Kings 2:9-15), would on occasion pass through Shunem. A Shunammite woman persuaded Elisha and his servant, Gehazi, to eat with her and her husband and to spend the night at their home whenever they would pass that way. Because of the woman's continual hospitality, Elisha asked her what he could do for her. [Similarly, Jesus said that whoever gives a cup of cold water to a man of God in Jesus' name would be rewarded (Mk. 9:41).] He offered to speak to the king or commander of the army on her behalf (these suggestions were things Elisha could provide out of his own natural ability), but she replied that she did not need these things. Therefore, Gehazi mentioned that she had no son and that her husband was old. So Elisha prophesied to the woman, "About this time next year you shall embrace a son" (verse 16). (This provision would obviously require divine intervention, and thus would bring greater glory to God than that which could be provided by natural means.) Though she maintained respect for Elisha, calling him a "man of God" and referring to herself as his "maidservant," still she doubted his words and replied, "No, my lord. Man of God, do not lie to your maidservant!" (verse 16). Her doubt was likely due, in part, to the shock of the promise that she would give birth. Although it is preferable, and often required, that the beneficiary of a particular miracle exercise faith, it is possible for a man or woman of God to stand in the gap and have faith on behalf the one being prayed for, and the miracle occurs. In verse 17, we see the fulfillment of the prophecy: she gave birth to a son.

After a few years, when the son was able to walk, he died, seemingly of an ailment in his head. The woman laid her dead son on the bed of the man of God and shut the door. Then she said to her husband, "It is well," and hurried to find Elisha. When Elisha saw her coming, he sent Gehazi to greet her. Again she replied, "It is well." (Incidentally, this is apparently the passage that inspired Horatio Spafford to write the famous hymn, *It Is Well with My Soul*, shortly after the sinking of a ship that claimed the lives of his four daughters.) To say "It is well" when one has just lost a child or children is a strong testimony to one's faith in the Lord who "comforts us in all our tribulation" and who Himself is "the resurrection and the life" (2 Cor. 1:4; Jn. 11:25). The woman, displaying deep distress, caught Elisha by the feet as she made reference to her son. So Elisha instructed Gehazi to quickly go to the child, avoiding any distractions, and to place Elisha's staff on the child's face. And as Elisha would not allow Elijah to leave him in 2 Kings 2 when Elijah was about to be taken to heaven, similarly the woman vowed that she would not leave Elisha, knowing that in a crisis a good place to be is in the presence of those whose prayers are heard by God. Gehazi's efforts were to no avail, and Elisha and the woman arrived at the woman's house and beheld the dead boy. Then Elisha prayed to the LORD. And in emulation of the prayer techniques of his predecessor, Elijah, he:

> lay on the child, and put his mouth on his mouth, his eyes on his eyes, and his hands on his hands; and he stretched himself out on the child, and the flesh of the child became warm. (35) He returned and walked back and forth in the house, and again went up and stretched himself out on him; then the child sneezed seven times, and the child opened his eyes (verses 34-35).

When the woman beheld her resurrected son, she "fell at his (Elisha's) feet, and bowed to the ground" (verse 37). As the widow of Zeraphath gained even more respect for Elijah and the Word of God in his mouth when her son was raised, so also the Shunammite woman would presumably gain great respect for Elisha as a man through whom God mightily worked. Certainly, we Christians today are not to seek glory for ourselves through miracles, but we are to glorify God and confirm God's Word through signs and wonders. Then many people will come to realize that God is not some distant, unconcerned, and impersonal force, but rather He tabernacled among His creation through the Lord Jesus Christ, and He tabernacles among us today by the Holy Spirit Who dwells in each member of Christ's church.

Later in 2 Kings 13, God's mighty anointing upon Elisha is also evidenced in the account of a dead man's body being hurriedly placed in the tomb that contained Elisha's dead body. When the dead man's body touched Elisha's bones, "he revived and stood on his feet" (verse 21). In a sense, Elisha was still raising the dead even after he himself had died. Furthermore, that two resurrections of dead people are attributed to Elisha and only one to Elijah points to the double portion of the Spirit of God that Elisha had received. For apart from Christ and His Spirit, one can do nothing (John 15:5).

The Healing of Naaman

Second Kings 5 contains the account of the healing of Naaman, the commander of the Syrian army, who was a leper. An Israelite girl who served in the house of Naaman, said, "If only my master were with the prophet who is in Samaria! For he would heal him of his leprosy" (verse 3). When the Syrian king sent a letter to the Israelite king requesting for Naaman to be healed, the Israelite king tore his clothes due to his personal inability to perform healings as well as his skepticism of the sincerity of the Syrian king's request. But Elisha sent word to the king of Israel to send Naaman to him so that the Syrian king "shall know that there is a prophet in Israel" (verse 8). Elisha's words revealed that he believed that God would heal Naaman through him, and that the healing would stand as a witness to Syria that Israel's God is the only true God. When Naaman arrived at Elisha's house, Elisha sent a messenger to instruct Naaman to "go and wash in the Jordan seven times, and your flesh shall be restored to you, and you shall be clean" (verse 10). But due to Naaman's pride and ignorance, he unwisely rejected Elisha's instructions. Naaman thought that Elisha's chosen method to heal was nonsensical. (Similarly today, many sick people ignore the instructions of James 5:14-16 which call for the sick to request that the church elders anoint them with oil and pray the prayer of faith for the healing of their bodies.) It could have been that Naaman's pride had opened the door for Satan to afflict his flesh with leprosy in the first place. Naaman's servants wisely advised Naaman to obey the prophet's instruction, especially since the instruction was not difficult to follow. Naaman heeded their advice, and when he had dipped seven times in the Jordan River, his skin was instantly and perfectly healed! What a double blessing for Naaman: 1) to be healed of a terminal disease, and 2) to realize that the God of Israel is the one and only God of the universe. It seemed Namaan lacked personal faith for healing; Elisha had faith on his behalf. [In Biblical numerology, seven is often seen as representing divine perfection. In Joshua 6, it was after the seventh lap on the seventh day of Israel's marching around Jericho, in accordance with God's instruction, that God caused the walls of Jericho to fall down flat. Such instructions may have seemed odd to Israel (as Elisha's instructions seemed odd to Naaman), but perhaps the work of obedience in their hearts needed to go to that extent for humility and faith to develop.] Naaman returned to Elisha, and this time he was allowed to speak with Elisha face to face. Displaying gratitude, Naaman offered a gift to Elisha for his being healed. But in accordance with what Jesus would later tell his disciples, "Freely you have received, freely give" (Mt. 10:8b), Elisha refused to receive any gift knowing that all credit for healings goes only to God. However, a warning is found in this passage in that Gehazi, Elisha's servant, yielded to greed and ran after Naaman, lied to him, and received gifts from his hand. By the Spirit of God, Elisha knew of Gehazi's deceit and pronounced God's judgment of leprosy to befall Gehazi and his descendants forever; immediately full-blown leprosy manifested on the skin of Gehazi. Our gracious God who heals the sick is also a "just judge" (Ps. 7:11). He can afflict with disease those who rebel against His Word—in Deuteronomy 32:39, God declares, "I kill and I make alive; I wound and I heal."

I have recounted here only three of the many miracles done by the prophets Elijah and Elisha. (Their ministries are recorded from 1 Kings 17 to 2 Kings 13.) The miraculous ministries of Elijah and Elisha foreshadowed the ultimate ministry of the One who was yet to come, the One who healed "every sickness and every disease among the people" (Mt. 9:35), and the One who rightfully declared Himself to be "the resurrection and the life" (Jn. 11:25), namely the Lord Jesus Christ.

Whether we consider the ten plagues and the parting of the Red Sea in Exodus, the Israelites' supernatural military victories over other nations in Joshua and Judges, or the miracles of Elijah and Elisha in 1 and 2 Kings, God used signs and wonders (demonstration) in the Old Testament to reveal His presence, power, and provision, as well as to attract people's attention to God's message (proclamation). In response, the people were to place their faith in, and give full obedience to, His holy Word. Second Corinthians 1:20 says, "For all the promises of God in Him (Christ) are yes, and in Him Amen, to the glory of God through us." This verse shows that all Biblical promises, including those of the Old Testament, are available to anyone who abides in Christ. Praise God!

Chapter 3

Healings throughout Church History

Adoniram Judson (A. J.) Gordon (1836 – 1895) was an American Baptist minister who served as pastor of Clarendon Street Church in Boston for over twenty-five years. The sick were regularly prayed for at his church. He was also a favorite speaker in Dwight L. Moody's Northfield conventions, and founded Boston Missionary Training Institute, which today is known as Gordon College. Gordon wrote an excellent book entitled *The Ministry of Healing: Miracles of Cure in All Ages* (1882), which testifies of healings that occurred throughout the history of the church. This chapter draws from that book.[10]

The Testimony of the Church

Gordon writes: "When we turn to the writings of the Christian Fathers...we find the testimonies abundant to the continuance of the miraculous powers. We will quote only a few as specimens from a larger number...."[11]

Justin Martyr (100-165 A. D.), a Christian apologist, said:

For numberless demoniacs throughout the whole world and in your city, many of our Christian men, exorcising them in the name of Jesus Christ, who was crucified under Pontias Pilate, have healed, and do heal…driving the possessing devils out of the men, though they could not be cured by all the other exorcists and those who used incantations and drugs.

Irenaeus (130 – 202 A. D.), who was a bishop, Church Father, and apologist, said:

the disciples receiving grace from Him do in His name perform miracles so as to promote the welfare of others, according to the gift which each has received from Him….Others still heal the sick by laying their hands upon them, and they are made whole.

Tertullian (160 – 220 A. D.), who was a theologian and Christian writer from Carthage, said:

For the clerk of one of them who was liable to be thrown upon the ground by an evil spirit was set free from his affliction….And how many men of rank, to say nothing of the common people, have been delivered from devils and healed of disease.

Origen of Alexandria (182 – 254 A. D.), who was a scholar and theologian (but some of his views contradicted the Bible), said:

And some give evidence of their having received through their faith a marvelous power by the cures which they perform, invoking no other name over those who need their help than that of the God of all things and of Jesus, along with a mention of His history. For by these means we too have seen many persons freed from grievous calamities and from distractions of mind and madness, and countless other ills which could be cured neither by men or devils.

Pope Clement (who died in 99 A. D.) was bishop of Rome and considered to be the first Apostolic Father of the Church. He said:

Let them, therefore, with fasting and prayer, make their intercessions, and not with the well-arranged and fitly ordered words of learning, but as men who have received the gift of healing confidently, to the glory of God.

Gordon says, "The weight of these and like testimonies is so generally acknowledged by Church historians that it seems little less than hardihood for scholars to go on repeating that well-worn phrase "the age of miracles ended with the apostles."[12]

Most church historians seem to agree that divine manifestations ceased to be recognized from the age of Constantine (Roman emperor from 306 – 337 A. D.) and onward for some time, probably due to an era of a more worldly Christianity when people ceased to depend wholly on the Lord but depended more on earthly rulers and earthly luxuries. Sadly, people seemed to believe one could be healed through contact with the bones of dead saints and martyrs rather than through faith in the living Christ.[13]

But it seems that throughout church history whenever revivals occurred miracles occurred also. The Waldenses, Moravians, Huguenots, Covenanters, Friends, Baptists and Methodists all had their record of miracles. The Johannis Lukawitz Waldensis Confession of 1431 said:

> Therefore, concerning this anointing of the sick, we hold it as an article of faith, and profess sincerely from the heart that sick persons, when they ask it, may lawfully be anointed with the anointing oil by one who joins with them in praying that it may be efficacious to the healing of the body according to the design and end and effect mentioned by the apostles; and we profess that such an anointing performed according to the apostolic design and practice will be healing and profitable.

Nicolas Zinzendorf, bishop of the Moravian Church (also called the United Brethren—an old denomination of Christians well respected for their piety and focus on missions) in the 1700s, wrote:

> I owe this testimony to our beloved Church, that apostolic powers are there manifested. We have had undeniable proofs thereof in the unequivocal discovery of things, persons, and circumstances, which could not humanly have been discovered, in the healing of maladies in themselves incurable, such as cancers, consumptions, when the patient was in the agonies of death...all by means of prayer, or of a single word.

Speaking of the year 1730, Zinzendorf wrote:

Various supernatural gifts were manifested in the Church, and miraculous cures were wrought....When, for example, a brother was cured of disease, even of the worst kind, by a single word or by some prayer, he viewed this as a very simply matter, calling to mind, even that saying of Scripture, that signs were not for those who believed, but for those who believed not.

The following is an account of a specific healing among the Moravians.

A married sister became extremely ill at Hernnhut. The physician had given up all hopes, and her husband was plunged in grief....Jean de Watteville made them sing some appropriate hymns under the window of the sick sister, at the same time praying in his heart to the Lord that He would be pleased, if He thought good, to restore her to health. What was the astonishment of those who surrounded the bed of this dying sister when they saw her sit up....To his great amazement and delight, he found her...quite well. She recovered perfectly, and not till thirty-five years after did he attend her earthly tabernacle to its final resting place.[14]

An amazing healing has been recorded among the Scotch Covenanters through the prayer of faith by John Welch. He prayed "over the body of a young man, who, after a long wasting sickness, 'has closed his eyes and expired to the apprehension of all spectators.'" After forty-eight hours it was insisted the "cold dead" body should be buried. Welch prayed for an hour and then "called upon his friends and showed them the dead young man restored to life again, to their great astonishment." The wonders recorded among the Scotch Covenanters are of every kind, and "theirs was a faith born and nourished of the bitterest persecution."[15]

Gordon writes of a man named Patrick Simpson: "whose insane wife, from raving and blaspheming as with demoniacal possession, was so wonderfully healed by his importunate prayers...the 16th of Auguest, 1601."

The following is a healing in Lincolnshire, England due to the prayer of faith by George Fox, whom Gordon calls "a worthy model is he for any minister, in any age."

Now there was in that town a great man that had long lain sick and was given over by the physicians: and some friends in that town desired me to go and see him, and I went up to him in his chamber and spoke the word of life to him and was moved to pray for him, and the Lord entreated and restored him to health.

And while George Fox preached in Hertfordshire, he was requested to pray for a sick woman. Fox says:

When we came in, there were many people in the house that were tender about her: and they told me she was not a woman for this world, but if I had anything to comfort her concerning the world to come I might speak to her. So I was moved of the Lord to speak to her, and the Lord raised her up again to the astonishment of the town and country.

Vavasor Powell was a Welch Baptist who was:

endued with such power of the Spirit that extraordinary revivals followed his preaching wherever he went. He was also a bitter sufferer for the faith having in the course of his life lain in thirteen different prisons for his testimony for Christ....It is recorded that 'many persons were recovered from dangerous sickness through the prayer of faith which he offered.'[16]

Gordon documents the healing of lame Ann Maather among the Methodists. Her father wrote the following testimony in his journal; the testimony also appeared in London Methodist Magazine.

My dear Ann yet remained without any use of either her limbs and indeed without the least feeling of them, or ability to walk a step...nor had she any use of them for upward of twelve months.... We prayed...that it would please the Lord, for the sake of her three little children, to restore her. (One day while in the presence of Ann and other Christians) I spoke of the certainty of God's hearing the prayer of his faithful people, and repeated many of His promises to that purpose. I also enlarged on Christ's being the same yesterday, today, and forever, and still both able and willing to give relief to His afflicted people....After singing (a hymn), we then kneeled down to pray....I prayed first, and then Mr. McDonald; all the company joining fervently in our supplications. We pleaded in prayer the Lord's promises (especially Mt. 18:19). Immediately on our rising from our knees, Ann beckoned to the nurse to take the child, and then instantly rose up, and said, "I can walk...and then walked three times over the floor. (Then they knelt down and gave God thanks.) She afterward, without any help, walked up stairs....She later said that while they sang the hymn she conceived faith that the Lord would heal her.[17]

The Testimony of Theologians

Gordon says of Augustine—the famous theologian, philosopher, and bishop (354 – 430 A. D.), that earlier in his career he denied the continuance of miracles, but he later retracted those assertions and affirmed their continuance. Augustine wrote about the healing of Innocentius, a devout Christian and man of high rank in Carthage. Innocentius suffered from "a painful malady" which led to several surgeries which did not help. An eminent surgeon declared there was no hope except possibly through an additional surgery. Innocentius agreed to one final surgery, and several officers of the church gathered with him for prayer the night before. Innocentius prayed out loud with such fervency in their midst that Augustine could barely pray himself. After prayer, Innocentius persuaded the officers to be with him the next day during his surgery. When the surgeon opened him up, he found the place perfectly healed. "Praise, thanksgiving, and tears...burst from the lips of all present."[18]

Concerning the great reformer, Martin Luther (1483 – 1564 A. D.), Gordon says: "The testimony of Luther's prayers for the healing of the body are among the strongest of any on record in modern times."[19] Luther said, "How often has it happened and still does that devils have been driven out in the name of Christ, also by calling on His name and prayer that the sick have been healed?"[20] Seckendorf's History of Lutheranism records how God worked through Luther's prayer of faith to heal Philip Melancthon, who had become ill on a journey.

Luther arrived and found Philip about to give up the ghost....His consciousness was almost gone...(and) he knew no one....Luther is filled with the utmost consternation...(and) called most devoutly to God....After this, taking the hand of Philip...he said, "Be of good courage, Philip, thou shalt not die...give not place to the spirit of grief, nor become the slayer of thyself, but trust in the Lord who is able to kill and to make alive." While he uttered these things, Philip began, as it were, to revive and to breathe, and gradually recovering his strength, is at last restored to health....Luther...writing to friends (says), "Philip is very well after such an illness, for it was greater than I had supposed. I found him dead, but by an evident miracle of God, he lives."[21]

Luthardt wrote of another healing that occurred in 1541 through the prayer of faith by Luther.

Myconius...was in the last stage of consumption, and already speechless. Luther wrote to him..."May God not let me hear, so long as I live, that you are dead, but cause you to survive me. I pray this earnestly, and will have it granted...." Myconius was...kept from the grave...and did not die till after Luther's death.[22]

Here is a healing of a man, told in his own words, who was reportedly so devout that he was referred to as "man of God, holy Richard Baxter."

I had a tumor rise on one of the tonsils...no bigger than a small button, and hard like a bone. The fear lest it should prove a cancer troubled me more than the thing itself. I used...medicines...for about a quarter of a year. At last my conscious smote me for silencing so many former deliverances, that I had had in answer of prayers....I was that morning to preach just what is here written: "How many times have I known the prayer of faith to save the sick when all physicians have given them up as dead?" When I went to church I had my tumor as before (for I frequently saw it in the glass, and felt it constantly). As soon as I had done preaching, I felt it was gone...and I saw that there was not the least...mark wherever it had been.[23]

John Albert Bengel, a well-respected commentator of the Bible, reported the following miracle:

At Leonberg, a town of Wirtembergh, 1644...a girl of twenty-three years of age was so disabled in her limbs as hardly to be able to creep along by the help of crutches. But whilst the Dean, Raumier was his name, was from the pulpit dwelling on the miraculous power of Jesu's name, she suddenly was raised up and restored to the use of her limbs....This happened in the presence of the Duke of Eberhard and his courtiers and was committed to the public records....[24]

Thomas Erskine, who was "deeply revered as a Christian...and walked so closely and constantly with God,"[25] wrote the following testimony:

In March 1830, in the town of port Glasgow...lived a family of MacDonalds, twin brothers, James and George, with their sisters. One of the sisters, Margaret, of saintly life, lay very ill, and apparently nigh to death. She had received a remarkable baptism of the Spirit on her sick bed, and had been praying for her brothers that they might be anointed in like manner. One day when James was standing by, and she was interceding that he might at that time be endowed with the power of the Holy Ghost, the Spirit came upon him with marvelous manifestations. His whole countenance was lighted up...he walked up to Margaret's bedside and addressed her in these words, "Arise and stand upright." He repeated the words, took her by the hand, and she arose. Her recovery was instantaneous and complete, and the report of it produced a profound sensation, and many came from great distances to see her. Mr. Erskine visited the house and made careful and prolonged inquiry into the facts, and put on record his conviction of the genuineness of the miracle.[26]

Dr. Horace Bushnell (1802 – 1876), American Congregational minister, theologian, and author, wrote of the healing of his friend's son. Bushnell said of his friend: "his character and veracity to be such as to put his story beyond question."

Before the doctor arrived, my mind was filled with revelation of the subject. I saw I had fallen into a snare by turning away from the Lord's healing hand to lean on medical skill. I felt grievously condemned in my conscious; a fear also fell on me that if I persevered in my unbelieving course my son would die, as his oldest brother had. The symptoms in both were precisely similar. The doctor arrived. My son, he said, was suffering from scarlet fever, and medicine should be sent immediately. While he stood, prescribing, I resolved to withdraw the child and cast him on the Lord. And when he was gone I called the nurse and told her to take the child into the nursery, and lay him on the bed. I then fell on my knees, confessing the sin I had committed against the Lord's healing power. I also prayed most earnestly that it would please my heavenly Father to forgive my sin, and to show that he forgave it by causing the fever to be rebuked. I received a mighty conviction that my prayer was heard, and I arose and went to the nursery...to see what the Lord had done, and on opening the door, to my astonishment, the boy was sitting up in his bed, and on seeing me cried out, "I am quite well and want to have dinner." In an hour he was dressed, and well, and eating his dinner, and when the physic arrived it (the medicine) was cast out of the window. Next morning, the doctor returned, and on meeting me at the garden gate he said, "I hope your son is no worse." "He is very well, I thank you," I said in reply. "What can you mean?" rejoined the doctor....I then told him all that had occurred, at which he fairly gasped with surprise....(The doctor examined the son and said) "Yes, he is quite well."[27]

The Testimony of Missions

Dr. Christlieb of Bonn, who was a theologian and professor and well-respected by Gordon, wrote the next three testimonies. The first is of God's working through Hans Egede, the first Evangelical missionary in Greenland.

He had given the Esquinmaux (people of the Arctic) a pictorial representation of the miracles of Christ before he had mastered their language. His hearers, who, like many in the time of Christ, had a perception only for bodily relief, urged him to prove the power of the Redeemer of the world upon their sick people. With many sighs and prayers he ventured to lay his hands upon several, prayed over them, and lo, he made them whole in the name of Jesus Christ! The Lord could not reveal himself plainly enough to this mentally blunted and degraded race my merely spiritual means, and therefore bodily signs were needed.[28]

At a Rhenish mission station in South Africa in 1858, an earnest native Christian saw an old friend who had become lame in both legs. Impressed with a peculiar sense of believing confidence, he went into the bushes to pray, and then came straight up to the cripple, and said, "the same Jesus who made the lame to walk, can do so still: I say to them, in the name of Jesus, rise and walk!" The lame man, with kindred faith, raised himself on his staff and walked, to the astonishment of all who knew him.[29]

This third testimony concerns Nommensen, a missionary from Rhineland working in Sumatra.

A heathen...managed secretly to mix a deadly poison in the rice which Nommensen was preparing for his dinner. Without suspicion, the missionary ate the rice, and the heathen watched for him to fall down dead. Instead of this, however, the promise contained in Mark 16:18 was fulfilled, and he did not experience the slightest inconvenience. The heathen, by this palpable miraculous proof of the Christian God's power, became convinced of the truth, and was eventually converted; but not until his conscience had impelled him to confess his guilt to Nommensen, did the latter know from what danger he had been preserved. This incident is well-attested, and the missionary still lives. 1873.[30]

Gordon writes:

A missionary of the Presbyterian Board who has been laboring for many years in China declares that with the New Testament in their hands the native Christians are constantly finding and putting in practice the promises for miraculous healing. This fact has led him to a careful revision of his opinions on the subject. He writes:

Fully believing that the gifts of the Spirit were not to be taken from the Church, I feel assured that our faith ought to exercise and claim their use now. The salvation aimed for by all should be present release from sin and the power of Satan. If this is attained, then the whole advantage of Christ's life, death, and resurrection will be secured. Healing is as much a part of this as any verbal proclamation of the good news. The ministry of healing, therefore, cannot be divorced from the duty of the missionary.[31]

Gordon writes of the experience of "an honored missionary about the Karens" (southern Myanmar):

While traveling in the Pegu district, I was strongly urged to visit an out of the way village, in which were only a few Christians. Entering the house of one of them, I had been seated but a little while when there came in a Karen, an entire stranger, but whose salutation proved him a Christian. He at once said that hearing that the teacher had come to visit the village, he came to beg that I would go and pray for his son who was very ill, he feared dying. He quoted James 5:14-15 as his excuse. Of course Mrs. _____ and myself went at once, accompanied by the three of four Christians of the house in which we were. The patient was found to be a child of about fifteen years of age…but through scrofula (a disease of glandular swellings) he was distorted and crippled so that he could not walk; indeed had never walked upright but crept painfully on knees and hands. He was greatly wasted, and had been much worse for some weeks, and at the time was perfectly helpless through extreme weakness. He had every appearance of one near death. We prayed, each in turn, the lad mingling short requests with ours. I think in all seven brethren offered petitions. A little bottle of medicine was left from our scanty supplies and we took leave of the poor little fellow. Six months afterwards the father came to the city, and on inquiring of him he said that his son was well—well as he had never been in his life, and was actually walking on his feet, that the heathen families living in the village were deeply impressed, and said unhesitatingly that our prayers had saved him. I asked him his own opinion. He most emphatically, in his strong Karen way, said: "God has done it; God has healed him." He then said, "Teacher this is no new thing; I was with your father-in-law many times when God, in answer to prayers, healed the sick, and that is why I asked you to pray with my boy, and now he is healed."[32]

Rev. Albert Norton wrote a letter to Dr. Stanton of Cincinnati, formerly the moderator of the General Assembly, which contained the following testimony of his own healing. Rev. Norton had been sick in Elichpoor, India in 1879 with "an abscess in his liver which had worked itself through the pleura and was discharging itself into the right lung— the most intense pain ever endured…."

I was thinking only of how I might die as easy as possible, when I was aroused by strong desire to live for my family, and to preach the unsearchable riches of the Gospel, and the thought came "why cannot God heal you?" My dear wife was the only Christian believer, except an ignorant Kerkoo lad, within eighteen miles. At my request she anointed me with oil, and united her prayers with mine that God might at once heal me. While I was praying vocally, before I felt any change in my body, I felt perfectly certain that God had heard and answered our prayers. When we were through praying we commenced praising; for the acute pain in my right side, and the fever, had left me. I was able at once to read some from the Bible, and to look out some passages from the Greek Testament. Neither the fever nor the acute pain returned, and from that hour I began rapidly to grow stronger. In a few days I was able to walk half a mile without fatigue. In this sickness I took no medicine, and had the help of no physician but Jesus. To Him be all the praise and glory. Why should it be thought a strange thing that He can heal our bodies? It is written of him, "Himself took our infirmities and bare our sicknesses." Is it not said of our Lord, "Who healeth all thy diseases," as well as "Who forgiveth all their iniquities"?[33]

The Testimony of the Healed

Miss Fancourt of London suffered from a severe hip disease which began in November of 1822. She was a cripple, confined to her bed most of the time. She also suffered from various medical treatments, from leeches to surgery, none of which helped her. She testified that the suffering continued until October 20, 1830, when a friend who had been led by God to pray for her recovery, remembered what is written, "Whatsoever ye shall ask in prayer, believing, ye shall receive" (Mt. 21:22, KJV). The friend said, "It is melancholy to see a person so constantly confined." Miss Fancourt answered, "It is sent in mercy." He replied, "Do you think so? Do you not think the same mercy could restore you?" Miss Fancourt said at that moment God gave her faith, so she answered "Yes." The man asked, "Do you believe Jesus could heal, as in old times?" She replied, "Yes." He asked, "Do you believe that Jesus could heal you at this very time?" She said, "Yes." The man then said, "Then rise up and walk: come down to your family." The man then took her hand and prayed to God to glorify the name of Jesus. Miss Fancourt said, "I rose from my couch quite strong. God took away all my pains, and we walked down stairs...." The next day, she walked more than a quarter of a mile, and on Sunday she walked one mile and a quarter. She said, "Up to this time, God continues to strengthen me, and I am perfectly well. To Jesus be all the glory. Nov. 13, 1830." Her father, a clergyman who until that point did not believe in modern miracles, made the following statement: "God has raised an impotent cripple, in the person of my youngest daughter, to instantaneous soundness of her bodily limbs by faith in the name of Jesus."[34]

Rev. Morgan Edwards, a New Jersey Baptist minister, told of a miracle that occurred in Hannah Carman. Around the age of twenty-five, Hannah had fallen off a horse and became crippled, and she remained in that condition for about ten years. Hannah testified:

> While I was musing on these words, "Aeneas, Jesus Christ maketh thee whole" (Acts 9:34, KJV), I could not help breathing out my heart and my soul…, "O that I had been in Aeneas' place!" Upon that I heard an audible voice saying, "Arise, take up thy bed and walk!" The suddenness of the voice made me start in my chair; but how I was astonished to find my back strengthening and my limbs recovering their former use….I got up, and to convince myself that it was a reality and not a vision, I lifted up my chair and whatever came in my way: went to my room and took up my bed, and put my strength to other trials, till I was convinced that the cure was real, and not a dream or delusion.[35]

Three individuals wrote and signed certificates affirming the healing of Hannah Carman. It was also affirmed by Miss Ketcham, who was Hannah's caregiver.

Dr. R of Philadelphia said his son fell off a bench and broke both bones of his arm below the elbow. Dr. R's brother, who was a professor of surgery at the College of Chicago, happened to be visiting and he set and dressed the arm, putting it in splints, bandages, and in a sling. The next day, the boy told his dad that he had been in great pain the night before so he asked Jesus to heal his arm, and Jesus did. The boy asked his dad to remove the splints and bandages. The dad said no; he said the boy had to wear them for at least five more weeks. The next morning, the boy begged his dad again to remove the bandages. Dr R. had his brother remove the bandages and the boy's arm was completely healed.[36]

Jennie Smith of Philadelphia had a mysterious and agonizing disease that was described by her pastor as "a narrative of suffering rarely if every equaled"; it left her a cripple for about sixteen years. One limb had such violent spasms that it had to be held down by heavy weights. But her faith in Christ was strong, and she shared the Word of God with those who came to visit. She also began to lay hold of the promise of God for bodily healing. She experienced small manifestations of healing, but began to ask God for full recovery. Some believers were gathered with Jennie and they had devoted the evening to prayer, led by Pastor Everett. A few of the people left after an hour, and one of them said to her, "You are too anxious to get well. The Lord can make better use of you upon your cot than upon your feet." After he left, Jennie replied to his accusations by saying, "No, I am not anxious to get well; I have gained the victory over that." Until that point in the meeting Jenny felt there was not oneness of mind. She said, "I feel that it must be by waiting that our Father will give us the blessing. Are we of one accord in this matter?" The physician, Dr. Morgan, was the first to say, "I will stay, and I fully agree with you." They continued waiting before the Lord; one would occasionally quote a Scripture or say a brief prayer. Jenny recalled:

> I lay in quiet expectancy, still suffering, but with a remarkable sense of the divine presence...so engaged was I in communion with my heavenly Father. About eleven p.m., I was led to vocally offer myself to God in fresh consecration, saying: 'I give this body anew—these eyes to see, these lips to talk, these ears to hear, and, if it be Thy will, these feet to walk—for Jesus. All that is of me—all, all is Thine, dear Father. Only let Thy precious will be done.'

She said up until that time, there had been no relief from the pain. Then she said she had a vision:

> A vivid view of the healing of the withered arm....I could see it being thrust out whole. At the same instant the Holy Spirit bestowed on my soul a faith to claim a similar blessing. It seemed as if heaven were at that moment opened, and I was conscious of a baptism of strength, as sensibly and as positively as if an electric shock had passed through my system. I felt definitely the strength come into my back, and into my helpless limbs....I raised myself to a sitting posture....While the hands of my friends were yet on my shoulders, I arose and stood upon my feet. (Then she knelt in reverence to God.)...I then arose and walked across the room with entire ease and naturalness.[37]

Reuben Archer (R. A.) Torrey (1856-1928) was a well-known American evangelist, pastor, educator, and writer. The following two testimonies are of God healing the sick through him.

How often God has given to me faith as I have prayed for some sick one, and healing immediate, complete and wonderful has followed. When I was Superintendent of City Missions in Minneapolis, I found on my desk one day a request to go to a home three miles distant. The people were unknown to me....I learned that the woman had been sick for four years and had had nine different physicians, none of whom could help her. She was helpless. She could move her hands, but she had to be lifted upon a sheet when they made the bed. I sat down by the sick-bed and asked the woman what she wished me to do. She replied that she wished me to pray that she might be healed....I read to the sick woman...James 5:14-15. Then I asked her, "Do you believe God will heal you?" She replied that she believed that He could heal her. "But," I said, "Do you believe that He *will* heal you?" After reading various promises from the Word she said she believed that He would. I then explained to her very fully the meaning of anointing and that on her part it meant a full surrender to God of all her physical powers. Then I knelt by her bedside and, "having anointed her with oil in the name of the Lord," I prayed that God would come in with the healing power of His Holy Spirit and restore her to perfect health then and there. As I prayed God gave me faith that He heard my prayer. I prayed "the prayer of faith," and as I arose I said to the woman, "I expect you as soon as I am gone to get up and go about your work." I went from that home with the full assurance that God had answered my prayer. The night of the day following...when the meeting was opened for testimony, a neighbor of this woman arose and said that God had completely healed the woman, and that immediately after my departure she did get up, dress, and go out for a call....She remained a strong, healthy woman as long as I remained in Minneapolis....Many years later, when I was holding meetings in Los Angeles...I told this story one afternoon....A man sprang up in the audience and said, "Mr. Torrey, that was my wife. We are living in Los Angeles, and she has been a well woman from that day, about thirty-five years ago, until this day.

There was an M. E. minister up in Dakota who had a child that was improperly formed. There was some defect in her backbone so that the little child was bent together and the abdomen protruded, causing constant pain, and the child could not sleep. The parents brought the child to Minneapolis to see what specialists could do, but the specialists told them that there was no hope for the child, that they might put her in a plaster-cast so that she might live, deformed, not longer than two or three years....Then the minister said to his wife, "Let us take her to Brother Torrey." They brought her over to my house, a little child of about two years of age, terribly misshapen and greatly suffering. I took the child in my arms and prayed for her. God gave the necessary faith and the child was healed. Relief came immediately. That night she slept normally for the first time; even the defective part of her body was made right. Something like eighteen years later I was holding meetings in Petoskey, Michigan. In one of the afternoon meetings, a Methodist minister from one of the neighboring towns came in. He got up in the meeting and told his story, saying he was the father of that daughter and that she was completely healed and a candidate for the mission field. She herself came in a few days later, a beautiful, perfectly-formed young woman. She was in our auditorium in Los Angeles at our Sunday morning services a few weeks ago.[38]

The healings throughout church history described in this chapter show that the miracle-working power of the Holy Spirit that was manifested throughout the gospels and Acts is still available today for those who would believe, for "Jesus Christ is the same yesterday, today, and forever" (Heb. 13:8).

In "The Conclusion" of Gordon's book, he said:

The prayer of faith...will be confessed to be the very highest attainment of the Christian life. And yet it is an attainment which comes...from decrease towards spiritual childhood rather than from increase towards the stature of intellectual manhood. To reach down and grasp the secret of simplicity of faith and implicitness of confidence is far more difficult than to reach up and lay hold of the key of knowledge. Hence, how significant it is that in the Scriptures children are made the heroes of faith....In proportion as we are emptied of self, and schooled back into that second childhood which should follow the second birth, will God be in us most fully and act through us most powerfully.[39]

Despite modern day critics of the healing ministry as well as any past failures to see healings manifest through our own ministries, may we embrace Gordon's concluding exhortation to pursue childlike faith and stand on our heavenly Father's wonderful promises which clearly bear out that healing of spirit, soul, and body is included in the atonement of Christ.

Chapter 4

Atonement

[I would like to credit F. F. Bosworth, author of *Christ the Healer*,[40] whose writing assisted me with some of the thoughts I share in this chapter.]

The Hebrew word for atonement is *kaphar* (from the root *kpr*), and it means "to cover." By its derivation, the English word "atonement" means "at-one-ment";[41] in other words—unity, harmony, reconciliation. It is also defined as: "reconciliation between estranged parties, bringing them into agreement…(or) God's way of bridging the gap…substitution, mediation…."[42] We see a type of atonement in Genesis 3:21, where the LORD God made tunics of skin *to cover* the nakedness of Adam and Eve. Blood had to be shed to make those tunics. Leviticus 17:11 says, "For the life of the flesh is in the blood, and I have given it to you upon the altar to make atonement for your souls; for it is the blood that makes atonement for the soul." Hebrews 10:22 says, "And according to the law almost all things are purified with blood, and without the shedding of blood there is no remission." The remission of sins is costly—it cost blood—one life for another. Non-blood atonements do occur in

Scripture (e.g. shekels paid as a ransom or a censor burning incense), but they point to certain aspects of the ultimate atonement—a particular blood atonement which we will soon discuss.

Kaphar is related to the word *kippur*, as in the Jewish term *Yom Kippur*, which means "Day of Atonement." Leviticus 23:27-28 says: "the tenth day of this seventh month shall be the Day of Atonement...to make atonement for you before the LORD your God." On the Day of Atonement, described in detail in Leviticus 16, the high priest entered the inner part of the tabernacle called the Holy of Holies (it was the only day of the year he was allowed to enter it) to offer blood to atone for his own sins and the sins of Israel. Hebrews 9:7 says: "But into the second part the high priest went alone once a year, not without blood, which he offered for himself and for the people's sins committed in ignorance." The high priest would also take a censer full of burning coals from the altar, put incense on the coals (incense representing the prayers of the saints, Rev. 5:8) which would create a smoke cloud above the mercy seat. God said He would appear in the cloud; the cloud served to shield the high priest from God's manifest presence, lest he die. The high priest would use his finger to sprinkle blood from a killed bull upon and in front of the mercy seat. Then outside of the Holy of Holies, the high priest would cast lots concerning two goats: one goat would be killed and its blood would be sprinkled inside the Holy of Holies; the other goat would be the scapegoat. The high priest would lay his hands on the head of the scapegoat and confess in the hearing of Israel all the sins of Israel, transferring Israel's sins onto the goat. Then the goat would be released into an uninhabited land, bearing away the sins of Israel.

Leviticus 14 details the law of the leper. An Israelite who contracted the deadly and highly contagious disease of leprosy was to go to the priest. The priest would examine the leper outside of the camp to see if the leprosy was healed in the leper. If the leprosy was healed, the priest would take two birds, kill one bird, then dip the feathers of the living bird into the blood of the killed bird, sprinkle the blood seven times on the leper and pronounce him clean. Then the priest would release the bird in an open field. The priest would also sprinkle oil seven times before the LORD, then apply oil to the tip of the right ear, to the thumb of the right hand, and to the toe of the right foot of him who was to be cleansed. As for the rest of the oil in the priest's hand, the priest would put it on the head of him who was to be cleansed. "So the priest shall make atonement for him before the LORD" (verse 18).

Let's imagine that a distinguished guest is coming to my house for dinner. Just before his arrival, one of my daughters spills spaghetti on the carpet. So I quickly rake the spilled spaghetti onto a plate and throw the spaghetti away. Then I place a small rug over the stain so that my guest will not see the stain. When my guest leaves, I remove the rug and apply soap and water to completely remove the spaghetti stain. The rug represents the blood atonement of animals—it temporarily covered over the stain until I could fully remove the stain at a later time. Similarly, the blood of bulls, goats, rams, lambs, birds, or any other animals could never take away sin. It simply covered sin—postponing God's dealing with sin until He dealt with it once for all when He poured His judgment and wrath upon His Son, the Lord Jesus Christ, on the cross. Collectively, the two goats (Lev. 16) and the two birds (Lev. 14) represent the ministry of the Lord Jesus. As one goat was killed as an atonement for sin and as one bird was killed as an atonement for a particular disease, so Jesus was killed, His blood was shed, as the ultimate and final atonement for all of mankind's sin, sickness, and disease. As the scapegoat bore the sins of Israel away from Israel, so Jesus bore our sins and sicknesses away from us, as far as the east is from the west (Ps. 103:12). As the living bird was released in the open field, so Jesus was bodily raised from the dead and, after He appeared to certain people for forty days, He flew up (ascended) into the heavens. Jesus Christ is the antitype of all Old Testament types of atonement. Furthermore, Jesus Christ is the ultimate High Priest. He did not enter a tabernacle made by the hands of men, but He entered heaven itself to present His own blood as the ultimate atonement for sin. His flesh was represented by the temple veil that was torn in two, so that we who have faith in His atoning blood have direct access to the presence of God.

Hebrews 9:11-15 speaks of Christ's atoning work:

But Christ came as High Priest of the good things to come, with the greater and more perfect tabernacle not made with hands, that is, not of this creation. Not with the blood of goats and calves, but with His own blood He entered the Most Holy Place once for all, having obtained eternal redemption. For if the blood of bulls and goats and the ashes of a heifer, sprinkling the unclean, sanctifies for the purifying of the flesh, how much more shall the blood of Christ, who through the eternal Spirit offered Himself without spot to God, cleanse your conscience from dead works to serve the living God? And for this reason He is the Mediator of the new covenant, by means of death, for the redemption of the transgressions under the first covenant, that those who are called may receive the promise of the eternal inheritance.

Again, Christ's atoning death and subsequent resurrection provide eternal salvation for the whole world. The blood of Christ also atoned for the sins of those who were faithful to God under the first covenant (Heb. 9:15; Rom. 3:25).

Exodus

The children of Israel were slaves in Egypt for 430 years. Through the words and rod of His servant Moses, God struck Egypt with ten miraculous plagues to demonstrate His unmatchable power. The tenth plague caused the death of the firstborn male of each Egyptian household, and even of their animals. The Israelites were spared such death as they followed God's instruction of applying blood from sacrificed lambs (an atonement) upon the doorposts of their homes. When God passed through Egypt on the appointed night, He *passed over* the Israelite homes—sparing them of His deadly judgment—if the blood of the lamb had been applied to the doorposts of their homes and if they remained in their homes on that night. So a blood atonement was the impetus for Israel's long-awaited deliverance from Egypt. Psalm 105:37 says of Israel's exodus from Egypt: "He also led them out with silver and gold, and there was none feeble among their tribes." So God granted Israel financial prosperity and physical strength, both linked to the atonement of Passover. Third John 2 can be seen as a New Covenant version of Psalm 105:37—"Beloved, I pray that you may prosper in all things and be in health, just as your soul prospers." Immediately, God began to lead Israel by a pillar of cloud by day and a pillar of fire by night, and He led them in this manner for approximately forty years. Similarly, the moment one is born again (through faith in the blood of Jesus, God's divine Lamb, John 1:36; Rev. 5:6), one should seek to be led daily by the Holy Spirit for the rest of one's life. In Exodus 14, Israel experienced a type of water baptism when God led them through the midst of the Red Sea and subsequently drowned, or washed away, the pursuing Egyptians. Similarly, each Christian should be immersed in water baptism following his conversion to Christ. In Exodus 15:26 (just three chapters after the Passover, thus in close proximity to the atonement), God revealed to Israel one of His covenantal names— *Jehovah Rapha*—"the LORD who heals you." This is the first covenant name of God following the atonement of Passover. God promised to be Israel's Healer if they would diligently obey all His commands. And because Jesus the Christ always perfectly obeyed the Father, through faith in Christ's atoning work on the cross we can experience God as *Jehovah Rapha*. The word *rapha* appears approximately fifty-five times in the Bible, and many of its appearances are in the context of divine physical healings (e.g. in Gen. 20:17; Num. 12:13; 2 Kings 8:29; 2 Kings 9:15; Ps. 103:3). So God made a never-ending promise, which He reiterated in Deuteronomy 7:15 and Psalm 103:3 (see also 2 Cor. 1:20), to be the Healer of the spirit, soul, and body (1 Thess. 5:23b) of His people who trust in Him.

Exodus 24:4-8 And Moses wrote all the words of the LORD. And he rose early in the morning, and built an altar at the foot of the mountain, and twelve pillars according to the twelve tribes of Israel. (5) Then he sent young men of the children of Israel, who offered burnt offerings and sacrificed peace offerings of oxen to the LORD. (6) And Moses took half the blood and put it in basins, and half the blood he sprinkled on the altar. (7) Then he took the Book of the Covenant and read in the hearing of the people. And they said, "All that the LORD has said we will do, and be obedient."(8) And Moses took the blood, sprinkled it on the people, and said, "This is the blood of the covenant which the LORD has made with you according to all these words."

In Exodus 24, we see the inauguration of the Old Covenant. There was a double cure, or a two-part work, of the atoning blood. The first part we see in verses 5-6: blood was applied to the altar, thus appeasing the wrath of God. This action pointed forward typologically to the offering of Christ's blood in the Holy of Holies of the true heavenly tabernacle (Heb. 9:11-12). Christ's dying on the cross as the divine Substitute for sinners allowed God's wrath to be carried out in full, so that those who trust in Christ might be justified and delivered "from the wrath to come" (1 Thess. 1:10). The second part we see in verse 8: the sprinkling of the blood on the people in order to cleanse the people from the defilement of sin that was upon them, so that their hearts could be in a position to obey God's law. James Grant says: "Here, in response to their verbal pledge in verse 7, the LORD officially adopts them as His covenant people."[43] The action of verse 8 pointed forward to New Testament sanctification, or purification, which delivers each believer from the power of sin (Rom. 6:6, 14).[44] We see this two-fold work of the atoning blood in the hymn *Rock of Ages, Cleft for Me*:

> Rock of Ages, cleft for me, let me hide myself in Thee; let the water and the blood, from Thy wounded side which flowed, be of sin the **double cure**; save from wrath and make me pure.

Exodus 30:11, 12, 15 is an example of an atonement preventing a plague.

> Then the LORD spoke to Moses, saying: (12) "When you take the census of the children of Israel for their number, then every man shall give a *ransom* for himself to the LORD, when you number them, that there may be *no plague* among them when you number them. (15) The rich shall not give more and the poor shall not give less than half a shekel, when you give an offering to the LORD, to make *atonement* for yourselves.

When a census was taken of the children of Israel, every man was to give a "ransom" of a half shekel for himself to the LORD "that there may be no plague among them." This ransom, or "offering," was to make "atonement" in order to prevent the plague (verse 15), which implies the healing of physical disease.

Numbers

Though Numbers 15 does not deal specifically with divine healing, it is instructive concerning atonement and provides a serious warning pertaining to sin. In Numbers 15, the Lord discusses two different types of sin: unintentional sin and presumptuous sin. In the discussion of unintentional sin (verses 22-29), some form of the word "unintentional" appears nine times, presumably for emphasis. When an Israelite or a stranger among the Israelites sins unintentionally, four offerings had to be made: a burnt offering (requiring the sacrifice of a bull), a grain offering, a drink offering, and a sin offering (requiring the sacrifice of a goat). Also in this passage, "priest" is mentioned, "atonement" is mentioned three times, and "forgiveness" is mentioned three times.

There is a cost for unintentional sin, but receiving divine forgiveness is possible.

Verses 30-31 reveal the Lord's view of presumptuous sin. No mention is made of offerings, a priest, atonement, or forgiveness. Instead, the one who sins presumptuously "brings reproach on the LORD, and he shall be cut off from among his people. Because he has despised the word of the LORD, and has broken His commandment, that person shall be completely cut off; his guilt shall be upon him."

My friend, James Grant, says of these passages:

This goes to show that the sacrificial system was never designed by God to be a set of indulgences—an automatic way, sort of through a commercial transaction, that people's sins could be forgiven. Instead, it was designed to emphasize the seriousness of even unintentional sin, and to emphasize the people's hearts' being directed toward the Lord.[45]

It seems the Numbers 15:30-31 passage is what the writer of Hebrews had in mind when he wrote Hebrews 10:26-39. Similar to the judgment that befell the presumptuous sinner in the Old Testament, Hebrews 10 reveals that an unimaginably horrible fate awaits the Christian who becomes a willful sinner.

For if we sin willfully after we have received the knowledge of the truth, there no longer remains a sacrifice for sins, (27) but a certain fearful expectation of judgment, and fiery indignation which will devour the adversaries. (28) Anyone who has rejected Moses' law dies without mercy on the testimony of two or three witnesses. (29) Of how much worse punishment, do you suppose, will he be thought worthy who has trampled the Son of God underfoot, counted the blood of the covenant by which he was sanctified a common thing, and insulted the Spirit of grace?... (38) Now the just shall live by faith; but if anyone draws back, My soul has no pleasure in him." (39) But we are not of those who draw back to perdition, but of those who believe to the saving of the soul." (Heb. 10:26-29, 38-39).

Committing willful sin, which is eternally dangerous, disrespects the blood of the covenant by which we were sanctified. Each of us should be willing to bend over backwards if need be to avoid committing sin

(Jn. 5:14; Jn. 8:11; 1 Jn. 2:1-2). Through the power of Christ which is available to each believer by faith, and through His holy Word which should dwell richly within each Christian, this is possible.

Numbers 16 contains the account of the rebellion of Korah. Korah, Dathan, Abiram, and On took 250 of the leaders of Israel and gathered together against Moses and Aaron, saying, "You take too much upon yourselves, for all the congregation is holy, every one of them, and the LORD is among them. Why then do you exalt yourselves above the assembly of the LORD?" (verse 3). They furthermore said, "you... keep acting like a prince over us [and]...you have not brought us into a land flowing with milk and honey" (verses 13-14). So "the LORD spoke to Moses and Aaron, saying, 'Separate yourselves from among this congregation, that I may consume them in a moment'" (verse 21). Verses 31-33 show that God opened the ground so that it swallowed up the rebels, with their households and goods, and then closed the earth in over them. The next day, the Israelites complained against Moses and Aaron because of the judgment, saying "You have killed the people of the LORD" (verse 41). (How ridiculous for them to think Moses and Aaron had the power within themselves to cause the earth's ground to split open. But when people's hearts and minds are warped with sin, such ridiculous ideas, here prompted by the desire to place blame, can occur.) Therefore, God again said, "Get away from among this congregation, that I may consume them in a moment" (verse 45). God struck Israel with a plague. Moses sent Aaron into the midst of the congregation to make "atonement" (verse 47) for them, and the plague was stopped. However, before the plague stopped, 14,700 died. The atonement made by Aaron on behalf of the congregation caused a profound physical benefit—it stopped the plague which had brought death.

In Numbers 21:4-9, the children of Israel grumbled against the LORD and against Moses. Therefore, the LORD sent fiery serpents among the people, and many of the people who were bitten died. This judgment by the LORD caused the people to confess their sins and have Moses pray for them. The LORD listened to Moses and provided a remedy: The LORD instructed Moses, whom they sinned against, to "make a fiery serpent [out of bronze], and set it on a pole; and it shall be that everyone who is bitten, when he looks at it, shall live" (verse 8). The bronze serpent on the pole foreshadowed Jesus on the cross.

Jesus said, "And as Moses lifted up the serpent in the wilderness, even so must the Son of Man be lifted up, that whoever believes in Him should not perish but have eternal life" (Jn. 3:14-15). In other words, the bronze serpent was a type of Calvary; it atoned for the sins of the people. If everyone who looked to this type of Calvary—the bronze serpent—was physically healed, then surely physical healing is available, along with forgiveness and every other covenantal promise, through Calvary itself. The Old Covenant provision cannot be greater than the New Covenant provision. Hebrews 8:6 says, "But now He (Jesus) has obtained a more excellent ministry, inasmuch as He is also Mediator of a better covenant, which was established on better promises." Physical healing was provided through the atonement in Numbers 21:4-9.

In Numbers 25, the children of Israel committed harlotry with the women of Moab, and they joined themselves to the false god, Baal. When an Israelite presented to his brethren a Midianite woman, Phinehas (the grandson of Aaron, the original Israelite high priest) thrust both the man and woman through with a javelin. "So the plague was stopped among the children of Israel…[thus, God made a covenant with Phinehas and his descendants] because he was zealous for his God, and made *atonement* for the children of Israel" (Num. 25:8b, 13). Again, atonement stopped a plague.

In 2 Chronicles 30, King Hezekiah reinstituted the Passover, for "they had not done it for a long time in the prescribed manner" (verse 5). Hezekiah prayed, "May the good LORD provide *atonement* for everyone who prepares his heart to seek God…And the LORD listened to Hezekiah and *healed* (*rapha*) the people" (verses 18-20).

The Year of Jubilee

Leviticus 25 refers to the year of Jubilee. This concept is based on the LORD's Sabbath. God mandated rest on the seventh day and the seventh year. Then after seven cycles of seven years began the year of Jubilee. Some of the notable benefits of the Jubilee year were as follows: 1) There was to be no sowing, reaping, or harvesting. All spontaneous fruit of the soil was to be left for the poor, slave, and stranger; 2) the land was to be returned to its original inherited line of ownership; 3) the slaves were to be released.[46] So the overall idea of Jubilee is freedom and release from debt. *The year of Jubilee always began on the Day of*

Atonement. In Luke 4:19, Jesus tells us in His inaugural sermon that He was anointed "to preach the acceptable year of the Lord," which refers to the Old Testament concept of the year of Jubilee. The gospel preached to the poor, the healing of the brokenhearted, the proclamation of liberty to the captives, the recovery of sight to the blind, the setting at liberty those who are oppressed, and all other gospel blessings fulfill the Old Testament type of the acceptable year of the LORD—the year of Jubilee. And the atonement is the basis for all of these blessings.

Isaiah 53: Who has believed our report? And to whom has the arm of the LORD been revealed? [2] For He shall grow up before Him as a tender plant, and as a root out of dry ground. He has no form or comeliness; and when we see Him, *there is* no beauty that we should desire Him. [3] He is despised and rejected by men, a Man of sorrows and acquainted with grief. And we hid, as it were, *our* faces from Him; He was despised, and we did not esteem Him. [4] Surely He has borne our griefs and carried our sorrows; yet we esteemed Him stricken, smitten by God, and afflicted. [5] But He *was* wounded for our transgressions, *He was* bruised for our iniquities; the chastisement for our peace *was* upon Him, and by His stripes we are healed. [6] All we like sheep have gone astray; we have turned, every one, to his own way; and the LORD has laid on Him the iniquity of us all. [7] He was oppressed and He was afflicted, yet He opened not His mouth; He was led as a lamb to the slaughter, and as a sheep before its shearers is silent, so He opened not His mouth. [8] He was taken from prison and from judgment, and who will declare His generation? For He was cut off from the land of the living; for the transgressions of My people He was stricken. [9] And they made His grave with the wicked—but with the rich at His death, because He had done no violence, nor *was any* deceit in His mouth. [10] Yet it pleased the LORD to bruise Him; He has put *Him* to grief. When You make His soul an offering for sin, He shall see *His* seed, He shall prolong *His* days, and the pleasure of the LORD shall prosper in His hand. [11] He shall see the labor of His soul, *and* be satisfied. By His knowledge My righteous Servant shall justify many, for He shall bear their iniquities. [12] Therefore I will divide Him a portion with the great, and He shall divide the spoil with the strong, because He poured out His soul unto death, and He was numbered with the transgressors, and He bore the sin of many, and made intercession for the transgressors.

The prophecy of Isaiah 53, which occurred approximately 700 B.C., is a primary passage concerning the ultimate and final atonement for mankind's sin—the substitutionary death of God's Messiah. In verse 1, the words "believed" and "revealed" are connected, for a person cannot believe in the saving work of the Messiah unless He and His work are revealed by God specifically to that person. Verses 2-3 emphatically state that the Messiah—the One through whom the world and its inhabitants were made—would be despised and rejected by men.

In verse 4, *nasa* means "borne"—"Surely He has borne (*nasa*) our griefs (*choli*)...." *Nasa* also appears in verses 11-12: "...My righteous Servant shall justify many, for He shall bear (*nasa*) their iniquities.... He was numbered with the transgressors, and He bore (*nasa*) the sin of many...." *Nasa* is also applied to the scapegoat of Leviticus 16:22: "The goat shall bear (*nasa*) upon him all their iniquities unto a land not inhabited...."

[Let's again look at Leviticus 16, which details the Day of Atonement. The killed goat and the live goat (or scapegoat) of Leviticus 16 should be viewed as together representing the atoning work of the Messiah. For the Messiah would be killed and His divine blood would atone for all sin. Then the high priest would "lay both his hands on the head of the live goat, confess over it all the iniquities of the children of Israel, and all their transgressions, concerning all their sins, putting them on the head of the goat, and shall send it away into the wilderness by the hand of a suitable man." (Lev. 16:21). This points to the fact that the Messiah would also carry our sins far away from each of us (represented by the live goat which bore the sins of Israel away). Likewise, if we, by faith in Christ's atoning work, confess and forsake our sins, "He is faithful and just to forgive us our sins and to cleanse us from all unrighteousness" (1 Jn. 1:9; Prov. 28:13).]

In Isaiah 53:4, "griefs" is the Hebrew word *choliy*. According to Strong's Concordance, *choliy* (#2483) occurs twenty-four times in the Bible and means disease, grief, and sickness.[47] The Assemblies of God General Presbytery of 1974 concurs, saying, "'griefs' is the same word used of physical sickness and disease (in numerous passages)...."[48] *Choliy* appears in the following passages: Deuteronomy 7:15—"And the LORD will take away from you all *sickness*, and will afflict you with none of the terrible diseases of Egypt which you have known..."; Deuteronomy 28:59— "then the LORD will bring upon you and your descendants extraordinary plagues—great and prolonged plagues—and serious and prolonged *sicknesses*"; Deuteronomy 28:61—"Also every *sickness* and every plague, which *is* not written in this Book of the Law, will the LORD bring upon you until you are destroyed"; 2 Chronicles

21:18—"After all this the LORD struck him (King Jehoram) in his intestines with an incurable *disease.*"

In verse 4, "sorrows" is the Hebrew word *makob.* According to Strong's Concordance, *makob* (#4341) occurs sixteen times in the Bible and means grief, pain, and sorrow.[49] *Makob* appears in Job 33:19: "Man is also chastened with *pain* on his bed, and with strong *pain* in many of his bones." (Job 33:21 further implies that the pain was physical in nature.) *Makob* also appears in Exodus 3:7: "And the LORD said: 'I have surely seen the oppression of My people who *are* in Egypt, and have heard their cry because of their taskmasters, for I know their *sorrows.*'" Here, *makob,* which is translated "sorrows," would include emotional, physical, and spiritual pain.

So Isaiah 53:4 can be translated: "Surely he hath borne our sicknesses, and carried our pains." The Gospel writer, Matthew, under the inspiration of the Holy Spirit, interpreted Isaiah 53:4 this very way: "He (Jesus) cast out the spirits with a word, and healed all who were sick, that it might be fulfilled which was spoken by Isaiah the prophet, saying: *'He Himself took our infirmities and bore our sicknesses'*" (Mt. 8:16-17). If questions are raised as to whether "infirmities" and "sicknesses" in Matthew 8:17 refer to the physical body, then we can point out the context. The preceding portion of Matthew 8 includes accounts of various physical healings: a leper being healed (8:1-4), the centurion's servant being healed of paralysis (8:5-13), Peter's mother-in-law being healed of a fever (8:14-15), and the healing of all among a multitude who were sick and many who were demon-possessed (8:16).

Isaiah 53:5 reveals that the Messiah would be wounded, bruised, chastised, and killed as an *atonement* for mankind. And the New Testament makes clear that all who believe in Jesus the Christ for the forgiveness of their sins are forgiven, and all who believe in Him for the healing of their bodies are healed. Franz Delitzsch, a great Hebrew scholar of the nineteenth century, said that in understanding the meaning of words such as "healing," "peace," and "wholeness," we ought not separate the natural from the spiritual because they are interrelated. Thus, if the word "healing" (or a form of "healing") appears in the Bible, *then all of what healing can mean is meant.* When Isaiah 53:5 says "the chastisement of our peace was upon Him," "peace" (*shalom*) means one's total well-being, including one's bodily health. The Hebrew word translated "healed" in Isaiah 53:5 is *rapha.* Any attempt to limit the healing mentioned in Isaiah 53:5 to spiritual healing only would be wrong. Instead, by the stripes laid on the back of the Messiah and by His murderous death, divine healing of the spirit, soul, and body (1 Thess. 5:23b) has been made available for all.

Jesus Christ, who embodied the fulfillment of this prophecy, would be scourged with the whip, would be crucified on a cross, but would also be bodily raised from the dead three days later. On the cross, Jesus entered into spiritual fellowship with our sins and sicknesses. Not only did Jesus bear our sins, but He also bore the consequences of those sins for us. Jesus' willingness to undergo such horrible sufferings on our behalf is the ultimate demonstration of God's love for this world (1 Jn. 4:9-10). On the cross, where He voluntarily assumed all of our sins and bore them far away from us, Jesus also assumed and bore away all of our sicknesses. Jesus died that we might be forgiven and healed.

Obviously, Jesus forgave sinners and healed people of diseases before Calvary. F. F. Bosworth says, "...these mercies were bestowed on the ground of the atonement in the future."[50] (For more explanation of Jesus' authority to heal, please refer to Chapter 6 of this book—Matthew 8:5-13, Authority.) Notice also that Isaiah 53:5 does not say "might be healed" or "some of us are healed," as if it were God's perfect will for some to be sick. But it says, "we are healed." So I can insert my name—"by His stripes Tom is healed."

F. F. Bosworth (1877 - 1958) was a great evangelist whom God used to preach the good news of salvation and healing through faith in Christ to many thousands in the early Twentieth Century. He has been one of my favorite authors, and I highly recommend his book, *Christ the Healer,* which has sold over 500,000 copies. He said:

> Disease, which is incipient death, entered into the world by sin. Since disease entered by sin, its true remedy must be found in the redemption of Christ.... Since disease is a part of the curse, its true remedy must be the cross. Who can remove the curse but God, and how can God justly do it except by substitution?...The Bible teaches...that disease is the physical penalty of iniquity. Since Christ has borne in His body all our physical liabilities on account of sin, our bodies are therefore released judicially from disease. Through Christ's redemption we may all have, as a part of the "earnest of our inheritance," the "life also of Jesus...made manifest in our mortal flesh" (2 Cor. 4:11)....If healing is not in the Atonement, why were

types of the Atonement given in connection with bodily healing throughout the Old Testament?...As in Leviticus the types show that healing was invariably through atonement, so Matthew 8:16-17 definitely states that Christ healed all diseases on the ground of the Atonement....Sin and sickness have passed from me to Calvary— salvation and health have passed from Calvary to me.[51]

God's Provision for the Spiritual and Physical Man

Bosworth has a chart that shows how Christ's atonement provides for the spiritual man (he calls "inner man") and the physical man (he calls "outer man"). The chart points out the similarities of God's provision for the spiritual aspect of man and the physical aspect of man. Here is much of his chart, with some changes and additions made by me.

<u>Spiritual Man</u>: Christ was made "sin for us" (2 Cor. 5:21) when He "bore our sins" (1 Pet. 2:24).

<u>Physical Man</u>: Christ was made "a curse for us" (Gal. 3:13) when He "bore our sicknesses" (Mt. 8:17).

> First Peter 2:24 relates back to Isaiah 53:5. Matthew 8:17 relates back to Isaiah 53:4. Isaiah 53 (called the fifth gospel) is the chapter on the atonement of the Messiah. So both of these works of Christ—that He "bore our sins" and "bore our sicknesses"—are clearly tied to His atoning death.

<u>Spiritual Man</u>: "As many as received him"...were born of God (Jn. 1:12-13).

<u>Physical Man</u>: "As many as touched him were made well" (Mk. 6:56).

<u>Spiritual Man</u>: Jehovah-Tsidkenu (THE LORD OUR RIGHTEOUSNESS) reveals God's redemption for our souls (Jer. 23:6, 33:16; 2 Cor. 5:21).

<u>Physical Man</u>: *Jehovah-Rapha* (The LORD our Healer) reveals God's redemption for our bodies (Ex. 15:26).

<u>Spiritual Man</u>: (God) "forgives all your iniquities" (Ps. 103:3a).

<u>Physical Man</u>: (God) "heals all your diseases" (Ps. 103:3b).

<u>Spiritual Man</u>: Christ "bore our *sins*" that we might be delivered from them. Not just SYMPATHY—a suffering with, but SUBSTITUTION—a suffering for. (—A. J. Gordon)

Physical Man: Christ "bore our *sicknesses*" that we might be delivered from them. Not just SYMPATHY—a suffering with, but SUBSTITUTION—a suffering for. (—A. J. Gordon)

Spiritual Man: "For you were bought at a price: therefore glorify God in your...*spirit*, which are God's" (1 Cor. 6:20). Your spirit has been redeemed.

Physical Man: "For you were bought at a price: therefore glorify God in your *body*...which are God's" (1 Cor. 6:20). Your body has been redeemed.

Man's spirit and body "were bought at a price," or redeemed, by Christ's shed blood (1 Pet. 1:18-19; Rev. 5:9).

Spiritual Man: Is remaining in sin the way to glorify God in your spirit?

Physical Man: Is remaining sick the way to glorify God in your body?

Spiritual Man: The first Adam, by his fall, brought sin into our souls. The last Adam (Christ) brought forgiveness and eternal life into the souls of all who believe in Him.

Physical Man: The first Adam, by his fall, brought disease into our bodies. The last Adam (Christ), brought healing into the bodies of all who believe in Him for healing—"your faith has made you well" (Mk. 5:34).

Spiritual Man: Sin is therefore the work of the devil.

Physical Man: Disease is also the work of the devil. But Jesus "went about...healing all who were oppressed of the devil" (Acts 10:38).

Spiritual Man: "The Son of God was manifested, that He might destroy the works of the devil" (1 Jn. 3:8) in the *soul*.

Physical Man: "The Son of God was manifested, that He might destroy the works of the devil" (1 Jn. 3:8) in the *body*.

Spiritual Man: "Himself bore our sins in His own body on the tree..." (1 Pet. 2:24a).

Physical Man: "...by whose stripes you were healed" (1 Pet. 2:24b).

Spiritual Man: The sinner is to repent as an aspect of believing the Gospel "unto righteousness."

Physical Man: James 5:16 says "Confess your trespasses...that you may be healed."

Spiritual Man: Christ's promise for the soul is in the Great Commission: "shall be saved" (Mk. 16:16).

Physical Man: Christ's promise for the body is in the Great Commission: "shall recover" (Mk. 16:18).

Spiritual Man: Preach the gospel [that "He bore our sins" (1 Pet. 2:24)] to every creature.

Physical Man: Preach the gospel [that "He bore our sicknesses" (Mt. 8:17)] to every creature.

Spiritual Man: Faith for salvation "comes by hearing" (Rom. 10:17)— we should hear that "He bore our sins" (1 Pet. 2:24).

Physical Man: Faith for healing "comes by hearing" (Rom. 10:17)—we should hear that Jesus "bore our sicknesses" (Mt. 8:17).

Spiritual Man: Ordinance of baptism: "he who believes and is baptized will be saved" (Mk. 16:16).

Physical Man: Ordinance of anointing with oil: he who is anointed by one praying the prayer of faith will be healed (Jas. 5:14-16).

Spiritual Man: We are commanded to baptize in Christ's name.

Physical Man: We are commanded to anoint "in the name of the Lord" (Jas. 5:14).

Spiritual Man: "Your faith has saved you. Go in peace" (Lk. 7:50).

Physical Man: "Your faith has made you well. Go in peace" (Lk. 8:48).

Spiritual Man: "Son, be of good cheer; your sins are forgiven you" (Mt. 9:2).

Physical Man: "Be of good cheer, daughter; your faith has made you well" (Mt. 9:22).

Bosworth said: "Why should not the 'last Adam' take away all that the 'first Adam' brought upon us?...Through the Fall we lost everything. Jesus recovered all through His Atonement."[52]

Testimony—God's Heals a Girl's Eyes

Rev. H. A. Maxwell Whyte begins his book, *The Power of the Blood*, with the following testimony.

"Pastor Whyte, will you pray for my eyes?" Betty...was a young girl of sixteen who worked in a Fish N' Chips store in Toronto. "Why, certainly, Betty...Let's just believe God together and plead the blood of Jesus."...She was totally blind in her right eye, and her left eye was wandering so that it was very difficult for her to focus at all. She was wearing very thick glasses....I began to pray for her, pleading the blood strongly and emphatically. Instantly, the Lord restored the sight of her right eye....She squealed, "I can see." Over a period of weeks, the wandering eye began to focus and in a matter of months, she had 20-20 vision. That was twenty years ago, and she is still healed.[53]

What Eminent Ministers Have Said on Atonement and Healing

Andrew Murray (1828 - 1917) was a South African pastor, teacher and writer. He was also an advocate of divine healing and testified that he was personally healed by God. He wrote:

By His own acts and afterward by the commands which He left for His disciples, He showed us clearly that the preaching of the Gospel and the healing of the sick went together in the salvation which He came to bring. He never taught one sick person to resign himself to being sick. The Name of Jesus both saves and heals....Healing and health are part of Christ's salvation....The health of our bodies is a fruit of the salvation which Jesus has acquired for us....Health as well as salvation are to be obtained by faith. Even the body has been saved by Christ.[54]

In this chapter (Isaiah 53), the expression "to bear" occurs twice, but in relation to two different things. It is said not only that the LORD's righteous Servant bore our sins (verse 12), but also that He bore our sickness (verse 4 RV). Thus His bearing our sicknesses as well as our sins forms an integral part of the Redeemer's work. Although He was without sin, He has borne our sins, and has done the same with our sicknesses....By bearing them, He triumphed over them and has acquired the right of delivering His children from them. Sin had attacked and ruined the soul and body equally. Jesus came to save both. Having taken sickness as well as sin on Himself, He is in a position to set us free from the one as well as the other. In order for Him to accomplish this double deliverance, He expects only one thing from us: our faith.[55]

I witnessed the blessed influence this truth exercised one day on a sick woman. She had spent almost seven years in bed. A sufferer from tuberculosis, epilepsy, and other sicknesses, she had been assured that no hope of cure remained for her. She was carried into the room where the late Mr. W. E. Boardman was holding a Sunday evening service for the sick, and was laid in a half-fainting condition on the sofa. She was too little conscious to remember anything of what took place until she heard the words, "Himself took our infirmities and bare our sicknesses" (Mt. 8:17). She then seemed to hear the words,

"If He has borne your sicknesses, why then bear them yourself?
Get up." "But," she thought, "if I attempt to get up, and fall on the
ground, what will they think of me?" But the inward voice began
again, "If He has borne my sins, why should I have to bear them?"
To the astonishment of all who were present, she rose, and although
still feeble, sat down in a chair by the table. From that moment, her
healing made rapid progress. At the end of a few weeks, she no longer
had the appearance of an invalid. Soon she was so strong that she
could spend many hours a day in visiting the poor.[56]

Rees Howells (1879 – 1950) was the founder of the Bible College of
Wales and was a missionary in Africa. *Rees Howells Intercessor* (the well-
known biography of Rees Howells) contains the following concerning
healing and the atonement.

> ...he (Mr. Howells) was arrested by that scripture, He "Himself took
> our infirmities, and bare our sicknesses" (Mt. 8:17), and realized
> for the first time that, through His atoning sacrifice, the Savior
> had provided not only for the forgiveness of our sins but for a full
> redemption from all the effects of sin and the Fall. Since He was
> "made a curse for us," why should these sufferers continue to bear
> the effects of that curse?

> Because he believed that Christ "bare our sins in His own body on the
> Tree," Mr. Howells always offered to sinners not only freedom from
> the guilt and penalty of sin but also from the power and domination
> of sin. "But," he reasoned, "if He also 'bare our sicknesses,' why do I
> not offer healing in His name just as freely? Why should there not be
> freedom from the power and domination of sickness?" Anything less
> than this, he felt, was not giving to the Savior the glory He deserved,
> and he resolved to pay any price to prove that this power was in the
> atonement.[57]

Adoniram Judson Gordon (1836 – 1895) was an American Baptist
minister who founded Gordon Bible Institute, and wrote a famous book
entitled *The Ministry of Healing*. In this book, Gordon asserts that healing
of the body is an aspect of Christ's atonement, citing especially Psalm
103:3 and Matthew 8:17. Here is an excerpt from his book:

We have Christ set before us as the sickness-bearer as well as the sin-bearer of His people. In the gospel it is written, "And he cast out devils and healed all that were sick, that it might be fulfilled which was spoken by Esias the prophet saying, 'Himself took our infirmities and bare our sicknesses'" (Mt. 8:17). Something more than sympathetic fellowship with our sufferings is evidently referred to here. The yoke of his cross by which he lifted our iniquities took hold also of our diseases; so that it is in some sense true that as God "made Him to be sin for us who knew no sin," so He made Him to be sick for us who knew no sickness."...Christ endured vicariously our diseases as well as our iniquities. If now it be true that our Redeemer and substitute bore our sicknesses, it would be natural to reason at once that he bore them that we might not bear them....Christ bore your sins (1 Pet. 2:24) that you might be delivered from them...Not sympathy—a suffering with, but substitution—a suffering for...In its ultimate consequences the atonement affects the body as well as the soul of man...."Thy sins are forgiven thee" and "Be whole of thy plague" are parallel announcements of the Savior's work which are found constantly running on side by side. Certain great promises of the gospel have this double reference to pardon and cure.[58]

Dr. T. J. McCrossan, who was a professor of Greek and Hebrew at Manitoba University, Manitoba, Canada, as well as pastor and author of an excellent book, *Bodily Healing and the Atonement*, points out that the following passages show that both the body and the spirit have been bought with a price.

Or do you not know that your body is the temple of the Holy Spirit who is in you, whom you have from God, and you are not your own? For you were bought at a price; therefore glorify God in your body and in your spirit, which are God's (1 Cor. 6:19-20).

The word for "bought" [*egorasthete*] comes from *agorazo*, meaning "I buy or redeem." Look at Revelation 5:9b: "You were slain, and have redeemed us to God by Your blood." The word for "redeemed" [*egorasas*] also comes from *agorazo*. Dr. McCrossan says:

Then these two passages together teach most clearly the blessed truth that, when Christ shed His blood at the awful scourging and on the cross, He redeemed both our bodies and our spirits by His blood, the price paid. No unprejudiced Greek scholar can possibly draw any other conclusion as he closely studies First Corinthians 6:19-20 and Revelation 5:9. Yes, praise God, Paul clearly teaches in First Corinthians 6:19-20 that bodily healing is in the Atonement.[59]

John G. Lake (1870 – 1935), who was a healing evangelist and church planter in Africa and in the United States, said:

> Everything there is in the redemption of Jesus Christ is available for man when man will present his claim in faith and take it. There is no question in the mind of God concerning the salvation of a sinner. No more is there any question concerning the healing of the sick one. It is in the atonement of Jesus Christ, bless God. His atonement was unto the uttermost; to the last need of man.[60]

E. W. Kenyon (1867 – 1948) was pastor of several churches including the New Covenant Baptist Church in Seattle, and he was founder and president of Bethel Bible Institute in Spencer, Massachusetts. He said:

> In the mind of the Father, we are perfectly healed and perfectly free from sin, because He laid our diseases and our sins upon His Son. His Son was made sin with our sins. He was made sick with our diseases.[61]

T. L. Osborn (1923 – 2013) was an American evangelist who preached internationally to large crowds for over thirty years. He said:

> In these Scriptures (Is. 53:4-5, 1 Pet. 2:24) we see that healing for the body is in the same atonement as salvation for the soul....You Substitute, Jesus Christ, (was) made sick and sinful for you....You will never have to bear the weight of that sin and sickness—Jesus bore it on the cross for you....Satan cannot legally lay on us what God laid on Jesus. Christ became sick with *our* diseases that we might be healed. He knew no sickness until He became sick for us....If Christ has borne our sicknesses and pains (Is. 53:4), and if He took our infirmities and bare our sicknesses (Mt. 8:17), that proves that we need not bear them. He, as our Substitute, has borne them in our place, so we are set free. Since Christ could say, "I have come to do Your will, O God" (Heb. 10:9), then when He bare our sicknesses and our diseases and suffered the stripes by which we are healed, we have the will of God revealed in the matter of the healing of our bodies. [62]

1 Peter 2:21, 24 ...Christ also suffered for us, leaving us an example, that you should follow His steps...(24) who Himself bore our sins in His own body on the tree, that we, having died to sins, might live for righteousness—by whose stripes you were healed.

The phrase "by whose stripes you were healed" (verse 24b) comes from Isaiah 53:5. The Greek word for "healed" is a form of the word *iaomai.* A form of *iaomai* also appears in each of the following verses, to name a few of its twenty-eight New Testament appearances: Mark 5:29: "Immediately the fountain of her blood was dried up, and she felt in her body that she was *healed* of the affliction"; Luke 6:19: "And the whole multitude sought to touch Him, for power went out from Him and *healed* them all"; Luke 7:7b: "But say the word and my servant will be *healed*"; Luke 8:2: "and certain women who had been *healed* of evil spirits and infirmities..."; Acts 3:11: "Now as the lame man who was *healed* held on to Peter and John...." The healings in these Scriptures are physical in nature and/or include deliverance from demonic possession or oppression. Twenty of the twenty-eight appearances of *iaomai* in the New Testament clearly refer to divine physical healing and/or deliverance from demonic oppression or possession. None of the other eight occurrences would preclude divine physical healing.

The verb tense of *iaomai* in 1 Peter 2:24 is aorist, indicating that the healing happened at a particular point in the past. Jesus the Christ paid the price for the divine healing of the spirit, soul, and body of each human when He was scourged with the whip and was crucified; God the Father bore witness to His acceptance of this payment when He raised Jesus from the dead. First Peter 2:24 clearly links physical healing, along with imputed righteousness, to the atoning work of Christ. Each of us may experience Christ's healing power through exercising personal faith in Christ as our Healer.

Propitiation

Let's look at some New Testament words that are related to the concept of atonement. In Romans 5:11, *katallage* is translated "atonement" in the King James Version and is translated "reconciliation" in the New King James Version—"...we also rejoice in God through our Lord Jesus Christ, through whom we have now received the *reconciliation*" (Rom. 5:11b, NKJV). *Hilasmos* is translated "propitiation" in 1 John 2:2 by the KJV and the NKJV—"And if anyone sins, we have an Advocate with the Father, Jesus Christ the righteous. And He Himself is the *propitiation* for our sins, and not for ours only but also for the whole world" (1 John 2:1b-2, NKJV). A related word, *hilasterion*, is translated "mercy seat" in Hebrews 9:5 and is translated "propitiation" in Romans 3:25 by the KJV and the NKJV—"being justified freely by His grace through the redemption that is in Christ Jesus, whom God set forth as a *propitiation* by His blood, through faith, to demonstrate His righteousness..." (Rom. 3:24-25, NKJV). Again, Christ's blood provides atonement, or propitiation, for our sins, so we, through faith, can receive God's mercy and be reconciled to Him. Praise the Lord!

Covenantal Promises

All covenantal promises / benefits found in the Bible are ultimately based on the atoning work of Jesus the Christ. Some of these wonderful promises are: divine forgiveness and healing (Ps. 103:3; Jas. 5:15); being a new creation in Christ (2 Cor. 5:17); the privilege of dying to sin and living to righteousness (1 Pet. 2:24); the newness of life and the abundant life in Christ in which we are created to walk (2 Cor. 5:17; Jn. 10:10; Rom. 6:4); love for God and others (1 Jn. 4:7-8; Jn. 15:9); peace (Rom. 5:1; Phil. 4:7); joy (Ps. 16:11; Rom. 15:13); strength (Ps. 18:1, 32; Phil. 4:13); prosperity (3 Jn. 2; Josh. 1:8; Ps. 1:3; Ps. 105:37. I interpret prosperity to mean one has enough for oneself and one's immediate family, and some extra with which to save and share.); power to obey Christ and be a witness for Christ (Acts 1:8; Rom. 1:16-17); through Christ, power and authority over demons and disease (Lk. 9:1-2; Lk. 10:19); hope (Rom. 5:4; Rom. 15:13); the baptism in the Holy Spirit (Mt. 3:11; Acts 1:5, 8); answers to prayers as one prays in faith and according to God's will (Jn. 14:14; 15:7, 16; 16:23-24; 1 Jn. 3:22; 5:14-15); divine deliverance from types of affliction, grave trouble, and disaster (Ps. 32:7; 34:19; 121:7-8; Prov. 12:21; Lk. 10:19); the Holy Spirit's daily guidance (Rom. 8:14); all of one's needs being met (Phil. 4:19); the desires of one's heart being fulfilled (Ps. 20:4; 37:4; 145:16, 19); all of one's purposes being fulfilled (Ps. 20:4); having peace with one's enemies (Prov. 16:7); being beneficiaries of all the blessings listed in Deuteronomy 28:1-14, and being divinely spared of all the curses listed in Deuteronomy 28:16-68 (since Christ was cursed for us, Gal. 3:13-14); all the gospel blessings that are typical of the year of Jubilee together with all other covenantal promises of the Old and New Testaments. Thus, 2 Corinthians 1:20 says: "For all the promises of God in Him (Christ) are Yes, and in Him Amen, to the glory of God through us." Hallelujah!

It has been estimated that the Bible contains thousands of promises, all of which are available to any believer on the basis of the atonement of Christ and are appropriated by faith. Concerning divine healing, if God is willing to heal one (and He is), He is willing to heal another, provided faith is present, for God is no respecter of persons.

Answering the Critics

It makes no sense to me for anyone who claims the Bible to be inerrant to say divine physical healing is not included in the atonement. I am at a loss as to how one can reject healing as a covenantal promise, given that so many Biblical statements are all-encompassing in what they promise. For example, Jesus said, "If you can believe, all things are possible to him who believes" (Mk. 9:23). Certainly, physical healing is included in "all things." The critic's twisted reading of this verse would seem to be: "If you can believe, some things are possible to him who believes." Again, Psalm 23:1 says, "The LORD is my shepherd; I shall not want" (or "I shall not lack"). It would be reasonable for a believer with cancer, for example, to *want* to be healed, and he can humbly remind the Good Shepherd that He supplies all his wants. But the critic's twisted reading of this verse would seem to be: "The LORD is my shepherd, but I shall want." Again, Psalm 37:4 says, "Delight yourself also in the LORD, and He shall give you the desires of your heart." If a believer is struggling with, for example, heart disease, then he can remind the Lord that a desire of his heart is to for his heart to be healed, and he can expect healing to manifest (as long as he maintains an abiding relationship with the Lord, a good diet, health, and hygiene—such healthy lifestyle choices would be included in his repentance, which is an aspect of faith). However, the critic might twist this Scripture to read: "Delight yourself also in the LORD, and He shall give you some (or most) of the desires of your heart." Again, Psalm 84:11b says, "No good *thing* will He withhold from those who walk uprightly." The critic might twist his reading of this verse to say: "One good thing might He withhold—namely divine healing—from those who walk uprightly."

Again, Philippians 4:19 says, "And my God shall supply all your need according to His riches in glory by Christ Jesus." If a believer suffers from diabetes or arthritis, then being healed of these ailments would constitute a legitimate need. But the critic would seemingly twist Philippians 4:19 to read: "And my God shall supply some (or most) of your needs according to His riches in glory by Christ Jesus." Critics and skeptics, quit leaning on your own understanding. Don't allow your experience, or lack thereof, to distort the truths of Scripture. Don't add to, take away from, or alter God's Word, for dire warnings are given to those who alter God's Word. Instead, acknowledge Scripture as the highest and perfect standard, and seek to understand your experiences on the basis of God's standard. Also, focus more on the Scriptural promises than on the sickly symptoms of yourself and others.

One may ask: "If a person never experiences God's healing power, would you say that person did not have enough faith?" I would say that with the understanding that faith is more than saying "God can heal me" [rather it is saying "God will heal me because on some level the revelatory word that He will do so is in me"], then, yes, if a person is not healed it is because that person has no faith to be healed. [It is possible to have faith in Jesus to be forgiven, or to have some other benefit, but not have faith to be healed. Faith for the particular benefit desired is needed.] Verses to support this include Matthew 21:22: "And **whatever** things you ask in prayer, **believing**, you **will** receive." Again, Matthew 17:20 says: "So Jesus said to them, 'Because of your **unbelief**; for assuredly, I say to you, if you have **faith** as a mustard seed, you will say to this mountain, 'Move from here to there,' and it **will** move; and nothing will be impossible for you." Again, Mark 11:22-24 says: "So Jesus answered and said to them, "Have **faith** in God. (23) For assuredly, I say to you, whoever says to this mountain, 'Be removed and be cast into the sea,' and **does not doubt in his heart, but believes** that those things he says will be done, he **will have whatever** he says. (24) Therefore I say to you, **whatever** things you ask when you pray, **believe** that you receive them, and you **will** have them." [In Acts 14:8-10, Paul observed that a man had faith to be healed before the healing manifest. It was when Paul told the man to stand up, and the man obeyed, that the healing manifest. Therefore, it is possible to have faith to be made well even though one has not yet experienced the outward manifestation.]

If It Is God's Will?

Some people include the phrase "if it is God's will" in their prayers for healing. F. F. Bosworth said:

> The greatest barrier to the faith of many seeking bodily healing in our day is the uncertainty in their minds as to it being the will of God to heal all....The sufferer must be convinced by the Word of God that his or her healing is the will of God. It is impossible to have real faith for healing as long as there is the slightest doubt as to it being God's will. We can't claim a blessing we are not certain God offers.... If it is God's will to heal only some...then none have any basis for faith unless they have a special revelation that they are among the favored ones....Faith begins where the will of God is known. Faith must rest on the will of God alone, not on our desires or wishes. Appropriating faith is not only believing God can, but that God will....Until a person knows God's will, he or she has no basis for faith....It is His will to take away my sickness and fulfill the number of my days, according to the promise—Exodus 23:25-26.[63]

Bosworth says that the Episcopalian Church (whose scholars Bosworth said were conservative in that era) appointed a commission on spiritual healing. Three years later, they reported: "The healing of the sick by Jesus was done as a revelation of God's will for man.... No longer can the Church pray for the sick with the faith-destroying, qualifying phrase 'If it be Thy will.'"[64]

When it comes to prayer for healing, the phrase "if it is God's will" typically indicates the existence of doubt in the heart of the one praying, and can sow doubt into the heart of the one for whom prayers are offered as well as anyone listening. How can you confidently ask God to intervene, to perform a particular task, to answer a prayer, if you are uncertain of God's will? You should never pray against the will of God. There are certain things that you can boldly and undoubtedly pray to receive because they reside within God's will of precept to be received by those who believe (typically they are reflected in the covenantal promises). But concerning matters that are not covenantal promises, you need to seek for God to lead you and to reveal His will. Therefore, Paul and Timothy did not cease to pray for the faithful brethren in Colossae to "be filled with the knowledge of His will..." (Col. 1:9).

James 4:13-16 says:

> Come now, you who say, "Today or tomorrow we will go to such
> and such a city, spend a year there, buy and sell, and make a profit";
> (14) whereas you do not know what will happen tomorrow. For
> what is your life? It is even a vapor that appears for a little time and
> then vanishes away. (15) Instead you ought to say, "If the Lord wills,
> we shall live and do this or that." (16) But now you boast in your
> arrogance. All such boasting is evil.

As the above passage points out, saying or praying "if the Lord wills" is
appropriate if you are talking about what you would like to do in the
future. In such cases, saying "if the Lord wills" is an aspect of humility
and is in accord with Proverbs 16:9—"A man's heart plans his way, but
the LORD directs his steps."

If you are telling someone how to be saved, do you tell him to
believe on the Lord Jesus Christ and he will be saved *if it is God's will*?
Could you imagine the evangelist Billy Graham preaching, "Repent,
and believe in the gospel, and God will save you, if He wills"? Neither
you nor Billy Graham should insert "If the Lord wills" as an add-on to
faith in Christ for salvation. Rather, if faith in Christ is present, then
salvation has occurred. T. L. Osborn wrote:

> How many sinners would be saved if the preacher...when he did
> speak on the subject of salvation, he chose as his main points: 1)
> Maybe it isn't God's will to save you. 2) Perhaps your sin is for God's
> glory. 3) Perhaps God is using this sin to chastise you. 4) Be patient
> in your sin until God wills to save you. 5) The day of miracles
> (conversion) is past. How many souls would be saved, and how many
> sinners would receive faith to be converted through such (unbiblical)
> messages? Yet these are about the only points many sick people hear
> concerning healing! It is easy to understand why many people are
> not healed today....[65]

Since divine healing is as much one of the benefits of the atoning work
of Christ as is the forgiveness of sins, then, likewise, one should not
insert the condition "if the Lord wills" into one's prayers for God to
physically heal.

Furthermore, if you are unsure it is God's will to heal you, then
shouldn't you avoid doctors and medicine? If you believe that God may

want you sick, then why combat the sickness using natural means? Are you then not saying God wants you to look to the natural realm to get your needs met instead of looking unto Him? I know of no Scripture where God says to His obedient children, "Don't look to Me; look elsewhere."

We Must Believe for Each Specific Benefit

Critic have said, "If divine healing were in the atonement, then once you are born again you would automatically get all the benefits of the atonement, including healing, immediately." I say, however, you need to believe God for each particular benefit/provision that you want. A person can acquire faith for God to forgive him, but fail to acquire faith for God to heal him. Also, one can acquire faith to know God's peace, but fail to acquire faith to receive God's supply of strength. During a particular season of my life I was praying for my knee to be healed so I could resume certain activities such as jogging. I knew God *could* heal my knee, but I had not received faith that He *would* heal my knee. Then one day while I was taking a walk, the Lord spoke to me, "Begin jogging and I will heal your knee." This was God's word (*rhema*) to me—thus faith came in to me for healing in that particular case. So I immediately began jogging and praising God, and my knee was healed!

On several occasions, Jesus said to individuals seeking healing, "Let it be to you according to your faith." If the persons whom Jesus healed on those occasions had not believed Him for healing, then they would not have received healing. Consider Mark 9:23b, where Jesus said, "All things are possible to him who believes." "All things" is plural and would seem to indicate you can believe for certain things, and whatever things you believe God to give you, those things will be possible for you. A similar statement occurs in Matthew 21:22: "And whatever things you ask in prayer, believing, you will receive." Again, "things" is plural; so you should ask God in faith for each particular thing you want, and that would include your needing to know that each particular thing you want is in accordance with His will to give it to you.

In conclusion to our discussion of the Old Testament types of atonement as well as the final atonement provided by Jesus Christ Himself, it is clear that Jesus died for the sins of the world and Jesus died for the sicknesses of the world. As anyone can receive the forgiveness of sins through faith in Jesus, it is also possible for anyone to receive physical healing through faith in Jesus. Galatians 3:5 corroborates this, saying "…He who supplies the Spirit to you and works miracles among you, does He do it by the works of the law, or by the hearing of faith?" Paul assures us it is by the hearing of faith. Conversely, one's failure to be forgiven, one's failure to be healed, one's failure to receive any of the covenantal promises of God ultimately boils down to one's lack of faith. But you can begin today to wholeheartedly seek God through meditation on, confession of, and obedience to His written Word, and thus you can position yourself to hear His revealed Word, including "By His stripes you were healed."

Chapter 5

F. F. Bosworth, a Healing Evangelist

I am devoting this chapter to the life and ministry of Rev. F. F. Bosworth, largely because I have found his book, *Christ the Healer*, published in 1924, to be instructional, inspirational, and a pure joy. Furthermore, there seems to be consensus that Rev. Bosworth was a man who maintained a high degree of humility and integrity throughout his entire ministry. Much of the material of this chapter, especially the newspaper reports and several testimonies, came from Eunice Perkins' biographical book, *Joybringer Bosworth, His Life Story*, published in 1921.[66] Roberts Liardon's excellent book *God's Generals: The Healing Evangelists*, published in 2011 (used with his permission), also aided my research on Rev. Bosworth, for which I am appreciative.[67]

Fred Francis Bosworth (1877 – 1958) was born on a farm in Nebraska, and had an older brother, a younger brother, and two younger sisters. Fred's father was a veteran of the civil war, and Fred later met a veteran of the war who told him that, while on the battlefields, Fred's father had led him to the Lord and instructed him on how to live the Christian life. Fred's parents were devout Methodists. Fred helped his father in the feed store his father owned, and Fred practiced his musical instrument, the cornet, during slow times. Before long, Fred was playing in the Nebraska State Band.

Once, Fred was in a room helping the doctors while they worked on a neighbor boy who had been shot. When Fred went out into the cold, winter air, he developed a severe cold which turned into serious lung trouble.

When Fred was sixteen, he and his older brother, Clarence, were hired to sell stereoscopic views during the summer. They sold throughout Nebraska and Kansas, committing thievery and lying along the way. At age seventeen, while selling in Omaha, an acquaintance, Miss Maude Greene, invited Fred to revival meetings at the First Methodist Church in Omaha. He attended three consecutive nights, and on the third night he went to the altar and accepted Jesus Christ, laughing with joy. Fred returned home, knowing he could not continue making money by dishonest means, so he quit his sales job and worked many short-term jobs over the next few years. About this time, his parents moved to Fitzgerald, Georgia, and Fred became engaged to a young lady.

Fred's lungs were growing worse. The doctor said there was nothing he could do to help Fred, so Fred decided to travel to Georgia to see his parents one last time before he died. His mother's care helped Fred find some strength. One night, Fred attended a Methodist Church meeting and coughed throughout the meeting. At the end of the meeting, he went forward for prayer. Miss Mattie Perry, who was ministering that night, told Fred that it was God's will to heal him, and she laid her hands on him and prayed. That hour, Fred began to heal, and within days his lungs were completely fine![68]

The woman with whom Fred was engaged wrote him and broke off the engagement. Fred operated a barber shop, and also directed the Empire State Band. He then became an assistant postmaster, and within two years he was elected city clerk. He met Miss Estella Hayde, who was eighteen years old and was living in Fitzgerald. Fred led her to the Lord, and they were married while she was still eighteen; he was twenty-three. Fred lost his re-election by one vote, presumably because he had openly supported a prohibition candidate for the legislature. He then became a bank's bookkeeper, and later became a teller.

A minister by the name of John Alexander Dowie, who had established a Christian church and community in Zion City, Illinois, had published a magazine, *Leaves of Healing*. Its contents so inspired Fred and Estella that they moved to Zion City. Fred became a bookkeeper for a food company, and he played in the church band. Rev. Dowie quickly recognized Fred's musical talent and made him director of the band, which was a full-time job. The band so flourished that, by invitation, they played ten consecutive days in Madison Square Gardens, New York City. As time passed, Bosworth developed strong reservations about the leadership of Rev. Dowie, and thus the Bosworths left that church.

In 1906, Charles Parham (considered to be a pioneer of Pentecostalism), visited Zion City and the Bosworth's home and taught about the baptism in the Holy Spirit. Bosworth said, "These words kept ringing in my ears: 'Seek ye first the kingdom of God and His righteousness, and all these thing shall be added unto you.' Then I promised the Lord I would obey Him if I starved to death."[69] Shortly thereafter, Bosworth attended a small meeting where the Holy Spirit fell on him and he spoke in tongues. He said he had a spot on his lung from too much cornet playing, and the spot instantly disappeared when he was baptized in the Holy Spirit.[70] When Bosworth was twenty-nine, he and Evangelist John Lake, who also lived in Zion City, traveled together to Azuza Street, Los Angeles to experience the great revival which was underway, and met William Seymour, the presiding minister. Later, Bosworth, reflecting on his earlier years of going from job to job, said, "I wish someone at that time would have told me about being baptized in the Holy Spirit. I did a great deal of drifting, not knowing what the right place was for me." Before Bosworth received the baptism in the Holy Spirit, he was afraid God might call him to preach. After he received the baptism in the Holy Spirit, he was afraid God might *not* call him to preach.[71] Later in his ministry, Bosworth said that he would not do anything else but preach the gospel.

After Bosworth preached his first sermon, he determined to not be secularly employed, but to trust the Lord to provide for his family's needs. At times he struggled with the verse, "But if anyone does not provide for his own, and especially for those of his household, he has denied the faith and is worse than an unbeliever" (1 Tim. 5:8). Nevertheless, he would return to his conviction that this was God's will for him. The times were lean, but God always provided. The Bosworths once lived on boiled wheat for a number of days. Bosworth preached revivals in Indiana, Georgia, South Carolina, and Texas. He asked nothing from man, but lived by faith and preached God's Word.

In 1910, Bosworth became pastor of First Assembly of God in Dallas, Texas. Perkins wrote, "His Dallas church, for almost the entire ten years of his pastorate, has been holding a constant revival, having meetings practically every night."[72] In the summers, they would pitch up to four tents in different areas around Dallas to preach the gospel. Bosworth said, "We held meetings every night and each night souls were saved. On Sunday afternoons I baptized the people who had been saved during the week. For eight months I baptized every Sunday, and the least I ever baptized in one week was twelve."[73] During his pastorate in Dallas, it is estimated that Bosworth traveled seventy-five thousand miles to hold evangelistic meetings around the country.

Once, Bosworth preached at a meeting where he stood on a platform between the tent where the African-Americans sat and the arbor where the whites sat. After the meeting, Bosworth was approached by a group of racist white men who announced they were going to shoot him for preaching to the African-Americans. Bosworth reasoned with them and they permitted him to go, providing he leave town on the first train. While waiting at the train station, another mob accosted Bosworth. They knocked him down and beat him in his back with boat-oars. Then they told him he couldn't wait for the train but had to leave town on foot. So he did, and walked perhaps 100 miles to get home, carrying his suitcase. Bosworth said, "When I finally reached home toward night of the next day, there was such exaltation in my soul that I could thank God for the awful ordeal through which I had passed, and pray for mercy on my persecutors. But it was a month before I could lie comfortably on my back."[74] Bosworth praised God that, in a small way, he could identify with the sufferings of Christ.

Bosworth was also selected as a delegate to the first General Council of the Assemblies of God in Hot Springs, Arkansas (April 1914), and became one of the sixteen members of the executive presbytery. Later, Bosworth concluded that speaking in tongues was not the only initial evidence of having received the baptism in the Holy Spirit. (The Assemblies of God says the initial physical evidence of the baptism in the Holy Spirit is speaking in tongues, and I agree.) So in 1918, Bosworth resigned his church, turned in his ordination papers, and parted ways with the Assemblies of God.

In 1919, Bosworth's wife, Stella, died of influenza and tuberculosis. Several years earlier, their only son, Vernon, died on his fourth birthday. So Bosworth was widowed with two daughters for whom he needed to care. He wrote, "My precious wife went triumphantly to sleep in Jesus yesterday....She had gone from a tent to a mansion....How sweet is the Christian hope at such a time as this! Many have found Christ and been baptized by Him because of the intercession of the Spirit through Mrs. Bosworth."

After the death of Stella, Bosworth made arrangements for the care of his daughters, and he began an evangelistic tour. Bosworth rejoined the Christian and Missionary Alliance Church, and asked his brother, Burt (called "B. B."; thus F. F. and B. B.), to be his worship leader. In the 1920s and 1930s, the Bosworth brothers were known for big tent revivals throughout the United States and Canada.

The Bosworth Meetings

In August 1920, Bosworth held meetings in Lima, Ohio. At first, attendance was sparse. Bosworth said, "We got a Ford car and put streamers on the sides, and then we went to the yards and got a big engine bell, and we drove all over the city ringing the bell, and large crowds began to attend." A pastor asked Bosworth to preach on divine healing. So Bosworth asked the Lord, "But suppose I preach healing, and the people come, and they don't get healed?" He said the Lord replied, "If people didn't get saved, you wouldn't stop preaching the gospel." Bosworth said:

> I studied the question and prayed about it, and at last I saw that it was God's will to heal as well as to save people. Before I had thought that it was His will only to heal **some**, and I was afraid if I prayed for anyone it might be the wrong one. The first night I preached on healing was the most wonderful night we had had at this campaign, and it was the beginning of a most marvelous revival....[75]

In *Christ the Healer*, Bosworth wrote:

> After witnessing the miraculous healing of thousands, I am convinced that the proofs of healing are as bright and convincing as are the proofs of regeneration. Yet I do not base any doctrine on these

answers to prayer. I, for one, will preach all the Gospel if I never see another man saved or healed as long as I live. I am determined to base my doctrines on the immutable Word of God, not on phenomena or human experience.[76]

Rev. F. Bertram Miller of Kenton, Ohio, wrote the following about the Lima, Ohio meetings, which was published by the National Labor Tribune of Pittsburgh:

Lima, Ohio is being unusually blessed with a mighty revival wave of salvation and Divine healing, which continues to rise higher and higher. Evangelist Bosworth…and his brother, B. B. Bosworth,… are wholly given up to God. Such humble, spiritual, simple men we have rarely seen. They are very particular to see that God gets all the glory for their labors….There has been no criticism from the public press, no fanaticism or carnal emotionalism at any of the services, as the Holy Spirit had full right of way, resulting in perfect harmony and fellowship….Many were saved and wonderfully healed, wondering why they had never heard the full gospel before….Many have been baptized with the Holy Spirit….At one service alone we were informed that ten doctors were present and took unusual interest in the meetings and healings, marveling at the mighty power of a living Christ. Some of their own patients, whom they had given up as hopeless, were healed before their very eyes. An infidel came thirty miles to be saved. God wonderfully met him….At one of these (services) thirty-three were baptized….A woman who had been unable to raise her hands up to her shoulders for twenty-three years, making it impossible to care for herself, was instantly healed, throwing her hands into the air and shouting the praises of God. Another woman jumped out of her seat, instantly healed of spinal trouble. A little girl came on crutches and came back a few days later without them, able to walk, perfectly normal. A young woman was totally blind in one eye. While she was at the altar, God restored sight in this eye. A traveling man doubted this girl's testimony, held his hand over the good eye, and told her to read that which was held on the envelope he held in his hand. This eye had been dead for ten years. She read what was on the envelop and the man believed….The meetings lasted close to the midnight hour….We feel safe in saying that most all who came for healing or salvation were very definitely helped....A woman who had undergone eleven operations was wonderfully saved and healed.... Another woman had a large goiter and was afflicted for over six weeks with a sore throat. She came for the healing of her throat, but doubted whether God could cure the goiter. The next morning her unsaved husband said, "What's the matter with you?" "Why nothing," she said. "Look in the mirror," he directed. This she did, and noticed that God had not only healed the throat but the goiter had been removed. This put her husband under deep, pungent conviction, so profoundly that he staggered under it. He was saved as a result of his wife's healing.

A traveling man, professing to be a lifelong infidel, came to the meeting and related the following: His brother had been afflicted for eighteen years with tuberculosis of the bone and other complications. He could break off pieces of his bones with his fingers, they were so brittle. He heard of the meetings, which instilled faith into his heart, and he began to pray for himself. He dreamed he could walk. The next morning he got out of bed and walked. The professed infidel said that if there were any who doubted it, he would take them to see for themselves in his own automobile, stating that this has cured him of his infidelity.

Perkins writes:

Only once a week Bosworth preaches on the subject of healing, as he does not wish to give as great prominence to physical benefits as to spiritual blessings. But every night, after the invitation to sinners at the close of the sermon, the sick are given opportunity to come up and be anointed and prayed for, according to the command of James 5:14-15....There has never yet been a large enough platform to hold all the sinners and sick folk who crowd forward every night without any urging. There is no chance for any undue coaxing or pleading on the part of the evangelist. The people respond because they already want to do so, even before the end of the sermon.[77]

After the Lima, Ohio meetings, the Bosworth team went to Pittsburgh, Pa., and the campaign was extended about five times, moving to larger quarters to accommodate the crowds. Mr. J. H. Vitchestain, who was a Christian as well as editor of the National Labor Tribune, published in Pittsburgh, became a great supporter of the Bosworth meetings, advertising them in his newspaper. As a result, hundreds came and heard the gospel. The following is one of the weekly stories written by Mr. Vitchestain, who was an eye-witness of much of what he reported.

Never in the history of this gigantic center of the world's industry has there been such a spiritual awakening as that now going on through the campaign conducted by the Rev. F. F. Bosworth, evangelist, of Dallas, Texas, in Carnegie Hall, Pittsburgh….Hundreds are crowding into these meetings each night with the hope that they may receive full salvation and bodily healing….All denominations crowd the hall….Nothing like it has ever before been witnessed in Pittsburgh. Doctors, lawyers, financiers, merchants, professional men of all types and caliber….Nurses, and head nurses from the hospitals and sanitariums, all seeking soul salvation or bodily healing. It is a sight that astounds the onlookers to see those multitudes seeking their way to God and being converted in the old-fashioned way. A practicing physician from another city came to be healed of a complication of diseases. He fell upon his knees, 'wept through,' as they say, got up rejoicing and declared he was perfectly healed. Physicians have joined in and are taking a deep interest in the phenomenal workings of the Holy Spirit and the miraculous healings of those who seek bodily healing. Practicing physicians, clearly realizing that medical skill has failed and that the cases are hopeless, advised their patients to be anointed and seek relief through faith in the Lord Jesus Christ….Cases of curvature of the spine, tuberculosis, cancers of the most revolting and foul-smelling type, limbs partly eaten away with some disease, eczema, heart failure, leaky heart, palsy, neuralgia, hemorrhoids, and all classes of disease—and these almost instantly healed. One man who had for years been afflicted with palsy sat in the rear of the Carnegie Music Hall, and Evangelist Bosworth was urged to go back and pray with him. He shook like an aspen leaf, almost doubled, body badly cramped through this disease. A prayer, the laying on of hands, and instantly the victim leaps to his feet acknowledging the saving and healing power…."The essential part of each service," Evangelist Bosworth stated, "was soul saving. Divine healing came second."[78]

After Lima and Pittsburgh, the Bosworth team went to Detroit. The following was reported:

Nothing like the evangelistic campaign now going on here has ever before swept this state. Rev. F. F. Bosworth, the very essence of simplicity, is attracting crowds equal to any ever aroused by Billy Sunday....The news of the power of God and the manifestation of the Holy Spirit, which are so remarkably astounding, have so spread that Toledo has caught the inspiration and preparations are being made to charter a car or an entire train...(for) those who are determined to attend the services....What at first was considered a matter for the Christian and Missionary Alliance has broken out all over Michigan and northwestern Ohio, and like a tornado, is sweeping everything before it....After seeing one healed, a sinner rushed down the aisle with tears pouring across his cheeks, saying, "Boys, there's something to this."...A lady who had been blind, without being prayed for, sprang to her feet and shouted aloud, "I can see all of your faces." Another lady who had been carried in, walked out after being prayed for. Another was a paralytic lady who for the first time in six years was able to walk, after prayer was offered in her behalf....B. B. Bosworth (the music leader)...prayed for a woman from East Liverpool with a cancer of the womb. She was healed instantly....A mother was overcome with joy as her daughter, now grown, received perfect hearing after being stone deaf, caused by an explosion when she was two years of age....A Methodist prayed for by the younger Bosworth had been deaf for twenty-eight years in the right ear. He said the drum was destroyed. He had no idea of asking God to restore it, but sought to be healed of insomnia. God, however, gave him instantly his hearing....The music leader also prayed for a young girl aged fourteen years who had suffered with a cataract on the left eye all her life and was unable to read, the trouble having occurred early after birth. After being prayed for she placed her hand over her good eye and read fine print without hesitation. Going to the front of the platform she told the audience. Another young lady, aged twenty years, was prayed for, having been totally deaf in the left ear from birth. Instantly she could hear a whisper while holding her hand over her good ear. She broke down and wept for joy over what the Lord had done for her."[79]

Before leaving Detroit, Bosworth baptized 248 people. He ministered there six weeks.

The Bosworth team then went to the Twin Cities of Minnesota for five weeks of revival meetings. The following is an excerpt from a report of these meetings, written by Rev. J. D. Williams, local pastor of the Christian and Missionary Alliance, St. Paul, for the Alliance Weekly.

Between ten and twelve thousand people were dealt with personally in the after-meetings for prayer and healing, as shown by the cards handed in. Also hundreds were prayed for who were seeking salvation and the Baptism with the Holy Ghost who did not hand in any cards.... The message was the old-time Gospel of the atoning blood and the all-sufficiency of Christ for every human need....The preaching was Scriptural and earnest and the truth presented covered the entire Fourfold Gospel, i.e., Christ as Savior, Sanctifier, Healer and Coming King. Special stress was laid upon the Atonement covering both spiritual and physical needs. Healing for the body was offered to all on the same basis as forgiveness....Thus a large number entered into both salvation for the soul and healing for the body, practically at the same time. This we had not seen in other revival campaigns. Another marked feature was the plain teaching on the Baptism of the Holy Ghost. Emphasis was also laid on the importance of baptism with water, as an act of obedience....About 175...observed this ordinance during the campaign. (There was) absence of emotionalism or sensationalism. The meetings were generally very quiet....It was evident, however, that each message was taking deep root in hearts.... There was no attempt upon the part of the Evangelist to produce an effect, or to urge anyone to hasty decisions by emotional appeals. We thank God for sending these workers to our cities....They live the Gospel. Bosworth said, "Christians are the salt of the earth because they make others thirsty."

The last Bosworth campaign before *Joybringer Bosworth* went to the printer was in Toronto, Canada, closing May 22, 1921. The following was reported by the Toronto Globe:

A plain man with a plain message of ruin in the fall, redemption in the blood of Christ, and regeneration by the Spirit, Evangelist Bosworth places little dependence on rhetorical effects to produce results, but believes in preaching the Word and leaving the Holy Spirit to drive home the truth to the hearts of his hearers....It was a moving sight when the evangelist invited all who wished to take Christ as Savior to come forward, and from the audience of almost three thousand people...scores after scores came up to the platform.... There were scores of testimonies of bodily healing...."We do not consider healing of the body nearly as important as the salvation of the soul," Mr. Bosworth stated....There were never two brothers who worked together more lovingly, more harmoniously, than the Bosworth Brothers...."

More Testimonies from the Bosworth Meetings[80]

Mrs. Baker had cancer of the face, and kept her face covered with cloths for two years. The following is her own words:

I heard that they were healing people at the Memorial Hall, so I went....God saved me, and after they prayed for me it seemed a rubber cap was drawn over my face, and it gradually slipped off, and I knew I was healed. I told a lady to remove the bandages...I shouted many times. It is so good to be without pain. God healed my broken foot too. My upper lip was eaten until you could see my teeth. Oh the pain was so great, but I have not had any pain since that night I was healed....The Lord had given me a new lip that night....That night I was healed the Lord told me to go under the water....I was baptized by Brother Bosworth....Many have come from other towns to see me....I am glad to tell them. My doctor came to see for himself, and all he said was it was wonderful.

The following testimony regards Mrs. Hutchinson of Lima, Ohio who had been afflicted for four years.

Five doctors had pronounced her case as hopeless....Her relatives had her funeral apparel prepared, expecting death. Doctors stated she had hardening of the arteries, a weak heart, and Bright's disease, and had blood pressure of 240. Both of her legs were swollen far beyond the natural and were cold below the knees, and were practically useless.... She could hit the afflicted limbs with her cane and not feel it. Never would a pin or needle prick have any effect....One night she was brought to the meeting held by Evangelist F. F. Bosworth....She was prayed with and anointed....The next morning...while...meditating, she thought of the man at the Beautiful Gate and silently said, "Lord, I believe."…While she was preparing herself for breakfast, the Lord witnessed to her heart, and she came out of the room shouting and jumping….That same day a new pair of shoes was purchased for her, because the swelling had gone down so rapidly (from a size eleven man's shoe to a size eight woman's shoe)….Her feet are now normal and perfectly warm, with blood circulating through them again.

Mrs. S. A. Wright of Pittsburgh wrote the following:

Nine years ago I was taken sick with a serious kidney disease. [(One of) her kidneys and uterus were surgically removed. Found within the kidney was a cancerous growth. The other kidney was also diseased. Finally this kidney sloughed off entirely.]…My tongue swelled until it filled my mouth. I could neither speak nor close my teeth to eat. October 30, 1920, I presented myself at the place of prayer and was anointed and prayed with by my pastor, Rev. E. D. Whiteside, and Evangelist F. F. Bosworth, according to James 5:14-15. The Lord wonderfully met me. From that hour vomiting was overcome, convulsions ceased, the need for morphine no longer existed and its power as a habit was broken by the Lord….I became normal and have been so ever since….The baptism of the Holy Ghost, which He gave me accompanying my healing, is more to me than the fact of healing and restoration of physical vigor.

Mrs. Kentor, a Roman Catholic of Detroit, wrote:

I have suffered for twelve years with internal troubles, having had five operations in 1912, but have had no relief. The doctors have been waiting for me to become strong enough for another operation….I… had rheumatism…varicose veins…neuritis…for days. I was out of my mind and the doctors called it temporary insanity. I was told that some day I would be in an insane asylum. But what troubled me more than all this was that my baby girl was suffering. She was five years old and had had infantile paralysis since she was six months of age. She could walk only by dragging one foot….I heard of the Bosworth meetings and having no faith, as I had never been told that Protestants had that power with God, yet for my baby's sake, I went, taking her to the morning meeting, January 17, 1921, to investigate. When two of the workers came to me and asked about my spiritual condition, I felt that I needed prayer for my lack of faith and for my spiritual needs, generally. We knelt, and the sister and brother prayed in the Name of Jesus that I might have a clean heart. God heard and answered the prayer. I made no mention of my physical condition, thinking only of my poor baby's need….They anointed and prayed for the baby with no immediate results. When I was again at home, I noticed I did not have the headache I had suffered for four years every time I had had my hair up for an hour. Then I found myself using my arm and hand with perfect ease, without any pain. That was odd, for they had been almost useless when I left home. When I found that for some reason I had no pain, I began investigating my previous symptoms and found that the knotted veins which had stood out an inch on my limbs had become normal; a rupture, which the doctors expected to remove at the next operation, was gone; and some torn ligaments which had caused much suffering for four years had been healed. Today I am a well woman; a new one, I might say, for God created almost a whole new body for me. I have not had one pain since, I praise His Holy Name. The result of the wonderful work He has completed in me is full consecration of myself to Him, forever. My husband has also given himself to God. Our baby can walk now without dragging her foot, and the tonsils and adenoids are healed without the use of the knife.

Rosalie Ullman of Detroit, Michigan wrote:

About six years ago, Jesus healed me instantaneously of ulcers of the stomach after nine physicians…had failed to give me even temporary relief. On the 25th of next April, it will be two years since, through the ministry of Rev. E. D. Whiteside of Pittsburgh, Pa., I accepted Jesus as my Healer for life….(I) had constipation for seven years and an enlarged liver. I was anointed and prayed for at the Bosworth evangelistic meetings in Detroit. I waited four weeks for the full manifestation of my healing and, in fact, became somewhat impatient, but as I knew that the fault did not lie with God, but with me, I asked God to search my heart. Consequently, He revealed to me several points along which I was not completely surrendered to Him, but just as soon as I had yielded unconditionally, Jesus performed a veritable operation on me—entirely exterminating the hemorrhoids and completely dispelling the catarrh in my head—for all of which I praise His precious Name....If anyone thinks my testimony of God's healing savors of the mythological, I will gladly refer him to the reputable physicians who can substantiate my statements.

Rev. Bosworth received the following letter from Mrs. Thomas Hughes of Bangor, Pennsylvania, who had attended one of his meetings:

More than three years ago, through sickness I completely lost my power of speech. I have had several physicians and all told me I could never regain my voice. Some of them told me that the vocal organs were paralyzed. During all this time I was never able to make an audible sound. I have also been a great sufferer from rheumatism and gall-stones. I came and was anointed and prayed for on February 2nd and was instantly healed! When I walked from the platform back to my seat I found my voice completely restored. After three years of total silence I could speak normally. Praise the Lord! I was also healed of my rheumatism and gall-stones.[81]

Mrs. B. Edwards of Camden, New Jersey sent in the following testimony to Rev. Bosworth:

Fifteen years ago...I was compelled to give up my work (as) my whole body seemed to be filled with some kind of poison that puzzled the doctors. For twelve years I suffered untold agony....I was later told I had cancer at the mouth of the large bowel and it had fastened to the spleen...and poison affected my left arm and side until I was drawn crooked....Later the cancer spread to my mouth...until it was as thick as another tongue...(and) was fastened to an artery. I came home to die. I thank God for Christian friends who persuaded me to go to the Bosworth meetings being held in Philadelphia....I then got the evangelist's book, *Christ the Healer*, studied the references, and found that healing was for me....I went to the platform and was anointed for healing. Praise God! He met me right there and I was instantly healed. When I was being prayed for, I felt a shock go through my body just like electricity. It seemed as though someone grasped the cancer under my tongue and was drawing it out of my mouth....I have taken no medicine since that time...and have no pain whatever.[82]

The following are more testimonies of healings reported by those who attended the Bosworth meetings.

Mrs. Clara Rupert, Lima, Ohio, had been blind in her right eye for twelve years....At the meeting one night the eye was perfectly healed, clear vision being given instantly.

Miss Elizabeth Guest of Avalon, Pa., suffering from a malignant exophathalmic goiter which had an inward development. (She had) at times lost consciousness because of intense pressure and pain.... Went to the meeting at Gospel Tabernacle, Pittsburgh, was prayed with and anointed for healing. The Lord healed her and filled her with His presence. The goiter was wholly removed.

Miss Genevieve Harris of Pittsburgh, when a girl of fourteen, fell on the ice, injuring her hip, which ceased to grow and caused her much pain. It was four inches smaller than the other hip, when on... December 4, 1920, she attended the meeting in Pittsburgh. As she knelt asking God for Christ's sake to save her soul, a burning sensation started in the hip bone....Upon examination she found the previously diseased hip entirely in proportion with the other one and wholly free from pain.

Miss Edith Watt of Detroit was cross-eyed for fifteen years. (She) had worn glasses for eleven years, having had terrible headaches if she tried to go without them. She was anointed and prayed for in the Detroit meetings and her eyes were instantly healed and straightened. She is no longer cross-eyed and no longer wears glasses.

Miss Alma Swarthout of Birmingham, Michigan had had ear trouble from infancy. When (she was) seventeen years of age, the left ear was operated upon and found to be so diseased that finally the entire inner ear was removed....At the Detroit meeting..."the organs which had been removed were perfectly recreated and restored, and she can now hear to the glory of God."

Miss Genevieve Beatty of Duluth, Minnesota had surgery "removing every natural possibility of hearing through this ear." (For more than a week, she went to the Bosworth meetings in St. Paul.) She went up to be anointed and prayed for. Instantly her hearing was restored and she praises God that now she can hear with both ears.

One woman with epilepsy nearly all her life came over a hundred miles to our meeting in Dallas. She had those awful fits ever day and her sister told me that at one time she had forty-two in one day and almost passed away....After listening to the truth, she came to the altar and the power of God struck her as soon as she knelt down. She was instantly saved and healed....

The following is Bosworth's testimony of his own healing.

I coughed much of the time for ten years...and went from Illinois to Georgia for the purpose of saying good-bye to my parents and brothers and sisters before going to heaven. I coughed violently all the way, and the jarring of the train was like knives piercing my lungs. But, praise God, when I found that Jesus had borne my sickness, I walked right out from under the whole thing and was healed. I didn't have to carry what Jesus carried for me. Twice since then, when I had a burning fever and was terribly sick, it came to my mind how Jesus bore my sicknesses and, without being prayed for, I crawled out of bed, counting God faithful to the work of Christ for me....As I began to praise God for the fact that Jesus bore my sickness, both times the sickness instantly passed off and I was well.[83]

Commendations of the Bosworth Meetings

The following are excerpts from a letter Bosworth received while in Toronto, from Rev. Joseph Hogue of Minneapolis, a Presbyterian minister and evangelist.

Through your earnest ministry, God has given me a fresh vision of the completeness and fullness of the plan of redemption. However, my greatest benefit was that I saw the need of a positive faith. I saw how simply and yet how confidently you took God at His word....I shall ever praise God for what your ministry has been to me in giving me a larger vision and confirming my faith in the whole truth of God....[84]

The following came from P. S. Campbell, Professor of Greek at McMaster University, Toronto.

All who had the privilege of attending the services conducted by the Bosworth Brothers will heartily endorse the statements I am about to make....His addresses are thoroughly biblical....His language is absolutely free from sensationalism....His sermons show that he possesses in a marked degree the teaching gift....Pungent conviction attends his preaching. No preacher could be clearer and sounder in his treatment of the subject of the new birth. The miracle of the new birth is to him the supreme miracle....He declares that no regenerated man is qualified for service unless he is filled with the Holy Spirit.... The evangelist holds that the command "Be filled with the Spirit" is as much a command of God as "repent," "believe," or any other command, and that no believer is fulfilling God's purpose unless he is anointed with the Holy Ghost and with power. His emphasis on divine healing is equally strong. He takes the ground that the text "Himself took our infirmities and bare our sicknesses" (Mt. 8:17) undoubtedly proves that healing is in the Atonement. His arguments from Scripture are so convincing that at the close of each address hundreds eagerly come forward for Divine healing. Toronto audiences, it will be admitted, never listened to more helpful and powerful sermons.[85]

Perkins writes:

Other ministers and consecrated laymen have gone out from the Bosworth meetings to conduct similar services, and God is working in mighty power through them....In practically every city where these meetings have been held, there has been some prominent professing Christian who has started a controversy.[86]

Excerpts from an F. F. Bosworth Sermon

Jesus included healing for your body as one of the benefits provided for you by His death on the cross....Everyone who meets His conditions can be healed. "Surely He hath borne our griefs (literally 'our sicknesses') and carried our sorrows (literally 'our pains')." In the next verse, salvation for the soul and body are linked together (verse 5). Rotherham translates the second clause of the tenth verse thus, "He hath laid on Him sickness." Praise God, our sicknesses were laid on Him just the same as our sins were. Peter, quoting from this chapter, also links healing with salvation: 1 Peter 2:24. Many good people say that this Scripture in Isaiah refers to spiritual disease and not to the diseases of the body, but this is easily shown to be an error. Matthew quotes Isaiah 53:4 and applies it to the healing of the body: Matthew 8:16-17.

The main hindrance to the acceptance of Divine Healing in our day is ignorance of the will of God in the matter. The word "Gospel" means "Good News," and the good news is the story of Calvary where Christ vicariously "bare our sins" (1 Pet. 2:24) and "bare our sicknesses" (Mt. 8:17).

One reason why many fail to get healed is because they have not been taught clearly enough, and they don't come to God with a real purpose in their hearts. They come and experiment (saying)... "I guess I will be prayed for, I may get healed."...A purpose of heart is an indispensable condition of faith in seeking salvation, and the Baptism in the Spirit, or anything God has promised. As soon as I know that God has something for me, it is not only my privilege but my duty to receive it, and anything short of a full purpose of heart in the matter is short of the spirit of obedience....The healing of the soul is a miracle as much greater than the healing of the body as eternity is greater than time....The reason more people are not healed is because that part of the Gospel has not been taught definitely enough for the people to have faith. "Faith cometh by hearing" (Rom. 10:17a); there is exactly the same basis for faith for physical healing as there is for the healing of the soul.[87]

Perkins indicates that Bosworth's ministry was in high demand: "Even at the present writing, May 1921, (Bosworth, age forty-four)...has in his possession letters recently received from more than one hundred parties, representing nearly...as many different cities, requesting him to come to them for series of meetings. Appeals for his services have also come from across the two oceans."[88]

After Perkins' *Joybringer Bosworth*

At age forty-five, Bosworth married Florence Valentine, who proved to be a loving and supportive helpmate during their thirty-six years of marriage. Bosworth's brother, Burton, eventually moved away to minister on his own, and Fred and Florence settled in the Chicago area. Bosworth often ministered with Paul Radar in Chicago's Gospel Tabernacle. On March 28, 1928, *the Chicago Daily News* printed the front-page headline, "Deaf Six Years, Faith Cures Her," including a photo of Bosworth teaching the sixteen year old girl, Ruth Peiper, how to use the telephone. She had been deaf in both ears due to diphtheria and scarlet fever, but she told the news reporter, "Something just suddenly happened to me as I stood on the platform being anointed by the Reverend Bosworth....It's all in the Bible. It is just believing what is there that has made me well."[89]

In the 1930s and 40s, Bosworth also evangelized via radio, creating "The National Radio Revival Missionary Crusaders," and his radio ministry received over a quarter million letters. In 1947, the Bosworths moved to Florida with the idea of slowing down. But in 1948, Bosworth met healing evangelist William Branham and began traveling the country ministering with him. Bosworth would teach during the daytime services and Branham ministered in the evenings.[90] In 1951 or 1952, Bosworth traveled with Branham and ministered in South Africa. The newspapers estimated that there were crowds of 75,000, with thousands turned away due to limited seating capacity. Bosworth returned to minister in Africa several times between 1952 and 1955, and also held campaigns in Cuba and Japan. He ministered with Branham in Switzerland and Germany.[91]

At age eighty-one, Bosworth said that the Lord had shown him that he had "finished his course," and it was time to go to his heavenly home. He retired to his bed in his home in Florida, and all his children came home to see him. Bosworth's son, Robert, indicated it was a great reunion as the family talked, laughed, and sang together. Bosworth said, "All I have lived for these past sixty years has been the Lord Jesus." Robert describes the final hours of his dad's life:

> (He) looked up; he never saw us again. He saw what was invisible to us. He began to greet people and hug people—he was enraptured. Every once in a while he would break off and look around, saying, "Oh, it is so beautiful." He did this for several hours. Finally, with a smile on his face, he put his head back and slept.[92]

Chapter 6

Healings in Matthew's Gospel

Matthew 4:23-25 And Jesus went about all Galilee, *teaching* in their synagogues, *preaching* the gospel of the kingdom, and *healing* all kinds of sickness and all kinds of disease among the people. (24) Then His fame went throughout all Syria; and they brought to Him all sick people who were afflicted with various diseases and torments, and those who were demon-possessed, epileptics, and paralytics; and He *healed* them. (25) Great multitudes followed Him—from Galilee, and from Decapolis, Jerusalem, Judea, and beyond the Jordan.

As stated in Chapter 1, I consider verse 23 to be the mission statement for Jesus' three and one-half year public ministry. The mission statement appears again in Matthew 9:35: "Then Jesus went about all the cities and villages, *teaching* in their synagogues, *preaching* the gospel of the kingdom, and *healing* every sickness and every disease among the people." Of the five-fold ministry offices mentioned in Ephesians 4:11—apostle, prophet, evangelist, pastor, and teacher—these passages, Matthew 4:23 and 9:35, highlight Jesus' operation in the third and fifth offices, evangelist and teacher. Jesus spread the Word of God far and wide through evangelistic preaching, probably in the streets and marketplaces. He also taught the Word of God (expounding upon the Word in a more in-depth manner) in the synagogues and other places such as on a mountaintop or from a boat (Mt. 5:1-2; Lk. 5:3). In Mark 1:38, Jesus said His *purpose* was to preach the gospel to many different people (which constitutes evangelism): "Let us *go* into the next towns, that I may *preach* there also, because *for this purpose* I have come forth."

What was Jesus' core message? Matthew 4:17 contains the first recorded words in Matthew's Gospel of Jesus' preaching: "Repent, for the kingdom of heaven is at hand." These were the same words that His forerunner, John the Baptist, preached (Mt. 3:2). The Greek word translated "repent" is *metanoia. Meta* can indicate change, as in "metamorphosis." The suffix *noia*, from *nous*, refers to the mind, as in the word "paranoia." To repent means to change one's mind—from carnal thinking to Christ-like thinking. Philippians 2:5 says, "Let this mind be in you which was also in Christ Jesus." We are called to think like Jesus—righteously. This comes by continuously meditating upon the words of Scripture (Ps. 119:97; Josh. 1:8) and by "bringing every thought into captivity to the obedience of Christ" (2 Cor. 10:5). Hear what Bosworth says of repentance in relation to healing:

> Our redemptive blessings are conditional....Jesus says, "Repent and believe in the gospel" (Mk. 1:15). Only those who are right with God can follow these instructions. When seeking healing for our bodies, there should be no compromise with the adversary of our souls, because it is he who is the author of our diseases. Jesus has promised to destroy the works of the devil in our bodies. He cannot legally do that while we are clinging to the work of the devil in our souls.... Until a man squarely faces and settles the question of obedience to God, he is not on believing ground....It is not proper to seek His (God's) mercy while rejecting His will.[93]

What is "the gospel of the kingdom," as referred to in verse 23? "Gospel" (Greek: *euaggelion*, similar to "evangelism") means good news, or a good message. Jesus personified and preached a message of salvation, blessing, and hope. Ultimately, the good news of the kingdom is that Jesus died for our sins and was raised from the dead. If we believe in Him, embracing Him as Lord, then we are forgiven of our sins and the Holy Spirit comes (the moment we believe) to reside in us. This good news of the kingdom includes, but is not limited to, healing of the sick and brokenhearted, liberation from the penalty and power of sin, and deliverance from the oppression of the devil (Lk. 4:19). The phrase "kingdom of heaven" is unique to Matthew's Gospel and occurs approximately thirty-three times. A kingdom consists of all subjects and objects under the dominion of a reigning king. And the Lord Jesus Christ, under whose feet are all things (Eph. 1:22), is the eternally reigning "KING OF KINGS AND LORD OF LORDS" (Rev. 19:16), and the second Person of the triune Godhead. The kingdom of heaven is manifest whenever and wherever God's Word, God's will, and God's ways prevail in the hearts and actions of God's people. Whenever one bears the fruit of the Spirit instead of the works of the flesh (Gal. 5:16-26), the kingdom of heaven is demonstrated. [Incidentally, it is more important for the believer to bear the nine-fold fruit of the Spirit than to operate in any of the nine gifts of the Spirit, including healing (1 Cor. 12:7-10)]. Romans 14:17 says "for the kingdom of God is...righteousness, peace, and joy in the Holy Spirit." Christians are to pray for His kingdom to manifest on earth as in heaven (Mt. 6:10). Since unrighteousness, injustice, poverty, sickness, strife, and stress do not exist in heaven, then Christians should pray for, and work for, righteousness, justice, good health, and peace through Christ to manifest on earth through the ministry of the church.

The Lord Jesus is our model evangelist. What He did, we ought to pursue. Jesus makes this evident in John 20:21b when, after His resurrection, He commissioned His disciples, "As the Father has sent Me, I also send you." In Matthew 4:23 and 9:35, we see that Jesus was *intentional* to pursue sinners for the purpose of saving them. In Luke 19:10, Jesus said, "for the Son of Man has come to *seek* and to *save* that which was lost." In Matthew 28:18-20 and Mark 16:15-20, Jesus commissioned the church to do the same—He said, "Go!" As He *went*, we are to *go*! We must *go* and find sinners where they are, be willing to help meet their practical needs, and give them the Word of God with the intention of making them disciples of Jesus Christ. In 2009, I participated in an Assemblies of God evangelistic outreach called "Invasion of America with the Gospel." The program called for each participant to commit to share his or her faith with at least one person for forty consecutive days, beginning on Resurrection Day. Because of my commitment to the program, I posted a sticky note in my car and on my computer at work, "Be a witness today!" And I was. Such intentionality to witness paid off as many seeds were planted and as I led one young mother to pray to receive Christ! When Jesus tells the church to *go*, He is telling the church to be intentional to witness and make disciples. Evangelism should be an integral part of our daily lifestyle and agenda. If we are not intentional, many of us will default to our comfort zones and hardly witness at all. I recommend your viewing the DVDs and reading the books of the evangelist, Mark Cahill; he is very intentional and inspirational in one-on-one evangelism. I also recommend handing out gospel tracts; I personally like the Chick Tracts best.

The word *all* appears in Matthew 4:23 and 9:35. Jesus was *thorough* in His evangelistic strategy, bringing the gospel to as many people as possible. Matthew 9:35 shows that Jesus focused on the areas of highest concentrations of people: "*all* the cities and villages...." Again, the church is to follow His example. We need to share the gospel and make disciples in the area(s) where God has planted us, including the neighborhood(s) surrounding our church building (and we should not omit sections, streets, or people groups). Since Jesus dined with tax collectors and sinners, since He said that the sick are those who need a doctor (Mt. 9:12-13), and since He said that the gospel is to be preached "to the poor" (Lk. 4:18), then the church should especially reach out to the following: homeless shelters, soup kitchens, orphanages, homes for troubled teens, retirement homes, hospitals, prisons, and those suffering in third world countries where the poorest people live (Mt. 25:31-46; Jas. 1:27). We see Jesus' evangelistic strategy of intentionality and thoroughness with His words to the church: "*Go* into *all* the world and *preach* the gospel to *every* creature" (Mk. 16:15).

Matthew 4:23 reveals that no sickness or disease existed in Galilee that Jesus did not heal. The list would include leprosy, blindness, deafness, paralysis, etc. Medical practices probably lost much business during Jesus' public ministry! On many occasions, entire multitudes were healed by Jesus; no one went home sick! Many of the healings were verifiable by sight. For instance, the lame would walk, the lepers were cured, and the dead were raised. Because of the many eyewitnesses to these miracles, no one could convincingly refute that they were happening. No wonder great multitudes flocked to Jesus! Could not the same occur today?

When Jesus sent the twelve on an evangelistic assignment in Matthew 10:1, notice that the wording is identical to Matthew 4:23 concerning what was to be healed: "And when He had called His twelve disciples to Him, He gave them power over unclean spirits, to cast them out, and *to heal all kinds of sickness and all kinds of disease*" (Mt. 10:1). Again, Jesus sent them to do what He did. They were to "do the work of an evangelist" (2 Tim. 4:5). Furthermore, the *magnitude* of the healings that the disciples were commissioned to perform in Jesus' name was commensurate with the magnitude of the healings that Jesus Himself performed: "Heal the sick, cleanse the lepers, raise the dead, cast out demons" (Mt. 10:8a). This goes along with John 14:12, where Jesus said, "he who believes in Me, the works that I do he will do also; and greater works than these he will do, because I go to My Father." These healings (demonstrations of the gospel) were to accompany the disciples' proclamation of the gospel: Matthew 10:7 says, "And as you go, preach, saying, 'The kingdom of heaven is at hand.'"

In Matthew 4:24, we see a result of Jesus' ministry. He became famous, and His fame spread through the large region of Syria, an area north of Palestine. Today, we also want Jesus to be famous—the kind of fame that causes people to repent of their sins and receive Jesus as their Lord and Savior. Certainly, Jesus was a great preacher and teacher of the Word of God and this contributed to His fame. However, I believe the main reason Jesus' fame spread so rapidly was because of His miracles (demonstration). After Jesus raised Lazarus from the dead, the Pharisees exclaimed, "Look, the whole world has gone after Him!" (Jn. 12:19). Many of today's churches obey a portion of the Great Commission in that they proclaim the gospel; praise God for that! But demonstrations of the gospel such as healings, miracles, signs and wonders occur in today's churches much less, both in frequency and in magnitude, than what was performed by Jesus and the early church. Today's churches should pursue a healing ministry in order to follow in the steps of Jesus.

John 3:34 says of Jesus, "For He whom God has sent speaks the words of God, for God does not give the Spirit by measure." Jesus had a limitless anointing of the Holy Spirit upon Him so that whenever someone came to Jesus with a need, whether for healing, deliverance, etc., Jesus could instantly meet that need. Jesus had perfect faith, and therefore, almost all of the healings He performed were instant and complete. On the other hand, we who are followers of Christ obviously do not possess perfect faith. Instead, we have "a measure of faith" (Rom. 12:3), and we can only perform miracles according to the measure of our faith in Christ. Therefore, we must enter into the process of *faith* cultivation—we must develop faith in our hearts that God will heal through us. Such faith comes, in part, by increasing our meditation upon healing Scriptures. Additionally, prayer, worship, and fasting can help prepare us to be able to *hear* a word from the Holy Spirit that indeed God will heal us, or heal through us (Rom. 10:17). This is one of the main purposes of this book—to cultivate faith in our hearts that God will heal us and will heal others through Christ in us, all to the glory of God.

The Principle of Asking and Receiving, and Stipulations to God's Answering One's Prayers

In Matthew 4:24, the phrase, "they brought to Him" introduces an important principle concerning divine healing that will recur throughout this book—*the principle of asking and receiving. The principle of asking and receiving refers to the fact that in Scripture if a person asked Jesus for healing, whether for himself or someone else, Jesus healed.* James 4:2b says, "...you do not have because you do not *ask.*" In Matthew 7:7a, Jesus said, "*Ask,* and it will be given to you...." In John 14:14, Jesus said, "If you *ask anything* in My name, I will do it." This principle is a promise of God that we believers should utilize.

But there are stipulations to God's answering our prayers, and I will name four. First, Psalm 66:18 says, "If I regard iniquity in my heart, the Lord will not hear." Unrepentant sin will impede one's prayers. (See also 1 John 3:22.) If we have sinned, the good news is that if we confess and forsake our sins, putting our full trust in Jesus as the propitiation for our sins, then God will show us mercy and forgive us (1 Jn. 1:9; 1 Jn. 2:1-2; Prov. 28:13). Second, in Matthew 21:22, Jesus said, "And whatever things you ask in prayer, believing, you will receive." So unbelief will impede one's prayers. (See also Mark 11:23-25.) Third, 1 Peter 3:7 says, "Husbands, likewise, dwell with them with understanding, giving honor to the wife, as to the weaker vessel, and as being heirs together of the grace of life, that your prayers may not be hindered." So if a husband dishonors his wife and is ungracious toward her, he must repent, and likely apologize, or his prayers will be hindered. Forth, 1 John 5:14-15 says, "Now this is the confidence that we have in Him, that if we ask anything according to His will, He hears us. And if we know that He hears us, whatever we ask, we know that we have the petitions that we have asked of Him." So praying contrary to the will of God will likely hinder one's prayers.

The principle of asking and receiving is a reminder that we believers are to look *first* to God (rather than to man or to the world) for the supplying of our every need (Mt. 6:33; Phil. 4:19). We look to God and put God first when we trust in Jesus Christ as our Savior; when we meditate upon the Word of God day and night (Ps. 1:2-3); when we commune with God through unceasing prayer (1 Thess. 5:17); and when we obey God in all that God calls us to do (1 Sam. 15:22). No one has perfectly obeyed God except Jesus; that is why we must trust in Him, being justified by faith and not by works. Because Jesus "is the same yesterday, today, and forever" (Heb. 13:8b), we who need healing (or any provision from God) should come to Jesus as our Good Shepherd and ask, for in Him we shall not lack (Ps. 23:1; Jn. 10:11).

Casting Out Demons

We see in Matthew 4:24 that among those who were brought to Jesus were the demon-possessed. Demons and disease are often linked in Scripture. Acts 10:38 says, "God anointed Jesus of Nazareth with the Holy Spirit and with power, who went about doing good and *healing all who were oppressed by the devil*, for God was with Him." Acts 10:38 implies that the devil had been oppressing those persons whom Jesus healed. In Mark 16:17-18, Jesus gave authority to the church to cast out demons and to heal the sick: "And these signs will follow those who believe: *In My name they will cast out demons...they will lay hands on the sick, and they will recover.*" Using the name of Jesus to exercise authority over demons and disease is not sufficient unless the believer abides in Jesus and allows the words of Jesus to abide in him (Jn. 15:7). Also, note what Jesus said in Matthew 17:21, "...this kind does not go out except by prayer and fasting." And, of course, the believer must submit to God's will. James 4:7 says, "...submit to God. Resist the devil and he will flee from you." If the believer had no authority over the devil, then he could try to resist the devil all day long and the devil would not have to flee. But when the believer submits to God, then the believer is properly positioned to cast out the devil.

Matthew 8:2-4 And behold, a leper came and worshiped Him, saying, "Lord, if You are willing, You can make me *clean*." (3) Then Jesus put out His hand and touched him, saying, "I am willing; *be cleansed.*" Immediately his leprosy was cleansed. (4) And Jesus said to him, "See that you tell no one; but go your way, show yourself to the priest, and offer the gift that Moses commanded, as a testimony to them."

The leper first worshiped Jesus. Our Lord, the Healer, inhabits the praises of those who worship Him (Ps. 22:3), which is conducive to being healed. Furthermore, the leper's calling Jesus "Lord" reminds us that submitting our will to the Lordship of Jesus should be our highest priority. When we yield to Jesus as Lord of our lives, then divine healing is one of the many benefits of which we can lay hold by faith.

The leper was unaware of *God's will* to heal—he said, "if you are *willing.*" Jesus replied, "I am *willing.*" Bosworth said: "The first thing Jesus did was correct his theology....The theology of this leper is almost universal today because this part of the gospel is so seldom and so fragmentarily preached."[94] In Scripture, when did Jesus ever say He was not willing to heal someone who asked Him to heal? In the four gospels, every time someone asked Jesus to heal, that person walked away having received the healing for which he or she asked. The leper did acknowledge Jesus' *ability* to heal, saying, "you *can* make me clean." The leper was correct—in Revelation 1:8, Jesus said, "I am... the Almighty." Jesus is willing and able to heal!

T. L. Osborn said, "How am I to know that a millionaire would make me a present of a thousand dollars unless he said that he would do it? His *ability* to do it would not prove his *willingness.* I must have his promise before I can expect such a gift." A man asked Osborn to pray for his ear to be healed which had been deaf for twenty years. He said, "I've been prayed for by the greatest people of faith in our country...and I have never received help." Osborn said, "Do you think God is willing to heal a fellow like you?" The man replied, "I don't know...I know that if it's His will to do it, He is able, but—well, I guess that's just one of those things we aren't supposed to know." Osborn said, "That's why you've never been healed....You don't know whether or not God has said He would heal you....Do you believe it is God's will to keep His promise?" The man replied, "Of course." Osborn said, "Well, He has promised to heal you. And if I can quote you His promise, then you should believe Him and be healed right here and now." Osborn quoted a few Scriptures regarding the healing of our bodies (Ex. 15:26; 1 Pet. 2:24; Ja. 5:14). Then Osborn asked, "Now, in the face of all of these Scriptures, which are promises made to all who will believe them, do you think God included you? The man replied, "Yes." Osborn said, "Is God willing to heal you, seeing that He has made provision for the healing of every sickness and every disease among all the people?" The man replied, "Yes. I do believe healing is for me tonight. I have never seen it like this before." Osborn said, "I had hardly touched his deaf ear before sound burst into it and he could hear me as well with that ear as with the other."[95]

Jesus utilized a particular method to heal that we will consider as another healing principle throughout this book—*the word of command.* Jesus did not beseech the Father to heal the man. Instead, Jesus, who is God the Son, pronounced, or commanded, the healing to occur, and the man was cleansed "immediately." The word of command is the predominant method used for healing in the four gospels and in *Acts.* (If and when we should use the word of command will be discussed at various places later in this book.)

Leviticus 14 and the Cleansing of the Leper

Leviticus 14:1 says, "This shall be the law of the leper for the day of his cleansing: He shall be brought to the priest." The leper did not go to a doctor but to the priest. [God has made each believer in Christ a king and a priest (Rev. 1:6). Therefore, God can use any believer to minister Jesus' healing power to others.] The priest was to take two living and clean birds, kill one bird, and then dip the living bird (along with hyssop, scarlet, and cedar wood) in the blood of the bird that was killed. He was to sprinkle the blood that was on the living bird seven times on him who was to be cleansed from leprosy, and then he was to pronounce him clean. He was to let the living bird loose in the open field. The killed bird represents the death of Jesus, whose divine blood atoned for our sins. The living bird that was released represents the resurrection of Jesus, who "flew" up out of the grave three days later, and ascended into the heavens over forty days later.

In Leviticus 14, the word "atonement" appears seven times and "blood" also appears seven times. Providing a blood atonement was a vital aspect of the cleansing of the physical disease of leprosy. According to the New Testament, Christ's shed blood on the cross constitutes the ultimate, final atonement on behalf of fallen mankind. Christ's atoning death and subsequent resurrection provide eternal salvation (including healing) for every human being who believes in Him.

Matthew 8:5-13 Now when Jesus had entered Capernaum, a centurion came to Him, pleading with Him, (6) saying, "Lord, my servant is lying at home paralyzed, dreadfully tormented." (7) And Jesus said to him, "I will come and *heal him.*" (8) The centurion answered and said, "Lord, I am not worthy that You should come under my roof. But only speak a word, and my servant *will be healed.* (9) For I also am a man under authority, having soldiers under me. And I say to this one, 'Go,' and he goes; and to another, 'Come,' and he comes; and to my servant, 'Do this,' and he does it." (10) When Jesus heard it, He marveled, and said to those who followed, "Assuredly, I say to you, I have not found such great faith, not even in Israel! (11) And I say to you that many will come from east and west, and sit down with Abraham, Isaac, and Jacob in the kingdom of heaven. (12) But the sons of the kingdom will be cast out into outer darkness. There will be weeping and gnashing of teeth." (13) Then Jesus said to the centurion, "Go your way; and as you have believed, so let it be done for you." And his servant *was healed* that same hour.

Let us consider the centurion in terms of his position and character. First, he was a *Roman.* The Romans were the dominating political and military empire in Palestine and beyond at that time. They were often oppressive and harsh, which is exemplified in that they instituted the extremely brutal form of capital punishment known as crucifixion, by which our Lord Jesus was murdered. The Romans served Caesar as king, and they would violently squash any challenge to Caesar's throne. But this Roman officer recognized Jesus as "Lord" and the ultimate King, not over Palestine politically, but over all of creation. Christ's rule will last forever.

Second, the centurion was a *Gentile.* The Jews were God's chosen people; the Gentiles, spiritually speaking, were considered outsiders and were relegated to an outer court in the temple, "the court of the Gentiles." However, Jesus found that this centurion, this Gentile, *had more faith than any other person Jesus had so far met in Israel.* (In verse 11, Jesus speaks of many Gentiles eating in the eternal heavenly kingdom with the patriarchs while many of the Jews will be rejected—a turning of the tables.)

Third, let us consider his position as a *centurion.* A centurion was a military officer in charge of one hundred men. So he held a position of authority and thus could positively influence the soldiers under him.

Perhaps he would influence many of them to also pledge their allegiance to the Lord Jesus.

Forth, the centurion was the *master of a servant*. This was not uncommon in New Testament days. We see in *The Epistle to Philemon* that Onesimus was the slave of Philemon, a Christian. Though this servant was, in a legal sense, the centurion's property and would be expected to follow the orders of the centurion (exemplified in verse 9b—"to my servant, 'Do this,' and he does it."), the centurion demonstrated compassion even in the context of the master-servant relationship. The centurion cared for his servant, who was "paralyzed, dreadfully tormented" (verse 6), and wanted alleviation of his servant's suffering.

So we should recognize another principle here, *the principle of love and compassion*. This is the most important of all biblical principles, and it is vital to a successful healing ministry. Jesus Himself demonstrated love and compassion in His healing ministry: "And when He went out He saw a great multitude; and He was *moved with compassion for them*, and healed their sick" (Mt. 14:14). Placed between two chapters which deal with the spiritual gifts is the great love chapter, which says, "though I have all faith, so that I could remove mountains, but have not love, I am nothing" (1 Cor. 13:2b). The proper collaboration of spiritual gifts and fruit is expressed in Galatians 5:6b: what avails is "faith working through love." Whatever we do for God will not be pleasing to God if it is not done from a heart of love. First Corinthians 16:14 says, "Let all that you do be done in love."

The centurion's actions also illustrate the Biblical principle of *intercession*, or *standing in the gap*. The centurion is standing in the gap for his servant, or coming to Jesus on behalf of his servant. If one lacks something such as faith for healing, this can be seen as a void, or gap, between that person and God's promise. Then someone else can pray to God on behalf of that person for his or her need to be met. Today, friends and loved ones should stand in the gap for each other, and also for others whom they do not know but for whom they feel burdened to pray. We can pray for God to bring to others the salvation, healing, strength, direction, etc. that they need.

Verse 7 shows *Jesus' willingness and eagerness* to heal, which is indicative of His heart of grace. This gets back to the principle of asking and receiving. Since I am to follow in Jesus' steps (1 Pet. 2:21), if someone asks me to pray for his or her healing, barring some check in my spirit or some known unrepentant sin in his or her life, I typically pray for healing to occur. If faith seems to be lacking, I may quote verses about God's provision to heal such as Isaiah 53:5b, "By His stripes I am healed," and Psalm 103:3, "who forgives all your iniquities, who heals all your diseases."

In verses 8-9, we read the words of the centurion that cause Jesus to commend the centurion *as having greater faith than anyone Jesus had so far met in Israel.* In verse 8, the centurion calls Jesus, "*Lord.*" Some called Jesus "Teacher" and "Rabbi," but no one should ever lose sight of the fact that Jesus is Lord. (See Matthew 7:21-22 and Revelation 19:16). Do you daily submit to the Lordship of Jesus?

In verse 8, the centurion says, "*I am not worthy....*" The centurion realizes that he is a sinner, and that he is not worthy to have Jesus, the absolutely holy Son of God, enter his residence. Earlier in Matthew's Gospel, another saint acknowledged his own unworthiness to perform an elementary act of service for Jesus. John the Baptist said of Jesus, "...He who is coming after me is mightier than I, whose sandals *I am not worthy* to carry" (Mt. 3:11). Jesus said that John the Baptist was the greatest man born among women (Mt. 11:11; that is, until the birth of Jesus). Since the man who displayed the greatest faith Jesus had so far seen in Israel—the centurion—and the man who was the greatest born among women until the birth of Jesus—John the Baptist—both humbly acknowledged their unworthiness in comparison to our Lord Jesus Christ, then certainly we should follow suit. We do not *deserve* any of the blessings of God, but rather we should appeal to the grace and mercy of God as grounds to receive His blessings, even as Bartimaeus cried out, "Jesus, Son of David, have mercy on me" (Mk. 10:47). Each of us can sow to this end by showing mercy to others (Mt. 5:7; Jas. 2:13).

But Only Speak a Word

The centurion told Jesus that He could simply speak a word from that very spot (perhaps "heal"), and such a one-word command would be sufficient to heal his servant. Similarly, we see in Matthew 8:16b that Jesus "cast out the spirits with *a word.*" Again, in Matthew 8:32, Jesus spoke a singular word, "Go," and the demons departed from the two men they had possessed. When Jesus was walking on water, He said one word to Peter, "Come," and Peter was able to walk on water (Mt. 14:28-29). The spoken words of Jesus have all power. Also, God's word spoken by us in faith has great power. Psalm 107:20 says, "He sent forth *His word* and *healed* them, and *delivered* them out of all their trouble."

Authority

In verse 9, the centurion seems to be saying: "Being in the military, I understand authority and the chain of command. I speak a few words of command such as 'go,' 'come,' and 'do this,' and those under my authority immediately obey. I recognize that You, Jesus, have absolute authority over everything. I know that You can speak a word or phrase such as 'be healed,' and even though You may be geographically distant from the one whom You command to be healed, nevertheless whatever You command will occur." Indeed, Jesus said, "All authority has been given to Me in heaven and on earth" (Mt. 28:18). In Jesus' earthly ministry, He demonstrated His authority in the spiritual and natural realm when He controlled winds and waves, when He defied gravity by walking on water, when He healed the sick, cast out demons, and raised the dead, including one who had been dead for four days.

James Grant (a friend of mine) said of Jesus' authority:

> Jesus healed through the anointing of the Holy Spirit that was upon Him, in accordance with Isaiah 61. Jesus also healed in His own name. He said, "Be healed," "be gone," or "come out of him," and demons and disease would obey on the basis of the command given in Jesus' own name. Furthermore, Jesus Christ's bodily resurrection from the dead declared the victory that Christ had won, and it gave a manifestation of His thoroughgoing authority. (Romans 1:4 says that Christ was "declared to be the Son of God with power according to the Spirit of holiness, by the resurrection from the dead.") Once Christ was raised from the dead, He was also given a name: "the name which is above every name…" (Phil. 2:5-11). But the actual root, the ultimate source of Jesus Christ's authority, was in Christ's deity—His being one with God the Father from eternity past, and in Christ's central role in the creation.[96]

Verse 9 of Matthew 8 points to the fact that Jesus Himself is under authority. Jesus said in John 5:19, "the Son can do nothing of Himself, but what He sees the Father do; for whatever He does, the Son also does in like manner." Jesus always depended on the Father, and thus Jesus always walked by faith. We also see a submission of the Son to the Father in 1 Corinthians 15:28: "Now when all things are made subject to Him, then the Son Himself will also be subject to Him who put all things under Him, that God may be all in all." Again, 1 Corinthians 11:3 says: "the head of Christ is God." So within the triune Godhead, there is a submission of the Son to the Father.

Jesus delegated much authority to the church. In Luke 9 and 10, Jesus delegated authority to the twelve and the seventy on the basis of His future death and resurrection which would constitute His ultimate victory over Satan and evil. Luke 9:1 says: "Then He called His twelve disciples together and gave them *power and authority* over all demons, and to cure diseases." In Luke 10:19, Jesus said to the seventy: "Behold, I give you the *authority* to trample on serpents and scorpions, and over all the power of the enemy, and nothing shall by any means hurt you." (Luke 9:1 and 10:19 are addressed in greater depth in Chapter 12.) In Mark 16:17-18, Jesus gave authority to all who believe in Him to cast out demons and to heal the sick: "And these signs will follow those who believe: In My name they will *cast out demons...*they will *lay hands on the sick, and they will recover.*" Notice our authority to heal and cast out demons is solely attached to faith in the name of Jesus.

Great Faith

In verse 8, we see that the centurion *makes a statement conducive to faith*, saying, "my servant *will* be healed." The centurion did not say, "my servant *might* be healed," or "my servant will be healed *if it is Your will.*" Similarly, the woman with the issue of blood said, "If only I touch His clothes, I *shall* be made well" (Mk. 5:28). One's confession should be supportive of faith in Christ.

Though the servant was healed because of who Jesus is, and His compassion and authority, still Jesus credits the centurion's faith for the healing. In verse 10, Jesus attributes *"great faith"* to the centurion; in verse 13, Jesus said, "as you have *believed*, so let it be done for you." Faith bridges the gap between Almighty God and all-needy man. Thus, "all things are possible to him who *believes*" (Mk. 9:23b); conversely: "without *faith*, it is impossible to please Him" (Heb. 11:6a).

The centurion's level of faith actually caused Jesus to *marvel*. Jesus said that the centurion had demonstrated the greatest faith that Jesus had ever seen. This stands in contrast to when Jesus *marveled* because of the *unbelief* of those in His own country, where He "could do no mighty work" (Mk. 6:5-6). Furthermore, notice the contrast of the centurion's great faith to the disciples' little faith or lack of faith: In Matthew 8:26, when Jesus calmed the storm, He said to the disciples, "Why are you fearful, O you of *little faith?*" In Matthew 14:31, concerning Peter's sinking into the water after he had walked on water, Jesus said to Peter, "O you of *little faith*, why did you doubt?" In Matthew 17:14-21, when the disciples could not cast a demon out of a boy, Jesus said of them, "*O faithless* and perverse generation...." The disciples were with Jesus day in and day out for His three and one half years of public ministry, and yet they often displayed little faith or no faith. But this Gentile, this outsider, who probably had never had a conversation with Jesus before this encounter, had "*great faith*." Christians today who are new to the faith and have not had much ministry experience can receive encouragement from this passage in that they can also demonstrate great faith and do great things for God.

Looking at verse 13 again, we see that this is another account of one with paralysis being healed (See also Mt. 4:24; Jn. 5:9; Acts 3:7; 9:33-34; 14:10). The healing of a paralytic is verifiable by sight—a real faith-booster! Think of how the healing of the centurion's servant must have served as a great testimony to those who knew him that Jesus is Lord!

Matthew 8:14-15 Now when Jesus had come into Peter's house, He saw his wife's mother lying sick with a fever. (15) So He touched her hand, and the fever left her. And she arose and served them.

Many Christians who have been sick have glorified Christ by displaying a consistent godly attitude despite their sickness. But we must also note that when a person is sick, he is often limited in how he can serve Jesus. Here, Peter's mother-in-law was likely confined to her bed, suffering with a fever. Her condition would have been a great concern for Peter's household; they would have been preoccupied with trying to help her overcome her fever, and thus not able to focus on other important matters. But when Jesus healed the mother-in-law, she was able to rise up and serve Jesus and His followers without restriction. Having good health allows a person to maximize the use of his time, talents, and resources for the advancement of the kingdom of heaven.

Jesus' touching the hand of Peter's mother-in-law can be seen as having a two-fold effect: 1) it was an act of compassion (see Mk. 1:40-42), and 2) it was a point of contact—a type of laying on of hands which can be conducive to faith for healing (Mk. 16:18). The touch from Jesus caused the fever to depart.

Matthew 8:16-17 When evening had come, they brought to Him many who were demon-possessed. And He cast out the spirits with a word, and *healed all* who were sick, (17) that it might be fulfilled which was spoken by Isaiah the prophet, saying: "He Himself took our infirmities and bore our sicknesses."

Here we see that people took initiative and brought the demon-possessed and the sick to Jesus. If we are sick, then in obedience to James 5:14 we should ask the elders to pray for us and anoint us with oil in the name of the Lord. Such obedience, and our taking those particular steps, are conducive to faith.

On that evening, Jesus cast demons out of anyone in the crowd who was possessed by them, and He did so by use of a singular "word," or by just a few words. Perhaps Jesus simply said "Go!" or "Be healed!" Such power-packed words of command spoken by the One who has all power and authority were sufficient to bring about deliverance and healing for those who needed it. In Matthew 12:28, Jesus said He cast out demons by the Spirit of God. Ephesians 6:17 says: "the sword of the Spirit...is the word of God." Jesus cast out demons and healed the sick by the Spirit of God and by His spoken Word. Likewise, today's church should boldly proclaim the Word of God, including the healing promises, and be Spirit-filled and Spirit-led so as to bring deliverance for God's people from sin, sickness, and Satan (Mk. 16:15-20).

Nowhere in Scripture do we see Jesus saying to a sick person, "You need to learn the lesson of patience (or some other lesson), so I am not going to heal you today. You need to endure this infirmity a while longer." Nor do we see Jesus saying to a sick person, "Sorry. It is not My will to heal you." Instead, we see in this passage that Jesus "healed all who were sick" (verse 16). He skipped over no one; He showed no partiality. On that particular evening, it could have been that a special anointing to heal the sick was present (see Luke 5:17), and every sick person who was in attendance, regardless of whether or not he or she had faith, was healed. That is the kind of power we need in our church services today!

Verse 17 reveals that Jesus' healing ministry fulfilled an Old Testament prophecy, Isaiah 53:4—"Surely He has borne our griefs and carried our sorrows." The Hebrew word for "griefs" is *choliy*, which also means "disease." Matthew translates Isaiah 53:4 in this way, emphasizing the physical aspect of Jesus' redemptive work. Matthew 8:17b says: "He Himself took our infirmities and bore our sicknesses." So when did Jesus take our infirmities and bear our sicknesses? He did this on the cross, where He died for the sins of the world. Isaiah 53, which has been called the fifth gospel, is a well-known prophetic passage about the sin-bearing Messiah. Jesus was scourged by the whip and crucified on the cross to pay for our sins and for our sicknesses. What a wonderful Savior! Pastor Chris Norman (a friend of mine) says, "We should see to it that Jesus receives all that He paid for." Healing (physical, spiritual, emotional, etc.) is included in the atoning work of Christ. All aspects of salvation, including healing, were purchased at the cross; all benefits are appropriated by faith.

In Matthew 8:16 we again see that healing and casting out demons are linked. Please note the close association of demons and disease in Acts 10:38, Luke 13:11, and Luke 9:1.

Matthew 8:28-34 When He had come to the other side, to the country of the Gergesenes, there met Him two demon-possessed men, coming out of the tombs, exceedingly fierce, so that no one could pass that way. (29) And suddenly they cried out, saying, "What have we to do with You, Jesus, You Son of God? Have You come here to torment us before the time?" (30) Now a good way off from them there was a herd of many swine feeding. (31) So the demons begged Him, saying, "If You cast us out, permit us to go away into the herd of swine." (32) And He said to them, "Go." So when they had come out, they went into the herd of swine. And suddenly the whole herd of swine ran violently down the steep place into the sea, and perished in the water. (33) Then those who kept them fled; and they went away into the city and told everything, including what had happened to the demon-possessed men. (34) And behold, the whole city came out to meet Jesus. And when they saw Him, they begged Him to depart from their region.

Ever since I received the baptism in the Holy Spirit (Chapter 13 of this book explains this), I have had many encounters with demons. Once, I attended a work-related conference at a hotel. I could sense a negative atmosphere at the conference. I had to spend that night in the hotel. As I was sleeping, I had a demonically-inspired dream which woke me up. Immediately, I felt an evil presence upon me and it was literally pressing me into my mattress. It was difficult to move, speak, or even breathe. However, I managed to proclaim the name "Jesus." The moment I did, the demon lifted off of me. In the name of Jesus believers will cast out demons (Mk. 16:17).

In this passage, Jesus encounters two demon-possessed men. This is a showdown between the divine Light and demonic darkness. John 1:4-5 says of Jesus: "In Him was life, and the life was the light of men. And the light shines in the darkness, and the darkness did not comprehend it." Again, 2 Corinthians 4:4 says, "the god of this age (the devil) has blinded (those) who do not believe, lest the light of the gospel of the glory of Christ, who is the image of God, should shine on them."

Demon possession is when a demon or demons have absolute control of a person. Demon oppression is when a demon is influencing a person, but does not have total dominion over the person. A Christian can be oppressed by a demon, but not possessed (unless, of course, the person has completely apostasized—departed from the faith). First John 4:4b says: "He who is in you (Christ) is greater than he who is in the world (the devil)."

Verse 28 says that the demon-possessed men were "exceedingly fierce, so that no one could pass that way." Demon possession may at times cause great physical strength in the person who is possessed because Satan is a supernatural being. In Acts 19:14-16, a demon who possessed a man gave the man supernatural power so that he was able to overpower and defeat seven other men. The demon-possessed man of this passage was able to tear shackles and chains in pieces and no human could tame him. In Mark's account of this story (Mk. 5:1-13), the demon-possessed man would cut himself with stones. This reflects the goal of demons—to steal, kill, and destroy (Jn. 10:10; Jn. 8:44).

In verse 29, the demons admit that Jesus could torment them "before the time." We also see in Luke 8:31 that the demons begged Jesus not to command them to go into the abyss. [The abyss is likely a prison for bound demons located in the center of the earth. Second Peter 2:4 and 9 say: "For if God did not spare the angels who sinned, but cast them down to hell and delivered them into chains of darkness, to be reserved for judgment...(9) then the Lord knows how to...reserve the unjust under punishment for the day of judgment." Again, Jude 6 says: "And the angels who did not keep their proper domain, but left their own abode, He has reserved in everlasting chains under darkness for the judgment of the great day." (See also Rev. 20:10, 15.)] Demons know that Jesus is Lord and the ultimate Judge. But since demons rejected His Lordship in time past, they now tremble (Jas. 2:19) when they ponder their upcoming eternal torment. In verse 29, the seemingly voluntary declaration by the demons that Jesus is the Son of God reminds us of Philippians 2:10-11, that "at the name of Jesus every knee should bow... and that every tongue (even the tongues of demons) should confess that Jesus Christ is Lord...." In Mark's account, the man with the demons "worshipped Him," that is, Jesus (Mk. 5:6).

Why did the demons desire to go into the pigs? As a parasite wants to dwell in a host body, demons want to inhabit a living being and turn the body of that being into a temple for ignoble purposes. Therefore, we must keep our bodies swept clean of sin and filled with the Holy Spirit so demons cannot gain access. Mark's version said there were about 2,000 pigs. With one word—"Go," Jesus cast the demons out of the men, and the demons entered the pigs. A violent suicide stampede of 2,000 pigs shows again the destructive nature of demons. Instead of rejoicing for the two men whom Jesus set free, all the people of the city begged Jesus to leave. They preferred the status quo over the prospect of change (repentance) that the revelation of Jesus as the Son of God would require of them.

Matthew 9:2-8 Then behold, they brought to Him a paralytic lying on a bed. When Jesus saw their faith, He said to the paralytic, "Son, be of good cheer; your sins are forgiven you." (3) And at once some of the scribes said within themselves, "This Man blasphemes!" (4) But Jesus, knowing their thoughts, said, "Why do you think evil in your hearts? (5) For which is easier, to say, 'Your sins are forgiven you,' or to say, 'Arise and walk'? (6) But that you may know that the Son of Man has power on earth to forgive sins"; then He said to the paralytic, "Arise, take up your bed, and go to your house." (7) And he arose and departed to his house. (8) Now when the multitudes saw it, they marveled and glorified God, who had given such power to men.

Jesus' identification of the paralytic as "Son" shows that Jesus included the man in the family of faith. We see a similar reference to familial belonging in Matthew 9:22, where Jesus said, "Be of good cheer, *daughter*; your faith has made you well." Conversely, in Matthew 15:28, Jesus spoke to the Canaanite woman in this manner: "O *woman*, great is your faith!" She was not an Israelite, so Jesus acknowledged her as being an outsider. But ever since Acts 10, when God ordained the gospel to be proclaimed to the Gentiles (this occurred at Cornelius' house), Jew and Gentile alike can be considered sons and daughters of God by faith in Christ. Galatians 4:6 says, "And because you are *sons*, God has sent forth the Spirit of His Son into your hearts, crying out, "Abba, Father!"

Jesus also told the man to "be of good cheer" because Jesus had forgiven his sins. There is no better reason for a person to be cheerful. Divine forgiveness comes through faith alone in Christ alone. And as a believer, you must forgive all others. Are you forgiven by God?

What did Jesus see that made Him say to the paralytic, "Son, your sins are forgiven you"? Jesus saw the faith of the friends of the paralytic. In other words, Jesus saw a certain action on their part that was indicative of their having faith: they carried the paralytic on a bed to Jesus. Mark's version (2:1-12) reveals some of their great effort in doing so—they climbed onto the roof and broke through it in order to gain access to Jesus. James 2:18b says, "I will show you my faith by my works." Their works, or actions, indicated that they expected their friend to be healed by Jesus. What you do demonstrates what you believe.

What is faith and how do you acquire it? Hebrews 11:1 says: "Now faith is the substance of things hoped for, the evidence of things not seen." Having faith is having substance and evidence in you now, which comes by the inner witness of the Holy Spirit concerning that for which you are hoping and believing. Romans 10:17 says, "So then faith comes by hearing, and hearing by the word of God." "Word" in Romans 10:17 is the Greek word *rhema*, which is the revealed Word of God. Faith comes by revelation from God. To say God can heal is a true statement, but not necessarily a statement of faith. To say God will heal because He has revealed to you that He will heal is more along the lines of faith. Consistent study of and obedience to the Scriptures that pertain to faith and healing, hearing testimonies of healings, and fasting are helpful ways to cultivate faith for healing. There is no limit to what miracles can occur if you have faith (Mk. 9:23, Mt. 17:20).

We should also note that a lack of faith hinders healing. For example, Mark 6:5-6 says of Jesus when He was in His own country: "Now He could do no mighty work there, except that He laid His hands on a few sick people and healed them. And He marveled because of their *unbelief.*" Their unbelief prevented His ability to heal on a larger scale.

We see here once again the principle of standing in the gap—the friends had faith on behalf of the paralytic. As the friends assisted the paralytic, we today should also "bear one another's burdens" (Gal. 6:2).

Verse 6 indicates that Jesus' healing of the man helped verify that Jesus has the authority to forgive sins. The following is my paraphrase of Jesus' words: "That you may know that I forgive, I heal!" Divine healing bears witness that Jesus is Savior; therefore it is a great evangelistic tool.

The scribes were scholars and teachers of the Old Testament Scriptures, and they copied Old Testament manuscripts by hand. In their hearts, the scribes accused Jesus of blasphemy. Blasphemy occurs when one slanders the name of God,[97] or when one who is not God claims to be God, or when one attributes the works of God to something or someone other than God. Only God can forgive sins; thus Jesus is claiming, and rightfully so, to be God. Many New Testament passages attest to Jesus being God (Mt. 1:23; Jn. 1:1, 14, 8:58; Col. 1:15-19, 2:9; 1 Tim. 3:16; Heb. 1:1-4; Rev. 1:8, to name some). As the scribes and other religious leaders did not believe Jesus' truthful claims but instead persecuted Him, today some religious leaders criticize and even persecute the healing ministry. In such cases, we are to love and pray for those who persecute us, and we are to keep our focus on Christ.

Verse 8 says, "when the multitudes *saw* it (the healing), they marveled...." The multitudes would likely not have "marveled" to the degree they did if Jesus had preached a powerful message but did not heal anyone. Scripture specifies that what they *saw*, rather than what they heard, caused them to marvel. Divine healings are marvelous. *Seeing* miracles can soften the heart of a lost person so that he will be open to hearing and believing the marvelous gospel (Jn. 4:48; Acts 3:1-4:4; Acts 9:35). [This is not always the case. See Acts 14:8-18.] The multitudes who witnessed the healing "glorified God, who had given such *power to men*" (verse 8). This implies that believing men and women can operate in such power. Paul said, "And my speech and my preaching were not with persuasive words of human wisdom, but in demonstration of the Spirit and of *power*" (1 Cor. 2:4. See also 1 Cor. 4:20). The power of God that we pursue should be used for glorifying God and serving others, not for self-exaltation.

Though Jesus forgives and heals so freely, we should never think we can become casual about sin. Each and every sin one commits will necessarily bring a negative consequence from the Lord (1 Cor. 5:10;

Heb. 2:2; Gal. 6:7). We must fully embrace Jesus' command to "sin no more" (Jn. 5:14; Jn. 8:11). We must also remember that if we sin "we have an Advocate from the Father, Jesus Christ the righteous" to whom we can confess and forsake our sins and receive His forgiveness (1 Jn. 1:9; 1 Jn. 2:1). We who believe will find victory in our battle against sin as we walk in the Holy Spirit and allow the Word of God to richly dwell within us.

Matthew 9:18-26 While He spoke these things to them, behold, a ruler came and worshiped Him, saying, "My daughter has just died, but come and lay Your hand on her and she will live." (19) So Jesus arose and followed him, and so did His disciples. (20) And suddenly, a woman who had a flow of blood for twelve years came from behind and touched the hem of His garment. (21) For she said to herself, "If only I may touch His garment, I *shall be made well*." (22) But Jesus turned around, and when He saw her He said, "Be of good cheer, daughter; your faith *has made you well*." And the woman *was made well* from that hour. (23) When Jesus came into the ruler's house, and saw the flute players and the noisy crowd wailing, (24) He said to them, "Make room, for the girl is not dead, but sleeping." And they ridiculed Him. (25) But when the crowd was put outside, He went in and took her by the hand, and the girl arose. (26) And the report of this went out into all that land.

The ruler, who had a prominent position in society and thus could be tempted to trust in his own vocational achievement, rightly humbled himself and "worshipped" Jesus, the Ruler of the universe. The Lord's Prayer models that we hallow God's name before we ask Him for our daily bread (Mt. 6:9-13). True worship of God will incline one's heart to submit to His Lordship.

We also see here the principle of asking and receiving—the ruler took the initiative and came to Jesus, making request of Him to raise his daughter from the dead. Matthew 7:7 says: "*Ask, and it will be given to you...*"

The ruler's confession was conducive to faith, saying that his daughter would be raised from the dead if Jesus would come and lay His hand on her. The ruler did not say "she *might* live"; he said "she *will* live." Proverbs 18:21 says: "Death and life are in the power of the tongue...." Nothing is beyond Jesus ability—He is Almighty (Rev. 1:8). Jesus complied with the man's request—He and His disciples began to follow the man toward the location of his dead daughter.

Suddenly, their journey is interrupted by another encounter. "A woman who had a flow of blood for twelve years" also took initiative and came to Jesus. She did not say, "For twelve years, I have tried everything I could think of to be healed, including the treatments of many doctors. However, I will give Jesus a try also; *maybe* Jesus will succeed." Instead, she made a confession of faith, as the ruler had done. She said, "If only I may touch His garment, I *shall* be made well" (verse 21). It is noteworthy that she approached Jesus from behind, because Jesus was unaware of her being there. This fact emphasizes her having faith. Jesus did not say to her, "My power has made you well," even though that would have been accurate. Jesus gave full credit to the woman's faith for her being healed. He said, "*Your faith* has made you well." [Verse 21: "I shall be made well" is rendered by the King James Version: "I shall be whole." Verse 22: "has made you well" is rendered by the King James Version: "hath made thee whole." Both expressions "made well" and "made whole" represent the Greek word *sozo*, which means "save." The benefits of salvation include wellness and wholeness of one's entire being—spirit, soul, and body, through faith in Jesus Christ.]

After the encounter with the woman, Jesus, the disciples, and the ruler arrive at the ruler's house. The crowd at the house is "noisy" due to their grieving, "wailing," and flute playing. When Jesus alludes to the fact that the girl's death would only be temporary (Jesus says "she is sleeping"), the crowd ridicules Him (verse 24). Such a nay-saying crowd produces a negative atmosphere, which is contrary to faith, so Jesus put them out of the house. Then Jesus, respecting the wishes of the ruler who had asked Jesus to lay His hand on his daughter, touched the hand of the dead girl. This is also the approach Jesus took when He healed Peter's mother-in-law—"He touched her hand" (Mt. 8:15). In Acts 3, Peter took the hand of the man who was "lame from his mother's womb" and "lifted him up" (Acts 2:2 and 2:7). Taking one by the hand can be seen as giving assistance, a touch of compassion, and a point of contact conducive to faith. Jesus, our Helper (Ps. 30:10), is willing to uphold us with His "righteous right hand" (Isa. 41:10) as we trust in Him. When Jesus takes the girl by the hand, He raises her from the dead! Hallelujah! And the report of this miracle is greatly circulated. Perhaps some of the nay-sayers would be converted to "yeah-sayers."

Matthew 9:27-31 When Jesus departed from there, two blind men followed Him, crying out and saying, "Son of David, have mercy on us!" (28) And when He had come into the house, the blind men came to Him. And Jesus said to them, "Do you believe that I am able to do this?" They said to Him, "Yes, Lord." (29) Then He touched their eyes, saying, "According to your faith let it be to you." (30) And their eyes were opened. And Jesus sternly warned them, saying, "See that no one knows it." (31) But when they had departed, they spread the news about Him in all that country.

Scripture records several accounts of Jesus healing the blind. In Matthew 20:29-34, Jesus healed a different set of blind men near Jericho. In Mark 8:22, Jesus led a blind man out of town, spat on his eyes, and touched him twice in order to heal him. In John 9, Jesus anointed a blind man's eyes with clay and told him to wash in the pool of Siloam. When the blind man washed, he could see. But more important than the physical sight that Jesus gave people is the spiritual sight that He gave people. The two blind men of this passage had enough spiritual sight to follow Jesus. Many people today have 20/20 vision physically, but they are blind to who Jesus is and they do not follow Him as Lord. Jesus pointed this out in John 9:39—"For judgment I have come into this world, that those who do not see may see, and that those who see may be made blind."

In verse 27, the blind men *cried out* (the principle of asking and receiving). They were desperate to gain Jesus' attention so that He would heal them. Such desperation for God's intervention is common throughout Scripture, and it often brings the desired results. Psalm 18:6 says, "In my distress I called upon the LORD, and *cried out* to my God; *He heard my voice* from His temple, and my *cry* came before Him, even to His ears." Again, Luke 18:7-8 says, "And shall God not avenge His own elect who *cry out day and night to Him*, though He bears long with them? I tell you that He will avenge them speedily." As a crying infant typically gets speedy attention and comfort from the parent, likewise, when we humble ourselves as little children and cry out in faith to our heavenly Father, we can expect Him to hear and respond.

In verse 27, the two blind men refer to Jesus as "Son of David." This was a common Messianic title in Jesus day, used only in the Synoptic Gospels. In Matthew 1, which lists the genealogy of Jesus, Jesus is referred to as "Son of David, Son of Abraham" (1:1). But we must regard Jesus as more than one who descended from a human king—Revelation 19:16 declares Him to be "KING OF KINGS AND LORD OF LORDS."

We also see in verse 27 that the blind men cry out to Jesus for *mercy*. Typically, God's mercy refers to His withholding judgment that we deserve, and His grace refers to His giving us the blessings that we do not deserve. We can never earn God's favor or blessings such as healing; they are gifts to us because God is gracious and merciful!

Twice Jesus indicated that whether or not the blind men would be healed depended on their having faith (see verses 28 and 29). In verse 28, Jesus asked if they believed He was *able* to heal them. This reminds me of the leper's words in Matthew 8:2, "Lord, if You are *willing*, You can make me clean." Jesus was and is willing and able to heal those who trust and obey.

Verse 29 indicates that Jesus laid His hands on the parts of their bodies that needed healing—"He touched their eyes." Then Jesus spoke a word of command with a contingency—He said, "According to your *faith, let it be to you*." Jesus was saying, "If you have faith, you will be healed"; "If you do not have faith, you will not be healed." (See Gal. 3:5.) Such commands for healing contingent upon faith are made by Jesus in other places in Matthew's Gospel (8:13; 15:28). Verse 30 indicates their healings were immediate—"And their eyes were opened."

In verse 31, we see that the newly healed men spread the news that Jesus healed them throughout all that country. Their unrestrained excitement actually caused them to disobey Jesus' instructions to them on this matter. Ironically, many Christians today often disobey Jesus by not taking full advantage of daily opportunities to witness to others of the Person and work of Jesus Christ, though Jesus commands us to do so (Mk. 16:15). As we see with these men, divine healings are highly effective in motivating people to spread the good news of the saving and healing power of our wonderful Lord Jesus.

Testimony—God Healed My Knee!

In August 2012, I had arthroscopic knee surgery due to a weight-lifting injury I experienced in 2010. About a month after my surgery, I resumed strenuous activities such as shooting basketball and jogging. This hasty return to exercise was a bad idea—I reinjured my knee. So I immediately began praying for the Lord to heal my knee. In late November 2012, as I was walking down the street, the words came to me, "Start jogging, and I will heal you knee." So I immediately began jogging, and continued jogging for months with no major difficulties. Praise the Lord!

Matthew 9:32-33 As they went out, behold, they brought to Him a man, mute and demon-possessed. (33) And when the demon was cast out, the mute spoke. And the multitudes marveled, saying, "It was never seen like this in Israel!"

We see here that the demon seemed to be the cause of the muteness of the man. When we pray for the sick, we need to discern if any demons are present, because demons are likely contributors to the sickness (or they may be the sole cause—Acts 10:38; Lk. 13:10-17). Believers are given authority to cast out demons in the name of Jesus (Mt. 10:7; Mk. 16:17; Lk. 9:1; 10:19). The people rightly acknowledged that the demonstration of Jesus' grace and power in casting out the demon was marvelous and unprecedented.

Matthew 9:35 Then Jesus went about all the cities and villages, teaching in their synagogues, preaching the gospel of the kingdom, and *healing* every sickness and every disease among the people.

The words of this verse are very similar to the words of Matthew 4:23. I consider 4:23 and 9:35 to be Matthew's mission statement for Jesus' three and one-half year public ministry. As in 4:23, in 9:35 Jesus is operating in the office of the evangelist—He is proliferating the Word of God through teaching and preaching. Jesus "went about all the cities and villages" in order to reach as many people as possible with the gospel message. The church should follow in Jesus' steps: 2 Timothy 4:5 says, "Do the work of an evangelist." Again, Titus 1:3 says, "God has in due time manifested His word through *preaching*...." Preaching and teaching God's Word should remain a top priority of the church. What an honor, and a responsibility, to preach God's Word!

What is the gospel of the kingdom? "Gospel" means good news. The good news is that God so loved the world that He sent His only begotten Son, Jesus the Christ, to be the final and sufficient offering to atone for humanity's sin by dying on the cross. Furthermore, Jesus was raised from the dead on the third day, and anyone who has faith in Him (embracing Him as Lord and Savior) is pardoned of his or her sins, and receives the indwelling of the Holy Spirit. The kingdom of heaven is wherever and whenever King Jesus reigns. Whenever you do God's will through the Holy Spirit, in accordance with Scripture, and with love in your heart, you are manifesting the kingdom of heaven on earth.

The healings and casting out of demons that Jesus performed comprise demonstration of the gospel which complements His proclamation of the gospel. This verse also indicates that no sickness or disease could withstand Jesus' power to heal. Today's church needs to implement the proclamation-demonstration model of evangelism by intentionally preaching and healing in Jesus' name in cities, villages, and wherever people are found.

Matthew 10:1, 7-8 And when He had called His twelve disciples to Him, He gave them power over unclean spirits, to cast them out, and *to heal* all kinds of sickness and all kinds of disease...(7) And as you go, preach, saying, "The kingdom of heaven is at hand." (8) *Heal* the sick, cleanse the lepers, raise the dead, cast out demons. Freely you have received, freely give.

In coming "to Him" (Jesus, verse 1), we receive "power" and everything else we need. *Exousian*—the Greek word used for "power" in verse 1—is the word from which "exorcism" (casting out demons) is derived. *Dunamis*—from which comes the word "dynamite"—is another Greek word that is translated "power" in the New Testament. For today as well as then, Jesus has given His followers power, both *exousian* and *dunamis* (see Luke 9:1), in order to cast out demons, heal the sick, be effective witnesses, and experience victory over the power of sin.

We may note from this passage that even Judas Iscariot, the betrayer (Mt. 26:46-49), the one whom Jesus called "a devil" (Jn. 6:70), and the one disciple who ended up in hell (Acts 1:25), also received power to cast out demons and to heal the sick. So one's operation in the gifts of the Spirit such as divine healing does not necessarily indicate that one is living (and will live) a life pleasing unto God (See Mt. 7:21-23). The Christian's top priorities include abiding in Christ, obeying His Word, walking in love, humility, and the fear of the Lord. Gift development is important, but character development is more important.

The phrase "to heal all kinds of sickness and all kinds of disease" in verse 1 is similar to a phrase in Matthew 4:23—"healing all kinds of sickness and all kinds of disease...." As Matthew 4:23 is a mission statement for the evangelistic ministry of Jesus, so Jesus commissioned the disciples to follow in His steps. Verse 8 confirms this in that the same types of miracles that Jesus performed are specified: "Heal the sick, cleanse the lepers, raise the dead, cast out demons." Apparently, the disciples even raised the dead during this outing! Jesus had been modeling for the disciples how evangelism was to be done. Now it was their turn; they were to employ the proclamation-demonstration model. They were to preach virtually the same message that Jesus and John the Baptist preached—"the kingdom of heaven is at hand" (See Matthew 4:17 and Matthew 3:2. However, the message of Matthew 10:7 does not include the word "repent," though both Jesus and John the Baptist included repentance in their messages. Mark 6:12, Acts 2:38, and Acts 3:19 shows that the disciples did preach repentance.) Reverend A. J. Gordon said the following about this passage:

> When our Lord gives command to the twelve, as he sends them forth "to heal all manner of sickness and all manner of disease" (Mt. 10:1), we might conclude that this was an apostolic commission, and one which we could not be warranted in applying to ourselves. But here the promise is not only to the apostles, but to those who should believe on Christ through the word of the apostles; or as Bullinger the Reformer very neatly puts it in his comment on this passage, to "both the Lord's disciples and the disciples of the Lord's disciples."[98]

Matthew 11:2-5 And when John had heard in prison about the works of Christ, he sent two of his disciples (3) and said to Him, "Are You the Coming One, or do we look for another?" (4) Jesus answered and said to them, "Go and tell John the things which you hear and see: (5) The blind see and the lame walk; the lepers are cleansed and the deaf hear; the dead are raised up and the poor have the gospel preached to them. (6) And blessed is he who is not offended because of Me."

John the Baptist had already identified Jesus as the Messiah. In John 1:29, John saw Jesus and said, "Behold! The Lamb of God who takes away the sin of the world!" But later, when John was incarcerated, his faith needed a boost. On account of his isolation in prison and other related hardships, John was tempted to doubt that Jesus was the Messiah. Therefore, John asked Jesus for confirmation of His identity. Rather than showing disappointment at John's lapse of faith, Jesus said of John: "among those born of women there has not risen one greater than John the Baptist..." (Mt. 11:11). What an outstanding testimony about John! He was the greatest man ever born until the birth of Jesus. If you struggle in your faith at times, you can be encouraged that John, the one whom Jesus highly commended, did also. As John the Baptist went directly to the Source—Jesus—for answers, we should do the same.

In this passage, Jesus mentions six results of His ministry, five of which are physical healings (demonstrations) and one is the poor hearing the proclamation of God's Word. Besides Christianity and Old Testament Judaism, are there any other world religions that can honestly claim healings of the blind, lame, deaf, leprous, and the raising of the dead? I know of none. But the Bible testifies that God worked through many Biblical characters to heal the sick, and God raised the dead through His servants Elijah, Elisha, Peter, Paul, and Jesus. There are testimonies of God raising the dead in contemporary times through Christians. For example, the video, *Raised from the Dead*, by Christ For All Nations, is a documentary of the bodily resurrection of Daniel Ekechukwu. He is a Nigerian pastor who was killed in an automobile accident, was certified dead by the coroner, was injected with embalming fluids, and then was revived three days later at a massive Christian worship service where Reinhard Bonnke was preaching and where there were an estimated 12,000 witnesses.

Verse 6 indicates that the Lord Jesus Christ is offensive to many people. Many religions use the term "God" which is typically not offensive. But use of the name "Jesus" is often offensive because it specifies that one is talking about the God of the Bible, which reveals that the way to God is narrow (one must die to sin, Rom. 6:11), the only Way is Jesus, so one must fully trust in Jesus to be saved.

Jesus confirmed His Messiahship to John by pointing out the healings that He performed (demonstration) as well as the gospel message that He proclaimed. Again, proclamation and demonstration of the gospel go hand-in-hand (Mk. 16:20).

Matthew 14:14 And when Jesus went out He saw a great multitude; and He was moved with compassion for them, and *healed* their sick.

In addition to Jesus' healing the sick in order to confirm His identity, perhaps the number one reason He heals is because He loves people. Divine healing is an expression of His compassion and grace. As Jesus "was moved with compassion," our motive for ministry ought to include possessing in our hearts Christ's love and compassion for others. First Corinthians 13:2b says, "...though I have all faith, so that I could remove mountains, but have not love, I am nothing."

Matthew 14:34-36 When they had crossed over, they came to the land of Gennesaret. (35) And when the men of that place recognized Him, they sent out into all that surrounding region, brought to Him all who were sick, (36) and begged Him that they might only touch the hem of His garment. And as many as touched it *were made perfectly well.*

Testimonies of Jesus' healings, which had been spreading like wild fire, created expectation in the men of Gennesaret that Jesus would also heal the sick among them. They took initiative to gather all the sick and bring them to Him. Their efforts, or works, demonstrated their faith.

The faith of those who were sick, as well as the faith of their friends who brought them, was such that they did not have to touch Jesus' skin or ask Him to lay His hands upon them. They believed that Jesus' power would heal them if they could simply touch something touching Him, such as His clothing. This is similar to Acts 5:15 where sick people believed that simply making contact with Peter's shadow was sufficient to produce faith for their healing; and they were all healed. No one who touched the hem of Jesus' garment remained sick. All were perfectly healed! Their faith, demonstrated by their effort, worked in harmony with Jesus' unlimited anointing to bring about the healing of all who were sick. This stands in contrast to the people of Jesus' own country where "He did do not many mighty works because of their unbelief" (Mt. 13:58).

Testimony—God Heals a Woman's Heart

Around 2001, Susan (who attended the same church I attended) developed a heart arrhythmia. A sincere and longtime follower of the Lord, Susan immediately sought the Lord for healing through prayer and quoting Scriptures. (She made flash cards of healing Scriptures and other prayer promises and constantly reminded God of His promises. What an excellent practice!) Susan also sought help from doctors, who, though they diagnosed her arrhythmia, were of little to no help in healing her. Around the thirty-ninth day of Susan's heart problem, the Lord spoke to her saying, "I am going to heal you." Hallelujah! The written Word of God (*logos*) became the revealed Word of God (*rhema*) to her. Susan continued to seek the Lord, thanking Him and waiting for her miracle. Approximately thirty-nine days after the Lord told Susan He would heal her, the healing manifested. The healing was thorough, divine in nature, and unrelated to medicine. Susan's healing is a testimony to the importance of persistence in the pursuit of faith. Jesus had perfect faith and thus He almost always healed instantly. The apostles, who were eyewitnesses to the countless miracles performed by Jesus, often saw instant miracles when they prayed. Today, however, because the healing ministry is not as prominent (at least in America) as it was during the ministry of Jesus and the early church, we may need to go through the process of cultivating faith through persistently standing on God's Word as Susan did, making God's Word the basis for our thoughts and confession.

Matthew 15:22-28 Then Jesus went out from there and departed to the region of Tyre and Sidon. (22) And behold, a woman of Canaan came from that region and cried out to Him, saying, "Have mercy on me, O Lord, Son of David! My daughter is severely demon-possessed." (23) But He answered her not a word. And His disciples came and urged Him, saying, "Send her away, for she cries out after us." (24) But He answered and said, "I was not sent except to the lost sheep of the house of Israel." (25) Then she came and worshiped Him, saying, "Lord, help me!" (26) But He answered and said, "It is not good to take the children's bread and throw it to the little dogs." (27) And she said, 'Yes, Lord, yet even the little dogs eat the crumbs which fall from their masters' table." (28) Then Jesus answered and said to her, "O woman, great is your faith! Let it be to you as you desire." And her daughter *was healed* from that very hour.

It is estimated that Sidon was one hundred twenty miles north of Jerusalem, Tyre was one hundred miles north, and Cana was eighty miles north. It was this region, outside of Galilee and in Gentile territory, that Jesus entered with his disciples. A woman of that region, a Canaanite, came to Jesus. She employed the principle of asking and receiving and "cried out" (verse 22) to Jesus for help because her daughter was severely demon-possessed. She was *standing in the gap* for her daughter—bringing her daughter's troubles to the only One who could heal her. (This text could be used for a Mother's Day sermon.) The woman's daughter was "severely demon-possessed," meaning a demon or demons had complete control of her daughter and intended to destroy her (Jn. 10:10). We who are parents should pray for our children to be strong in the Lord and protected by the Lord so as to overcome any and all temptations and demonic influences of this present world. We should leave our children the legacy of a genuine faith in Christ, as Timothy's grandmother and mother did for him (2 Tim. 1:5). The Canaanite woman is now looking to Jesus as her "Lord" (verses 22, 25, 27), Healer, and overall Provider, even as 1 Peter 5:7 says: "casting all your care upon Him, for He cares for you."

Verse 23 says of Jesus: "He answered her not a word…." He explains His silence to His disciples: "I was not sent except to the lost sheep of the house of Israel" (verse 24). Jesus was apparently commissioned by the Father to minister only to the Jews during that time period. Verse 26 shows that the Jews were considered the children, the people of the covenant, whereas the Gentiles were by comparison "little dogs" (verse 26), because they were not in covenant with God. The Gentiles had no hope—Ephesians 2:12 says: "that at that time you were without Christ, being aliens from the commonwealth of Israel and strangers from the covenants of promise, having *no hope* and *without God* in the world." Israel was given the first opportunity to hear the gospel. Romans 1:16 says: "For I am not ashamed of the gospel of Christ, for it is the power of God to salvation for everyone who believes, for the *Jew first and also for the Greek*." The Jews will be the first to suffer God's judgment if they reject the gospel. Romans 2:8-10 says: "…but to those who are self-seeking and do not obey the truth, but obey unrighteousness— indignation and wrath, tribulation and anguish, on every soul of man who does evil, *of the Jew first and also of the Greek*; but glory, honor, and peace to everyone who works what is good, *to the Jew first and also to the Greek*." In Matthew 10:5, Jesus gave the same commission to His twelve disciples that the Father gave Him: "Do not go into the way of the Gentiles, and do not enter a city of the Samaritans. But go rather to the lost sheep of the house of Israel." However, in *Acts* we see that the Gentiles—even those as far away as "the end of the earth" (Acts 1:8), became included, along with the Jews, as those who would be invited to believe the gospel message and thus be saved. In Acts 10, God ordained for the gospel to be preached and received at the household of Cornelius, a Gentile. Peter later reported this event to the church in Jerusalem, and the church concluded: "Then God has also granted to the Gentiles repentance to life" (Acts 11:18). In Acts 14:46, Paul boldly told the Jews in Antioch in Pisidia: "It was necessary that the word of God should be spoken to you first; but since you reject it, and judge yourselves unworthy of everlasting life, behold, we turn to the Gentiles." But the Canaanite woman of Matthew 15 called upon Jesus for help during the dispensation when the gospel was not intended for the Gentiles. (Another possible explanation as to why Jesus did not want to minister to this woman can be seen in Mark's version of this story. Mark 7:24-25 says, "From there He arose and went to the region of Tyre and Sidon. And He entered a house and wanted no one to know it, but He could not be hidden." Jesus did not want anyone to know His location, and this woman was drawing attention to his presence in the house and in that region.)

The Canaanite woman asked for help three times: verse 22: she cried out for Jesus; verse 25: she came and worshipped Jesus, saying, "Lord, help me"; and verse 27: she asked for help a third time. Twice Jesus declined to assist her; we see this in verses 23 and 26. This is the only place in Scripture where I see Jesus declining to help someone who is asking for His help. This reminds us that God is under no obligation to fulfill His promises to someone who is not in covenant with Him. Being in covenant with God comes only through faith in His Son, Jesus. [Incidentally, the disciples would have acted wisely if they would have refrained from telling Jesus how to handle the situation (verse 23).] But the Canaanite woman is to be commended in that she did not exhibit pride and show offense at Jesus' words. She called Him "Lord" in her third plea to Him (in verse 27), even though He called her people "little dogs." She did not resist the label "little dogs," but accepted it because it came from the Lord's mouth. And the woman was *persistent*. She was determined to have Jesus heal her daughter. This reminds me of Luke 18 where the widow kept troubling the unjust judge in her continual pleas for his assistance. The judge finally granted her request because, he said, "lest by her continual coming she weary me" (verse 5). That parable highlights that God will "avenge His own elect who *cry out day and night to Him*" (verse 7).

It was the Canaanite woman's *great faith*, demonstrated by her persistence and humility, that caused Jesus to cast the demon out of her daughter. Similarly, Jesus commended the centurion of Matthew 8 for having greater faith than He had so far seen in Israel. The two greatest displays of faith (other than Jesus' own faith) recorded in Matthew's Gospel were by Gentiles (outsiders). Today, one can be brand new to the Christian faith—an outsider to the traditions of the church, not having grown up in it—yet one can have great faith in Jesus for deliverance and healing from demons and diseases for oneself or for another.

The Canaanite woman acquired what she desired by *faith*. And you can acquire what you desire by faith, as long as what you desire pleases God. Faith comes by hearing the revealed Word of God (Rom. 10:17). John 15:7 says, "If you abide in Me, and My *words* abide in you, you will ask what you *desire*, and it shall be done for you." In reference to God's willingness to grant us our desires, Psalm 37:4 says, "Delight yourself also in the LORD, and He shall give you the *desires* of your heart." Again, Psalm 20:4 says, "May He grant you according to your heart's *desire*, and fulfill all your purpose." Again, Psalm 145:19 says, "He will fulfill the *desire* of those who fear Him; He also will hear their cry and save them."

Matthew 15:30-31 Then great multitudes came to Him, having with them the lame, blind, mute, maimed, and many others; and they laid them down at Jesus' feet, and *He healed them.* (31) So the multitude marveled when they saw the mute speaking, the maimed made whole, the lame walking, and the blind seeing; and they glorified the God of Israel.

Again, the people came to Jesus for healing, as Matthew 7:7 advocates. Here, Jesus healed people who had a variety of sicknesses, and these healings would have been verifiable by sight. How could one plausibly refute such miracles as the lame suddenly walking, the blind suddenly seeing, the mute suddenly talking, and the maimed suddenly being made whole? (I believe this is the only Biblical reference to Jesus healing the maimed. Perhaps short legs lengthened, skin grew over exposed areas, and wounds instantly healed. Amazing!) Any onlooker (atheist, agnostic, or other) would not be able to refute the legitimacy of these healings by Jesus. Matthew 9:35 says that Jesus healed "*every* sickness and *every* disease among the people." We need to pursue such a healing ministry today—that verifiable healings will manifest through our prayers, to the glory of Christ. As the healings caused "great multitudes" to marvel and glorify God, such healings today could also cause great multitudes to marvel at the power of the gospel, glorify God, and believe.

Matthew 17:14-21 And when they had come to the multitude, a man came to Him, kneeling down to Him and saying, (15) "Lord, have mercy on my son, for he is an epileptic and suffers severely; for he often falls into the fire and often into the water. (16) So I brought him to Your disciples, but they could not *cure him.*" (17) Then Jesus answered and said, "O faithless and perverse generation, how long shall I be with you? How long shall I bear with you? Bring him here to Me." (18) And Jesus rebuked the demon, and it came out of him; and the child *was cured* from that very hour. (19) Then the disciples came to Jesus privately and said, "Why could we not cast it out?" (20) So Jesus said to them, "Because of your unbelief; for assuredly I say to you, if you have faith as a mustard seed, you will say to this mountain, 'move from here to there,' and it will move; and nothing will be impossible for you. (21) However, this kind does not go out except by prayer and fasting."

Many people who are sick look first to the doctor's office for treatment rather than seek Jesus for healing. But this caring father came to Jesus on behalf of his sick son. (He first went to Jesus' disciples because Jesus was away on the mountain.) Indeed, an aspect of being a godly husband and father is bringing the needs of your family to Jesus in prayer because Jesus is the only One who can perfectly meet every need.

At the beginning of this encounter, the father rightly humbled himself by kneeling before Jesus and acknowledging Jesus' Lordship. He asked the Lord for mercy. Any blessing you might receive from God is never merited; rather, it is a gift based on God's grace and mercy.

Verse 15 says that the boy had epilepsy, an illness that is characterized by out-of-control convulsions and seizures. Verse 18 reveals that the cause of the epilepsy was a demon. When the demon was cast out, the boy was healed. How often today do doctors prescribe medication or do surgery for the treatment of illnesses when the root cause may be demonic? Acts 10:38 links Satan and sickness: "...Jesus...went about... healing all who were oppressed by the devil...."

Jesus seemed exasperated with his disciples' inability to cure the boy—He called them a "faithless and perverse generation" (verse 17). When believers today fail to heal the sick, I imagine Jesus is likewise disappointed. Each of us should strive to live in such a way that we may one day hear Jesus say to us, "Well done, good and faithful servant" (Mt. 25:21, 23). The disciples wisely came to Jesus to ask why they had failed to heal the boy. Their teachability was commendable. Jesus said the sole reason the disciples failed to cast out the demon was their unbelief. Jesus said that if you possess even a very small amount of faith, an amount resembling a mustard seed (which, in Mark 4:31, Jesus describes as "smaller than all the seeds on earth"), then "nothing will be impossible for you" (verse 20).

Jesus illustrated this truth by saying, "if you...say to this mountain, 'Move from here to there,'...it will move...." This figurative example of moving the mountain contains a word of command. The command is to be spoken directly to the mountain as if it had ears. Keeping in mind the need to pray according to the will of God (1 Jn. 5:14-15), you may, in faith, command the mountain-sized obstacle to the will of God to move, and it will.

It would serve us well to be reminded of the nature of faith. Faith is not wishful thinking. Faith is not saying, "I know God can heal, but I do not know if God will heal in this circumstance." Instead, faith is more along the lines of truthfully saying, "I know that God will heal me because the Spirit of God has born witness to me that He will do so." (See Romans 10:17.)

In verse 21, Jesus indicated that certain spiritual disciplines are necessary in order to have the faith to cast out "this kind," or this caliber of demon. Prayer, which is one of the two disciplines Jesus mentioned, should be a vital component of one's preparation for dealing with "the devil" and "the evil day" (Eph. 6:11, 13, 18). The Lord exhorts believers to develop a lifestyle of prayer—"pray without ceasing" (1 Thess. 5:17; Eph. 6:18). In the Garden of Gethsemane, Jesus urged His disciples to pray for one hour while He was in the throes of sorrow in anticipation of His upcoming crucifixion (Mt. 26:40). Had they obeyed the Lord and prayed for that one hour, then perhaps they would have reacted more courageously when Jesus was arrested. Perhaps Peter would not have denied Jesus three times.

Jesus also mentioned fasting as a vital spiritual discipline which is conducive to faith. The topic of fasting appears just after the topic of prayer in Matthew 6, as fasting should sometimes accompany prayer. In Matthew 6:16-17, Jesus says, "when you fast," indicating that all of His followers should fast. In Matthew 9:15, Jesus says that when the bridegroom (who is Jesus) is taken away, then the disciples will fast. Fasting is an indispensable method of humbling oneself and keeping oneself from being weighed down in the flesh by food so that one is spiritually sharper. Since we typically do not know when we might encounter a situation which involves demons and mountain-sized obstacles, we ought to be people of regular prayer and fasting so that we are spiritually prepared when such situations arise.

Matthew 20:30-34 And behold, two blind men sitting by the road, when they heard that Jesus was passing by, cried out, saying, "Have mercy on us, O Lord, Son of David!" (31) Then the multitude warned them that they should be quiet; but they cried out all the more, saying, "Have mercy on us, O Lord, Son of David!" (32) So Jesus stood still and called them, and said, "What do you want Me to do for you?" (33)

They said to Him, "Lord, that our eyes may be opened." (34) So Jesus had compassion and touched their eyes. And immediately their eyes received sight, and they followed Him.

The actions of two blind men expressed their hearts of faith. When Jesus passed by, they "cried out" to Him (principle of asking and receiving) because they were certain that He could heal them. They were willing to "raise a ruckus" to get Jesus' attention, and no amount of pressure from the multitudes to silence them was going to hinder their pursuit of Jesus. Those in the multitudes who were trying to hinder the blind men were probably not blind themselves. And since they were not in the shoes of the blind men, they should not have been so quick to define what would constitute appropriate actions on the part of the blind men. Hurting and broken people are typically more fervent in their pursuit of the Lord than those who are comfortable. And when hurting and broken people are healed, they are often more radical in their praise and service of the One who granted them such a great deliverance. Sadly, many people who have great needs look to the world for solutions rather than crying out to the One who created them and who can supply their every need, namely the God and Father of our Lord Jesus Christ (Phil. 4:19; Col 1:3). They called Jesus "Lord," which hopefully reflected genuine submission to Him on their part, and they rightly appealed to His mercy. Jesus "is Lord of all" (Acts 10:36), and "His tender mercies are over all His works" (Ps. 145:9).

When Jesus heard their cry, He stopped what He was doing and attended to their need. Since it was obvious that the men were blind, why did Jesus ask, "What do you want Me to do for you?" Jesus wanted the blind men to be specific in their request. Likewise, we should be specific in what we ask of our heavenly Father. Based on the Spirit's leading, we should include details in our prayer requests. Furthermore, we should verbalize our prayers as the blind men did. Even if we whisper, our lips should move when we pray. Even Hannah moved her lips when she prayed for God to grant her a son (1 Sam. 1:13). Mark 11:23 and Romans 10:9 also emphasize the importance of speaking words in prayer. When the blind men specified what they wanted, then Jesus "had compassion and touched their eyes." Jesus' touch "immediately" healed them (verse 34). The men also had spiritual sight, for they followed Jesus.

Matthew 21:14 Then the blind and the lame came to Him in the temple, and *He healed them.*

After Jesus purged the temple of corruption—of those who were buying and selling, using the house of prayer as a market place (Mt. 21:12-13)—then He soulc procedd with His healing ministry in the temple. The body of the Christian is the temple of God, and we need to "cleanse ourselves from all filthiness of the flesh and spirit, perfecting holiness in the fear of God" (2 Cor. 7:1). Then the Spirit of God can minister through us as He did through Jesus in the temple. The healing the blind and lame were irrefutable miracles; they were undeniable testimonies to anyone who knew them as formerly blind and lame.

Matthew 21:18-22 Now in the morning, as He returned to the city, He was hungry. (19) And seeing a fig tree by the road, He came to it and found nothing on it but leaves, and said to it, "Let no fruit grow on you ever again." Immediately the fig tree withered away. (20) And when the disciples saw it, they marveled, saying, "How did the fig tree wither away so soon?" (21) So Jesus answered and said to them, "Assuredly, I say to you, if you have faith and do not doubt, you will not only do what was done to the fig tree, but also if you say to this mountain, 'Be removed and be cast into the sea,' it will be done. (22) And whatever things you ask in prayer, believing, you will receive."

Though this passage does not directly refer to healing the sick, it does deal with the related issue of faith. But before we look at that aspect of the passage, let us first consider its prophetic meaning. The fig tree represents Jerusalem, which in turn represents the nation of Israel. The Israelites were God's chosen people in whom God had invested His favor and blessings to an unprecedented degree. God delivered the Israelites from captivity in Egypt, gave them His law, and then drove out the inhabitants of Canaan so that Israel could occupy that good land. In view of His mercy upon Israel, God expected Israel to produce the fruit of righteousness and to be a holy people, set apart unto Him. However, even as the fig tree that Jesus approached contained no fruit, so Israel throughout its history in the Promised Land bore little if any godly spiritual fruit. An example of their unfruitfulness appears in the religious leaders' starkly negative reaction to the presence of their Messiah, Jesus, who is God in the flesh. They hated Him and eventually murdered Him. So Jesus' word of command to the fig tree to never bear fruit again can be seen as a pronouncement of judgment against unfaithful, natural Israel. The withering of the fig tree was an outward sign of that judgment which would include eventual loss of land and dispersion of the people among the nations. History reveals that around 70 A.D., Jerusalem and its temple were destroyed by the armies of the pagan conqueror, Nero of Rome. So from the prophetic meaning of this passage, each of us is warned to "bear fruits worthy of repentance," for "even now the ax is laid to the root of the trees…(and) every tree which does not bear good fruit is cut down and thrown into the fire" (Mt. 3:8, 10).

The literal meaning of this passage pertains to the unlimited potential one has through faith in Christ. The disciples marveled at the immediate withering of the fig tree due to Jesus' pronouncement of a curse against it, and they asked, "How did the fig tree wither away so soon?" Jesus could have replied, "I commend you for acknowledging the miracles I do. Yes, I can do all things; I am the Messiah." But Jesus turned the moment into an opportunity to teach His disciples and us today about faith. (For what the disciples could do, we can do.) He told them that they could perform miracles of the same caliber that He performed, if they had faith in Him. Jesus cursed a fig tree and it immediately withered; likewise, we can curse fig trees and see them immediately wither. But our miracle-working potential through faith in Christ is not limited to fig trees. Jesus added that we can also command the mountain to "be removed and be cast into the sea," and if we "have faith and do not doubt," then "it will be done" (verse 21). This is the second reference by Jesus in Matthew's Gospel to one's ability to move a mountain through faith. In 17:20, Jesus said, "if you have faith as a mustard seed, you will say to this mountain, 'Move from here to there,' and it will move; and nothing will be impossible for you." Jesus' analogy—that of moving a mountain—may seem extreme, but He chose it for a purpose.

From 1973 to 1987, the Army Corps of Engineers literally moved a mountain in what is known as the Pikeville, Kentucky cut-through. The cut-through is reportedly the world's second largest earth-moving project, with only the Panama Canal project being larger. The project allowed for a four lane highway to be created, a river to be rerouted, and a key railroad line to be moved. The relocation of the river was critical to ending the devastating flooding that historically plagued the city. The moving of the mountain in Pikeville, which cost close to seventy-seven million dollars, undoubtedly required a large team of people and heavy machinery. The project took fourteen years to complete.[99]

A mountain can be seen as any large obstacle that stands in the way of the advancement of the kingdom of heaven and one's having victory in any area of life. A mountain can be bitterness in your heart toward someone who has wronged you. A mountain can be a physical ailment or disease. A mountain can be depression due to a military deployment or a lengthy prison sentence. Jesus is challenging the body of Christ to be mountain-movers, not by utilizing bulldozers and other heavy equipment, but by cultivating and utilizing faith in Him, even mustard seed-sized faith (Mt. 17:20). Then love, joy, and peace in the Holy Spirit can replace stress and strife.

God can do anything (Mk. 10:27; Lk. 1:37). His name is El-Shaddai, or Almighty God (Gen. 17:1). Jesus is telling the body of Christ that through faith in Him, the believer can also do anything. Philippians 4:13 says: "I can do *all things* through Christ who strengthens me." Again, in John 15:7, Jesus says: "If you abide in Me, and My words abides in you, you will ask what you desire, and it shall be done for you." And Jesus twice referenced such unlimited potential by humans through faith in Him in the following Matthew passages: "nothing will be impossible for you" (17:20), and "*whatever* things you ask in prayer, believing, you will receive" (21:22).

This is not the first time in Matthew's Gospel that Jesus challenged the disciples to do miracles of such a high caliber. In Matthew 10:8, Jesus sent the disciples out with the instruction to "heal the sick, cleanse the lepers, raise the dead, cast out demons." So the disciples even raised the dead!

Matthew 21:21 emphasizes the word of command. If you have assurance concerning God's will in a particular matter, then you should speak a word of command. You should not command God, but rather you should command the obstacle, the sickness, or the demonic spirit to be removed from your life. You can say, "In Jesus' name, be gone!," or "Be healed!," or "Be removed and be cast into the sea!" (verse 21), and it will happen.

On the other hand, verse 22 emphasizes asking. If we ask in prayer, we are speaking to God. So though we who are believers can "come boldly to the throne of grace" (Heb. 4:16), at the same time we should remain humble and reverent, seeking to be led by the Holy Spirit concerning what to pray, and seeking to be empowered by God so we will submit to His will. For example, Jesus prayed "O My Father, if it is possible, let this cup pass from Me; nevertheless, not as I will, but as You will" (Mt. 26:39). Whether asking or speaking a word of command, if we have faith and do not doubt (verse 21), then whatever we speak "will be done."

Chapter 7

Healing Evangelists and Testimonies–Part 1

"And Stephen, full of faith and power, did great wonders and signs among the people"—Acts 6:8

The eleven healing evangelists I discuss in this book make up only a small percentage of the healing evangelists whom God has raised up over the decades and centuries to proclaim and demonstrate His gospel. As I have read their life stories and healing testimonies, and as I have seen videos of some of their evangelistic meetings, faith for healing has risen within me.

Smith Wigglesworth

Smith Wigglesworth (1859 – 1947) was born again at age eight, but due to his having to help provide for his family as a kid, he did not learn to read until after he married (1882). His wife, Polly, taught him to read the Bible, and he stated that the Bible was the only book he would read, even shunning the newspaper. During the Sunderland Revival in 1907, hands were laid on Wigglesworth and he spoke in tongues. No matter what the primary text for his sermon was, Wigglesworth prayed for the sick after he preached. Wigglesworth's ministry emphasized salvation for the lost, divine healing, and the baptism in the Holy Spirit. Having been healed of a ruptured appendix himself, Wigglesworth believed healing came through faith in Christ, and he anointed the sick with oil and distributed handkerchiefs (see Acts 19:11-12). Wigglesworth received credentials with the Assemblies of God in the United States, and developed an international ministry, preaching in the United States, Australia, New Zealand, South Africa, the Pacific Islands, India, Ceylon, and in several countries in Europe. In praying for others, his methods often involved hitting, slapping, or punching the afflicted part of the body. He said, "I don't hit them; I hit the devil. I am not dealing with the person; I am dealing with the satanic forces that are binding the afflicted."[100] There were reports of God using Wigglesworth to raise the dead. Here are three testimonies of the Lord's using Wigglesworth.

> Wigglesworth was being shown around a farm by the owner, who was his friend. Wigglesworth commented on the beauty of one field in particular. But his friend said, "It's not what it looks. The whole field is ruined by blight." Wigglesworth...stretched out his hand over the field and prayed in the name of Jesus. The field was completely cleansed of blight and the entire crop was saved. In fact, it was the best crop his friend had ever had from any field!

> Wigglesworth...had an appointment with a man whose wife was dying of abdominal cancer....Wigglesworth said, "Jesus is up. Jesus is down. Jesus is up." Wigglesworth explained that John 3:13 says: "No one has ascended to heaven but He who came down from heaven, that is, the Son of Man who is in heaven." Wigglesworth continued, "Jesus is in heaven with all power. I reach out the hand of faith and touch Him. His power flows down through me. I stretch out the hand of compassion and faith and touch the sick and the needy." Wigglesworth stood up in the train and prayed, "Pour your life into this man." Wigglesworth told the man, "Go home and lay your hands on your wife's stomach, and she will be healed." Months later, the man's pastor testified that the wife was healed just as Wigglesworth had said.[101]

A young man was dying, so his friends asked Wigglesworth to come and pray for him. When Wigglesworth arrived, the young man's mother told him he was too late. The young man's heart was failing, he had difficulty breathing, and he had lost much weight and was expected to die within a few days. Wigglesworth went into the young man's room and fell to his knees. He fasted and prayed all through the day and night. The next day Wigglesworth went to a nearby field to continue praying, and he saw a vision. He returned to the house and announced that the young man would be healed the next day. On the following day, Wigglesworth had all of the young man's family and friends leave the room. Then he knelt by the young man's bed and said to him, "When I touch you, God's power is going to come all over you. It will be nothing like you or even I have ever seen before. Don't be afraid. This is all happening to bring glory to God." He prayed for another hour or so, then laid his hands on the young man. Instantly the man rolled over in his bed and began crying. The young man said, "For Your glory, God, for Your glory." Then the young man stood up and walked around the room. The young man cried out to his family, "I've been healed." The father and mother both collapsed to the floor. The entire village was affected by the healing and many people repented and put their faith in Christ.[102]

For two years, Evangelist Lester Sumrall was discipled by Wigglesworth, who was perhaps sixty years older than him. Sumrall said Wigglesworth's morning ritual was as follows:

I jump out of bed! I dance before the Lord at least ten or twelve minutes—high-speed dancing. I jump up and down and run around my room telling God how great He is…how glad I am to be associated with Him and to be His child.[103]

John G. Lake[104]

John Graham Lake (1870-1935) was born in Ontario, Canada, and he and his family moved to Michigan in 1886. Lake was one of sixteen children, and eight of his siblings died young due to illness. At an early age, Lake prayed to receive Jesus as his Lord and Savior at a Salvation Army meeting. Lake said God called him to be a preacher, and he chose the Methodist church through which he would prepare. In 1891, Lake married Jennie Stevens of Michigan; they had six children naturally and one child by adoption. Less than five years into their marriage,

Jennie developed tuberculosis and heart disease, and became an invalid. During his earlier years, Lake struggled with a strange digestive disease for nine years that nearly killed him. He also had rheumatism which caused his legs to grow out of shape and distort his body. Lake's pastor and other church members made comments to him about his ailments such as "Brother, you are glorifying God," and "Be patient and endure it." Lake wrote: "There was nobody to pray for me…. As I sat alone, I said, 'Lord, I am finished with the world and the flesh, with the doctor and with the devil. From today, I lean on the arm of God." (I personally endorse the use of doctors.) Lake also wrote, "I laid down everything and went to Chicago…to John Alexander Dowie's Divine Healing Home." In Chicago, Lake was healed! In 1899, Lake took his brother who was an invalid for twenty-two years to a Dowie healing room. Healing ministers laid their hands on his brother and he was healed and walked out! Then Lake's thirty-four year old sister who had cancer visited a healing room. She had to be carried there on a stretcher, but God healed her! Another of Lake's sisters who was bleeding to death was healed by the Lord through the prayers of Dowie! God inspired Lake through Acts 10:38: "how God anointed Jesus of Nazareth with the Holy Spirit and with power, who went about doing good and healing all who were oppressed by the devil, for God was with Him." Lake believed that God was with him as He had been with the Lord Jesus, John Dowie, and others who operated in the gift of healing. Lake recruited friends to agree with him in prayer for the healing of his wife. They would all pray at a certain time, April 28, 1898 at 9:30 a.m. At the appointed time, Lake laid his hands upon Jennie, and she was healed! Her paralysis left, her coughing left, her heart became normal, and her temperature and breathing became normal. Word spread of Jennie's healing, and many sick people sought out Lake to have him pray for their healing. Lake said, "We were forced into it. God answered, and many were healed." Lake's healing ministry was born!

In 1891, eight months after Lake had married Jennie, the Methodist church asked him to pastor a church in Wisconsin. But Lake declined and went into business for himself—he started a newspaper in Harvey, Illinois. But when Jennie's health began to fail, they moved to Michigan and Lake went into real estate. Lake also helped start another newspaper. Lake was hired by a group of investors to form and manage a large life insurance company. It is reported that Lake became a millionaire through these various business ventures, but historians have not substantiated these claims. During those business years, Lake also began preaching and holding healing meetings in Chicago. In 1901, he moved his family to Zion City, Illinois so he could further learn about divine healing through Dowie's ministry which was headquartered there. Lake witnessed the power of God (though eventually Lake developed reservations about some of Dowie's practices), and that created a desire in him to draw closer to God. Lake ministered part time for about ten years. At the end of those years, Lake said, "I believe I was the hungriest man for God that ever lived."

For the first nine months of 1907, Lake frequently fasted and cried out to God for the baptism in the Holy Spirit. In October, he and his preaching partner, Tom Hezmalhalch, visited the home of an invalid woman to pray for her healing. While Hezmalhalch was instructing the woman about healing, Lake said the Lord spoke to him, "I have heard your prayers, I have seen your tears. You are now baptized in the Holy Spirit." "A downpour of electrical-like currents surged through his body...and moments later, he began speaking in tongues."[105] Lake began operating more in the gifts of the Spirit, and the healing gift in him became more pronounced. Lake began preaching to crowds of thousands in his healing meetings. He lost his desire to run the insurance company as he wanted to focus on ministry full-time. So in April 1907, Lake abandoned his business. Furthermore, he and Jenny disposed of all their wealth and decided to never disclose any financial needs that might arise; instead they would trust God.

In 1908, Lake, his family, Tom Hezmalhalch, and a group of missionaries (seventeen people in all) went to Africa. Lake left with $1.25 in his pocket, but when they arrived in Johannesburg, South Africa, he had been given $200, plus a fully furnished house. A South African pastor took a leave of absence and Lake was asked to fill his pulpit. His first Sunday, Lake preached to 500 people and God performed miracles. Over the next few weeks hundreds were healed, revival spread, and a door opened for Lake to preach throughout South Africa. It was reported that the anointing on Lake was so strong that at times people would fall down when coming within six feet of him. While Lake was away preaching, many sick people would come to his home and sleep in his yard, waiting for him to return and pray for them. It is reported that within eighteen months of being in Africa, Lake had established his own church and had started and was overseeing many churches in the surrounding area. Lake also publicly denounced the racism that was prevalent in South Africa.

Within his first year in Africa, Lake returned from a preaching tour and found that his wife of seventeen years, Jenny, had died of a stroke (1908) just twelve hours before his return. This devastated Lake, who wrote: "God gave us a marvelous unity in the Spirit. I adored her, and she me, likewise." In 1909, Lake went to America, and in 1910, he returned to Africa with $3,000 and eight more missionaries. Lake's sister, Irene, helped him raise the seven children. Lake and Thomas Hezmalhalch co-founded the Apostolic Faith Mission of South Africa. By 1913, Lake's ministry reportedly included 1,250 preachers, 625 congregations, and 100,000 converts. (Such success has been disputed.)

In February 1913, Lake (age forty-two) and his seven children returned to the United States. Lake married Florence Switzer in November, and they had five children. Lake became an itinerant preacher for one year and then moved to Spokane, Washington where he ministered in The Church of Truth. There he founded The Divine Healing Institute and opened Lake's Divine Healing Rooms, which he oversaw for the next five to six years. Lake also oversaw the International Apostolic Congress—the parent organization to his church. So by age fifty, Lake was an apostle, bishop over a denomination, pastor, and teacher. The healing rooms were once offices that he converted to classrooms where he taught men and women how to operate in Christ's healing power. Lake called the students "healing technicians" because he wanted to emphasize taking their knowledge beyond the classroom. He assigned each technician to the home of a sick person to regularly teach the sick person God's Word and build faith for healing. Over 100,000 healings occurred through the world-famous Healing Rooms ministry, and a report out of Washington D.C. said: "Rev. Lake, through divine healing, has made Spokane the healthiest city in the world, according to United States statistics." It was reported, in a healing room a thirty-five year old woman who had a thirty-pound fibroid tumor in her abdomen was healed—the mass dematerialized!

In 1920, Lake moved to Portland, Oregon and started another Apostolic Church and Healing Rooms ministry, and had similar success. During this time, Lake had a vision of an angel who opened a Bible to the book of Acts and spoke the following to him:

This is Pentecost as God gave it through the heart of Jesus. Strive for this; contend for this. Teach the people to pray for this. For this alone will meet the necessity of the human heart and have the power to overcome the forces of darkness.

For the next eleven years, Lake continued to establish healing rooms and plant churches throughout the West Coast and as far as Houston, Texas (he took one year off for rest). In 1931, Lake returned to Spokane where he began a final church and healing room. In 1935, Lake, age sixty-five, had a stroke and died two weeks later.

William Branham

William Marion Branham (1909-1965) was born near Burksville, Kentucky. His parents were farmers, his father was an alcoholic, and Branham grew up in extreme poverty. At an early age, Branham heard a voice say to him, "Do not drink or smoke or defile your body in any way, for when you get older I'll have a work for you to do." Later, Branham became seriously ill and thought he would die, and thus he began to seek God. While Branham was in the hospital, he heard a voice say three times to him: "I called you and you would not go." Branham prayed, "If you let me live, I will preach the gospel." Branham felt somewhat better that day, left the hospital, went to a church where the elders anointed him with oil and prayed for him, and he was instantly healed. From that point, Branham was committed to the Lord. For six months he cried out to God to receive the baptism in the Holy Spirit. At the age of twenty-four, the Spirit of God came upon him and he heard God's call to preach the gospel and pray for the sick. Branham began holding tent meetings and saw many come to Christ. In 1933, Branham preached to 3,000 people in a tent meeting in Jeffersonville, Indiana, and that same year he built a church building there initially called the "Pentecostal Tabernacle" and later called "Branham Tabernacle." He was a bivocational minister of this church until 1946. Branham married Hope Brumback and they had two children. Branham attended a Pentecostal convention and was asked to join the team as a traveling evangelist. Some of his friends spoke against his going, so he decided not to join the team. From that point, things began to go wrong for Branham. His church began to fail. Then his father died of a heart attack at age fifty-two. His brother died. Then his wife and his daughter died as a result of the Ohio River flood of 1937. He believed he was under God's judgment for not joining the evangelistic team. Then Branham worked as a game warden, a logger, and he occasionally preached. He married Meda Marie Broy and they had three children.

In 1946, Branham said he was visited by an angel of God who told him that he would be able to detect illness and sins in people. Thus Branham began a healing ministry and traveled throughout the United States.

> Branham went to minister at the Bible Hour Tabernacle in Jonesboro, Arkansas. It was estimated that 25,000 attended the meetings. On the last night of the meetings, a blind girl was pushing through the large crowd crying, "Daddy, Daddy," for she had become separated from him. Branham stopped her and asked "Where are you from?" "Memphis," she replied. Branham asked, "What are you doing here?" She replied, "I came to see the healah...Cataracts blinded me. The doctor said they're wrapped around the optical nerve of my eye. If he should try to operate I would be worse off and my only hope is to get to the healah, and then God will heal me. I am told that this is his last night here." Tears rolled down Branham's cheeks, and he said, "Lady, perhaps I'm the one you're looking for." She grabbed his coat lapel and said, "Is you the healah? Don't pass me, suh. Have mercy upon me, a blind woman." Branham replied, "I am not the healer, I am Brother Branham. Jesus Christ is your Healer." Then he prayed: "Lord, some 1900 years ago, an old rugged cross was dragging the streets of Jerusalem, dragging the bloody footprints of the Bearer. On the road to Calvary, His frail body fell under the load of the cross. Then came along Simon of Cyrene, and helped Him bear it. Now, Lord, one of Simon's children stands here staggering in the darkness...." At that moment, the girl screamed. "I can see." At that point, an old man with a twisted leg, leaning on a crutch, said, "Brother Branham...I've been standing in this rain for eight hours; have mercy on me!" Branham replied, "In the name of Jesus Christ, the Son of God, you're healed! You may throw away your crutches." Immediately the man's crooked limb was made straight, and he began leaping and screaming.[106]

The following is a testimony written by Rev. Robert Daugherty of St. Louis, Missouri.

Our little girl, Betty, had been sick for three months. We had two noted doctors of the city, but seemingly they could not find the cause of her sickness. We also had many outstanding ministers of the city and country around, praying for her. She steadily grew worse. Then we sent to Jeffersonville, Indiana, for...Rev. William Branham, who has the gift of divine healing. Brother Bill, as he is called, came to us at once. After hours of praying, he came in and told us that the Lord had showed him a vision of what to do for our little Betty. She was mere skin and bones and shook all the time as if she had palsy. Brother Bill asked us if we would believe God and would obey what He said to do. After he had prayed and called over her the name of Jesus, our little girl was immediately healed. That has been about ten months ago. Our little Betty is now in perfect health and is as fat as she can be.[107]

Branham filled auditoriums and stadiums.[108] "Historians generally mark the 1946 (Branham) meetings as inaugurating the modern healing revival....Along with Oral Roberts, Branham was the most revered leader of the healing revival."[109] Branham teamed up with Jack Moore (a Louisiana pastor) and Gordon Lindsay (an Oregon pastor), and Lindsay became Branham's campaign manager. The three of them began an organization and magazine called "The Voice of Healing," headquartered in Shreveport, Louisiana. Its original purpose was to report on the Branham meetings but later expanded to report on the meeting of other healing evangelists. F. F. Bosworth joined the organization in 1950. Bosworth told of one Branham meeting where nine deaf-mutes were in the prayer line, and all nine were healed.[110] U. S. Congressman William Upshaw from California had remained crippled from a farming accident when he was a youth. In 1951, Branham prayed for Upshaw who was then sixty-six years old and he was healed. Upshaw sent a letter describing his healing to every member of Congress. The miracle was also widely reported by the media.[111]

Branham held some unorthodox and unbiblical beliefs which either originated or became accentuated in the 1950s and 1960s. He embraced Oneness, and insisted that those who had been baptized by the Matthew Trinitarian formula (Mt. 28:19) would have to be rebaptized in the name of the "Lord Jesus Christ." Branham also spoke of the "serpent's seed," saying that Eve had sexual relations with the serpent, bore Cain, that some humans descended from the serpent's seed, and that central sins of the modern culture were a result of the serpent's seed. By 1957, Branham denied an eternal hell. Branham also proclaimed himself the angel of Revelation 3:14 and 10:7. Branham claimed that denominationalism was the mark of the beast and all denominations were synagogues of Satan. He "prophesied" that by 1977 all denominations would be consumed by the World Council of Churches under the dominion of the Roman Catholic Church, and then the rapture would occur. (I disagree with Branham on all these points.) Many said that Branham "had stepped out of his anointing."[112]

Even though Branham did not have an extravagant lifestyle, in 1955 he began having financial problems, including struggling to cover the expenses of his evangelistic meetings. The Internal Revenue Service reviewed Branham's finances and found that he had not kept good records, and he ended up owing the government $40,000 in back taxes.[113] In 1948, Branham refused to conduct any more large meetings, saying he was burned out. This stunned many people, including Gordon Lindsay who had already scheduled Branham to conduct meetings in major cities throughout the country. However, after a few months, Branham declared he had recovered and he resumed his ministry. In 1965, Branham was driving in Arizona when he was struck by a drunk driver. He lived a few days longer and then died. Gordon Lindsay wrote in *The Voice of Healing* that in Branham's latter years, he had likely fallen into delusion similar to that which befell faith healer John Alexander Dowie.

A. A. Allen

Asa Alonzo Allen (1911 - 1970) grew up among alcoholic parents and step-parents, left home when he was fourteen, and began partying and bootlegging. At age twenty-one, Allen happened across a Methodist church where the congregants were singing and dancing. He wanted what they had, and on his second night in attendance he received Jesus Christ as His Lord and Savior. Allen became filled with the Holy Spirit in a home meeting, and he desired to preach the gospel that had saved him. He married Lexie Scriven in 1936 and they had four children. This was during the Great Depression, and Allen would chop wood to earn money and then preach in small towns. In 1936, Allen accepted a pastorate of an Assemblies of God church in Holly, Colorado. He later left the pastorate to hold meetings as a singing, healing evangelist. The eyes of a blind coal miner were healed through his ministry. But Allen's constant travel as an evangelist began to wear on Lexie and the children, so in 1947 Allen decided to settle down and accept a pastorate at an Assemblies of God church in Corpus Christi, Texas. Inspired at an Oral Roberts tent meeting in Dallas in 1949, Allen felt he was called to the same type of ministry. So he resigned his pastorate in 1950 and began holding evangelistic healing meetings. In 1955, Allen purchased a large tent and became a major healing evangelist. Allen received a drunk driving charge in Knoxville, Tennessee, and thus parted ways with the Assemblies of God as well as with the Voice of Healing Association with which he had been involved. He became an independent minister and began his own magazine, *Miracle Magazine*, which had over 200,000 subscribers by the end of 1956. Allen also developed a national television and radio ministry which aired his healing lines.[114] (I have enjoyed viewing some of those services on Youtube.) In 1958, Allen said he felt called to build a Bible school in Arizona. Someone donated 1,250 acres, which he called Miracle Valley, and in 1960 he built a 4,000 seat church building on the property. In 1970, Allen co-authored with Walt Wagner his autobiography *Born to Lose, Bound to Win*.[115]

Evangelist Don Stewart testifies of a miracle he witnessed firsthand at an Allen crusade in Paramount, California.

> They brought a woman in on a stretcher; she was dying of cancer. When Allen pulled the sheet off of her, there was an audible gasp from the ministers on stage. The odor was unbelievable....Her whole front was a mass of blood, puss, and cancer. The open wound extended from her chest down to her intestines....When Allen prayed, the color and texture of that mass up by her chest began to change to that of normal skin. It just kept changing and changing and moving down the body. The wound started to close....We had all seen healings every night for years, but we had never seen anything like this. When the woman began to see it happening, she jumped up off that stretcher and started shouting, "Thank You, Jesus! Thank You, Jesus." Everyone was crying.[116]

In his book *Miracles*, R. W. Schambach reports the following testimony that he witnessed at an Allen meeting.

A woman brought her four year old boy from Knoxville, Tennessee to Alabama to attend a week's worth of the A. A. Allen crusade meetings which were held in the Birmingham Fairgrounds Arena. The boy had multiple major diseases including being born blind, deaf, and mute; both of his arms and legs were crippled and deformed, and he had clubbed feet. Around the end of the week, the woman came up to Rev. Schambach and said, "I'm down to my last twenty dollars….My baby has not been prayed for." Schambach encouraged her to come back to one more service and if her boy wasn't prayed for, he would personally take her and her boy to Rev. Allen's trailer for prayer. In the next service, Rev. Allen said "Tonight we are going to receive an offering of faith….give God something you cannot afford to give." That woman came running down the aisle and put her final twenty dollars in the offering bucket even though she didn't know how she would pay for her drive back to Knoxville or for food. Later, Allen launched into his sermon. But after about fifteen minutes, he stopped and said, "I'm being carried away in the Spirit. I'm being carried away to a hospital. I see doctors around a table. A baby has been born with twenty-six diseases. The doctors said he'd never live to see his first birthday. But that's not so; that boy is approaching four. Now I see the mother packing a suitcase. They're going on a trip. The boy's in a bassinet which is in the back seat of an old Ford. I see the Alabama-Tennessee border….Lady, you're here tonight. Bring me that boy! God is going to give you twenty-six miracles." That lady came running again and put her boy in Allen's arms. As Allen prayed, with the three thousand in attendance standing and agreeing in prayer, that boy was healed! His tongue, which usually hung out of his mouth, came back into his mouth. His eyes were healed and his arms stretched out. Allen placed the boy on his feet, and the boy ran for the first time in his life. He saw his mother for the first time and spoke for the first time, saying "Mama." This miracle sparked many more miracles in the Birmingham crusade and the Allen team remained there an extra week holding services. About fifteen people who were brought on stretchers from the local hospital were healed, along with about twelve people in wheelchairs, six blind people, and many others—all healed by the power of Jesus. Later, Schambach received a letter from the mother of the boy who had been healed. She had taken him to the hospital on the following Monday and the doctors kept him there all week. They called in many doctors to examine the boy. They pronounced him cured of twenty-six major diseases. Affidavits were collected from the doctors certifying that the boy was genuinely healed. The mother also testified that the night her boy was healed, those in the crowd gave her $235.[117]

Chapter 8

Healings and Related Themes in Acts

"Jesus the Christ heals you" Acts 9:34

Peter and Paul

The main mortal human characters in Acts are Peter and Paul. It is interesting to note that God worked through both Peter and Paul to perform miracles comparable in magnitude to Jesus' miracles, which fulfill Jesus' words in John 14:12: "...he who believes in Me, the works that I do he will do also; and greater works than these he will do...." At times, Jesus healed all who were present (Mt. 4:23-24; Mt. 8:16). Likewise, Scripture records two occasions in which Peter or Paul healed all who were present. Peter was the one person mentioned in a healing crusade in Acts 5:12-17 where "they were *all* healed" (verse 17). God used Paul to heal all who were sick on the island of Malta—Acts 28:9 says: "the rest of those on the island who had diseases also came and were healed." Furthermore, as Jesus healed by unusual methods, such as spitting on eyes or anointing eyes with clay (Mk. 8:23; Jn. 9:6), Scripture records two occasions in which Peter or Paul also healed by unusual methods. In Acts 5:15, Peter's shadow became a point of contact for those who were seeking to be healed, and indeed all were healed. Paul healed by unusual methods in that "handkerchiefs and aprons were brought from his body to the sick, and diseases left them and the evil spirits went out of them" (Acts 19:12). Finally, as Jesus raised the dead, Peter raised Dorcas from the dead (Acts 9:40), and Paul raised Eutychus from the dead (Acts 20:10; the Holy Spirit working through Peter and Paul did this). Since divine healing was a major vehicle, or sign, through which God confirmed His Word to a largely skeptical and unbelieving society (Mk. 16:20), we should pray for God to raise up Christians within our ranks today who will likewise minister God's Word with accompanying miracles comparable in magnitude to those performed by Jesus, Peter, and Paul. "God shows no partiality" (Acts 10:34); God can heal the sick through you!

Healings in Acts

Healing the sick is mentioned approximately thirteen times in Acts: 3:6-8 (at the Gate Beautiful, the man lame from his mother's womb was healed); 4:30 (a corporate prayer solicited God to grant healings, signs and wonders and to embolden His servants to preach His Word); 5:14-16 (a healing crusade occurred, where the sick sought to touch Peter's shadow—all were healed); 8:7 (Philip evangelized in the city of Samaria—"many who were paralyzed and lame were healed"); 9:18 (Saul's eyes were healed); 9:32-35 (Aeneas, who had been bedridden eight years and was paralyzed, was healed); 9:36-43 (Dorcas was raised from the dead); 10:38 (Peter testified to Cornelius' household of the healing ministry of Jesus); 14:8-10 (in Lystra, a man crippled from his mother's womb was healed); 19:11 (God healed the sick and cast out demons as people touched handkerchiefs and aprons taken from Paul's body); 20:9-10 (Eutychus was raised from the dead); 28:8-9 (Publius' father was healed of a fever, and then all the sick on the island were healed). The various and frequent miracles in Acts are perhaps why the book is entitled *Acts* and not merely *Words*. First Corinthians 4:20 says: "For the kingdom of God is not in word but in power." Likewise, today's church should seek to become a church of acts where manifestations of God's power confirming God's Word occur regularly. Also, today's church should employ acts of loving service toward others, and of course should proclaim the Word of God boldly and without compromise.

The four passages below contain perhaps the most narrative detail among accounts of healings in Acts. Studying these four passages together is beneficial in order to discover recurring themes that can instruct us and boost our faith as we pursue a healing ministry.

Acts 3:6-8 Peter said (to a man lame from his mother's womb), "Silver and gold I do not have, but what I do have I give you: In the name of Jesus Christ of Nazareth, rise up and walk." (7) And he took him by the right hand and lifted him up, and immediately his feet and ankle bones received strength. (8) So he, leaping up, stood and walked and entered the temple with them—walking, leaping, and praising God.

Acts 9:33-34 Then he (Peter) found a certain man named Aeneas, who had been bedridden eight years and was paralyzed. (34) And Peter said to him, "Aeneas, Jesus the Christ heals you. Arise and make your bed." Then he arose immediately.

Acts 9:36-42 Dorcas…became sick and died…(40) But Peter put them all out, and knelt down and prayed. And turning to the body he said, "Tabitha, arise." And she opened her eyes, and when she saw Peter she sat up. (41) Then he gave her his hand and lifted her up; and when he had called the saints and widows, he presented her alive. (42) And it became known throughout all Joppa, and many believed on the Lord.

Acts 14:8-10 And in Lystra a certain man without strength in his feet was sitting, a cripple from his mother's womb, who had never walked. (9) This man heard Paul speaking. Paul, observing him intently and seeing that he had faith to be healed, (10) said with a loud voice, "Stand up straight on your feet!" And he leaped and walked.

In all four passages, the infirm could not walk. In Chapter 3, the man was *lame* from his mother's womb; in Chapter 9, Aeneas "had been *bedridden* eight years and was *paralyzed*"; in Chapter 9, Dorcas was *dead*; in Chapter 14, the man was "*without strength in his feet…a cripple* from his mother's womb, who *had never walked.*" In all four accounts, Peter or Paul (Peter was the human agent through whom God healed in the first three accounts, and Paul in the fourth account) commanded the person to do something he or she could not do before, namely to arise: "rise up and walk" (3:6), "Arise and make your bed" (9:34), "Tabitha, arise" (9:40), and "Stand up straight on your feet!" (14:10). In all four accounts, the word of command to arise was given before there was any evidence of healing. In all four accounts, the infirm person obeyed the command to arise (or stand). Chapter 3 specifies that the feet and ankle bones received strength *after* the man obeyed the word of command from Peter and attempted to stand.

Chapter 3 and Chapter 14 specifically mention that the infirm were both crippled from their mother's womb (the man in Chapter 3 was over forty years old, 4:22). Also, Chapter 3 and Chapter 14 specifically mention that both men leaped and walked. The similar wording seems to point to an intentional effort on Luke's part to relate the two passages. Both men epitomized lameness (from their mother's womb), and both men epitomized being physically healed (they leaped and walked, thus indicating instant and complete healing). No matter how severe of a condition of paralysis, bondage, oppression, or illness (spiritually, physically, or mentally) one might have, God can grant one instant and complete healing through one's faith (or the faith of someone else on one's behalf) in Jesus Christ.

In Chapter 3, Peter assisted the man in his rising up. Also, in Chapter 9, Peter assisted Dorcas in her rising up. These acts of assistance remind us to lovingly serve others, even in practical ways. As in 3:11, when the healed man "held on to Peter and John," those whom God heals in our churches might cling to us, and we need to be patient and supportive. Furthermore, we may need to disciple those whom God heals through us, and teach them to ultimately hold on to Jesus—the One who completes us (Col. 2:10), and the One in whom lies "all things that pertain to life and godliness" (2 Pet. 1:3).

Only in the 9:36-42 passage (the raising of Dorcas) is there any evidence that the one giving the word of command, namely Peter, first prayed to the Father before he gave the word of command. Chapter 9, verse 40 shows that Peter "knelt down and prayed" before he "turned to the body" to give the word of command: "Tabitha, arise." It is likely that in Chapter 3 and Chapter 14, the circumstances did not allow the apostles to pray about the situation before issuing the word of command. This should remind each of us of the importance of walking in the Spirit and remaining ready to be used of God at any given moment. It is noteworthy that the predominant method used for healing the sick by Jesus and by the disciples in Acts was to speak a word of command to the sick person. Speaking a word of command requires having faith in one's heart (which is given by the Holy Spirit) that God will heal in that situation.

In Chapter 3 and in 9:34, the name of Jesus Christ was invoked in conjunction with the word of command. For emphasis, the name of Jesus is twice expressed in 3:16: "And *His name*, through faith in *His name*, has made this man strong..." (See also 4:10 and 4:12). This is in accordance with Mark 16:17-18, where Jesus said: "*In My name* they will cast out demons...they will lay hands on the sick, and they will recover." When Christ was raised from the dead, He was given a "*name* which is above every name, that at *the name of Jesus* every knee should bow...and that every tongue should confess that Jesus Christ is Lord..." (Phil. 2:9-11). Jesus delegated to the church His authority over demons and disease by the use of His name in faith (Lk. 9:1; 10:17; Mk. 16:17). Furthermore, since it is His name, His power, and His finished work on the cross which serve as the sole basis for faith when one prays for the sick, then certainly all glory for today's healings and other victories should go to Him—Jesus the Christ.

Let's now look at the vital role of faith in the Chapter 14 account. After the lame man had heard the gospel message from Paul's mouth, verses 9-10 say: "Paul, observing him (the lame man) intently and *seeing that he had faith to be healed*, said with a loud voice, 'Stand up straight on your feet!'" You might typically think of faith as being intangible— something you cannot see or touch. So in verse 9, how did Paul see the man's faith? Perhaps Paul's sermon included testimonies of people being healed, and Paul observed in the man hope and anticipation that God would also heal him. God likely gave Paul revelatory insight that the man had faith to be healed. Once the man had acquired faith, all that was needed was for the man to act on it. So Paul strongly exhorted him to do this, saying: "Stand up straight on your feet!" The man heard and believed the gospel message (that Christ died for our sins and rose again, and that through faith in Him one is redeemed), and now the man would act—"he leaped and walked." Such action is important because "faith by itself, if it does not have works, is dead" (Jas. 2:17). He did not slowly or gradually get up; he leaped up! How amazing this miracle must have been for those who witnessed it—a man lame from birth suddenly leaped up and began walking! How absolutely joyful this realization must have been for the healed man, that now he would be able to enjoy walking and running as others do. Now he could embrace the prospect of earning a living for himself instead of always having to depend on others. God is awesome! When faith is present, "all things are possible" (Mk. 9:23). But when faith is absent, one cannot please God (Heb. 11:6), nor can one accomplish anything of heavenly value (Jn. 15:5b).

Let's take a closer look at the related evangelistic results from the healing in Chapter 3 as well as the results from the tongues phenomenon and Peter's sermon in Chapter 2.

Acts 3:9-11 And all the people saw him walking and praising God. (10) Then they knew that it was he who sat begging alms at the Beautiful Gate of the temple; and they were filled with wonder and amazement at what had happened to him. (11) Now as the lame man who was healed held on to Peter and John, all the people ran together to them in the porch which was called Solomon's, greatly amazed.

A crowd recognized that the man who had been lame and had been a daily fixture as a beggar at the Beautiful Gate was now walking and leaping. Thus the crowd, "filled with wonder and amazement," ran to the healed man who was holding on to Peter and John, to take in the full explanation of this obvious miracle. Miracles are often called "wonders" in Acts (2:19; 2:22; 2:43; 4:30; 5:12; 6:8; 7:36; 14:3; 15:12). Miracles also cause "amazement." (See 2:7 and 2:12, where onlookers were "amazed and perplexed" and "marveled" at the supernatural phenomenon of tongues.) Such amazing miracles often set up prime opportunities for the gospel to be preached. Even those religious rulers who would persecute Peter and John could say nothing against the healing since the undeniable evidence—the healed man—was standing in front of them (4:14). They even admitted "that a notable miracle has been done through them (Peter and John) is evident to all who dwell in Jerusalem, and we cannot deny it" (4:16).

In 3:16, Peter gave the attentive audience the explanation for the healing: that faith in Jesus "made this man strong" and gave "him this perfect soundness in the presence of you all." Peter capitalized on the opportunity—he preached the gospel message including the identity of Jesus, that He is "the Holy One and the Just" (verse 14), "the Prince of life" (verse 15), and "the Christ" (verse 18). Peter confronted them with the fact that they had "denied" that Jesus is the Christ, and they were guilty of murdering the Messiah (verses 14-15). But God had raised Jesus from the dead!, preached Peter (verse 15). Peter preached a similar message in Chapter 2, focusing on many of the same themes—the death and resurrection of Jesus, their guilt in murdering Him, Old Testament prophecies foretelling the death and resurrection of the Messiah, and the sovereignty of God in the matter—"Him (Jesus), being delivered by the determined purpose and foreknowledge of God, you have...crucified..." (2:23); (but) "God has made this Jesus, whom you crucified, both Lord and Christ" (2:36). In 3:18-26, Peter again explained that the death and resurrection of the Christ were the fulfillment of Old Testament prophecy, and he specifically mentioned Moses, Samuel, and Abraham as examples of Old Testament saints through whom the prophecies came. Also in Chapter 2, Peter quoted from Psalm 16 and Psalm 110, authored by the highly regarded former king of Israel, David, to support his truthful claims of the death and resurrection of the Christ (2:25-35). In chapters 2 and 3, the anointed preaching of the gospel by Peter, utilizing the Old Testament Scriptures which the Jews acknowledged, and confirmed with the signs of speaking in tongues and healing (demonstration), proved persuasive to many in the Jewish crowds. In both 2:38 and 3:19, Peter calls for all within the sound of his voice to repent. Repentance, which is a changing of one's mind from carnal thinking to Christ-like thinking (agreeing to obey God and His Word), is inherent in one's having faith in Christ. Bosworth says, "Faith always implies obedience."[118] Peter said that the man was not healed by Peter's or John's "own power or godliness," but by faith in Jesus (3:12 and 3:16). Likewise we cannot be divinely forgiven of our sins through our own power, godliness, good works, charity, etc., but only through faith in Jesus Christ's death on our behalf (to pay for our sins) and His bodily resurrection. If the Jews (and anyone else for that matter) would repent and believe the gospel, then their sins would be "blotted out, so that times of refreshing...(would) come from the presence of the Lord" (3:19). Indeed, the Holy Spirit, who is given to those who obey God (5:32), refreshes, empowers, and helps those who follow Christ.

A result of this evangelistic opportunity in Chapter 3, where miraculous demonstration set up gospel proclamation, was that "many of those who heard the word believed; and the number of the men came to be about five thousand" (4:4). The number of believers was initially "a hundred and twenty" in Acts 1:15. Then the number grew by "about three thousand" on the Day of Pentecost (Acts 2:41). In Acts 4:4, the number grew to "about five thousand." That is phenomenal church growth! The following list of verses shows church growth continuing throughout Acts:

(2:41b) that day about three thousand souls were *added* to them;
(2:47b) And the Lord *added* to the church *daily* those who were

being saved; (4:4) many of those who heard the word believed; and the number of the men came to be about five thousand; (5:14) And believers were *increasingly added* to the Lord, *multitudes* of both men and women; (6:1) Now in those days, when the number of the disciples was *multiplying...*; (6:7) Then the word of God spread, and the number of the disciples *multiplied greatly* in Jerusalem, and a *great many* of the priests were obedient to the faith; (9:31) Then the churches throughout all Judea, Galilee, and Samaria had peace and were edified. And walking in the fear of the Lord and in the comfort of the Holy Spirit, *they were multiplied*; (9:35) So *all* who dwelt at Lydda and Sharon saw him and *turned to the Lord*; (9:42) And it became known throughout all Joppa, and *many believed on the Lord*; (11:21) And the hand of the Lord was with them, and a *great number believed and turned to the Lord*; (11:24b) And a *great many people were added* to the Lord; (12:24) but the word of the Lord *grew and multiplied*; (17:4) And some of them were persuaded; and a *great multitude* of the devout Greeks, and *not a few* of the leading women, joined Paul and Silas; (17:12) Therefore *many of them believed*, and also *not a few* of the Greeks, prominent women as well as men; (18:8) Then Crispus, the ruler of the synagogue, believed on the Lord with all his household. And *many* of the Corinthians, hearing, believed and were baptized.

Notice the accelerating growth rate in Acts. *Added* appears in 2:41b; *added...daily* appears in 2:47b; *increasingly added* appears in 5:14; *multiplying* appears in 6:1; and *multiplying greatly* appears in 6:7. As the story of Acts extends beyond Jerusalem, church growth continues but perhaps not always as rapidly as in the first six chapters. Also note that an entire household is saved in 16:31 and another entire household is saved in 18:8. This can encourage us that God can bring salvation to all within our households. Such astounding church growth in Acts is one reason why churches today should regard Acts as its main textbook for any contemporary church growth plan. Other church growth books can be used as supplements, but they should not be regarded more highly than Acts, for Acts is God's inerrant Word.

In summary, the Acts model for church growth unfolds in Acts 2 and 3 with demonstrations of divine power (tongues in Acts 2 and healing in Acts 3) which amazes many people and draws a crowd seeking explanation. This is followed by bold proclamation of the gospel message which includes the call unto repentance and faith in Jesus Christ. The result is phenomenal church growth!

Testimony—God Heals a Man of a Staph Infection

At the request of a friend, my uncle, Doug Tweed, went to a hospital and prayed for a man who had a staph infection in his foot due to a spider bite. The doctors were planning to amputate the next morning. But the next morning, the infection was completely gone and no surgery was needed.

Themes in Acts

I would like to mention a few themes in Acts which relate to divine healing. One important theme is the fear of the Lord. In 2:43 and in 5:11-12, the fear of the Lord precedes signs and wonders: 2:43: "Then fear came upon every soul, and many wonders and signs were done through the hands of the apostles"; 5:11-12: "So great fear came upon all the church and upon all who heard these things. And through the hands of the apostles many signs and wonders were done among the people." The fear of the Lord is the conviction in one's heart that God is holy, that all sin will be judged by God, and therefore one should always seek to remain obedient to God in all matters. The fear of the Lord does not come naturally; one must pursuit it—Proverbs 23:17b says, "be zealous for the fear of the LORD all the day." Again, Proverbs 16:6b says, "by the fear of the LORD one departs from evil." So the fear of the Lord is necessary to drive sin out of one's heart, for unrepentance will certainly hamper the effectiveness of one's prayers (Ps. 66:18).

Several other themes, all of which relate to the highest spiritual quality one can possess—love—appear in Acts. One such theme is unity within the body of Christ, often referred to as being in "one accord." The believers were in one accord preceding Pentecost (1:14), on the day of Pentecost (2:1), during corporate prayer (2:46; 4:24), during times when signs and wonders took place (5:12), and during an important business meeting, the Jerusalem Council (15:25). Another theme is Christian generosity: church members would often share their material possessions with those in need (2:44-45; 4:32-37). Also, close friendships were formed within the body of Christ, for they spent much time together, even daily (2:46; 5:42). They often spent time in one another's homes and in the temple, focusing on things of God: "the apostles' doctrine and fellowship...the breaking of bread, and... prayers" (2:42). Such themes of unity, generosity, frequent fellowship, and spiritual devotion within the body of Christ imply great love of the brethren. Love—the first and greatest of the nine fruit of the Spirit (Gal. 5:22-23)—never fails, even as God, who is love, never fails (1 Cor. 13:8; 1 Jn. 4:8). Any church which consistently demonstrates God's love within its membership as well as toward those outside the church will prosper in its mission. The church's mission should include worshipping God, edifying the body, and making disciples of all nations. However, if churches allow factions, strife, and selfishness to develop and go unchecked, then those churches will not fulfill God's mission, and the prospect of signs, wonders, and healings occurring will be diminished.

One more theme in Acts which I will mention is persecution. While Peter was preaching the gospel to the crowd in Chapter 3, he and John were seized by "the captain of the temple, and the Sadducees" (4:1). Peter and John were taken into custody until the next day and were brought before religious leaders including the high priest. These leaders severely threatened Peter and John saying they should no longer speak to any man about Jesus. The leaders likely would have physically punished Peter and John, but they feared a backlash from the Jews since all of Jerusalem knew that an irrefutable miracle was performed by God through Peter and John. Unlike Peter's cowardly reaction to persecution when he denied Jesus three times (Lk. 22:54-62), here Peter, "filled with the Holy Spirit" (4:8), *boldly proclaimed* to his captors that Jesus Christ, whom they crucified, had been raised from the dead, and that faith in the resurrected Jesus was the sole reason that the lame man was healed.

A Corporate Prayer for Proclamation and Demonstration

After Peter and John reported to the church the persecution they had endured, the church came together and "raised their voice to God with one accord" (4:24). Let's look at a portion of their prayer:

Acts 4:29-31 "Now, Lord, look on their threats, and grant to Your servants that with all boldness they may speak Your word, (30) by stretching out Your hand to heal, and that signs and wonders may be done through the name of Your holy Servant Jesus." (31) And when they had prayed, the place where they were assembled together was shaken; and they were all filled with the Holy Spirit, and they spoke the word of God with boldness.

The church showed no signs of being intimidated by the persecution they were undergoing; instead, the church petitioned God to grant them boldness to continue speaking God's Word. Such boldness had been demonstrated by Peter in his sermons in Acts 2 and 3, as well as in his and John's response to the religious leaders in 4:19-20. Their boldness stands as a testimony to God's great power available through the baptism in the Holy Spirit which believers first received on the Day of Pentecost. The boldness of the early church testifies to the words of Jesus in John 16:7: "It is to your advantage that I go away; for if I do not go away, the Helper will not come to you." Indeed, being baptized in the Holy Spirit, and subsequently being refilled with the Holy Spirit (Eph. 5:18), are vital, not only to preaching the gospel boldly, but to experiencing all of the joy-filled, abundant life that comes through knowing our Lord Jesus Christ (Jn. 10:10; Jn. 15:11; Eph. 3:19).

The believers' corporate prayer links bold proclamation to signs and wonders in general, and to healing specifically (again, I consider healing the premier miraculous sign of the New Testament). David Yonggi Cho, former pastor of the world's largest church, Yoido Full Gospel Church in Seoul, Korea, has said that he makes room in every worship service at his church for the elders to pray for the sick to be healed. It is significant that the ministry of divine healing has been made a high priority in the largest church body today.

The conclusion to the corporate prayer was a physical shaking of the place where they were and "they were all filled with the Holy Spirit, and they spoke the word of God with boldness" (verse 31). Hebrews 12 speaks of God's shaking the earth and heaven to remove "things that are made, that the things which cannot be shaken may remain" (Heb. 12:27). We as the church need to regularly ask God to remove the worldly "things," or ungodly desires, from our hearts so that what is of true, heavenly value may remain the focus of our affections.

Acts 5:12-16 And through the hands of the apostles many signs and wonders were done among the people. And they were all with one accord in Solomon's Porch. (13) Yet none of the rest dared join them, but the people esteemed them highly. (14) And believers were increasingly added to the Lord, multitudes of both men and women, (15) so that they brought the sick out into the streets and laid them on beds and couches, that at least the shadow of Peter passing by might fall on some of them. (16) Also a multitude gathered from the surrounding cities to Jerusalem, bringing sick people and those who were tormented by unclean spirits, and they were *all healed.*

News spread that a powerful healing ministry was under way in the Jerusalem church. Therefore, believers were bringing the sick and "those tormented by unclean spirits" from long distances—"surrounding cities"—to where Peter and the other apostles were ministering. They believed that their great effort to transport the sick to the Jerusalem church would be rewarded (their works would demonstrate their faith)— the sick would be healed. The anointing to heal, and consequently the reputation to heal, must have been tremendous upon the apostles, and especially Peter, since the sick were being laid in the streets for the purpose of getting close enough to Peter so that his shadow would touch them. This is reminiscent of Jesus ministry in the land of Gennesaret: "the men of that place sent out into all that surrounding region, (and) brought to Him all who were sick, and begged Him that they might only touch the hem of His garment. And as many as touched it were made perfectly well" (Mt. 14:35-36). In the case with Peter, the sick did not think it necessary to touch his skin or even a piece of his clothing; rather they believed that simply touching Peter's shadow would be a sufficient point of contact to support their faith that the Spirit of Christ would heal them. As all were healed by Jesus in Gennesaret, likewise all were healed through the Holy Spirit in Peter and the other apostles in the streets of Jerusalem. Sick people who had to be carried to the streets where the healing crusade was located were now able to walk back home on their own. That Peter's shadow "might fall on *some* of them" (verse 15) indicates that the crowds must have been huge. Perhaps thousands were there daily. God was doing a great work in and through the early church.

Immediately following the section describing the healing crusade in the streets, persecution occurred as the high priest and other religious leaders put the apostles in prison. But an angel of the Lord freed them and commanded them: "Go, stand in the temple and speak to the people all the words of this life" (verse 20). The believers obeyed, and once again the captain and his officers, at the request of the religious leaders, brought the disciples before the counsel. When the disciples were interrogated, they boldly replied, "We ought to obey God rather than men." Many national leaders and even church leaders today wrongly place too much value on pleasing man, and in doing so they disobey God. In 1 Samuel 15:24, we see that King Saul replaced the fear of God with the fear of man, and it cost him everything. Once again, the disciples, under interrogation, preached the gospel: that Jesus was Prince and Savior (5:31), that they had murdered Him (verse 30; actually the sins of each of us put Jesus on the cross), that God had raised Jesus from the dead (5:30-31), and that through repentance and faith in Jesus the forgiveness of sins is offered (5:31). Therefore, the religious leaders plotted to kill them. But God raised up a highly respected Pharisee, Gamaliel, who made a reasonable appeal to the religious leaders to refrain from killing the believers. His wisdom and cool-headedness prevailed, so the disciples were beaten and released. But in keeping with Matthew 5:11-12 and James 1:2-4, they "rejoiced that they were counted worthy to suffer shame for His name" (5:41). Indeed, "our light affliction, which is but for a moment, is working for us a far more exceeding and eternal weight of glory" (2 Cor. 4:17).

Acts 6:1-10 Now in those days, when the number of the disciples was multiplying, there arose a complaint against the Hebrews by the Hellenists, because their widows were neglected in the daily distribution. (2) Then the twelve summoned the multitude of the disciples and said, "It is not desirable that we should leave the word of God and serve tables. (3) Therefore, brethren seek out from among you seven men of good reputation, full of the Holy Spirit and wisdom, whom we may appoint over this business; (4) but we will give ourselves continually to prayer and to the ministry of the word." (5) And the saying pleased the whole multitude. And they chose Stephen, a man full of faith and the Holy Spirit, and Philip, Prochorus, Nicanor, Timon, Parmenas, and Nicolas, a proselyte from Antioch, (6) whom they set before the apostles; and when they had prayed, they laid hands on them. (7) Then the word of God spread, and the number of the disciples multiplied greatly in Jerusalem, and a great many of the priests were obedient to the faith. (8) And Stephen, full of faith and power, did great wonders and signs among the people. (9) Then there arose some from what is called the Synagogue of the Freedmen (Cyrenians, Alexandrians, and those from Cilicia and Asia), disputing with Stephen. (10) And they were not able to resist the wisdom and the Spirit by which he spoke.

Verse 8 is the only place in Acts where someone is described as having done wonders and signs that were "great" in magnitude. And these "great wonders and signs" were done by Stephen, who was not one of the twelve apostles. (In 2:43 and 5:12, the signs and wonders were done through the apostles.) Stephen was one of seven men chosen to oversee the daily distribution ministry. Let's consider the listed qualities of Stephen (the main character of Acts 6 and 7). First, Stephen was "a man full of faith" (verse 5). If you have "faith as a mustard seed," then you can move a mountain (Mt. 17:20; Mk. 4:31). Yet, Stephen was "*full* of faith" (this is mentioned twice about him, verses 5 and 8), so he was able to perform "great wonders and signs among the people" (6:8). Similarly, we should seek to be "full of faith," and to have "great faith" (Mt. 8:10), so that the church and nonbelievers can witness "great wonders and signs."

A helpful means for cultivating "great faith" is to sit under a great pastor. We see the role of the apostles described in verse 4. (In that context, an apostle could be likened to a pastor in that he was especially responsible for the spiritual welfare of his flock.) The apostles felt it would be right to give themselves to nothing less than continual prayer and continual study and ministry of the Word of God. They did not feel it wise to divert their attention from these vital matters in order to oversee administrative matters that could be handled by others. After all, out of the 5,000 or so new believers in Jerusalem, there were only twelve apostles, and God expected the twelve to fulfill their weighty responsibility of being the spiritual overseers and human shepherds of that huge flock. Hebrews 13:17 alludes to the responsibility before God that spiritual leaders have: "Obey those who rule over you, and be submissive, for they watch out for your souls, as those who must give account." (See also James 3:1.)

Pastors of smaller churches may have to do the bulk of the administrative responsibilities and therefore they cannot focus strictly on prayer and the ministry of the Word. (I salute pastors who are willing to serve smaller churches, perhaps serving bi-vocationally, and must operate this way.) But if at all possible, I highly recommend that administrative responsibilities be delegated to other responsible church members so that the pastor can spend more time in the Word of God and prayer, preparing excellent and anointed messages for his flock, tending to their spiritual needs, and seeking God's will concerning vision and direction for the church. Incidentally, those to whom administrative responsibilities are delegated should take note of the qualifications for those who oversaw the daily distribution: "good reputation, full of the Holy Spirit, and wisdom" (Acts 6:3).

Stephen is not only "full of faith" but he is also "full of the Holy Spirit" (verse 5) and full of "power" (Gk. *dunameos,* verse 8). Faith is necessary to connect one to God (Heb. 11:6). And God the Holy Spirit is He who empowers the believer to live victoriously, dead to sin, and to be God's effective witness to those who are lost. First Corinthians 4:20 says: "For the kingdom of God is not in word but in *power,*" and such power will be upon the pastor who, through abiding in Christ, teaches and preaches God's Word, and who continually prays. (We will focus more on power in Acts 8.)

After the reference to the "great signs and wonders" performed by Stephen (verse 8), we again see the theme of persecution by the religious leaders and others. The devil, working through these people, brought swift opposition to the progress of this Spirit-filled church. But Jesus had already said that the "gates of Hades" would not be able to stop the advancement of His church (Mt. 16:18). The Synagogue of the Freedmen compelled others to bear false witness against Stephen, saying he blasphemed. [Caiaphas and other religious leaders had likewise accused Jesus of blasphemy (Mt. 26:65).] Their false accusations stirred up "the people, the elders, and the scribes" who brought Stephen before "the council" (verse 12). Verse 10 indicates these persecutors could not resist Stephen's words, for he spoke with "wisdom and the Spirit," and they saw that his face was as the face "of an angel" (verse 15).

I will not spend much time on Stephen's speech in this writing. It is found in Acts 7 and is largely a synopsis of Jewish history. (Stephen spoke from Scripture to convict the Jewish leaders of their habitual rejection of God's will which culminated in their rejection of the Messiah. Peter had also quoted from the Old Testament in his sermons in Acts 2, 3, and 4 for the same purpose.) I do want to focus on some of the words Stephen spoke just before his death because they parallel words that Jesus spoke just before His own death. While on the cross, Scripture records Jesus making seven statements, two of which are: "Father, forgive them, for they do not know what they do" (Lk. 23:34), and "Father, into Your hands I commit My spirit..." (Lk. 23:46). Similarly, Stephen, while being stoned to death, said: "Lord Jesus, receive my spirit" (8:59), and "Lord, do not charge them with this sin" (8:60). The obvious parallel of these sayings by Jesus and Stephen, both martyrs for the fulfillment of God's purpose, conveys an important message. As Jesus' death brought greater life—abundant and eternal life to all who would believe in

Him, likewise, Stephen's death brought greater life in that the increased persecution that resulted from his death propelled the believers beyond Jerusalem, and they preach God's Word wherever they went! That helped fulfill the Great Commission of Acts, which I believe is Acts 1:8: "But you shall receive power when the Holy Spirit has come upon you; and you shall be witnesses to Me in Jerusalem, and in all *Judea and Samaria,* and to the end of the earth." Certainly those within the council, including Saul of Tarsus, thought that killing Stephen would be a major victory in their all-out war against Christianity. Not so! As 8:1 is the numerical reciprocal of 1:8, 8:1 is also the beginning of the fulfillment of 1:8. Acts 8:1 says: "they were all scattered throughout the regions of *Judea and Samaria,*" and verse 4 continues this thought saying: "those who were scattered...went everywhere preaching the word." Again, many of those who were persecuted preached the gospel wherever they were scattered! God is in control. If one is "persecuted for righteousness sake" (Mt. 5:10), or if one dies for one's obedience to God, then God will reward that person in this life and / or in the life to come. God will use one's righteous sacrifice to bring greater life and blessing to others. (See John 12:24 and Revelation 2:10b.) For this biblical promise, we should rejoice!

Acts 8:5-24 Then Philip went down to the city of Samaria and preached Christ to them. (6) And the multitudes with one accord heeded the things spoken by Philip, hearing and seeing the miracles which he did. (7) For unclean spirits, crying with a loud voice, came out of many who were possessed; and many who were paralyzed and lame were healed. (8) And there was great joy in that city. (9) But there was a certain man called Simon, who previously practiced sorcery in the city and astonished the people of Samaria, claiming that he was someone great, (10) to whom they all gave heed, from the least to the greatest, saying, "This man is the great power of God." (11) And they heeded him because he had astonished them with his sorceries for a long time. (12) But when they believed Philip as he preached the things concerning the kingdom of God and the name of Jesus Christ, both men and women were baptized. (13) Then Simon himself also believed; and when he was baptized he continued with Philip, and was amazed, seeing the miracles and signs which were done. (14) Now when the apostles who were at Jerusalem heard that Samaria had received the word of God, they sent Peter and John to them, (15) who, when they had come down, prayed for them that they might receive the Holy Spirit. (16) For as yet He had fallen upon none of them. They had only been baptized in the name of the Lord Jesus. (17) Then they laid hands on them, and they received the Holy Spirit. (18) And when Simon saw that through the laying on of the apostles' hands the Holy Spirit was given, he offered them money, (19) saying, "Give me this power also, that anyone on whom I lay hands may receive the Holy Spirit." (20) But Peter said to him, "Your money perish with you, because you thought that the gift of God could be purchased with money! (21) You have neither part nor portion in this matter, for your heart is not right in the sight of God. (22) Repent therefore of this your wickedness, and pray God if perhaps the thought of your heart may be forgiven you. (23) For I see that you are poisoned by bitterness and bound by iniquity." (24) Then Simon answered and said, "Pray to the Lord for me, that none of the things which you have spoken may come upon me."

The Samaritan people received Philip's preaching about "things concerning the kingdom of God and the name of Jesus Christ" (proclamation) because they witnessed the miracles he performed (demonstration, verses 6 and 12). The miracles included casting out demons and healing those who had been "paralyzed and lame" (irrefutable healings—verifiable by sight). The result of Philip's evangelistic ministry in the city of Samaria was "great joy" (verse 8) as "multitudes...both men and women" (verses 6 and 12) came to Christ. Being divinely forgiven, healed, and delivered from demonic oppression so that one can fully serve Christ is a most joyous reality—"Now may the God of hope fill you will all *joy* and *peace* in believing. (Rom. 15:13).

In this passage, we see a head-to-head confrontation between the all-powerful gospel preached by Philip and sorcery practiced by a local resident, Simon. In Acts, opposition to the gospel comes not only through persecution by hypocritical religious leaders but also through those involved in the occult and sorcery (see also Acts 13:6-12). Simon had previously "astonished the people of Samaria" (verse 9) so that "all gave heed...saying this man is the great power of God" (verse 10). Simon claimed that he himself "was someone great" (verse 9). Such boasting should be a red flag to observers; Proverbs 27:2 says: "Let another man praise you, and not your own mouth." Before Philip arrived, the city of Samaria had been deceived, thinking that "the great power of God" was manifested in the person, Simon.

People are attracted to power. The gospel "is the power of God to salvation for everyone who believes" (Rom. 1:16). When a particular people group has not yet been reached with the gospel, they will often embrace some other power, whether it be witchcraft, new age spirituality, or some other false religion. Also, people can embrace the deceitful power of wealth, prestige, etc. But the all-powerful gospel preached and demonstrated by Philip trumped the power of Simon's sorcery and usurped Simon's hold on city. What if Philip had only preached the gospel but had not healed any sick or cast out any demons? Would as many Samaritans have "heeded the things spoken by Philip"? Probably not. For an evangelist to maximize his impact, both proclamation and demonstration of the gospel are needed. Again, Romans 15:18-19 say: "Christ has...accomplished through me, in word and deed, to make the Gentiles obedient—in mighty signs and wonders, by the power of the Spirit of God...." Again, 1 Thessalonians 1:5-6 say: "For our gospel did not come to you in word only, but also in *power*, and in the Holy Spirit and in much assurance...."

Were the Samaritans born again in verse 12? Yes. They "believed" (Gk. *episteusan*) Philip as he preached "Jesus Christ." Believing on Jesus Christ is the singular requirement for being saved (Acts 16:31). Also, the Samaritan believers were baptized. For a baptism to be legitimate, it must occur *after* one is born again. This text gives no indication that the baptisms of verse 12 were premature or illegitimate. Even Simon believed and was baptized (verse 13). However, we shall later see that Simon had not repented of certain prideful desires, and his unrepentance would prove costly to him.

Did the Holy Spirit regenerate and indwell the believers in verse 12? Yes. They could not have been saved if they were not regenerated and indwelt by the Holy Spirit. Romans 8:9b says: "Now if anyone does not have the Spirit of Christ, he is not his." So how does one explain what happened in verses 14-17? The apostles in Jerusalem sent Peter and John to the city of Samaria to pray for the Samaritan believers that they "might receive the Holy Spirit. For as yet He had fallen upon none of them" (verses 15-16). There is a difference between the Holy Spirit's indwelling a person (the Holy Spirit "within" or "in" a person) and the Holy Spirit's "falling upon" or "coming upon" a person. I believe the Samaritans were born again and thus indwelt with the Holy Spirit in verse 12. However, not until verse 17 when Peter and John laid their hands on the Samaritan believers, did the believers receive the baptism in the Holy Spirit. [I am making a distinction between one's being indwelt by the Holy Spirit (thus one is born again / saved) and one's receiving the baptism in the Holy Spirit (thus one is empowered).

These separate functions of the Holy Spirit will be discussed in depth in Chapter 13.]

Though Acts 8 does not mention speaking in tongues, can tongues be inferred? Verse 18 says: "And when Simon *saw* that through the laying on of the apostles' hands the Holy Spirit was given, he offered them money." What did Simon see? Perhaps he saw them speaking in tongues since speaking in tongues accompanied the believers who received the baptism in the Holy Spirit in Acts 2, 10, and 19. Speaking in tongues is available to every Christian for the purpose of empowerment and self-edification (Mk. 16:17; 1 Cor. 14:4-5.)

Simon had apparently developed an idol of prestige in his heart. Since he had been highly esteemed by the Samaritans for his demonstrations of spiritual power—albeit sinful sorcery power, here again Simon sought the ability to bestow power—the baptism in the Holy Spirit. However, Simon's offering of money to Peter and John—seeking to buy the ability to demonstrate divine power, was a sin against God. The gifts of God are not for buying and selling; instead, God freely gives the Holy Spirit "to those who obey Him" (5:32). Peter had earlier witnessed the perishing of Ananias and Sapphira for their lying to the Holy Spirit because of their love of money (Acts 5). Here again, Peter becomes the messenger for God's rebuke of Simon for his impure motive and lust for power displayed in his attempt to buy the gift of God. Peter called such desires of Simon "wickedness," and urged Simon to "repent" (verse 22). Peter warned Simon that he might "perish" and that "perhaps" God would forgive Simon, which insinuates that "perhaps" God would not forgive Simon (verse 20, 22). We have been warned in Acts to not love money, to not love the praises of men, and to not trifle with the Holy Spirit. "Do not grieve the Holy Spirit of God" (Eph. 4:30), "do not quench the Spirit" (1 Thess. 5:19), do not lie to the Holy Spirit (Acts 5:1-10), and do not blaspheme the Holy Spirit (Mk. 3:29). The Holy Spirit is the third Person of the triune God; He is the One who is directly manifest on earth during this age of the church.

Acts 9:17-18 And Ananias went his way and entered the house; and laying his hands on him he said, "Brother Saul, the Lord Jesus, who appeared to you on the road as you came, has sent me that you may receive your sight and be filled with the Holy Spirit." (18) Immediately there fell from his eyes something like scales, and he received his sight at once; and he arose and was baptized.

These verses lie within the well-known testimony of the conversion of the man, Saul, who once terrorized Christians but became an apostle of Jesus Christ, full of God's love; who was once an accomplice to murder but became a missionary to the Gentiles; who was once a Pharisee blind to God's grace but became the author of approximately thirteen books of Holy Scripture, which articulated the wonderful doctrine of justification by faith. Saul, later named Paul, is the primary human character of Acts 13-28. The Lord Jesus apprehended Saul when Saul was persecuting His followers. I believe the moment when Saul was born again was when Jesus said "I am Jesus" in response to Saul's question "Who are you, Lord?" (verse 5). My reasons are: 1) Saul had revelation that Jesus is Lord in verse 5; 2) Saul showed his submission to the lordship of Jesus when he said in verse 6 "Lord, what do you want me to do?"; 3) when Ananias first greeted Saul in verse 17, he called him, "Brother Saul." When Ananias laid his hands on Saul, who had been blind for three days, at least two things happened: 1) "there fell from his eyes something like scales, and he received his sight at once" (verse 18)—thus he acquired spiritual and physical sight in Chapter 9; 2) presumably Saul was "filled with the Holy Spirit," since Ananias stated that would happen (verse 17). Since in 1 Corinthians 14:18, Paul (who was Saul) said, "I thank my God I speak with tongues more than you all," it seems likely that Paul spoke in tongues for the first time when he was filled with the Holy Spirit at the laying on of Ananias' hands. So it is likely that Saul was born again (thus indwelt with the Holy Spirit) in verse 5, and baptized in the Holy Spirit in verse 17. These dramatic events: Saul's encounter with the resurrected Lord Jesus on the road to Damascus, His eyes being healed, and his being filled with the Holy Spirit inspired Saul to immediately begin preaching the very gospel message that he, just a few days before, had tried to destroy. What an awesome God we serve!

Acts 9:32-35 Now it came to pass, as Peter went through all parts of the country, that he also came down to the saints who dwelt in Lydda. (33) There he found a certain man named Aeneas, who had been bedridden eight years and was paralyzed. (34) And Peter said to him, "Aeneas, Jesus the Christ *heals* you. Arise and make your bed." Then he arose immediately. (35) So all who dwelt at Lydda and Sharon saw him and turned to the Lord.

Though no mention is made of Aeneas having faith, Aeneas was probably a believer as he was found amongst the saints in Lydda. Aeneas was "bedridden" and "paralyzed"; thus he was quite limited in his ability to serve the Lord and others. But his medical status would suddenly change as a result of Peter pronouncing, "Aeneas, Jesus the Christ heals you." Then Peter commanded Aeneas to do two things he had not been able to do for the last eight years: "Arise and make your bed" (verse 34). The word of command was indicative of faith in Peter: he had a certainty within himself (which came from the Holy Spirit) that healing would manifest, and thus he boldly proclaimed healing for Aeneas before he saw any evidence of healing. Also, Aeneas obeyed the word of command—he made the effort to stand—and his obedience, which demonstrated faith, led to his healing. Peter rightly gave full credit to Jesus the Christ for Aeneas' healing. Later, Peter would write of Jesus the Christ's scourging and atoning death: "who Himself bore our sins in His own body on the tree, that we, having died to sins, might live for righteousness—by whose stripes you were healed" (1 Peter 2:24). Again, this type of irrefutable healing (verifiable by sight)—the healing of a paralytic—would prove extremely effective for evangelism. Everyone who lived in the two towns of Lydda and Sharon "saw him and turned to the Lord" (verse 35). Their turning suggests they repented.

Acts 9:36-42 At Joppa there was a certain disciple named Tabitha, which is translated Dorcas. This woman was full of good works and charitable deeds which she did. (37) But it happened in those days that she became sick and died. When they had washed her, they laid her in an upper room. (38) And since Lydda was near Joppa, and the disciples had heard that Peter was there, they sent two men to him, imploring him not to delay in coming to them. (39) Then Peter arose and went with them. When he had come, they brought him to the upper room. And all the widows stood by him weeping, showing the tunics and garments which Dorcas had made while she was with them. (40) But Peter put them all out, and knelt down and prayed. And turning to the body he said, "Tabitha, arise." And she opened her eyes, and when she saw Peter she sat up. (41) Then he gave her his hand and lifted her up; and when he had called the saints and widows, he presented her alive. (42) And it became known throughout all Joppa, and many believed on the Lord.

Today, if a church member dies, does the church usually pray for the dead person to be resurrected, or call for a faith healing evangelist to come and pray for the person to be resurrected? No; a funeral is held. But when Dorcas, who was a Christian disciple in Joppa, died, the church in Joppa did not bury her. Instead, verse 37 says they washed her body and laid her in an upper room. Then they sent for Peter who was in the nearby town of Lydda. I do not think they sent for Peter to come and preach Dorcas' funeral. Presumably they expected Peter to pray for Dorcas to be raised from the dead. Why is this mindset rare or absent today? One reason is because finding a believer today who has faith and power to the degree that Peter had is rare.

God had already worked through Peter to heal on a number of occasions: the healing of a man who had never walked (3:6-8); the healing of all who were sick and demon-possessed in the streets of Jerusalem (5:15-17); and most recently, healing Aeneas who had been paralyzed and bedridden for eight years (9:34). Peter had a reputation for being one through whom God performed the miraculous. Peter had personally witnessed Jesus performing miracles on a daily basis. Also, Peter was among the twelve that Jesus sent out in Matthew 10, when Jesus commissioned them to "preach" and to "heal the sick, cleanse the lepers, *raise the dead*, cast out demons..." (Mt. 10:6-8). I imagine that the disciples raised some dead people back to life on that outing, and Peter was likely involved in that.

Peter came to Joppa and found weeping widows. (In Luke 7:13, Jesus said to the widow at Nain whose son was being carried in a coffin, "*Do not weep*," because Jesus was about to raise her son to life.) The weeping widows seemed to focus more on the works of Dorcas' hands than the works of God's hands as found in Scripture. Peter put all the people out of the room, probably to eliminate doubt and distraction. (Jesus had also done this when He resurrected Jairus' daughter, Lk. 8:54) Instead of immediately giving a word of command as in other healing accounts, Peter first "knelt down and prayed" (verse 40). He may have been worshipping *Jehovah Rapha*, quoting healing promises, and waiting on the Holy Spirit to cause faith to rise in his heart. [In Matthew 14, Peter wisely did not attempt to walk on water until he had first asked and received from Jesus the "word of faith" (Rom. 10:8)]. During the prayer, faith came to Peter, so he turned to the corpse and spoke a word of command. He spoke to the corpse as if the ears worked. This is similar to speaking to a mountain (Mk. 11:23), or to a fever (Lk. 4:39), or to deaf ears (Mk. 7:34). Peter said to the corpse, "Tabitha, arise," and she did! This is the first Scripturally recorded resurrection of the dead performed by the church. In verse 41, Peter "lifted her up." This is similar to Acts 3:7, where, pertaining to the lame man,

Tom Caldwell

Peter "lifted him up." (See also Mark 1:31.) In Matthew 14, Jesus lifted Peter up when he failed to walk on water. Such assistance—lifting up others—testifies to the importance of demonstrating love within the body of Christ. Note the great evangelistic fruit from this miracle: "it became known throughout all Joppa, and many believed on the Lord" (verse 42).

Acts 10:38 how God anointed Jesus of Nazareth with the Holy Spirit and with power, who went about doing good and healing all who were oppressed by the devil, for God was with Him.

Due to divinely ordained circumstances, Peter was given the opportunity to preach the gospel to a gathering of Gentiles at Cornelius' house (Acts 10). He preached (verses 34-43) that Jesus was murdereded by being hung on a tree, but God raised Jesus from the dead on the third day, and thus Jesus Christ "is Lord of all" (verse 36) and "Judge of the living and the dead" (verse 42). Peter said he was one of many eyewitnesses to Jesus' resurrection from the dead as well as to the numerous healings performed by Jesus throughout His earthly ministry. Verse 38 (above) lies within Peter's sermon and describes much of the earthly ministry of Jesus—that by the Holy Spirit and power (Gk. *dunamei*) Jesus did good and healed "all who were oppressed by the devil."

This verse reveals, in part, that the devil himself was behind the various sicknesses and infirmities that oppressed those whom Jesus healed. Acts 10:38 closely links Satan to sickness. And this is congruent with the account in Luke 13:10-17, where Jesus healed a woman who was bent over for eighteen years due to "a spirit of infirmity"—a demon spirit that caused the sickness in the woman. The divine antidote to the devil's tactics is Jesus, as 1 John 3:8b expresses: "For this purpose the Son of God was manifested, that He might destroy the works of the devil." Through the anointing of the Holy Spirit upon Jesus and ultimately through His death and resurrection, Jesus destroyed the works of sickness caused by the devil. Christ partook of "flesh and blood…(so that) through death He might destroy him who had the power of death, that is the devil" (Heb. 2:14). Sickness is a form of death in that it drains people of life and vitality.

At times, Jesus healed *all* sick persons who were present (Mt. 8:16; Lk. 4:40); Acts 10:38 affirms this—"healing *all*...." Jesus can likewise heal *all* today if faith is present, for "God is no respecter of persons"

(Acts 10:34, KJV). Mark 9:23 says, "*all* things are possible for him who believes"; Philippians 4:19 says, "My God shall supply *all* your need according to His riches in glory by Christ Jesus." As Jesus was "anointed...with the Holy Spirit and with power," we believers also "have an anointing from the Holy One" (1 Jn. 2:20) and we have power through the Holy Spirit (Acts 1:8) so that we can "follow His steps" (1 Pet. 2:21).

Acts 13:6-12 Now when they had gone through the island to Paphos, they found a certain sorcerer, a false prophet, a Jew whose name was Bar-Jesus, (7) who was with the proconsul, Sergius Paulus, an intelligent man. This man called for Barnabas and Saul and sought to hear the word of God. (8) But Elymas the sorcerer (for so his name is translated) withstood them, seeking to turn the prosonsul away from the faith. (9) Then Saul, who also is called Paul, filled with the Holy Spirit, looked intently at him (10) and said, "O full of all deceit and all fraud, you son of the devil, you enemy of all righteousness, will you not cease perverting the straight ways of the Lord? (11) And now, indeed, the hand of the Lord is upon you, and you shall be blind, not seeing the sun for a time." And immediately a dark mist fell on him, and he went around seeking someone to lead him by the hand. (12) Then the proconsul believed, when he saw what had been done, being astonished at the teaching of the Lord.

This encounter occurs near the beginning of Paul's first missionary journey, and he is accompanied by Barnabas and his nephew, John Mark. In Paphos, which is on the island of Cyprus in the Mediterranean Sea, the three missionaries encounter a sorcerer named Elymas. This is the second sorcerer so far mentioned in Acts; Simon, mentioned in 8:9-24, was also a sorcerer. God condemns sorcery, witchcraft, and the like in Deuteronomy 18:9-14. Thus Christians should have nothing to do with Harry Potter and similar witchcraft literature. Thus, Christians should have nothing to do with Harry Potter literature and similar "entertainment." They also find a proconsul (a type of Roman official who oversaw a province),[119] Sergius Paulus, who "sought to hear the word of God" (verse 7), and who would become the first recorded Gentile ruler to believe the gospel. But Elymas, whom Paul calls a "son of the devil" and "enemy of all righteousness," does what Paul had been doing just a few chapters earlier—he hinders the preaching of the gospel. The Lord had struck Paul (then called Saul) with temporary blindness in order to chastise and humble him. Then the Lord commissioned Saul to preach the gospel of Christ. Here, Paul commands blindness to befall

Elymas "for a time." Again, the filling of the Holy Spirit precedes the sign and wonder, in this case the curse of blindness befalling Elymas due to its pronouncement by Paul. Perhaps the chastening and humbling of Elymas would cause him to eventually turn to the gospel as Paul did; we are not told the outcome. In any case, the proconsul witnesses this demonstration of divine power, and he believes the gospel message.

Answering the Critics

One critic said to me: "Perfect health could easily lead to pride and a lack of compassion for others who are ill, whereas illness might lead to humility and a caring attitude." I responded, "It is not perfect health that leads to pride and a lack of compassion; rather it is a sinful, prideful heart that causes a lack of compassion. Similarly, preaching the gospel effectively could be a factor that allows a preacher to become prideful, but that does not negate the fact that the gospel must be preached. God's use of sickness to bring one to the godly quality of humility is an aspect of Romans 8:28. Just because 'all things work together for good' does not mean that 'all things'—including sickness—lie within God's perfect will." Bosworth said:

> Does not God sometimes chasten His people through sickness? Decidedly yes! When we disobey God, sickness may be permitted, through the Father's loving discipline....When we see the cause of the chastening, and turn from it, God promises it shall be withdrawn.... Divine healing is not unconditionally promised to all Christians, regardless of their conduct. It is for those who believe and obey.[120]

Acts 14:8-10 And in Lystra a certain man without strength in his feet was sitting, a cripple from his mother's womb, who had never walked. (9) This man heard Paul speaking. Paul, observing him intently and seeing that he had faith to be *healed*, (10) said with a loud voice, "Stand up straight on your feet!" And he leaped and walked.

Paul spoke the Word of God to a crowd in the town of Lystra, a stronghold for Greek mythology. Similar to Acts 3, this account includes a man who had been a cripple from birth. He was among the crowd listening to Paul's preaching. Paul likely preached that Jesus is Healer as well as Savior (Acts 10:38), and the lame man believed the gospel message. Verse 9 implies that if the man did not have faith to be healed, he would not have been healed. When Paul saw that the man believed, Paul spoke a word of command to him—"Stand up straight on your feet!", something the lame man had never before done. The man obeyed God's Word which came through Paul and attempted to stand before there was any outward evidence of healing. The man "leaped and walked"! So we have accounts in Acts 3 and Acts 14 of men who were crippled from the womb, and then were immediately and thoroughly made whole—both "leaped and walked." These healings were irrefutable demonstrations of divine intervention, bearing witness that Jesus is Lord.

Unlike Acts 3 when many converted to Christ, the evangelistic response to this divine healing was not impressive. The onlookers were so steeped in their pagan religion that they could not discern the true Source of the healing. Instead of believing that the Son of God had become incarnate in the Person of the Lord Jesus, who had died for man's sin and rose again, they thought that "the gods," specifically Zeus and Hermes, had come down to them in the forms of Paul and Barnabas. And despite the efforts of Paul and Barnabas to try to change their pagan thinking, the citizens of Lystra persisted in trying to sacrifice to them. Then we see in verse 19 how easily these citizens of Lystra could be deceived. Jews from Antioch and Iconium came there and quickly persuaded the citizens of Lystra to stone Paul. Within a short time span, the citizens of Lystra went from worshipping Paul to attempting to murder Paul, which shows how easily they could be swayed. James 1 describes the person who acts like this as a doubter who "is like a wave of the sea driven and tossed by the wind...he is a double-minded man, unstable in all his ways" (Jas. 1:6, 8). Though signs and wonders bear witness to the Word of God's grace (14:3), it is not automatic that signs and wonders will cause people to repent and believe the gospel message.

Acts 16:16-19 Now it happened, as we went to prayer, that a certain slave girl possessed with a spirit of divination met us, who brought her masters much profit by fortune-telling. (17) This girl followed Paul and us, and cried out, saying, "These men are the servants of the Most High God, who proclaim to us the way of salvation." (18) And this she did for many days. But Paul, greatly annoyed, turned and said to the spirit, "I command you in the name of Jesus Christ to come out of her." And he came out that very hour. (19) But when her masters saw that their hope of profit was gone, they seized Paul and Silas and dragged them into the marketplace to the authorities.

The girl of this passage was a slave in three different ways. First, she was a slave within the societal structure of that day, owned as property by other human "masters." Her masters did not care about her well-being; rather they preferred she remain demon-possessed so they could make money from her demonically-inspired abilities. Second, this girl, because she did not know Jesus, was a slave of sin. Anyone who is without Christ is a slave of sin (Jn. 8:34). Third, she was enslaved to a demonic spirit. Perhaps she had in the past spent time with other diviners which led her to increasingly dabble in divination, and thus she ended up being possessed by a demon of divination. "Evil company corrupts good habits" (1 Cor. 15:33). This girl was undoubtedly discontent with her life's circumstances since her spiritual and social conditions were defined by bondage. Only through Christ would she find forgiveness, deliverance, and peace (Rom. 5:1).

The demon in the girl spoke the truth that Paul and his companions were servants of the Most High God and were proclaiming the gospel message of salvation that only comes through faith in Christ. This is compatible with Philippians 2:11, that "at the name of Jesus...every knee should bow...and that every tongue should confess (even the tongues of demons, against their will) that Jesus Christ is Lord...." Despite the truthfulness of the demon's words, Paul was greatly annoyed by the demon and commanded the demon to come out of the girl in the name of Jesus Christ. The demon obeyed Paul's words.

The result, however, was that once again the followers of Christ, here Paul and Silas, would suffer persecution. So far in Acts, the persecution has primarily come from religious authorities and those of the occult, but here the persecution comes from government authorities and slave owners. Paul and Silas were beaten with rods, were locked in the inner prison of the jail, and their feet were fastened in the stocks. Though they were Roman citizens, Paul and Silas did not benefit from due process, had no legal defense, and had no trial. But Paul and Silas refrained from grumbling and complaining (Phil. 2:14) about their circumstances; instead they chose prayer and praise unto God. We should emulate this, counting it all joy when we fall into various trials and are persecuted for righteousness' sake, knowing that our reward in heaven will be great. God sent a mighty earthquake which caused all the prison doors to open and all the chains to fall off all the inmates. Yet none of the inmates ran away. Perhaps the inmates remained because they did not want to leave the presence of the Lord who was inhabiting the praises of Paul and Silas. The end result was that the jailer and his household received salvation, and the other inmates were exposed to the gospel message. Also, future inmates in that jail would benefit from having a compassionate Christian jailer. The following day, Paul and Silas were released from jail by the magistrates. Once again, God intervened into the activities of His faithful followers and gave them victory and a testimony.

Acts 19:11-20 Now God worked unusual miracles by the hands of Paul, (12) so that even handkerchiefs or aprons were brought from his body to the sick, and the diseases left them and the evil spirits went out of them. (13) Then some of the itinerant Jewish exorcists took it upon themselves to call the name of the Lord Jesus over those who had evil spirits, saying, "We exorcise you by the Jesus whom Paul preaches." (14) Also there were seven sons of Sceva, a Jewish chief priest, who did so. (15) And the evil spirit answered and said, "Jesus I know, and Paul I know; but who are you?" (16) Then the man in whom the evil spirit was leaped on them, overpowered them, and prevailed against them, so that they fled out of that house naked and wounded. (17) This became known both to all Jews and Greeks dwelling in Ephesus; and fear fell on them all, and the name of the Lord Jesus was magnified. (18) And many who had believed came confessing and telling their deeds. (19) Also, many of those who had practiced magic brought their books together and burned them in the sight of all. And they counted up the value of them, and it totaled fifty thousand pieces of silver. (20) So the word of the Lord grew mightily and prevailed.

During Paul's third missionary journey, he spent over two years in Ephesus ministering the Word of God in the school of Tyrannus. During that time, the anointing of the Holy Spirit to heal the sick was upon Paul so mightily that articles of clothing (handkerchiefs and aprons) which were taken from his body had remnants of the anointing attached to them. When those pieces of clothing made contact with people who were sick or demon-possessed, they were healed! [Second Kings 13 also contains a dramatic example of the anointing of God lingering, in this case beyond the life of the anointed prophet, Elisha. When a dead man was lowered into Elisha's tomb and touched the bones of Elisha, the dead man "revived and stood to his feet" (verse 21).] These unique types of miracles [including Peter's shadow being a point of contact to boost faith for healing (Acts 5:15)] fulfill to a certain degree Jesus' words that those who believe in Him would do works comparable to His works, and would do even greater works (Jn. 14:12).

In the accounts of the itinerant Jewish exorcists and the seven sons of Sceva, we see the necessity of having one's own faith in the Lord Jesus if one is going to successfully cast demons out of people (see Mark 16:17-18). The seven sons of Sceva possessed only head knowledge of Jesus, so they tried to minister from the vantage point of Paul's faith rather than having acquired their own faith in Jesus. The devil is a supernatural being, and no man can simply rely on his own natural strength to defeat the devil. (See Mark 5:1-20 for another example of demons giving a man supernatural strength.) Only if the Holy Spirit dwells in a man can that man have the power and authority he needs to cast out the devil.

An indicator of spiritual revival is confession of sin and repentance. We see this happening in Ephesus during Paul's two year ministry there. Many people came confessing their sins and demonstrating repentance by burning their magic books—being more concerned about holiness than about the monetary value of the magic books. The Holy Spirit was doing a great work in the hearts of the people so that "the name of the Lord Jesus was magnified" (verse 17), and "the word of God grew mightily and prevailed" (verse 20).

Answering the Critics

A critic once said to me that if divine physical healing was included in the atonement and received by faith, then one would never die. I responded by saying God has set limits on the length of man's life on earth, and divine physical healing does not disregard those limits. People will still die of old age, but they do not have to die of, say, cancer or heart disease. Nevertheless, many saints have died and will continue to die of disease because saints are imperfect. Remnants of sin likely remain our members such as our ongoing battle with pride. Furthermore, there is that spiritual enemy, the devil, who opposes God's people. Though in Jesus' name we have total authority over the devil, he has at times successfully landed some fiery, sickly darts on believers. F. F. Bosworth says of this: "Divine healing goes no further than the promise of God. He does not promise we shall never die, but He says: 'I will take sickness away from the midst of you....I will fulfill the number of your days' (Ex. 23:25-26); 'The days of our lives are seventy years; and if by reason of strength they are eighty years...' (Ps. 90:10); 'O my God, Do not take me away in the midst of my days' (Ps. 102:24); 'Why should you die before your time?' (Eccl. 7:17). How is man going to die? 'You take away their breath, they die and return to their dust'" (Ps. 104:29).[121] Rev. P. Gavin Duffy writes:

> He has allotted to man a certain span of life, and His will is that life shall be lived out. I want you to recall that all those He called back from the dead were young people who had not lived out their fullness of years; and in that very fact we may well see His protest against premature death...if the allotted span has not been spent we have a right to claim God's gift of health; and, even though it be past, if it be His will that we should continue here for a time longer, it is equally His will that we should do so in good health.[122]

Acts 20:7-12 Now on the first day of the week, when the disciples came together to break bread, Paul, ready to depart the next day, spoke to them and continued his message until midnight. (8) There were many lamps in the upper room where they were gathered together. (9) And in a window sat a certain young man named Eutychus, who was sinking into a deep sleep. He was overcome by sleep; and as Paul continued speaking, he fell down from the third story and was taken up dead. (10) But Paul went down, fell on him, and embracing him said, "Do not trouble yourselves, for his life is in him." (11) Now when he had come up, had broken bread and eaten and talked a long while, even till daybreak, he departed. (12) And they brought the young man in alive, and they were not a little comforted.

In Troas, Paul taught the Word of God to a group of believers in an upper room three stories high. Many lamps were burning in the upper room, so it was likely warm. Eutychus, who was in attendance and presumably was a church member, sat in a window ledge and eventually fell asleep during Paul's lengthy message. I cannot fault Eutychus for sleeping in church, for I have occasionally drifted to sleep in church myself. However, since I married in 2001, my wife, Kim, has made sure I remain awake in church.

I do fault Eutychus for his unwise choice to sit in a third floor window ledge. He could get bumped and lose his balance, or he could become dizzy. If he began to get sleepy while sitting in a third floor window ledge, it was certainly time to move to a safer seat. Eutychus' tragedy was avoidable.

Eutychus may represent church members today who drift away from being in the center of the activities of the church. For some reason, they become complacent and less attentive to the things of God. Perhaps a brother does not prefer the style of music, so he becomes less involved in church. Or perhaps he remains offended by the actions of a fellow church member. Or perhaps he is married, but he develops too friendly of a relationship with a lady in the church who is not his wife. Or perhaps he has a history of gambling and is given unchecked oversight of the finances of the church. Proverbs 16:18 says: "Pride comes before destruction, and a haughty spirit before a *fall.*" Eutychus' willingness to sit in a third floor window ledge can represent a person who has allowed pride to develop within. A person with pride can place himself in a risky position, whether physically or spiritually, and falsely think that he will be fine. As Eutychus may have had one foot inside the window and the other foot dangling outside the window, a church member may be straddling the fence, keeping one foot in the world and the other foot in the church. Eutychus could have fallen inward towards the believers and into the safety of the room. Instead, Eutychus fell outward. He was likely leaning more outward than inward, so he fell in the direction of death, not safety.

I also find fault with the church of Troas. During that lengthy upper room service, someone should have noticed Eutychus sitting in a dangerous place. A fellow church member should have gone to Eutychus and gently urged him to come out of the window ledge and sit in a chair. Eutychus could sit beside the window where he could still feel the breeze. Or the concerned church member could have invited Eutychus to sit beside him, more towards the middle of the room. Galatians 6:1 says: "Brethren, if a man is overtaken in any trespass, you who are spiritual restore such a one is a spirit of gentleness...." But no one urged Eutychus to find a safe seat. Eventually, Eutychus suffered a fatal fall.

Much of what I have shared has been typological, or figurative, in interpretation and application. But we should also consider the literal account. Eutychus literally died. If this tragedy had happened in most other churches, then a funeral for Eutychus would likely have been held a few days later. But there happened to be an exceptionally anointed and faith-filled man of God who was in attendance at this church service in Troas—Paul. Before his conversion to Christ, Saul (same person) may have murderously shoved Eutychus out of the window if given the opportunity. Saul had persecuted Christians; he was an evil man. But beginning in Acts 9, God did a wonderful work in Saul. God converted

Saul from being a hater of Jesus to a lover and preacher of Jesus, and a lover of others. He became a new creation in Christ and later received a new name, Paul. It was the on-fire apostle and evangelist, Paul, who, with great concern for his brother in Christ, rushed down to the dead man Eutychus, fell on him, and embraced him. Ecclesiastes 4:9-10 says: "Two are better than one...for if they *fall*, one will lift up his companion. But woe to him who is alone when he *falls*." The Lord performed such a healing miracle through Paul that Paul was able to declare to the onlooking church, "Do not trouble yourselves, for his life is in him" (verse 10). God worked through Paul's faith to raise Eutychus from the dead! The old Saul was an instrument of death, but the new creation—Paul—was an anointed man of God through whom the life of Christ abundantly flowed!

We saw in Acts 9:36-41 that Peter also raised the dead. Our study of these texts may prompt us to ask ourselves, "Are there any Peters or Pauls in today's church?" As Jesus commanded the twelve to "raise the dead" (Mt. 10:8), the church today should fulfill Jesus' words in John 14:12, that "he who believes in Me, the works that I do he will do also; and greater works than these he will do, because I go to My Father." We, in whom Christ the Healer dwells, are called by God to heal the sick (Mk. 16:18). If the church consistently fails to heal the sick, we should seriously investigate the reasons for our failure. The early church had a vibrant healing ministry, and today's church should also.

If a brother makes unwise decisions, and if no one in the church warns him, then the brother could bring tragedy upon himself as well as bring great sorrow upon the church. We fellow believers, as "iron sharpening iron" (Prov. 27:17), need to look out for each other, hold each other accountable, and do so with an attitude of love. But if failure or tragedy does befall a brother, then the church, in whom Christ the Healer dwells, must rally around and embrace the fallen brother and seek to raise him up. As Christ raised up Peter who was sinking in water, Christ can also raise each of us up spiritually, physically, and in any way needed. Luke 14:11 says: "he who humbles himself will be exalted." If tragedy befell you today, what would be your eternal destination? We must abide in the Lord Jesus Christ (Jn. 15:1-8) and remain on-fire for Him (Rev. 3:15-16), for salvation is found in none other. The Lord Jesus is "the resurrection and the life" (Jn. 11:25).

Testimony—God Confirms a Call to Ministry Through a Healing!

In 1970, when Randy Clark (founder of Global Awakening, a ministry of healing and impartation) was eighteen, just after his miraculous recovery from a serious car wreck, he sensed the Lord was calling him into the ministry. He asked the Lord to confirm this call, and the Lord did so twice. But Randy prayed for one more confirmation. About that time, his thirty-three year old youth pastor, Fred, suffered a stroke. After Fred left the hospital and was at home recuperating, Randy visited him. Fred had limited mobility in his left hand, and any movement of it was very painful. Randy went home and prayed, "God, if you will cause Fred to play the piano tomorrow night in church, without pain, I will stand up and immediately announce my call to preach." The next night at church, Randy saw Fred play the piano! Fred told Randy, "When I was sitting in the pew, I had a strong impression of the Lord saying to me, 'If you will try to play the piano, I will heal you.' So I went to the piano, and when I touched the keys, I was instantly healed....All the pain left the moment I touched the keys.'" That night, Randy announced he would become a preacher.[123]

Divine Protection

The latter chapters of Acts contain several occurrences of divine protection for Paul, who in Acts 21 was arrested by the Romans and remained in their custody for the remainder of Acts. In Acts 23, more than forty Jews "banded together and bound themselves under an oath, saying that they would neither eat nor drink till they had killed Paul" (verse 12). What hatred those Jews had toward Paul, despite their knowledge of the Sixth Commandment—"You shall not murder" (Deut. 5:17). Paul's nephew became aware of their plans and informed Paul. Then Paul sent word of the plot to the Roman commander. So the commander ordered 270 soldiers and horsemen to take Paul to Caesarea (many miles away) for Paul's own safety, and also so Paul could appear before Governor Felix. God's protection of Paul was manifested through His causing Paul's nephew to overhear of the assassination plot, and His using a Roman commander to send Paul out of harm's way.

In Acts 27, Paul and 275 other people (many of them prisoners, including Paul) were traveling on a ship heading toward Italy. But a tempestuous head wind arose and made sailing treacherous for days, to the point that almost all on the ship lost hope that they would survive. But an angel of God appeared to Paul, saying, "Do not be afraid, Paul; you must be brought before Caesar, and indeed God has granted you all those who sail with you" (27:24). So God's protection for Paul extended to all 275 of Paul's traveling companions, whether they were friends or foes. Paul's relationship with Christ saved their lives! Paul encouraged those on the ship by telling them the message of the angel. Later, Paul did so again, saying, "not a hair will fall from the head of any of you" (verse 34, which is a reminder of God's sovereignty over even the minutest of details. See Mt. 10:29-31). When the ship began breaking up, the guards wanted to kill all the inmates (including Paul) to prevent them from escaping. But the captain saved all the inmates because the captain wanted to save Paul. So lives of the inmates were spared twice because of God's favor upon Paul.

All 276 travelers successfully reached the shore of an island called Malta. The natives of Malta were very hospitable (28:2, 7, 10), which was quite refreshing in light of the Jew's treatment of Paul—persecution [thus they persecuted Christ as Paul himself had done (Mt. 25:40; Acts 9:4)]. Perhaps these Gentile islanders would be open to the gospel of Jesus Christ; the majority of the Jews had rejected the gospel. As Paul was laying a bundle of sticks on a fire, a poisonous snake driven out by the heat fastened onto Paul's hand. This reminds us that, as the devil is likened to a serpent, any believer who has the fire of the Holy Spirit can drive the devil away. Paul shook the snake off and into the fire, and he suffered no ill effects from the snake bite. (See Mark 16:18, where Jesus said that His believers would have authority over serpents and protection from poison.) That Paul was unharmed amazed the natives, who thought Paul to be a god. (In Acts 14, the citizens of Lystra thought Paul and Barnabas were gods due to Christ's healing a crippled man through Paul). Miracles do not always lead onlookers to faith in Christ; they must hear and believe the gospel message in order to be saved.

God saved Paul from death at least four times in the last eight chapters of Acts. Paul likely anticipated his own preservation since Jesus said to him in Jerusalem, "Be of good cheer, Paul; for as you have testified for Me in Jerusalem, so you must also bear witness at Rome" (23:11). This message was reiterated by the Lord's angel to Paul in Acts 27:24, "Do not be afraid, Paul; you must be brought before Caesar...."

Furthermore, the Bible contains many passages that promise divine protection for those who trust and obey God. Psalm 121:7-8 says, "The LORD shall preserve you from all evil; He shall preserve your soul. The LORD shall preserve your going out and your coming in from this time forth, and even forevermore." Psalm 91 also promises divine protection for those who know, love, and abide in God. (See also Lk. 10:19, Ps. 12:5b, Ps. 23:4, and Ps. 97:10.)

Testimony—God Shrinks a Huge Tumor!

When Randy Clark was about thirteen years old, his Sunday School teacher had a tumor the size of a watermelon in her abdomen. The church prayed for her the night before her surgery, and at the beginning of surgery the doctors noticed the tumor had shrunk to the size of an orange. Also, the tumor's roots were not attached to any organs, so the tumor was easily removed. The teacher lived over forty more years.

Acts 28:7-9 In that region there was an estate of the leading citizen of the island, whose name was Publius, who received us and entertained us courteously for three days. (8) And it happened that the father of Publius lay sick of a fever and dysentery. Paul went in to him and *prayed*, and he laid his hands on him and *healed* him. (9) So when this was done, the rest of those on the island who had diseases also came and were *healed*.

Because Publius was the leading citizen of the island, the healing of his father was reliable news to the rest of the islanders. As a result, everyone who had diseases on the island came to Paul to be healed, and they were all healed. Though the text is silent on this, hopefully these magnificent healings on the island of Malta, as well as the testimony that God saved Paul from the poisonous snake bite and the 276 travelers from the tumultuous sea, opened the hearts of many of the islanders so that they embraced the gospel message.

Christ through Peter *healed all* in the streets of Jerusalem (Acts 5:16)—the hub of Judaism, and Christ through Paul *healed all* on an obscure, Gentile island. Christ's ministry of salvation and reconciliation was spreading to the uttermost parts of the world, with signs confirming His Word. Since "God is no respecter of persons" (Acts 10:34, KVJ), each of us can be used of God, as Peter and Paul were, to do mighty works so as to advance God's glorious kingdom.

A List of Signs, Wonders, and Miracles in Acts

We have repeatedly seen through Acts, as we did in the gospels, that demonstration of gospel power through healing the sick, casting out demons, and other miracles often opens the door for greater reception of the gospel message. In order to remind ourselves of what God can do and wants to do in and through today's church in terms of evangelism and making His power known, let's take a final look at the variety and frequency of miracles, signs, wonders, and divine interventions that occur in Acts.

2:4 Approximately 120 people spoke in tongues on the Day of Pentecost.

2:22 In Peter's evangelistic sermon on the day of Pentecost, Peter acknowledged that Jesus' miracles pointed to His Messiahship: "Jesus of Nazareth, a Man attested by God to you by *miracles, wonders, and signs* which God did through Him in your midst...."

2:43 "and many *wonders and signs* were done through the apostles."

3:6-8 A man lame from birth was instantly healed.

4:29-31 The disciples prayed: "Now, Lord, look on their threats, and grant to Your servants that with all boldness they may speak Your word, (30) by stretching out Your *hand to heal*, and that *signs and wonders* may be done through the name of Your holy Servant Jesus. (31) And when they had prayed, the place where they were assembled together was shaken; and they were all filled with the Holy Spirit, and they spoke the word of God with boldness."

5:3, 9 Peter received a word of knowledge about Ananias' and Saphira's lying to the Holy Spirit, and God killed them.

5:12 "And through the *hands* of the apostles many *signs and wonders* were done *among the people*...."

5:15-16 Many divine healings occurred in the streets of Jerusalem. All of the sick were healed and demons were cast out.

5:19 An angel freed the apostles from prison.

6:8 "And Stephen, full of faith and power, did *great wonders and signs among the people*."

7:36 Stephen testified of Israel's exodus from Egypt: "He brought them out, after he had shown *wonders and signs* in the land of Egypt, and in the Red Sea, and in the wilderness forty years."

8:6-8 In the city of Samaria, Philip healed the sick and cast out demons. Verse 6 says, "And the multitudes with one accord heeded the things spoken by Philip, hearing and seeing the *miracles* which he did."

8:13 "Then Simon himself also believed; and when he was baptized he continued with Philip, and was amazed, seeing the *miracles and signs* which were done."

8:17 At the laying on of Peter's and John's hands, the Holy Spirit came upon the believers in the city of Samaria.

8:26-40 An angel of the Lord gave Philip directions. The Spirit spoke to Philip. A eunuch from Ethiopia was converted. The Spirit of the Lord took Philip away.

9:1-18 Saul had a vision of Jesus and was converted. The Lord spoke to Ananias in a vision, and sent him to Saul. At the laying on of Ananias' hands, Saul's eyes were healed, and he was filled with the Holy Spirit.

9:32-35 Aeneas was healed of paralysis, and all who dwelt in Lydda and Sharon saw him and turned to the Lord.

9:36-43 Dorcas was raised from the dead. Verse 42 says, "And it became known throughout all Joppa, and many believed on the Lord."

10:10-16 Cornelius was visited by an angel. Peter saw a vision from heaven and heard the Spirit speak to him. When Peter preached the gospel to those at Cornelius' house, they spoke in tongues.

12:1-24 Due to the prayers of the church, an angel freed Peter from prison. An angel killed Herod.

13:6-12 Paul pronounced blindness upon Elymas the sorcerer, and it occurred. Verse 12 says, "Then the proconsul believed, when he saw what had been done...."

14:3 "Therefore they (Paul and Barnabas) stayed there a long time, speaking boldly in the Lord, who was *bearing witness* to the word of His grace, granting *signs and wonders* to be done by their hands."

14:8-10 In Lystra, a man lame from birth was healed.

15:12 "Then all the multitude kept silent and listened to Barnabas and Paul declaring how many *miracles and wonders* God had worked through them *among the Gentiles.*"

16:26 Paul cast a demon out of a slave girl. God sent an earthquake at Philippi. The jailer and his family were saved.

19-1-7 Twelve men were converted. Verse 6 says, "And when Paul laid hands on them, the Holy Spirit came upon them, and they spoke with tongues and prophesied."

19:11-12 "Now God worked *unusual miracles* by the *hands* of Paul, (12) so that even handkerchiefs or aprons were brought from his body to the sick, and the diseases left them and the evil spirits went out of them."

19:13-20 God did a mighty work in Ephesus—many confessed their deeds and burned their magic books.

20:9-10 Eutychus was raised from dead.

21:8-11 Agabus prophesied to Paul.

<u>23:11</u> "But the following night the Lord stood by him and said, 'Be of good cheer, Paul; for as you have testified for Me in Jerusalem, so you must also bear witness at Rome.'"

<u>27:23-24</u> "For there stood by me this night an angel of the God to whom I belong and whom I serve, (24) saying, 'Do not be afraid, Paul; you must be brought before Caesar; and indeed God has granted you all those who sail with you.'"

<u>28:3-6</u> Paul was bitten by a viper, but not harmed by the venom.

<u>28:8-9</u> God used Paul to heal Publius' father as well as all who were sick on the island of Malta.

Note the following observations from the above list. "Signs and wonders" occur together eight times. Similar phrases include: "miracles and signs" (8:13), "miracles and wonders" (15:12), "unusual miracles" (19:11), "miracles, wonders, and signs" (2:22), and "great wonders and signs" (6:8). Miracles done "by their hands," or similar wording, is also common. God's hand is linked with the apostles' hands in 4:30. This alludes to the partnership of God and man (with the Holy Spirit obviously being the Senior Partner, as Rev. David Yongee Cho says) in the advancement of God's kingdom on earth. In 4:30, healing is shown to be the premier sign. "Among the people" is a common phrase, which alludes to the evangelistic role of signs and wonders. "Among the Gentiles" appears in 15:12, which is partial fulfillment of Acts 1:8: "and to the end of the earth." Notice that the laying on of hands occurs at times in connection with the filling of the Holy Spirit, speaking in tongues, healing, and in the sending of Paul and Barnabas on their first missionary journey (13:3).

Chapter 9

Healing Evangelists and Testimonies–Part 2

Oral Roberts

Granville Oral Roberts (1918 - 2009) was born in Oklahoma and was the son of a Pentecostal Holiness preacher. At age seventeen, he developed tuberculosis and was bedridden for about five months, but the Lord healed him of tuberculosis and of stuttering under the ministry of evangelist George Moncey. Roberts apprenticed under his father, was ordained by the Pentecostal Holiness Church in 1936, and pastored four churches until 1947. At that time, Roberts launched a healing ministry which was headquartered in Tulsa, Oklahoma. He broadcast his messages over the radio and started a monthly magazine entitled *Healing Waters*. In 1948, Roberts preached all across America utilizing a portable tent that would seat 12,500.[124] The following testimonies came from the early days of Roberts' healing ministry.

Roberts held his first healing crusade under a tent in Tulsa. The crowd was small the first night. But as God anointed Roberts' preaching and a few sick people were healed, word spread through Tulsa and within days the one-thousand-seat tent was packed and hundreds were standing around the edges. Steve Pringle, who owned the tent, said,

"Oral, you can't close this meeting. God is with you, and you must stay another week." But the revival continued for nine weeks, with standing room only. Roberts testified, "I felt the greatest anointing I had ever known. I preached for an hour and a half in each service."

Shortly after the Tulsa crusade, Roberts preached at a church service in Nowata, Oklahoma to an overflow crowd of three hundred. A mother came to the prayer line with her little boy who was deaf. While Roberts was looking at the boy, the Lord spoke to Roberts: "Son, you have been faithful to this hour, and now you will feel My presence in your right hand. Through My presence, you will be able to detect the presence of demons. You will know their number and name, and will have My power to cast them out." Roberts immediately felt the presence of God, like a strong warmth and an electrical charge, coming into his right hand. Roberts put a finger of his right hand in one ear at a time of the boy and said, "In the name of Jesus Christ of Nazareth, you tormenting spirit of deafness, come out!" The boy put his hands over his ears, cried, and stared at his mother. Roberts said, "He is apparently hearing noise and voices for the first time, and it scares him." Roberts asked her to stand behind her son where he couldn't see her and speak to him to test his hearing. Each time, the boy turned around and said her words back to her as best he could, demonstrating that a measure of healing had occurred.

Then a woman was brought to him who had trouble walking. Roberts laid his right hand on her forehead and again felt the presence of God flow through his hand and into her body. She leaped up, raised her legs up and down a few times, and ran through the crowd, praising God and crying! Those in the church began dancing and shouting!

A few days later, Roberts ministered in Tulsa's Faith Tabernacle Church. Irma Morris, who was a close friend of Roberts and his wife, came to the service expecting to be delivered from tuberculosis. Irma came through the healing line "burning up with fever" and emanating the smell of tuberculosis. Roberts recognized that smell from when he had the disease. Roberts placed his right hand on Irma and spoke a word of command to the disease: "Loose her body and let her go free in the name of Jesus of Nazareth." Irma's body "almost jumped," and she asked, "Oh Oral what did you do to me?" "What do you mean, Irma?" he replied. "Your right hand. It felt on fire when it touched me….Something in your right hand is causing a warmth to go through my lungs. My lungs are opening up. I believe I am healed!"

At home, Roberts' wife, Evelyn, asked him, "Do you suppose if you put your hand on my head, Oral, I could feel it?" Roberts replied, "So far, it's come only as I have preached and as I have touched some of the sick people." Evelyn said, "Maybe if you prayed for this thing in my body I have been suffering with, it would come." He began to feel the presence of God run down his elbow and right arm and into his hand. When he laid his right hand on her, she exclaimed, "Oh, Oral, you are right. It is in your right hand. It is God!" And her pain was "totally gone."

In Durham, North Carolina in 1948, Roberts conducted a twenty-one day crusade, with an estimated crowd of nine thousand on the final night. Each night, many deaf children from a school for the deaf would come into the healing lines. Roberts said, "Not everyone received the same measure of healing, but everyone received some hearing and speech."[125]

From 1947 to 1968, Roberts conducted more than 300 crusades on several continents. In 1955, Roberts began a weekly national television program that showed excerpts of his healing crusades. His healing ministry was broadcast on about 500 radio stations; his monthly magazine, renamed *Abundant Life*, reached a circulation of over a million; his devotional magazine, *Daily Blessing*, had about 250,000 subscribers; his monthly column was featured in 674 newspapers; about fifteen million copies of his eighty-eight books were in circulation; his yearly mail from supporters was about five million letters; his Sunday morning television show was considered the top syndicated religious program in the nation for almost thirty years! In 1963, Roberts opened a liberal arts university in Tulsa—Oral Roberts University—which has over 3,000 students. Historian Vinson Synan said Roberts was considered the most prominent Pentecostal in the world.[126]

Roberts once held a sixteen day crusade in Goldsboro, North Carolina in a B-29 hanger which could seat 10,000 people. Roberts said a healing crusade had never come to Goldsboro, and news stories planted doubt about healing being possible today. Roberts felt he was in hostile territory, that the thousands in the crowd were like one doubting person. The following occurred on the fifth night:

In the healing line were a mother and her son (Douglas Sutton, about age eleven). He was on crutches, with one leg lifted and supported in a brace that was strapped to his shoulder....Faith leaped in my spirit that the confirmation of the Word I had preached was about to happen. His mother told me he had Perthes' disease since he was quite young. (This is a flattening of the hip bone.)..."Jesus, heal!" I prayed as I touched the little boy....I felt the presence of God run down my arm into my right hand and flow into that little boy's flat hip bone. Inwardly, I knew God was working His healing power in the boy's entire body.... (The mother) leaned down, unstrapped her boy's leg, and took his crutches. He put his foot to the floor.... "What do you want to do, son?" I asked. "I want to run!" He looked at his mother. She nodded, and he took off from the lower platform on which he stood in front of me. In a split second he was racing down one of the long aisles....Men and women were jumping, running down the aisles, shouting at the top of their voices, and crying....For fifteen full minutes, they were rejoicing and praising God as I had never seen them before....The rest of the crusade was totally unlike its beginning. Extra crowds broke through the lines the fire marshal had erected. Joy swept over the people and over eastern North Carolina. The boy's healing and the healings that came so often every night until the end of the crusade were the talk of the radio, on television, in newspapers, in factories, in warehouses, on the streets....I was told over 25,000 had gathered for the final service.[127]

Kathryn Kuhlman[128]

Kuhlman (1907 - 1976) was born in Missouri and was born again at age fourteen at an evangelistic meeting in a Methodist church. When she was sixteen, her older sister, Myrtle, and Myrtle's husband, Everett Parrott, an evangelist, took Kathryn with them as Parrott preached in various places. Kathryn often shared her testimony at the meetings, and traveled with them for five years. Once Everett missed a meeting, and Myrtle and Kathryn preached in his place. The pastor of the church encouraged Kathryn to step out as an evangelist. She and pianist Helen Gulliford did so for five years, ministering in Idaho, Utah, and Colorado. In 1933, she established the Kuhlman Revival Tabernacle in Denver, in a paper company's warehouse. In 1935 she established the Denver

Revival Tabernacle, in an abandoned truck garage, and the church grew to about 2,000. She also began a radio show called "Smiling Through," and one of her guest speakers was evangelist Burroughs Waltrip. Waltrip and his wife divorced (they had two children); he moved to Iowa and established a revival center, called Radio Chapel. Kuhlman married Waltrip in 1938, and they traveled back and forth between the Denver church and the Iowa church, preaching. She eventually gave up the Denver church to be in Iowa. Radio Chapel went into bankruptcy around 1939. They became traveling evangelists for a while, but they separated, probably in 1944. They divorced in 1948.

In 1946, Kuhlman was asked to preach in Franklin, Pennsylvania. She decided to live in the area and began preaching on the radio, and her sermon content included the healing power of God. Healings occurred as people listened to Kuhlman preach. [Incidentally, the year was 1947, which is considered the beginning of the Healing Revival that would last ten years. Other big names related to the Healing Revival were William Branham, Oral Roberts, and A. A. Allen.) In 1948, Kuhlman began preaching in Carnegie Hall in Pittsburg and continued preaching there until around 1970. She held famous miracle services there and the auditorium was typically filled to capacity. Her services were broadcast on radio and television, and people reported being healed in their homes while tuned in. She also traveled around the United States holding healing crusades, and her weekly television program was called "I Believe in Miracles." Around 1970, Kuhlman moved her ministry headquarters to Los Angeles, and she regularly filled the Los Angeles Shrine Auditorium which seated 7,000. In addition to divine healing, a phenomenon associated with her ministry was people "going under the power" or being "slain in the Spirit." The following are two healing testimonies from Kuhlman services.

In 1925, George Orr was injured in a foundry where he worked in Grove City, Pennsylvania. Red-hot liquid iron splashed onto his right eyelid, burned through it, and "lay inside his eye—just cooking it." The liquid iron quickly hardened into a solid splinter of metal which the company nurse removed from his eye. An eye specialist told George, "You'll never see out of this eye again." Several other doctors looked at George's eye and came to the same conclusion. The eye quickly became infected, and George suffered great pain for six months. As time went on, George noticed his other eye going bad. A doctor examined his eye and explained that the blind eye had cast too heavy a burden on the left eye, and so the left eye was heading toward total blindness. In 1947, George's oldest daughter heard one of the Kuhlman broadcasts over the radio and suggested he attend a Kuhlman service. George was skeptical of healing ministries, but beginning in March 1947 he and his wife attended several of the Kuhlman services. George said, "My doubts were all removed when I saw the scope and depth of this ministry. I knew it was the real thing." During a Kuhlman service on May 4, 1947, George heard Kuhlman say that healing is available for everyone just as salvation is. George said, "That's it! God, please heal my eye." George recalls, "Immediately...the blinded eye began to burn intensely." Tears began streaming from his blinded eye. As his friend drove them home, George closed his left eye and for the first time in over twenty-one years he could see out of his right eye—the formerly blind eye. George turned to his wife and said, "I can see everything!" He covered his left eye and demonstrated to his wife that he could see. She responded, "Oh, thank God, it's true. You can see!" An optometrist examined George's formerly blind eye and said the scar that had covered that eye had disappeared. He said George's other eye had also been healed. Two year later, George had another eye exam: his left eye was eight-five percent normal, and his right eye was one hundred percent normal![129]

Carey Reams of Florida was a father of three who served as a chemical engineer in World War II. While driving to Manila, Carey's vehicle hit a land mine, and he was "crushed from the waist through the pelvis." He was unconscious for thirty-one days. "His right eye was gone; he had lost all his teeth; his jawbone was fractured; his neck was broken; and his back was broken in two places. The lower part of his body was completely paralyzed. His legs...hung entirely without sensation, but in those parts of his body in which he still retained feeling, the pain was incredibly intense." Carey, who had endured forty-one surgeries, said life didn't seem worth living, except for his children. In December of 1950, Carey had not walked unaided since 1945. He had heard of Miss Kuhlman's healing ministry through a magazine article. At the prompting of a few friends, Carey made a bus trip from Florida to Pennsylvania to attend one of her services. At the end of the service, Miss Kuhlman pointed at Carey and asked, "Are you from Florida?" Carey replied, "Yes." Then Miss Kuhlman asked Carey to stand up. He replied, "I can't." Then she said, "In the name of Jesus, stand up and look up, and walk!" So Carey stood up on his crutches! Then Miss Kuhlman said, "Take that right crutch away." Carey dropped it. He said at that moment, the pain in his body "instantly vanished." Carey dropped the other crutch. Miss Kuhlman told him to come up on the platform which would require his climbing twelve steps. Carey said, "I walked onto the platform like a bird flying up...I ran." Three days later, his two youngest children for the first time saw their father walk without crutches. Eleven years later, at the writing of this book, "Carey has been the picture of perfect, robust health."[130]

T. L. Osborn[131]

Tommy Lee Osborn (1923 – 2013) was born in Oklahoma and raised on a farm. He was the seventh son of a family of thirteen children. At age twelve, he went to a revival meeting at Faith Tabernacle and he was saved. At age fourteen, while Osborn was walking in the woods, God revealed to him that he was to preach the gospel. At age fifteen, Osborn left the farm to accompany a minister for the next two and one-half years as the minister conducted church revivals. At a revival service in California, Osborn met Daisy Washburn of Los Banos, California. He married Daisy one year later, when he was seventeen. For two years, the Osborns traveled throughout California preaching the gospel. They gave birth to a daughter, Marie, in 1943, but little Marie only lived seven days. The grief was "almost unbearable," but they determined to press on with the gospel and recompense their loss with spiritual births in the kingdom of heaven. In 1944, Osborn became a pastor in Portland, Oregon. In 1945, their son, Tommy Lee, Jr., was born. Three weeks later, they resigned the church, itinerated seven months in several states, and then sailed to India to serve as missionaries. They came home within a year due to sickness, and Osborn later said he greatly regrets that they did not understand the ministry of divine healing while in India. In the fall of 1946, Osborn became a pastor again in Oregon, and during that time they gave birth to their daughter, LaDonna Carol. Soon thereafter, Osborn learned of the recent death of the evangelist, Dr. Charles S. Price. He thought of the passing of other great healing evangelists such as Wigglesworth, McPherson, Dowie, and Kenyon. He prayed:

Lord, those great heroes are gone now, and millions are still dying. Multitudes are still sick and suffering. To whom will they now go for help? Who will now stir our large cities and fill our large auditoriums with the magnetic power of God, healing the sick and casting out devils?

A few days later, when Osborn was about twenty-two years old, he was awakened by an amazing vision from God. Osborn saw the cross and the angel Gabriel with his trumpet; then Jesus entered Osborn's room. Osborn said, "I lay as one dead, unable to move...awe-stricken by His presence....When I walked out of that room, I was changed.... Jesus became Master of my life." A few months later, Osborn witnessed divine healings and deliverances through a visiting evangelist. Osborn said: "That's the Bible way....My wife and I determined to be channels through which God would minister His mighty works of deliverance today....We began immediately to preach deliverance for all and to pray for the sick. Needless to say, God began immediately to work miracles because we had dared to take Him at His Word." As Osborn sought the Lord in an upstairs room, God answered his questions concerning the recent deaths of heroes of the faith. The Spirit said to him:

My son, as I was with Price, McPherson, Wigglesworth, and others, so will I be with you. They are dead, but now it is time for you to arise, to go and do likewise. You cast out devils; you heal the sick; you raise the dead; you cleanse the lepers. Behold, I give unto you power over all the power of the enemy. Be not afraid. Be strong. Be of good courage. I am with thee as I was with them. No evil power shall be able to stand before thee all the days of thy life as you get the people to believe My Word. I used those people in their day, but this is your day. Now I desire to use you.

Over the next three decades, Osborn preached the gospel in nearly seventy nations, including to crowds of over 200,000 people, and:

have seen literally tens of thousands of the most amazing miracles perhaps ever witnessed...and have been able to lead tens of thousands of sinners to accept Jesus Christ as Savior....We have seen deaf-mutes by the hundreds perfectly restored...great numbers of the blind instantly receive their sight...those in wheelchairs as long as forty-two years, arise and walk...goiters and tumors leave in a flash, cancers die and vanish, lepers cleansed....In a single campaign which we have conducted, as many as 125 deaf-mutes, 90 totally blind, and hundreds of other equally miraculous deliverances have resulted.[132]

The following is a sampling of the healings that occurred through Jesus Christ on January 5, 1980 at a crusade led by Osborn at the Moi Stadium grounds in Embu, Kenya.

A blind man mounted the steps (of the crusade platform). His eyes were open, and he could see everything. Then an old man with crippled feet was healed. He jumped and stomped across the platform with such joy! He was well! Then a mother came with her daughter who had been out of school for two years because she lost her eyesight....Now her eyes were clear! She and her mother were weeping for joy. One old woman was healed of terrible suffering in her bladder....There was a woman who had been bedfast for six years, unable to walk and to help herself. Carried there in a bed and laid where she could hear us, she had been healed. They came up the steps with her, and we all marveled at her testimony. Her name was Fosana. She was so thrilled because she could stand, and even talk. She had not been able to talk for a long time. Evidently, she had suffered a stroke...Now she walked back and forth, and everyone praised God as she told her story of deliverance. A woman with a deaf ear was healed. She could hear a faint whisper in the ear that had been stone deaf for many years....An old woman came whose hips and chest were so bad that she had barely been able to walk. Also, she was almost blind. For three weeks she had been lying at home. Now she could walk and jump and run and see clearly!...An epileptic lady said she knew when the epileptic spirit left her as I prayed. She knew she was healed....(A cripple man) was well-known in the town. When he was healed, he took off his braces and threw down his crutches. But, instead of coming to the platform, he and a large group paraded out of the grounds and up the road by the market place to show the city what God had done. A great commotion is sweeping through the town! They sent usher to catch him and bring him back to testify, but he said: "No, Mr. Osborn said to go tell the people, so I'm doing that." The whole town is in an uproar and the man is well—running, walking, jumping.[133]

R. W. Schambach

Robert W. Schambach (1926 – 2012) was born in Philadelphia and was born-again as a youth on a street corner under the preaching of evangelist C. M. Ward. After serving in World War II, Schambach attended Central Bible College, Springfield, Missouri. In the 1950s, he served as an apprentice to A. A. Allen for five years. Schambach went on to preach in tent meetings of 2,000 to 8,000 in major cities throughout the United States. Often he brought in truckloads of food to give to the inner-city poor. He was a pastor in Tyler, Texas and had a television program, *Power Today*. It is reported that Schambach ministered in over 200 nations. "Schambach devoted his life to preaching the gospel of Jesus Christ (and) believing for signs and wonders to confirm the Word. Through his ministry, the lame walked, the blind saw, the deaf heard, and many captives were set free by the power of the Holy Ghost...."[134]

In 1993, Schambach conducted a ten-day revival, sponsored by Rev. Joe Martin, pastor of a church in Virginia Beach. Schambach wrote the following testimony:

> On October 7, the night before the crusade began, their (the Martin's) eighteen-month old daughter, Elisha Ann, started having difficulty breathing. By Sunday night, the problem had grown more severe, and they noticed a rattle in her lungs. She could hardly breathe and couldn't drink milk....Four specialists at the hospital...listened to her lungs and looked at the heart on a special heart sonogram. (The doctors said) "Your daughter has a congenital heart defect, a cardiac myopathy, and all four chambers of the heart have failed. This is blood in her lungs." They told him that his daughter would live on increasing doses of medicine until she died unless she had a heart transplant. Brother Martin walked in (my trailer) crying and told me about it. "Brother Schambach, she's going to be the first one over the ramp. You're going to lay hands on her on this Children's Blessing Night, and she'll be the first one healed." "That's exactly right," I said. The second I laid hands on her that night, she began to recover. Praise God! As they were driving home that night, Elisha drank a whole bottle in three minutes, which she hadn't done in four whole days. The rattle in her breathing was gone as well. The next morning, they went back to the same doctors. Within a short period of time, they all agreed that her heart was normal. There was no leakage in

any of her heart's chambers. She was totally healed! Once again, the doctors were astounded....After four weeks they returned again to the doctor, who congratulated them and told them that she would be off all medication....[135]

One night in Philadelphia, a lady gave Schambach some candy, not to eat, but to wear. She explained that her sister was in a mental institution and had been there for thirty years. She had sent her sister prayer cloths (Acts 19:12) for her healing but the staff had thrown them in the trash. Recently the staff said she was welcome to send her sister candy. So Schambach put the candy in his coat pocket, preached, then returned it to the lady at the end of the worship service. Six months later, Schambach returned to Philadelphia to preach. During the offering, the same woman came up to him and introduced him to her sister. She said, "I sent that candy to the hospital, and the moment my sister bit into the candy, she bit into the power of God. The demons came out of her instantly, and she was in her right mind for the first time in thirty years." The hospital staff examined her for two weeks, then released her, for there was nothing wrong with her anymore. She went on to hold down a job and live a normal life. (Certainly the candy did not heal the woman. God honored the faith of her sister.)[136]

Chapter 10

Scriptures Related to Healing In the Epistles

Dr. T. J. McCrossan, who was professor of Greek and Hebrew at Manitoba University, Manitoba, Canada and author of *Bodily Healing and the Atonement* (1930), offers the following insights on Romans 8:11 and Romans 8:26.

Romans 8:11 But if the Spirit of Him who raised Jesus from the dead dwells in you, He who raised Christ from the dead will also give life to your mortal bodies through His Spirit who dwells in you.

"Mortal" is *thneta*. Some may try to interpret *thneta* as "dead," but it is not. *Thneta* appears also in Romans 6:12: "Therefore do not let sin reign in your mortal [*thnetos*] body, that you should obey it in its lust." Paul does not say, "Do not let sin reign in your dead body." *Thneta* also appears in 2 Corinthians 4:11: "For we who live are always delivered to death for Jesus' sake, that the life of Jesus also may be manifested in our mortal [*thnetosa*] flesh." Again, the life of Jesus is not manifested in our dead bodies, but in our mortal bodies—bodies that are alive but will one day die. Therefore, John Calvin correctly says of Romans 8:11, "The quickening of the mortal body here cannot refer to the resurrection of the saints, but must mean a giving of life to their bodies, while here upon the earth, through the Spirit."

Romans 8:26 Likewise the Spirit also helps in our weaknesses. For we do not know what we should pray for as we ought, but the Spirit Himself makes intercession for us with groaning which cannot be uttered.

"Weaknesses" [*astheneiais*] comes from *astheneia*, which is the most common word in the Greek language for "sickness." "Helps" is *sunantilambanetai*: *sun* means "together with," *anti* means "against," and *lambano* means "I take hold of." Romans 8:26a says "the Holy Spirit takes hold against our sicknesses together with us." "Together with us" is under what condition? It is under the condition that we abide in Christ and His Word. McCrossan says, "Romans 8:26 teaches us that it is just as much the work of the Holy Spirit today 'to take hold against our sicknesses' as it is to convict sinners of their sin."

"Give life" of Romans 8:11 is *zoopoiese*, from *zoe* [life] and *poieo* [I make]. So the Holy Spirit makes, or gives, life. We also see this in 2 Corinthians 3:6: "...for the letter kills, but the Spirit gives life." McCrossan says of Romans 8:11 along with Romans 8:26:

> While it is the work of the Spirit to keep making life in your mortal bodies (bodies subject to sickness and death), yet He will not do this blessed work unless we, God's saints, do our part, and take hold together with Him. What is our part? John 15:7 gives the explanation, "If you abide in Me, and My words abide in you, you will ask what you desire, and it shall be done for you." In other words, we must let the Holy Spirit control us in thought, word, and deed, and then He "will take hold against our sicknesses together with" ourselves (literal reading of Romans 8:26). The result will be that He (the Holy Spirit) will keep making life (the exact meaning of *zoopoieo*) in these mortal bodies.[137]

The presence of the Holy Spirit within the believer not only gives spiritual life to that believer, but also gives life to the mortal body of that believer.

1 Corinthians 11:23-26 For I received from the Lord that which I also delivered to you: that the Lord Jesus on the same night in which He was betrayed took bread; (24) and when He had given thanks, He broke it and said, "Take, eat; this is My body which is broken for you;

do this in remembrance of Me." In the same manner He also took the cup after supper, saying, "This cup is the new covenant in My blood. This do, as often as you drink it, in remembrance of Me." (26) For as often as you eat this bread and drink this cup, you proclaim the Lord's death till He comes.

In Exodus 12, God commanded the Israelites to observe the Passover throughout all generations. The Israelites were to put the blood of the Passover lamb on the doorposts of their houses to spare them of the divine judgment of death of the firstborn male; they were also to eat the flesh of the Passover lamb for nourishment. The Passover lamb was a type of Christ, Who is our Passover (1 Cor. 5:7), Who is "the Lamb slain from the foundation of the world" (Rev. 13:8), Who said "Whoever eats My flesh and drinks My blood has eternal life..." (Jn. 6:54). So Jesus instituted the Lord's Supper as a replacement for the Passover. In the Lord's Supper, we recognize that Jesus' blood was shed for our redemption, including the remission of our sins. We also recognize that Jesus' body was broken for our redemption, including the healing of our bodies—"by whose stripes you were healed (1 Pet. 2:24). We see these joint benefits of the atoning work of Christ in Psalm 103: "Who forgives all your iniquities, Who heals all your diseases" (verse 3). Incidentally, in Psalm 103:2, David wrote: "**forget not** all His benefits," which is similar to what Paul expressed as the purpose of the Lord's Supper: "This do, as often as you drink it, **in remembrance** of Me." I see the Lord's Supper as a God-ordained reminder, like a picture, of the suffering and atonement of Christ for the purpose of the encouragement and quickening of our faith in Him. So ingesting the bread and wine (or juice) in the Lord's Supper, when we do so in a worthy manner, can very much be conducive to believing for the healing of our bodies as well as believing for the forgiveness of our sins.

A sermon by F. F. Bosworth inspired me concerning this concept. The following are testimonies he shared of individuals being healed while partaking of the Lord's Supper.

> Brother Birdsall (of Texas)...was all run down in health, having the jaundice and weeping eczema....I was asked to talk on the atonement, and...showed them that the bread stood for our healing just as definitely as the blood for our salvation...Brother Birdsall saw how certain this made his healing. The next day when we had the Lord's Supper, he put the bread in his mouth, really appropriating the

Lord's body for the first time in his life. What was the result? God's lightning struck his body, made him whole, and he gained twenty pounds in the next thirty days. The weeping eczema left his body and he has been well ever since.

One Sunday afternoon just preceding the communion service, I made the statement, "You can be healed when you put the bread in your mouth, if not before, by discerning the Lord's body broken for your healing." A woman in the audience, Mrs. Rosa McEvoy, had paralysis of the optic nerve for fifteen years. She told me that she could not tell white from black three feet from her eyes, and was not able to distinguish her husband that far away. She ate the Lord's Supper, discerned the Lord's body with faith, and was healed. She does not even have to wear glasses.[138]

1 Corinthians 12:7-11 But the manifestation of the Spirit is given to each one for the profit of all: (8) for to one is given the word of wisdom through the Spirit, to another the word of knowledge through the same Spirit, (9) to another *faith* by the same Spirit, to another *gifts of healings* by the same Spirit, (10) to another the *working of miracles*, to another prophecy, to another discerning of spirits, to another different kinds of tongues, to another the interpretation of tongues. (11) But one and the same Spirit works all these things, distributing to each one individually as He wills." [v. 9 gifts—*charismata*]

Though Christ can heal the sick through any believer, this passage shows that each believer has a gift or gifts distributed by the Holy Spirit that provide him or her with a special endowment of faith and/ or anointing to minister with effectiveness in particular areas. Three of the gifts: "faith," "gifts of healings," and "working of miracles" are especially relevant to our topic of healing the sick. It is important to seek the Lord to ascertain which spiritual gift(s) you possess so that you may cultivate the full use of your gifts. For example, if you are called to the office of the evangelist (Eph. 4:11), then you likely possess certain gifts that work well with that office: "gifts of healings" and "working of miracles." "Philip the evangelist" (Acts 21:8) operated effectively in these two gifts in his ministry in the city of Samaria (Acts 8:5-13).

2 Corinthians 4:8-11 (8) We are…(10) always carrying about in the body the dying of the Lord Jesus, that the *life of Jesus* also may be manifested *in our body*. (11) For we who live are always delivered to death for Jesus' sake, that the *life of Jesus* also may be manifested *in our mortal flesh*.

The believer, in his body, experiences sufferings and persecutions in this hostile world, as Jesus did. But as Jesus was bodily raised from the dead, the believer may also experience the resurrection power of Jesus even in his or her body. Similar to Romans 8:11 in application, the believer can declare that "the life of Jesus" is "manifested in" the "mortal flesh" (or in the living "body," not the dead body) of the believer. Such declarations are conducive to faith for divine healing and health.

Galatians 3:13 Christ has redeemed us from the curse of the law, having become a curse for us (for it is written, "Cursed *is* everyone who hangs on a tree....")

The word for "curse" is *katara*. In Deuteronomy 28:15-47, we see that many awful sicknesses and diseases are included in the curse of the law. For example:

> But it shall come to pass, if you do not obey the voice of the LORD your God, to observe carefully all His commandments and His statutes which I command you today, that all these curses [*katarai* in the *Septuagint*] will come upon you and overtake you:...(21-22) The LORD will make the plague cling to you until He has consumed you from the land which you are going to possess. The LORD will strike you with consumption, with fever, with inflammation, with severe burning fever, with the sword, with scorching, and with mildew; they shall pursue you until you perish....(27-28) The LORD will strike you with the boils of Egypt, with tumors, with the scab, and with the itch, from which you cannot be healed. The LORD will strike you with madness and blindness and confusion of heart (Deut. 28:15, 21-22, 27-28).

Dr. McCrossan says:

> Since sickness was one of the curses (*katara*) of the law, and Christ died to redeem us from the curse (*katara*) of the law, by becoming a curse (*katara*) for us (substitutionary Atonement); therefore, according to Paul's teaching, bodily healing is in the Atonement.[139]

Bosworth concurs, stating:

> Every form of sickness and disease known to man was included, and many of them even mentioned particularly, in "the curse of the law"

(Deut. 28:15-62). In Galatians 3:13, we have the positive statement that "Christ hath redeemed us from the curse of the law, being made a curse for us...." What plainer declaration could we have than that Christ, Who was born under the law to redeem us, bore its curse, and therefore did redeem us from all sickness and disease?...Redemption is synonymous with Calvary. Therefore, we are redeemed from the entire curse, body, soul, spirit, solely through Christ's atonement.[140]

Amen! And we appropriate this wonderful benefit by faith.

Ephesians 2:5-6 (God) <u>made us alive together</u> with Christ (by grace you have been saved), (6) and <u>raised us up together</u>, and <u>made us sit together</u> in the heavenly places in Christ Jesus....

Notice the three underlined phrases are past tense—God has already performed these works in the one who believes in Christ. Spiritually the believer is already occupying a place of authority, in a sense ruling with Christ even now. For Christ is now sitting at the right hand of God, and the abiding Christian is spiritually positioned in Christ. Colossians 3:3 supports this, saying: "For you died, and your life is hidden with Christ in God."

1 Thessalonians 5:23 Now may the God of peace Himself sanctify you completely; and may your whole spirit, soul, and body be preserved blameless at the coming of our Lord Jesus Christ.

Here is mentioned the three aspects of a person's being: spirit, soul, and body. The spirit and soul are eternal, but the body is temporal. God desires that all three parts of the person, including one's body, be preserved blameless. A blameless body is a healed and healthy body. Being blameless in one's spirit and soul (which is certainly more important than being blameless in one's body) includes steadfastly trusting in Christ and His righteousness which is imputed to us by faith, walking in His Spirit, and bearing the fruit of righteousness. Such a victorious Christian walk is conducive to one's having a blameless body. Generally, sin can open the door for Satan and sickness to come in, but righteousness leads to all aspects of life and blessing, including physical healing and health.

Hebrews 12:12-13 Therefore strengthen the hands which hang down, and feeble knees, (13) and make straight paths for your feet, so that what is lame may not be dislocated, but rather *healed.*

Believers are to strengthen whatever parts of their being have so far proven to be weak, and also endeavor to walk in paths of righteousness. This focus on improving oneself holistically, through the power of Christ, will allow for healing in the body, instead of there being an increase of sickness and weakness in certain areas due to one's remaining in the flesh and in disobedience.

Hebrews 13:8 Jesus Christ is the same yesterday, today, and forever.

People have protested that Hebrews 13:8 should not be used to support contemporary healing ministries. However, James Grant has responded in the following way:

> Hebrews 1:10-12 is talking about specifically God the Son. To the Son He says, "You LORD, in the beginning laid the foundation of the earth, and the heavens are the work of Your hands....You are the same...." This statement, "You are the same" (pertaining to Christ), was not simply dealing with the incarnate Christ, but it shows that He has been unchanging even from the foundation of the earth. The fact that this sort of statement—that Christ is the same—appears both in relation to His role in creation and in His relation to working through Christian leaders and believers, to me, shows that we should not separate one from the other. We should not try to apply this statement "Jesus Christ is the same yesterday, today, and forever" only to Christ as a disembodied, divine Person, but we should see Him as one Person from eternity past to eternity future....The same Jesus who has been working through the Christian leaders you have known—some of the original apostles, Peter, Paul, and others—is able to work through you. He's unchanging. As He was working through them, He's the same now and will remain the same.

Regarding Hebrews 13:8, Bosworth said:

> I maintain that God's law for the healing of the body is just as absolutely dependable as His law for the salvation of the soul....Jesus never refused one case during His ministry on earth and "He is the same yesterday and today and forever"[141]

James 5:13-20 Is anyone among you suffering? Let him pray. Is anyone cheerful? Let him sing psalms. (14) Is anyone among you sick? Let him call for the elders of the church, and let them pray over him, anointing him with oil in the name of the Lord. (15) And the prayer of faith will *save the sick*, and the Lord will raise him up. And if he has committed sins, he will be forgiven. (16) Confess your trespasses to one another, and pray for one another, that you may be *healed*. The effective, fervent prayer of a righteous man avails much. (17) Elijah was a man with a nature like ours, and he prayed earnestly that it would not rain; and it did not rain on the land for three years and six months. (18) And he prayed again, and the heaven gave rain, and the earth produced its fruit. (19) Brethren, if anyone among you wanders from the truth, and someone turns him back, (20) let him know that he who turns a sinner from the error of his way will save a soul from death and cover a multitude of sins.

Prayer is the main theme in this passage as the words "pray" or "prayer" are mentioned seven times. The culminating verse is 16b—"the effective, fervent prayer of a righteous man avails much."

"Anyone" is another recurring word; it is mentioned four times. When it comes to the promises of God, no one is excluded. Romans 10:13 says, "For *whoever* calls on the name of the LORD shall be saved." *Anyone* in Christ who prays in faith should expect his or her prayers to be answered because God is faithful to keep His promises. God is a miracle-working, mountain-moving, merciful God, Who is no respecter of persons. The key to the promises of God being manifest in your life is whether or not you abide in Christ and allow His words to abide in you (Jn. 15:7).

Because our heavenly Father loves us and wants to commune with us, each of us should regularly spend time in private prayer. In Matthew 6:6, Jesus makes mention of this, saying, "But you, when you pray, go into your room, and when you have shut the door, pray to your Father who is in the secret place; and your Father who sees in secret will reward you openly." We may have heard the secret place of prayer referred to as our "prayer closet." But in James 5:14-16, where the Lord gives us specific instructions concerning how to pray for the sick, no mention is made of retreating to one's prayer closet. Instead, verses 14-15 say, "Is anyone among you sick? Let him call for the elders of the church...." The sick person is to *ask* the elders for assistance, utilizing the faith of his fellow believers, in whom Christ the Healer resides, to complement his own measure of faith for the pursuit of his healing.

When believers come together to agree in prayer and to anoint with oil, a synergistic effect occurs. Synergy is when the power of coming together is greater than the sum total of the power of each individual if they were to remain separate. For example, Deuteronomy

32:30 indicates that one can "chase *a thousand* (to flight)," but two can "put *ten thousand* to flight." Again, in Matthew 18:19-20, Jesus says, "if *two of you agree* on earth concerning *anything* that they *ask*, it will be done for them by My Father in heaven. For where *two* or *three* are gathered together in My name, I am there in the midst of them." (This is an important spiritual principle that married couples should utilize!) Churches today should regularly put into practice the instruction of James 5:14-15. Such obedience to the Scriptures and pursuit of faith ought to take precedence over holding out for a doctor's appointment. Doctors are a blessing from God and I utilize them myself on occasion. But we should not seek first the doctor; rather we should seek first God who is the Supplier of every good and perfect gift (Jas. 1:17).

In verse 14, the word for "sick," *astheneo*, typically means a physical infirmity or debility, as we will see in its appearance in the following verses: Matthew 10:8: "Heal the *sick*, cleanse the lepers, raise the dead, cast out demons..."; Matthew 25:36: "I was *sick*, and you visited me"; Luke 7:2: "And a certain centurion's servant, who was dear to him, was *sick* and ready to die"; John 11:1: "Now a certain man was *sick*, Lazarus of Bethany." So various physical sicknesses are included in the meaning of "Is anyone among you *sick*?" (verse 14).

Principle of Asking and Receiving

If someone who is sick fails to call the elders to pray for him or her, then that sick person is disregarding the exhortation found in this passage. The sick person's request for prayer for healing is conducive to having faith for healing whereas a sick person's failure to request prayer is indicative of having no faith for healing. In the preceding chapter, verse 2b affirms this: "Yet you do not have because you do not *ask*." (See also Matthew 7:7 and John 14:14.)

Who Are the Elders?

The elders of the church (verse 14) refer to those within the church who consistently display spiritual maturity over a period of time; they are usually recognized by the church body as elders. In every corporate worship service, the elders ought to be spiritually ready to anoint and pray for the sick when asked, just as Jesus always healed when He was asked.

If no elders are available, then according to Mark 16:17-18, any believer in Christ can pray for the sick: "And these signs will follow *those who believe*...they will lay hands on the sick, and they will recover." All believers in Christ have Christ the Healer living inside of them.

Anointing with Oil

Rev. A. J. Gordon says the following regarding anointing with oil in this passage:

> Oil is applied as a symbol of the communication of the Spirit, by whose power healing is effected...As in baptism the disciple confesses his faith in the cleansing power of Christ's atonement, by the use of water; or, as in the communion he declares his dependence on Christ for the spiritual sustenance, by the use of bread; so here he avows his faith in the saving health of the Spirit by the use of oil.[142]

Anointing with oil is ordained by God to support one's faith, that as one anoints and prays God does a spiritual work. (In a similar way, water baptism, the Lord's Supper, and the laying on of hands are God-ordained "pictures" or "visuals" to support, or undergird, one's faith.) The outward action of anointing with oil is a means of supporting and boosting the believer's faith that the Holy Spirit will come upon that person for a particular purpose such as healing. We see the link between anointing with oil and the anointing of the Holy Spirit in 1 Samuel 16:13: "Then Samuel took the horn of oil and anointed him in the midst of his brothers; and the Spirit of the LORD came upon David from that day forward." We also see anointing with oil linked to the atonement and the cleansing of the physical disease of leprosy in Leviticus 14:18:

> The rest of the oil that is in the priest's hand he shall put on the head of him who is to be cleansed. So the priest shall make atonement for him before the LORD.

How much oil should you apply? I believe it is best to apply enough oil on the top of the head so that it runs down upon the edge of the garments, as is mentioned in Psalm 133:1-2: "Behold, how good and how pleasant it is for brethren to dwell together in unity! It is like the precious oil upon the head, running down the beard, the beard of Aaron, running down on the edge of his garments." When an Old Testament prophet would anoint a man to be king, the prophet would typically pour an entire flask of oil upon his head. Again, when one sees oil flowing (and an abundant amount would be easier to see), then one's faith may be boosted that God's Spirit of healing and power will flow upon the person being anointed. Jesus' disciples anointed the sick with oil: "And they cast out many demons, and anointed with oil man who were sick, and healed them" (Mk. 6:13).

The Necessity of Faith

Verse 15 says, "And the prayer of *faith* will save the sick, and the Lord will raise him up." The only reason God is ever obligated to move on your behalf is if you, or someone praying for you, has faith. Hebrews 11:6 says, "But without *faith*, it is impossible to please Him (God), for he who comes to God must *believe* that He is, and that He is a rewarder of those who diligently seek Him." (Faith and belief are synonymous; both come from the Greek word, *pisteuo*.) Faith is necessary for all aspects of the Christian life: Ephesians 2:8 says: "For it is by grace that you have been saved, through *faith*...." Mark 9:23 says: "...all things are possible to him who *believes*." Second Corinthians 5:7 says: "For we walk by *faith*, not by sight." Habakkuk 2:4, Romans. 1:17, Galatians 3:11, and Hebrews 10:38 say: "the just shall live by *faith*."

The Definition of Faith

What is faith? Hebrews 11:1 says, "Now faith is the substance of things hoped for, the evidence of things not seen." Faith must contain "substance" and "evidence." The New American Standard Bible uses the terms "assurance" and "conviction." So faith is having substance, evidence, assurance, and conviction of things for which you hope to receive and have asked to receive, but do not yet see (have not yet outwardly received). A person will have this substance, evidence, assurance, or conviction because of a quickening, or a knowing, by the Holy Spirit in the deepest part of his or her being that God is doing or will do a particular work, such as regenerate, heal, give victory, etc. Consider the following statement: "I know God can heal me; God can do anything." That is a true statement, but it is not necessarily a statement expressing faith that healing will occur. It acknowledges that God *can* heal, but not that God *will* heal. (The leper made this sort of statement in Mt. 8:2). Praying that God *might* heal me expresses uncertainty, which is doubt. But praying, "God *will* heal me" because the Holy Spirit has imparted knowledge to me that God indeed will heal me—that constitutes a prayer of faith. This is the type of assurance spoken of in Hebrews 11:1. In the prayer of faith, there is no place for "doubt," "might," "maybe," or "if it be God's will." The woman healed of the issue of blood had said, "If only I may touch His clothes, I *shall* be made well." Her words expressed her internal, Spirit-produced assurance of her upcoming healing; she had no doubt about the matter. Romans 10:17 says "…faith comes by hearing, and hearing by the word of God." "Word" in Romans 10:17 is the Greek word *rhema*, which means a revealed word. This is different from *logos*, which also means "word" in the Greek, often referring to Scripture. (*Logos* also means reason, thought, or pattern and refers to the person Jesus Christ in John 1:1, 1 John 1:1, 1 John 5:7, and Rev. 19:13.) For a Christian to cultivate faith for healing, it is best to spend much time in the Scriptures (*logos*) which deal with divine healing. Through frequent meditation upon the *logos* pertaining to healing, you position yourself to receive *rhema* for healing—that is faith. Bosworth says of faith:

> Faith refuses to see…anything contrary to the Word of God. It sees the health and strength bequeathed to us as already belonging to us because of the death of the Testator. By His (Christ's) death, the will is in force.…Faith is believing you have what God says you have and acting accordingly before you either feel or see that you have it. Faith is believing what God says in the face of contrary evidence of the senses.[143]

"Save the Sick"

The fundamental New Testament word "save" appears in verse 15a: "And the prayer of faith will *save* the sick, and the Lord will raise him up"; also in verse 20, "he who turns a sinner from the error of his way will *save* a soul from death.…" In both places, the Greek word for "save" is *sosei*. It also appears in Mark 3:4 where Jesus heals a man with a withered hand—"Is it lawful on the Sabbath to do good or to do evil, to save (*sosei*) life or to kill?" The word "salvation" is holistic in nature. It means being delivered from sin and many of the negative effects of sin, including any bondage or oppression of a spiritual, physical, emotional, or even financial nature. The greatest aspect of salvation is specified in verse 15b: "And if he has committed sins, he will be forgiven." What would it profit a man if he were healed, say of cancer, but he remained in spiritual darkness, died, and went to hell? Nothing. It is infinitely more important that we receive God's forgiveness (being pardoned of the guilt of our sins) than for us to receive physical healing of a disease. Thankfully, we do not have to choose between these wonderful benefits. Psalm 103:2-3 says, "Bless the LORD, O my soul, and forget not all His benefits: who forgives all your iniquities, who heals all your diseases." Forgiveness and healing are two sides of the same coin, and the coin is the atonement of Christ. Through faith in the blood of Jesus Christ, which He shed when He was scourged with the whip and when He was crucified on the cross, we can receive forgiveness, healing, and every other Biblical promise. In Matthew 9:2-8, Jesus granted a paralytic both forgiveness and healing, saying to him, "your sins are forgiven" and "arise, take up your bed, and go to your house." (See Chapter 12, my exposition of Luke 8, for more on the meaning of salvation.)

Leaning on One Another

In verse 16, the phrase "one another" appears twice, emphasizing the importance of love, connectedness, unity, and mutual support within the body of Christ. Verse 16 says: "Confess your trespasses to one another...." Though in the New Testament, primary importance is placed on confessing one's sins directly to God (1 Jn. 1:9), there is also value in confessing one's sins (as well as sharing one's struggles and prayer concerns) to a fellow Christian. A Christian friend of mine who struggled with pornography for many years finally began to experience victory over that sin when he started confiding in a fellow Christian about his struggle. Christ, the One who forgives and heals, dwells within each believer. So a fellow believer can come alongside you with his or her faith and assist you through prayer to experience the forgiveness and/or healing you seek from God. (See also Matthew

18:19-20.) Galatians 6:2 says: "Bear one another's burdens, and so fulfill the law of Christ."

"The Effective, Fervent Prayer of a Righteous Man Avails Much" (16b)

Effective prayer includes one's knowing or sensing by the Spirit what God's will is in a given situation and then lining up one's prayer with God's will. In prayer, as well as in all aspects of our lives, we ought to be sensitive to the leading of the Holy Spirit, and we should seek to know what the Lord wants to do. In 1 Kings 17, God had revealed to Elijah that He wanted to hold back the rain. God put that Word in Elijah. It's important to have Christ's Words abiding in us so that our desires are His desires. John 15:7 says: "If you abide in Me, and My words abide in you, you will ask what you desire, and it shall be done for you."

Our prayers should also be "fervent." Fervency conveys the idea of fire or burning. Spiritually speaking, when one is fervently praying, one's inner man is on fire by the Holy Spirit, and the Word of God within him must be spoken. The LORD said to the prophet Jeremiah, "Behold, I will make My words in your mouth fire, and this people wood, and it shall devour them" (Jer. 5:14). Later, Jeremiah said, "But His word was in my heart like a burning fire shut up in my bones; I was weary of holding it back, and I could not" (Jer. 20:9b). Therefore, in prayer we ought not to say words merely out of ritual or a sense of duty. Instead, we should cause the Word of God to abide in us richly so that we will pray effectively, fervently, and with conviction.

"Righteous" means to be in right standing with God, which is necessary for having a powerful prayer life. First Peter 3:12a says: "For the eyes of the LORD are on the *righteous*, and His ears are open to their prayers...." One aspect of righteousness is the transference of the righteousness of Christ to a person. This comes when the Holy Spirit produces faith within a person's heart in the atoning work of Jesus Christ on the cross on one's behalf and that God raised Christ from the dead. The purpose of Christ's death was to pay the penalty for the sins of the world. If we have such faith, then we have Christ's righteousness transferred to us so that we are "the righteousness of God in Him" (2 Cor. 5:21). A second aspect of righteousness concerns one's daily walk—that one walks according to the Holy Spirit who lives within each believer and desires to lead the believer in "paths of righteousness." This includes obedience to God's Word (Gal. 5:16-26; Ps. 23:3) so the believer will be "filled with the fruits of righteousness which are by Christ Jesus" (Phil. 1:11a).

Unrepentant sin is a deterrent to effective, fervent prayer. It is a road block, a kink in the hose; it will render one's prayer life ineffective. Psalm 66:18 says, "If I regard iniquity in my heart, the Lord will not hear." (See also Isaiah 59:2.) First John 3:21-22 states, "Beloved, if our heart does not condemn us, we have confidence toward God. And whatever we ask we receive from Him, because we keep His commandments and do those things that are pleasing in His sight." Keeping God's commandments, thus pleasing Him, allows us to have confidence and faith in our hearts so that when we petition the Father, whatever we ask we receive. What a wonderful promise!

Just Like Elijah

What is meant by "avails much"? Verses 17-18 contain an example.

Elijah was a man with a nature like ours, and he prayed earnestly that it would not rain; and it did not rain on the land for three years and six months. And he prayed again, and the heaven gave rain, and the earth produced its fruit" (James 5:17-18).

Elijah was a bold prophet of God who confronted wicked King Ahab of Israel for leading Israel into grave sin. Elijah pronounced in the hearing of Ahab that, due to Israel's sin, rain would not fall again in Israel until Elijah called for rain. Therefore, a three and one half year drought ensued, bringing great distress upon Israel. After that period, Elijah, who had been in hiding, once again presented himself to Ahab (at the LORD's instruction) and told Ahab he wanted to hold a contest between Baal (a false god whom Ahab and many other Israelites worshipped) and the God of Israel (who is the God of all creation, the God and Father of our Lord Jesus Christ whom Elijah worshipped). The contest would be on Mt. Carmel and all Israel was summoned to attend. Two altars would be built, one for Baal and the other for God. Baal's prophets would petition Baal to send fire from heaven to consume the sacrifice on Baal's altar. Then Elijah would petition God to send fire from heaven to consume Elijah's altar. The One who would answer that prayer would prove Himself to be the true God. Baal's prophets cried out to Baal all day long, obviously to no avail. Then it was Elijah's turn. Elijah ordered men to pour twelve pots of water on his altar so that there would be no question as to the supremacy and power of the One to whom he would pray. When Elijah petitioned the LORD God, fire fell from heaven with such intensity that it consumed the burnt sacrifice, the wood, the stones, and the dust! Therefore, all of Israel fell prostrate and cried out, "The LORD, He is God! The LORD, He is God!" The false prophets were executed, and many in Israel turned back to God that day due to a spectacular demonstration of divine power in response to the effective, fervent prayer of one righteous man who heard and obeyed the voice of God (1 Kings 17-18).

Verse 17a states: "Elijah was a man with a nature like ours." In other words, Elijah was subject to personal weakness, failure, and sin as we all are. And yet Elijah was blessed to know God and be used of God. Likewise, each of us can know God by being born again and abiding in Jesus Christ. And God can perform miracles through us to His glory. Jesus said, "he who believes in Me, the works that I do he will do also; and greater works than these will he do, because I go to My Father" (Jn. 14:12). Hallelujah! So one who is committed to the Lord Jesus and His Word can be used of God to turn many in our nation and world toward God. Pray with me, "Lord, use me!"

1 Peter 2:24 who Himself bore our sins in His own body on the tree, that we, having died to sins, my live for righteousness—by whose stripes you were healed.

The latter part of this verse is a quotation from the fifth verse of Isaiah 53, the outstanding chapter on the atonement of the Messiah. Here, the Greek word for heal is a form of the word *iaomai*. The verb tense of *iaomai* in 1 Peter 2:24 is aorist, meaning the healing happened at a particular point in the past. Jesus the Christ, God's Messiah, purchased healing for the spirit, soul, and body for every human when He was scourged with the whip just prior to His crucifixion. First Peter 2:24 clearly links divine physical healing to the atoning work of Christ. (Please see Chapter 4 "Atonement" in this book for more on *iaomai* in 1 Peter 2:24.)

1 John 3: 5, 8 (Christ) "was manifested to take away our sins" (and to) "destroy the works of the devil."

One work of the devil is to afflict humans with physical disease. For example, in Luke 13 the woman who was bent over had a "spirit of infirmity," which was a demonic spirit. Also, Acts 10:38 says "...Jesus...went about...healing all who were oppressed by the devil...." So the removal of our sins and the destruction of the works of the devil are attributed to the manifestation of Christ, whose ultimate work in defeating the devil was His atoning death and resurrection. Hebrews 2:14b says: "that through death He (Christ) might destroy him who had the power of death, that is, the devil." Sickness is a form of death in that it saps the body of vitality. Dr. McCrossan says: "Is not sickness one method by which Satan causes death? Then Christ died to destroy (annul the power of) sickness."[144]

3 John 2 Beloved, I pray that you may prosper in all things and be in *health*, just as your soul prospers.

In addition to prosperity and health in one's soul (which is the eternal aspect of a person and includes one's mind, will, and emotions), there is also the desire in the heart of God for His beloved children to prosper in every area of life and have blessed physical health. Again, God is concerned about the whole being of a person.

Testimony—God Heals a Heart

One day in September 2008, when Vance (an acquaintance of mine) finished his P90X workout, he felt flu-like symptoms. He eventually went to the doctor who performed an EKG. The results showed that Vance was having a heart attack at that moment. More tests revealed that Vance had myocarditis—an infection that attacks the heart wall; it was likely caused by the flu. The seriousness of his medical condition caused Vance to assess the direction of his life, and Vance committed his life to Jesus in December 2008. Before that date, Vance gave lip-service to the Christian faith, but he was not saved.

In December 2008, Vance's doctor told him that his heart was functioning at twenty percent, and that no doctor could fix his heart. By December 2009, Vance's heart had been built up to function at forty-two percent. In December 2010, the results of an MRI, a CAT scan, and the report of four different cardiologists revealed that a hole had developed between two chambers of Vance's heart. The doctors later told him that blood clots were passing through the hole and traveling to the brain, causing him to have headaches. In July 2011, at least twenty blood clots were in Vance's brain. He had mini-strokes, slurred speech, and physically debilitated. In the coming weeks, the number of blood clots in Vance's brain grew to well over one hundred. He suffered sharp pain in his head. A doctor agreed to try an experimental medicine on Vance that would take an estimated six to eight weeks to work, but the doctor said he did not think Vance would live that long. Vance and his wife, Sherrie, began planning his funeral. On September 16, 2011, Vance went on a men's weekend retreat with his church, Church of the Savior, of Lexington, Kentucky. Vance did not want to go, but his wife strongly urged him to go, saying "I believe God will heal you on the retreat if you will just go." At the time, Vance could not walk, and he could not speak well. On the first day of the retreat, Vance met a fellow church member, Stephen, who was the retreat's keynote speaker. They fellowshipped for about three hours that first day, and twice Stephen laid his hands on Vance's shoulder and prayed for him to be healed. Stephen asked Vance to listen to a song by Michael W. Smith called *Healing Rain*. Vance stayed up most of the night and listened to that song for hours. The next morning, after Stephen finished his talk to the men, he began to play the song *Healing Rain* for all those gathered. He knelt beside Vance and put his hands on Vance's shoulders. He told Vance, "This song is for you. This is God's healing for you." When the song was over, Vance no longer had a headache. He could focus and he could walk. He felt better than he had in years. Vance's neurologist was shocked at Vance's recovery and thought he would have been dead by then. Vance's body had been rejecting the experimental medication. Around early November, the doctor said he was going to slowly wean Vance off the medication over the next eight to ten months. But while Vance was on a prayer walk in April, God told him he no longer needed any medication. So Vance quit taking medication that day, which was contrary to the doctor's advice.

In July 2012 the doctors performed a comprehensive exam on Vance, including an EKG, MRI, CAT scan, and blood work. Two days later, the doctor said, "There is no hole in your heart, the damage in your heart is gone, and your heart has the strength of the heart of a twenty year old. Your diabetes is gone. Your rheumatoid arthritis of the last eight years is gone. Your blood work is 100 percent perfect!" Hallelujah! In December 2012, a doctor performed follow-up tests, and had the same results: Vance had no physical problems! Now, in April 2013, Vance (age forty-one) feels great. He rides his bicycle ten miles per day, is happily married to Sherrie, and is active in his church.

Chapter 11

Healing Evangelists and Testimonies–Part 3

John Wimber

John Wimber (1934-1998) was born again in 1963 and went into full-time ministry. He initially opposed any contemporary use of the charismatic gifts (1 Cor. 12:7-11), including tongues. However, when his three-year-old son was repeatedly stung by a swarm of bees, John, to his own surprise, broke out praying in tongues while he held his son, and his son was healed! Even after that, John was slow to embrace the charismatic gifts. His wife, Carol, who also was critical of the gifts, began praying for God to change some of the people around her including John who was quite discontent in several areas of his life. One night, through a dream Carol was filled with the Holy Spirit and awoke speaking in tongues. Carol repented of having a negative attitude toward the Holy Spirit's gifts. Soon thereafter, Carol waited until John was asleep, placed his hand on her shoulder and prayed for God to heal her shoulder from painful rheumatoid arthritis. A surge of heat came into her shoulder and she was healed! So on two occasions the charismatic gifts had operated through John independent of his will. A short time later, while John was at an low point emotionally, due to poor health and burn out, he prayed in an airport hotel for God to show him what was wrong with his life. In the middle of the night the Lord spoke to John: "John, I've seen your ministry, and now I'm going to show you Mine." In 1977, John became pastor of Yorba Linda Friends Church (later called Vineyard Christian Fellowship). The Lord told him, "Most people are hesitant, even fearful, to pray for other's healing because they misunderstand My compassion and mercy. They know about Me, but they do not always know Me." John preached through Luke's gospel and many sermons dealt with divine healing. He had an altar call after every sermon to pray for the sick. During the first ten months, no one was healed and many left the church. John became despondent and said to God, "I will not teach about healing anymore." God replied, "Either preach My word or get out." John repented. Then God spoke again, "Preach My word, not your experience." John took the Lord's admonition seriously and continued to preach Christ the Healer and pray for the sick. One morning, John received a call from one of the newest church members. The man's wife was sick. The man had to be at his brand new job and they couldn't find a babysitter, so he asked John to come and pray for her to be healed. John went and prayed for her, and God instantly healed her! John drove home and exclaimed "We got one!" Healings began occurring within their church, and the church began growing. By 1984, Vineyard Christian Fellowship had grown to about 4,000 in attendance. John Wimber reported that in 1986 thirty-two percent of all people prayed for in their church were completely healed, and eighty-six percent showed evidence of some significant healing. Wimber also taught a class at Fuller Theological Seminary, entitled "The Miraculous and Church Growth," which became the most popular class, as well as the most controversial, in Fuller Seminary history. Wimber established a "signs and wonders" ministry, and held conferences and workshops attended by thousands of people, many of whom had dramatic encounters with the Holy Spirit. The Vineyard Christian Fellowship Church planted over 500 Vineyard churches.[145]

The following is an example of how a word of knowledge (1 Cor. 12:8) that Wimber received brought life transformation to a husband and wife.

On an airplane, John saw a middle-aged man sitting across the aisle from him. John had a word of knowledge—he saw written across the man's face the word "adultery." When the man asked John, "What do you want?", a woman's name came clearly to John's mind. He quietly said to the man, "Does the name 'Jane' (not her real name) mean anything to you?" The man replied, "We've got to talk." As John and the man went to the jumbo jet's upstairs cocktail lounge, the Holy Spirit said to John, "Tell him if he doesn't turn from his adultery, I'm going to take him." The man asked John, "Who told you that name?" John said, "God told me....He also told me to tell you...that unless you turn from this adulterous relationship, He is going to take your life." The man asked, "What should I do?" John explained the gospel of Christ and the man's need to repent. The man confessed his sins and prayed to get saved through faith in Jesus Christ. Then John said the man needed to confess his sin to his wife. The man went back to his seat and confessed his adulterous affair to his wife who was sitting beside him, and told her he had repented and believed on Christ. Before the plane landed, the wife also prayed to receive Christ![146]

Jack Deere was a Dallas Seminary professor and pastor who believed that God had withdrawn the supernatural gifts of the Holy Spirit at the death of the first apostles since we now have the completed Bible. However, at the recommendation of a friend, Deere went one night to hear John Wimber speak at Lake Country Baptist Church in Fort Worth. Deere was skeptical of anything charismatic so he took ten people from his church along as witnesses in case anything "weird" happened, so they could verify he had merely gone to evaluate, not participate. Wimber preached on the kingdom of God and Deere genuinely liked the message. Then Wimber announced it was "clinic time." He continued, "I have no idea what direction we are supposed to take, but I believe the Lord will show us what He wants to do tonight. I am going to ask the Holy Spirit to come now." So Wimber asked the Holy Spirit to come, and there was silence for about sixty seconds. Then Wimber said, "He has given me some words of knowledge for healing," and said that God wanted to heal people with back pain. Several people came forward and were met by prayer teams. Minutes later Wimber said, "There is a woman here who has severe back pain, but you haven't come forward yet. Come forward; I think the Lord will heal you right now." But no woman came forward. Then Wimber said, "You went to the doctor several days ago; you have had this pain for years. Please come forward." Still no woman came forward. Then

Wimber said, "Your name is Margaret." A lady got up and walked to the front. As Deere was stewing in disgust over this "clinic time," the man sitting next to him whom he had known for fifteen years, said, "That's Margaret, my sister-in-law!" Indeed Margaret Pinkston was healed that night of a condition she had for years. Deere knew the family and thus he knew there was nothing fake about the healing. So God began to melt away Deere's skepticism about the contemporary use of the Holy Spirit's gifts, and that evening marked the beginning of a close friendship between Deere and Wimber. In 1987, Deere quit his position at the seminary and joined the staff of the Vineyard Christian Fellowship Church in Anaheim, California where he ministered until 1992. He also began teaching throughout the world and became an advocate for the use of gifts of the Spirit today.[147]

Reinhard Bonnke

Reinhard Bonnke (1940 - present) was born in Germany to a Pentecostal pastor, and was born again at the age of nine. At age ten, Bonnke received the baptism in the Holy Spirit and heard God's call to preach in Africa. In 1964, he married Anna Sulzle, and they bore three children. After ministering as a pastor and an evangelist in Germany for seven years, the Bonnkes relocated to Africa in 1967.

On four consecutive nights Bonnke had visions from God saying to minister to the whole of Africa and that "Africa shall be saved." But initially Bonnke's ministry was quite small. Bonnke said, "I believed the signs that followed Jesus as He walked the earth could—and should—be true in our lives today....But I was not seeing miracles in Maseru (a city in Lesotho, Africa where he ministered) and it distressed me." He invited a minister, John Bosman, whom God used in the miraculous, to come preach at Maseru. The church building was packed with people, but after Rev. Bosman's sermon he told Bonnke to close the service. Bonnke was flabbergasted, knowing the people expected Bosman to pray for them. He said to Bonnke, "Tell them the sick will be prayed for tomorrow." The next morning, Bosman told Bonnke he was leaving. Bonnke protested, "You had me tell the people you would pray for them today." Bosman replied, "I promised the sick would be prayed for. You promised that I would do the praying." As Bonnke drove to the church without Bosman, faith arose inside him, and he said to the Lord, "Now

I will go and do the preaching and praying for the sick and You will do the miracles." Bonnke said of his preaching that day, "I spoke with an authority I had never known before." Half way through Bonnke's sermon, the interpreter was overcome by the power of the Spirit and fell to the floor. The Lord said to Bonnke: "My Word in your mouth is as powerful as My Word in My mouth. Call those who are totally blind, and speak the Word with authority." Bonnke asked all who were totally blind to stand. Then he proclaimed, "In the name of Jesus, blind eyes open!" A woman began screaming and rushed forward from the back of the crowd exclaiming, "I see!" The church erupted with celebration! Then a young child who had "twisted legs" was passed, hand-to-hand, over the heads of the crowd to Bonnke. The child began to vibrate in Bonnke's arms. Then the child stood on his own feet, and began running! The Holy Spirit later said to Bonnke, "You will plunder hell and populate heaven for Calvary's sake."

Soon thereafter, the Lord said to Bonnke, "Go to the city of Gaborone in Botswana." In Gaborone, the Lord led Bonnke to the Botswana National Sports Stadium, and the Lord said, "You will preach My name there." Initially, Bonnke rented a sports hall that could hold 800 people. But because he received little help from the local churches, the first night of the Gaborone crusade only drew 100 people in attendance. But after Bonnke had preached about ten minutes, a woman stood up and shouted, "I've just been healed." Then about four others stood and claimed they had just been healed. When Bonnke gave an altar call and began to lay hands on people, a phenomenon unusual to him began to occur—each person collapsed to the floor. Then a woman rose from the floor and exclaimed "I can see!" Another man who had relied on crutches got up from the floor and started running. Within two nights, the sports hall was filled to capacity, and 2,000 more were standing outside listening to Bonnke on loudspeakers. Bonnke moved his crusade to the Sports Stadium, and by the second night there were upwards of 10,000 in attendance. Bonnke saw that many of the pastors who had initially refused to help him came to the crusade. During the service the Lord said to Bonnke, "I want you to pray for the people to receive the baptism of the Holy Spirit." So Bonnke invited those who wanted to receive the baptism to come forward, and nearly 1,000 people gathered before him. Bonnke's partner gave instructions to the crowd about the baptism in the Holy Spirit, but he didn't mention speaking in tongues, which grieved Bonnke. Nevertheless, while their hands were lifted toward heaven, Bonnke prayed for them. Suddenly he saw "a transparent wave coming from the right to the left, sweeping over the stadium…(like) a mighty rushing wind (and) blew them to the ground in masse. All of them were speaking in tongues and prophesying." Five hundred converts were baptized in water that day. That was the end of the first Bonnke campaign.[148]

In 1977 Bonnke purchased a 10,000 seat tent, and in 1984 he purchased a 37,000 seat tent. Accompanying Bonnke's crusade sermons were healings and deliverances from demons; also bonfires were set by new converts to burn witchcraft paraphernalia. Bonnke regularly encouraged converts to receive the baptism in the Holy Spirit with the evidence of tongues. Bonnke wrote: "The healings are signs that follow the preaching of the gospel. They open the door for salvation on a large scale."[149] In 1986, Bonnke's team reported 1,500,000 responses to the invitation to receive Jesus as Lord and Savior. In the mid-1980s, Bonnke began holding leadership conferences called "Fire Conferences" throughout Africa and Europe. In 1987, the Bonnkes moved from Johannesburg to Frankfurt, Germany, which served as the headquarters for his ministry called Christ for all Nations. In the 1990s, Bonnke attempted a mass mailing of a gospel booklet, *From Minus to Plus*, and 20,000 converts to Christ were reported through that initiative. In 1991, due to purported anti-Islamic comments made by Bonnke, Muslim-led riots occurred in Kano so that Christians were killed and church buildings were burned. In February 2013, Bonnke proclaimed from a Florida airport "America Shall Be Saved," and he has included American cities for many of his recent crusades sites.[150]

The following is a healing testimony from a Bonnke crusade in Khartoum, Sudan.

> Omar Mohammed and his father were caught in a terrible storm and were struck by lightning that killed the father and left Omar deaf and dumb. The medical diagnosis was that the lightning bolt had caused irreversible damage, destroying the vocal and aural capacities of Omar's nervous system. For the following five years, Omar was a beggar on a busy street corner outside Khartoum University. Then Omar read a poster advertising an Easter Celebration with Reinhard Bonnke—"Come expecting miracles of healing." So Omar attended the crusade on its first night, but he could not hear anything despite

the crusade's use of high-powered amplifiers. But Omar could see that people were being healed, so Omar attended the second meeting. When the time came for Bonnke to pray for the sick, Omar raised his hands with hope. Bonnke shouted: "Deaf ears open! Dumb mouths speak!" Omar said he suddenly felt like lightning had struck him again, knocking him to the ground, but he did not know it was the power of the Holy Spirit. Omar was immediately healed, able to hear and speak! Many in the crowd recognized him as the one who regularly begged at the University; they began shouting that a miracle had occurred, and rushed him to the platform.[151]

Benny Hinn

Toufik Benedictus Hinn (1952 - present) was born in Jaffa, Israel and was raised in the Eastern Orthodox tradition. Around 1968, the Hinn family immigrated to Toronto, Ontario, Canada. Around age nineteen, Hinn was born again and developed a deep relationship with the Holy Spirit. In 1974, Hinn had a vision in which he saw a man enveloped in flames. The Lord spoke to him during the vision, "Preach the gospel." Later Hinn had a dream in which he saw thousands of people falling into a fiery abyss, and the Lord said, "If you do not preach, every soul who falls will be your responsibility." Soon thereafter, Hinn preached his first sermon, and the moment he opened his mouth to preach God healed him of stuttering which had plagued him his entire life. After his sermons, Hinn would lay hands on people who came forward and "they began falling under God's anointing." Soon thereafter, Hinn's father secretly came to hear him preach, and later that night asked him, "Tell us how we can have what you have." That night Hinn led his parents to pray to receive the Lord Jesus Christ. In 1979, Hinn married Suzanne Harthern, with whom he would have four children. In 1983, Hinn relocated to Orlando, Florida and founded a church, The Orlando Christian Center. From 1983 to 1990 his church services were taped and aired on television, and by 1992 the church claimed over 7,000 members. In 1990, the Lord spoke to Hinn to take the saving and healing message of Christ to the whole world through television and crusades. About that time, Hinn began a television show, *This is Your Day*, which showed highlights of the crusades, especially the healings, and the show reportedly reached an audience of sixty million homes world-wide. In response to critics, Hinn recruited five volunteer doctors to attend the crusades and verify all healings people claimed they received before they were allowed to come on the platform and testify. In 1994, heavyweight boxing champion Evander Holyfield was completely healed of a serious heart condition at a Hinn meeting. In 1999, Hinn stepped down as pastor of the Orlando Christian Center and moved his headquarters to Grapevine, Texas. In 2005, Hinn held a crusade entitled *Festival of Blessings* in Bangalore, India in which an estimated seven million people attended, including three million on the final night.[152]

The following is a testimony that occurred at a Hinn crusade.

Around 1990, Ray Scott was in his mid-thirties and worked as a restaurant manager in Bakersfield, California. When he went to the hospital for an appendectomy, the medical team discovered and removed a fist-sized tumor which they think had damaged what was his healthy appendix. Ray's follow-up treatment included two and one-half years of chemotherapy, radiation, and surgery. During this time, the cancer had spread to the base of Ray's aorta. The doctors told Ray that remission would not be possible. Ray also suffered from short bowel syndrome, two hernias, and depression, but the love and care of his wife, children, and church helped sustain him. A friend encouraged Ray to travel to Sacramento (five hours from Bakersfield) to attend a Benny Hinn Crusade. On the way, Ray was so ill that he thought he may need to go to the hospital. At the crusade, when Ray prayed for a sick baby nearby, he said, "God went right through me." An usher led Ray on stage where Ray publicly testified: "A warmth came through my side where it was herniated once before." Ray said all of his pain was gone, even as Hinn pressed his hand strongly against Ray's abdominal area. Hinn declared, "Standing here in God's presence, the cancer is dead." Ray called his doctor the next day and said, "I am healed. I want to run blood work." Ray's blood work was examined, and the doctor wrote: "He has no evidence or recurrence of cancer in his body. He now has the ability to stand as a testament to his faith and religion." At the time this video was produced (eight years later) Ray had remained cancer-free, was physically active, and appeared strong. Ray testified, "What God has done for me, He will do for you."[153]

Lord, because of your great mercy, please raise up many more evangelists and ministers who will boldly proclaim your full gospel message, with signs following, to bring You glory! In Jesus' name, Amen.

Chapter 12

Healings in Luke's Gospel

Luke 4:16-19 So He came to Nazareth, where He had been brought up. And as His custom was, He went into the synagogue on the Sabbath day, and stood up to read. (17) And He was handed the book of the prophet Isaiah. And when He had opened the book, He found the place where it was written: (18) "The Spirit of the LORD is upon Me, because He has anointed Me to preach the gospel to the poor; He has sent Me to heal the brokenhearted, to proclaim liberty to the captives and recovery of sight to the blind, to set at liberty those who are oppressed; (19) to proclaim the acceptable year of the LORD."

This passage lies at the beginning of Jesus' three and one-half year public ministry that He began when He was thirty years old. Jesus had recently been baptized in the Jordan River by John. He overcame temptations from the devil during His forty day fast in the wilderness. Then Jesus "returned in the power of the Spirit to Galilee, and news of Him went out through all the surrounding region" (4:14). In His hometown, while in the synagogue on the Sabbath, Jesus was handed the book of the prophet Isaiah so that He could publicly read from it. He read Isaiah 61:1-2a (quoted in Luke 4:18-19, with some variation), and then told those in attendance that He was the One of whom the passage spoke. He was the fulfillment of it's prophesy. Notice that the particular benefits mentioned in this quotation encompass liberties of a physical, spiritual, social, and emotional nature. God is certainly concerned about ministering to all aspects of a person's being (1 Thess. 5:23; 3 Jn. 2).

Jesus' proclamation of "the acceptable year of the LORD" is likely a reference to the Year of Jubilee (Lev. 25:10). It occurred every fifty years (the year after seven sabbaths of years) and began on the Day of Atonement. The fiftieth year was a year of special liberties made available for all Israelites; the benefits included debts being forgiven and slaves being set free. Jesus announced in the synagogue that His coming can be seen as an ongoing time of jubilee. Jesus' coming inaugurated God's new covenant and the kingdom of heaven being at hand. This new covenant is made available through the ministry of Jesus which began in Luke 4 and culminated in His atoning death and bodily resurrection three days later. Jesus' ministry continues through His ongoing intercession for the saints (Rom. 8:34; Heb. 7:25), as well as His equipping all members of His church today with the indwelling Holy Spirit. By having faith in Christ, one's spiritual debt is cancelled, and one can enjoy a myriad of blessings and liberties including having beauty instead of ashes, the oil of joy instead of mourning, and a garment of praise instead of a spirit of heaviness (Isa. 61:3). Furthermore, one who abides in Christ can and should help rebuild and repair the lives of others who have so far been damaged by sin and Satan.

Also, the Isaiah 61:1-2a quotation specifies that the beneficiaries of God's kingdom are "the poor," "the brokenhearted," "the captives," "the blind," and "the oppressed." Though God's grace and benefits are available to all people (Rom. 10:13), those who will likely be the most receptive to God's kingdom are those who are broken and especially struggling in this life. Their tribulations often make them open to conforming to the will of the One who makes all things new.

Those in the synagogue "marveled at the gracious words which proceeded out of His mouth" (verse 22). However, their attitude quickly changed when Jesus pointed out that the Old Testament prophets, Elijah and Elisha, were sent by God to minister to those *outside* of Israel because Israel had been unfaithful to God, indicating that the Israel of Jesus' day had continued to hold to their ancestors' pattern of unfaithfulness to God. Thus those in the synagogue did not receive Jesus' rebuke, and they sought to kill Him.

Luke 4:33-37 Now in the synagogue there was a man who had a spirit of an unclean demon. And he cried out with a loud voice, (34) saying,

"Let us alone! What have we to do with You, Jesus of Nazareth? Did You come to destroy us? I know who You are; the Holy One of God!" (35) But Jesus rebuked him, saying, "Be quiet, and come out of him!" And when the demon had thrown him in their midst, it came out of him and did not hurt him. (36) Then they were all amazed and spoke among themselves, saying, "What a word this is! For with authority and power He commands the unclean spirits, and they come out." (37) And the report about Him went out into every place in the surrounding region.

The demon seemed to have fully possessed the man, even using the man's voice. The demon spoke in the first person plural, so perhaps more than one demon was in the man (or the demon was speaking on behalf of other demons). In verse 35, Jesus rebuked the demon (not the man); thus the demon came out of the man without hurting him. In verse 36, the people acknowledged that Jesus possessed authority (Greek: *exousia*) and power (Greek: *dunamei*) over "unclean spirits." Referencing Christ's victory over all demons, which He achieved at the cross, the Apostle Paul said, "Having disarmed principalities and powers, He made a public spectacle of them, triumphing over them in it" (Col. 2:15). Similarly, through our union with Christ, we believers have power and authority over all demons, and to cure diseases (Lk. 9:1; 10:19; Mk. 16:17-18; Eph. 1:22).

In verse 34, the demon's confession that Jesus is "the Holy One of God" reminds us that one day "every knee should bow" and "every tongue should confess that Jesus Christ is Lord" (Phil. 2:10-11). Verse 34 also reveals that the demon acknowledged that Jesus has the power to destroy demons, as one day Jesus will destroy all demons and Satan himself (Mt. 25:41; Jude 6; Rev. 20:10).

Once again, we see that a manifestation of God's power—in this case an exorcism—brought amazement to all onlookers and caused Jesus' fame to spread. It was also a sign that confirmed God's Word: "What a word this is!" (verse 36; Mk. 16:20).

Testimony—God Heals a Leg!

When Brian, a friend of mine, was fifteen years old, he had a life-changing experience while on vacation with his family in Wyoming. One day, Brian's knee began hurting. Initially, he thought he had pulled a muscle, but then his leg began swelling and was accompanied by excruciating pain. At the hospital, an ultrasound revealed that blood was not flowing properly through Brian's leg. The doctor said that he would likely have to amputate Brian's entire leg within a few days. The doctor said the next day a CAT scan would be performed and a specialist would assist with the final decision. When the doctor left Brian's room, Brian said to his mother, "I came into this world with two legs, and I am checking out with two legs. Mom, I believe God is real, and your God needs to heal my leg!" Brian's mother replied, "It doesn't work like that. You need to first get your heart right with God." She explained the gospel to Brian, and Brian prayed to receive Jesus as His Lord and Savior! Then Brian spent the entire night crying out to God to heal his leg. The next morning, a CAT scan was performed on Brian's leg. When the specialist came to Brian's room with the results of both the CAT scan of that morning and the ultrasound from the previous day, the specialist was amazed. He said the results from the previous day's ultrasound indeed revealed that Brian's leg would have to be amputated, but the results of that morning's CAT scan revealed that Brian's leg was completely fine! All glory be to God our Healer! Brian was immediately released from the hospital and had no more problems with that leg, which is still the case today, over twenty years later.

Luke 4:38-39 Now He arose from the synagogue and entered Simon's house. But Simon's wife's mother was sick with a high fever, and they made request of Him concerning her. (39) So He stood over her and rebuked the fever, and it left her. And immediately she arose and served them.

The people asked Jesus to heal. Matthew 7:7a says, "Ask, and it will be given you." Notice how Jesus positioned Himself when He healed Peter's mother-in-law. His standing over her can represent His authority over the fever. Then Jesus spoke to the fever as if the fever had ears and the ability to comprehend. Similarly, in Mark 11:23 Jesus exhorts believers to speak directly to the mountain, or obstacle, in one's life. Through faith we should command to be gone illnesses, demons, barriers, and obstacles that we know oppose God's will and are hindering the advancement of God's kingdom. We should speak to them, rebuking them as if they can hear us. In faith we should exercise dominion over them. (See Luke 10:19.)

When Peter's mother-in-law was healed, she served them. God is glorified when we are healed and utilize our full potential in serving Him and others.

Luke 4:40-41 When the sun was setting, all those who had any that were sick with various diseases brought them to him; and He laid His hands on every one of them and *healed* them. (41) And demons also came out of many, crying out and saying, "You are the Christ, the son of God!" And He, rebuking them, did not allow them to speak, for they knew that He was the Christ.

The people displayed faith in Jesus as Healer by bringing those who were sick to Jesus (the principle of asking and receiving). "Any" who were sick were brought, just as "anyone" is mentioned in James 5:13 pertaining to those who are eligible to be anointed by the elders for healing. Jesus was not selective about whom He healed; He healed everyone who was brought to Him. Nor was Jesus too busy or preoccupied, for He took time to lay His hands on every one of them that needed healing. Acts 10:34 says, "God is no respecter of persons" (KJV). If Jesus healed all the sick who were brought to Him then, why wouldn't Jesus heal all the sick who are brought to Him in faith today? We should confess Scriptures which promise that Jesus is our Healer. If healing does not manifest quickly, we should persist in our Scripture meditation and confession and "imitate those who through *faith and patience* inherit the promises" (Heb. 6:12).

Jesus healed "various diseases." Matthew 4:23 reiterates this, saying Jesus "went about...healing every kind of disease and every kind of sickness among the people" (NASB). Jesus is willing and able to heal every kind of physical sickness and disease today, and Jesus is also willing and able to deliver us from all other afflictions, including those of a spiritual and emotional nature. Psalm 34:19 says: "Many are the afflictions of the righteous but the LORD delivers him out of them all." Stipulation to receiving complete victory is having faith (1 Jn. 5:4) as well as not allowing sin to remain in our hearts (Ps. 66:18).

In verse 41, Jesus rebuked demons, casting them out of people and commanding the demons not to speak. The demons obeyed, and once again they confessed that Jesus is Lord (Phil. 2:10-11). By faith in the name of Jesus, Christians can command demons to be quiet and be gone and expect the same result.

Mark 16:15-20 says all believers are commissioned to cast out demons and heal the sick. The singular requirement for healing the sick is *faith* in Jesus. John 14:12 says, "He who *believes in Me*, the works that I do he will do also; and greater works than these he will do, because I go to the Father. And whatever you ask in My name, that I will do." Those who abide in Christ have exceedingly great and precious promises!

Luke 5:12–16 And it happened when He was in a certain city, that behold, a man who was full of leprosy saw Jesus; and he fell on his face and implored Him, saying, "Lord, if You are willing, you can make me clean."(13) Then He put out His hand and touched him, saying, "I am willing; be cleansed." Immediately the leprosy left him. (14) And He charged him to tell no one, "But go and show yourself to the priest, and make an offering for your cleansing, as a testimony to them, just as Moses commanded." (15) However, the report went around concerning Him all the more; and great multitudes came together to hear, and *to be healed* by Him of their infirmities. (16) So He Himself often withdrew into the wilderness and prayed.

The leprous man prostrated himself—"he fell on his face"—to demonstrate reverence and humility before Jesus as he made his request. Though leprosy is contagious, Jesus did not worry about contracting leprosy Himself, but He instead touched the leper, displaying compassion and utilizing the laying-on-of-hands method to heal. [See Matthew 8:2-4 in Chapter 6 of this book for more on *God's will* as it pertains to healing.]

In verse 13, Jesus pronounced the healing (a word of command): "be cleansed," which can refer to physical, spiritual, and emotional cleansing. Jesus desires to heal and to cleanse the whole person (1 Thess. 5:23b).

Verse 15 indicates a sense of anticipation, or expectation, among the multitudes, for they came to Jesus for two reasons. They expected: 1) to hear the Word of God and 2) to be healed. (This dual expectation by the people also appears in Luke 6:17.) The church today should strive to create a similar expectation among its members and within its community by pursuing a vibrant teaching, preaching, and healing ministry (Mt. 4:23). Worship services should be filled to capacity as many people come to hear and to be healed. Regular testimonies should be given that miracles are occurring, prayers are being answered, and the spiritual fire of the Lord is burning in the hearts of God's people. (Luke 5:17 says, "the power of the Lord was present to heal them." Likely, the expectation of the people to hear and to be healed by Jesus contributed to the Lord's power to heal being present in that special way. Typically, what is in your heart will determine what God will do for you. If you maintain a heart of faith that God will bless you in a particular way, then in due time He will.)

Verse 16 reveals that Jesus' prayer life helped Him maintain the spiritual strength and faith He needed to minister effectively. In Mark 9:29, Jesus indicated that certain miracles can only occur through "prayer and fasting." Certainly, an increase in effective, fervent prayers by Christians and church congregations today, as well as fasting and the commitment to walk in Christ's righteousness, will avail much (James 5:16).

God's Will and Prayer for the Sick

I have heard people pray for healing by saying, "If it is Your (God's) will to heal this person, then please heal him." By praying this way, they are implying that there are two categories of people: 1) those people whom God wills to heal, and 2) those people whom God wills to remain sick or diseased. In Category Two, they might say God's will is for the sick person to remain sick and glorify God through having a good attitude and perhaps a good ministry despite his or her being sick. I certainly agree that a Christian with a sickness, disease, or debility can glorify God through bearing the fruit of the Spirit and ministering to others despite his or her sickness. Joni Eareckson Tada, who has been a quadriplegic since 1967 as a result of a diving accident, now serves God as an artist (holding the brush with her mouth), a singer, a radio host, and she has authored approximately seventeen books. First Corinthians 10:31b says, "Whatever you do, do all to the glory of God." If we are sick, poor, divorced, or incarcerated—no matter our condition—we are expected to glorify God. But I disagree with the view that we should pray, "Lord, heal this person if it is Your will." Nowhere in Scripture did Jesus ever reply to someone requesting Him to heal, "I am *not* willing to heal you. I will for you to remain sick. Serve and glorify Me despite your sickness." Words of this effect are not in Scripture. But we do read Jesus' words to the leper "I am willing; be cleansed" (Lk. 5:13), and to the centurion "*I will* come and heal him" (Mt. 8:7). Jesus is the same today as He was then (Heb. 13:8). T. L. Osborn corroborates this, saying:

Since Christ could say, "I have come to do *Your will*, O God (Heb. 10:9), then when He bare our sicknesses and our diseases and suffered the stripes by which we are healed, we have *the will of God* revealed in the matter of the healing of our bodies.[154]

Instances of All Being Healed

There are many instances in Scripture where Jesus healed *all* who were in a crowd. If there is a Category Two—those whom God wills to remain sick—then surely some within that great multitude would have been in Category Two and would not have been healed. But that is not the case because Jesus "healed them all." Jesus also healed all in Matthew 4:23, 8:16, 9:35, 12:15, 14:14, 14:34-36, 15:30, 19:2, Mark 6:53-56, Luke 4:40, 9:11, 17:11-19, and Acts 10:38. Also, all were healed in Jesus' name through His followers in Acts 5:15-16 and 28:8-9.

In Matthew 10, Jesus commissioned His twelve disciples to preach "The kingdom of heaven is at hand" (verse 7) and to "Heal the sick, cleanse the lepers, raise the dead, cast out demons" (verse 8). Jesus did *not* say, "Heal *some of* the sick, cleanse *some of* the lepers, raise *some of* the dead, cast out *some of* the demons, and discern which persons I will to remain sick."

In Luke 17:11-19, Jesus did *not* say to the ten lepers, "I will that the first five of you be healed, and you other five are to remain lepers." Jesus healed all ten.

James 5:15 says, "And the prayer of faith will save the sick." It does *not* say, "And the prayer of faith will save *some of* the sick." If faith is present, the sick will be healed.

In Matthew 17:14-21, when a man brought his demon-possessed, epileptic son to Jesus' disciples so they could heal the boy, the disciples failed to heal him. Should we therefore conclude that it was not God's will to heal the boy? No, because Jesus healed the boy. Jesus told the disciples they failed to heal the boy not because it was not God's will to heal him, but because of their unbelief.

If Christians today pray for healing, but it does not manifest, many conclude that it must not be God's will to heal. Their failure to heal does not mean it is not God's will to heal. Healing is available for all if a particular condition is met. That condition is faith in the Lord Jesus Christ to heal. Inherent to the word "faith" is brokenness, repentance, and the cross.[1] If today's church will embrace and consistently preach Christ as Savior, Healer, Deliverer from demonic oppression and possession, Baptizer in the Holy Spirit, and the Good Shepherd who supplies all our needs, and if the church will consistently incorporate prayer and fasting, then healings will manifest and people will be on-fire for God.

Testimony—God Heals a Woman of Ankylosing Spondylitis!

In 2013, my wife, Kim, received the following text message:

> A few months ago in Tom's healing class, we prayed for my healing of ankylosing spondylitis. (A. S. is a disease that causes pain and inflammation of the joints of the spine, particularly where it meets the pelvis.) Well, my A.S. is in remission!!! I am off my infusion treatments!...I had been taking those treatments for years. I stopped after Tom's classes were over, and now I don't need them.

Luke 5:17-26 Now it happened on a certain day, as He was teaching, that there were Pharisees and teachers of the law sitting by, who had come out of every town of Galilee, Judea, and Jerusalem. And the power of the Lord was present to *heal* them. (18) Then behold, men brought on a bed a man who was paralyzed, whom they sought to bring in and lay before Him. (19) And when they could not find how they might bring him in, because of the crowd, they went up on the housetop and let him down with his bed through the tiling into the midst before Jesus. (20) When He saw their faith, He said to him, "Man, your sins are forgiven you." (21) And the scribes and the Pharisees began to reason, saying, "Who is this who speaks blasphemies? Who can forgive sins but God alone?" (22) But when Jesus perceived their thoughts, He answered and said to them, "Why are you reasoning in your hearts? (23) Which is easier, to say, 'Your sins are forgiven you,' or to say, 'Rise up and walk'? (24) "But that you may know that the Son of Man has power on earth to forgive sins"; He said to the man who was paralyzed, "I say to you, arise, take up your bed, and go to your house." (25) Immediately he rose up before them, took up what he had been lying on, and departed to his own house, glorifying God. (26) And they were all amazed, and they glorified God and were filled with fear, saying, "We have seen strange things today!"

Verse 17b says, "And the *power* (Greek: *dunamis*) of the Lord was present to *heal* them." In other words, a special anointing to heal was present that day, which implies that there are times when a special anointing to heal is not present. This may explain why Jesus, on occasion, healed entire multitudes, and left no one sick. When a special anointing to heal was present, it would likely override a person's lack of faith, and all would receive healing. On other occasions, when such an anointing to heal was not present, there was more of a need for an individual to have faith in order to be healed by Jesus.

Notice the persistence of the friends of the paralytic in their transporting the paralytic into the presence of Jesus. They carried the paralytic on a bed to the house where Jesus was. Perhaps this was a long distance and required extraordinary effort on their part. When they could not access Jesus because of the crowd, they hoisted the paralytic onto the roof, made a hole in the roof, and lowered him into the presence of Jesus. It was a labor of love. The friends worked diligently to get their friend into the presence of Jesus (they *stood in the gap* for him) because they believed there would be a pay-off—Jesus would heal their friend. It is also noteworthy that the friends viewed the prospective healing of the paralytic as more important than the condition of the roof. Roofs can be fixed, and the friends recognized that the health and salvation of the paralytic was much more valuable than any temporal item. [An example of this is when I apply anointing oil to a sick person. I often apply a significant amount, (pouring it rather than just applying a drop) despite any concerns of messing up the hair or clothes of the one for whom I am praying. Hair and clothes can be washed. But when I pray for the sick, I want to maximize the opportunity for faith to be present so that the Holy Spirit will minister healing.] The effort of the friends demonstrated their faith (see Jas. 2:14-26). Verse 20 verifies that it was "their faith" that caused Jesus to say, "Man, your sins are forgiven you."

Also notice in this passage that Jesus' words "your sins are forgiven" and "rise and walk" are closely connected, basically used interchangeably. Indeed, physical healing and forgiveness of sins are often linked in Scripture. Psalm 103:3 says: "Who forgives all your iniquities, who heals all your diseases." (See also Jas. 5:15.) Through His being scourged by the whip and crucified on the cross, Jesus purchased for us the forgiveness of our sins and the healing of our bodies (Isa. 53:4-5; Mt. 8:17; 1 Pet. 2:24; 3 Jn. 2). We appropriate these wonderful benefits by faith.

Jesus pronounced forgiveness of the man's sins before He said "rise up and walk." Receiving God's forgiveness is infinitely more important than receiving physical healing. Your physical body may last perhaps eighty or ninety years, whereas your spirit and soul will exist forever. Certainly, you can receive both: God's forgiveness of your sins and God's healing of your body.

Verse 24 indicates that Jesus' healing of the man helped verify that Jesus has the authority to forgive sins. A paraphrase of Jesus' words is as follows: "That you may know that I forgive, I heal!" Divine healing is a great evangelistic tool, pointing to Jesus as Savior.

The crowd's reaction to the healing (verse 26) emphasizes their realization that God is not far-removed from the affairs of man. Instead God is in our midst, and we are accountable to Him for all He has entrusted to us.

Luke 6:6-11 Now it happened on another Sabbath, also, that He entered the synagogue and taught. And a man was there whose right hand was withered. (7) So the scribes and Pharisees watched Him closely, whether He would heal on the Sabbath, that they might find an accusation against Him. (8) But He knew their thoughts, and said to the man who had the withered hand, "Arise and stand here." And he arose and stood. (9) Then Jesus said to them, "I will ask you one thing: Is it lawful on the Sabbath to do good or to do evil, *to save life* or to destroy?" (10) And when He had looked around at them all, He said to the man, "Stretch out your hand." And he did so, and his hand *was restored* as whole as the other. (11) But they were filled with rage, and discussed with one another what they might do to Jesus.

Once again, the reaction of the scribes and Pharisees to the healing of the man by Jesus on the Sabbath reminds us that there will be resistance, even from the religious community, to any full gospel ministry, especially the more that the ministry resembles Jesus' ministry. In John 15:18, Jesus said, "If the world hates you, you know that it hated Me before it hated you." The frequent persecutions against the early church in Acts from the scribes and Pharisees attest to this point.

In verse 9, Jesus described divine healing as "to do good" and "to save life." Part of the abundant life that Jesus came to impart is our victory through Him over disease and demons. Jesus affirms that doing good and saving life, both of which characterize divine healing, are lawful acts to perform on the Sabbath. Though the scribes and Pharisees had no healing ministry of their own with which they could help the sick, they did not seem impressed with the healings and other miracles performed regularly before their eyes by Jesus, nor did they appear happy for those who were healed. Instead, they were deceived because of their own man-made traditions and pride. Their hearts were corrupt—they were "filled with rage" and jealousy at the success and growing popularity of Jesus. He posed a huge threat to their impotent religious system through which they sought esteem in the eyes of men. But Jesus did not let those haters hinder the fulfillment of His God-given mission.

Luke 6:17-19 And He came down with them and stood on a level place with a crowd of His disciples and a great multitude of people from all Judea and Jerusalem, and from the seacoast of Tyre and Sidon, who came to hear Him and be *healed* of their diseases, (18) as well as those who were tormented with unclean spirits. And they were *healed*. (19) And the whole multitude sought to touch Him, for power went out from Him and *healed* them all.

Jesus spent the entire previous night in prayer on the mountain (verse 12). Such communion with the Father and the Holy Spirit would 1) strengthen Jesus to endure the persecution of the Pharisees (verse 11), 2) give Jesus wisdom and direction concerning whom He should choose to be His twelve apostles (verse 13), 3) empower Jesus to heal all the sick who came to Him (verse 19).

A "great multitude" came to Jesus in full anticipation of receiving from Him blessings of a spiritual and physical nature: they "came to hear" the Word of God from His mouth and "be healed of their diseases" (verse 17). Such anticipation also appeared in Luke 5:15: "great multitudes came together *to hear,* and *to be healed* by Him of their infirmities." Typically, one is healed by hearing and believing God's revealed Word, so it makes sense that hearing precedes healing in these verses. If I pray for the sick in a setting other than a worship service (where the Word is preached), I usually speak the Word of God to the person before I pray for him. I want to give the person the opportunity to believe in Christ for salvation (if he is not already saved) as well as share Scriptures pertaining to faith and healing so the person has the best opportunity to believe and be healed. Psalm 107:20 says, "He sent His Word and healed them…." Today's church would do well to embrace the proclamation-demonstration model of ministry so that those who attend services would come with great anticipation to hear the powerfully preached Word of God as well as be the beneficiaries of the prayer of faith for healing if they need it. Since our Lord Jesus ministered to the physical and spiritual needs of people, so should the church today.

This text says every sick person was healed. Physically touching Jesus seemed to be especially effective for those who were sick, serving as a contact point conducive to faith. Power went out of Jesus and healed everyone who needed healing. This passage encourages us to lay hands on the sick when we pray for them, as Mark 16:18 advocates. Also, anointing the sick with oil, as James 5:14 and Mark 6:13 advocates, is worthwhile.

Answering the Critics

Healing being linked to the atonement and appropriated by faith is a threat to some people because they despise the idea that if someone is not healed it is because of a lack of faith. Instead of admitting they lack faith and instead of being willing to pursue the faith they lack (perhaps due to laziness, uncertainty as to how to pursue such faith, and pride), they would rather place blame on God and say God did not provide healing as a benefit of the atonement. Thus they reject a wonderful benefit for which Christ died.

Why do some exclude divine healing from the list of covenantal promises that can be rightfully claimed by all believers? Is it because peace, joy, forgiveness, and many of the other covenantal promises are intangible spiritual qualities and benefits and are not verifiable in the way that physical healing is? Perhaps the failure of a person to receive divine physical healing (or a person prays for others to be healed but they are not healed) and the ability to verify such failure, can be threatening to a person. Perhaps certain critics seek to remove divine healing from the promise list so that in their minds they are released from the responsibility to believe for healing.

Luke 7:2-10 And a certain centurion's servant, who was dear to him, was sick and ready to die. (3) So when he heard about Jesus, he sent elders of the Jews to Him, pleading with Him to come and *heal* his servant. (4) And when they came to Jesus, they begged Him earnestly, saying that the one for whom He should do this was deserving, (5) "for he loves our nation, and has built us a synagogue." (6) Then Jesus went with them. And when He was already not far from the house, the centurion sent friends to Him, saying to Him, "Lord, do not trouble Yourself, for I am not worthy that You should enter under my roof. (7) Therefore I did not even think myself worthy to come to You. But say the word, and my servant *will be healed.* (8) For I also am a man placed under authority, having soldiers under me. And I say to one, 'Go,' and he goes; and to another, 'Come,' and he comes; and to my servant, 'Do this,' and he does it." (9) When Jesus heard these things, He marveled at him, and turned around and said to the crowd that followed Him, "I say to you, I have not found such great faith, not even in Israel!" (10) And those who were sent, returning to the house, found the servant *well* who had been sick.

Verse 3 reminds us of the necessary prerequisite for faith—hearing (Rom. 10:17). Had someone not testified of Jesus as the Healer, then the centurion could not have heard nor believed this good news. Today, we should readily preach, teach, and testify to the good news that Jesus is willing and able to forgive sinners who repent and believe in Him, save people from the power of sin, heal those who are sick, deliver people from the devil's oppression, fill believers with the Holy Spirit, and give abundant and eternal life to all who come wholeheartedly to Him.

In verse 4, the Jewish elders spoke as if it were possible to deserve God's blessing—"the one for whom He should do this was deserving." But as Jewish elders, they should have been aware of Old Testament Scriptures like Isaiah 64:6: "But we are all like an unclean thing, and all our righteousnesses are like filthy rags...." The whole of Scripture testifies that if we would receive from God what we deserve, then we would receive eternal punishment. Instead, *every* good and perfect blessing that comes to us is a gift from God (James 1:17), and He gives these gifts to us because He is gracious, merciful, and loving; not because we deserve them.

In contrast to the pride of the Jewish elders, we see the humility of the centurion. Rather than agreeing with them that he was deserving, the centurion said, "I am not worthy that You should enter under my roof" (verse 6). Perhaps he recognized that Jesus (God the Son) is the holy co-Creator of the universe (along with God the Father and God the Holy Spirit), and in comparison to Jesus, the centurion was a wretched sinner not even worthy to stand in His presence. Remember the seraphim of Isaiah 6: they kept their faces and feet covered with their wings while in the presence of the all-holy God as a demonstration of their unworthiness to be in His presence. Likewise, an attitude of humility, reverence, and gratitude should be evident in all of us who would follow the Lord Jesus Christ, who is holy, yet also rich in mercy and grace toward those who trust in Him.

The centurion's words also demonstrated "great faith" in the power and authority of Jesus"—greater faith than anyone in Israel, including the Jewish elders. He believed that Jesus did not even need to be present to heal, but that Jesus could simply "say the word" and his servant would "be healed" (verse 7). All authority in heaven and on earth has been given unto Jesus (Mt. 28:18), so any command spoken by Him cannot be thwarted by any force, whether natural or spiritual. (Please see the Matthew 8:5-13 section in this book for more on Jesus' authority.)

Jesus came with the Jewish elders toward the centurion's house, not because the Jews were so persuasive about the worthiness of the centurion, but because they asked. In John 14:14, Jesus said, "If you *ask anything* in My name, I will do it."

Luke 7:11-17 Now it happened, the day after, that He went into a city called Nain; and many of His disciples went with Him, and a large crowd. (12) And when He came near the gate of the city, behold, a dead man was being carried out, the only son of his mother; and she was a widow. And a large crowd from the city was with her. (13) When the Lord saw her, He had compassion on her and said to her, "Do not weep." (14) Then He came and touched the open coffin, and those who carried him stood still. And He said, "Young man, I say to you, arise." (15) So he who was dead sat up and began to speak. And He presented him to his mother. (16) Then fear came upon all, and they glorified God, saying, "A great prophet has risen up among us"; and, "God has visited His people." (17) And this report about Him went throughout all Judea and all the surrounding region.

Here, we see two large crowds, each of quite a different nature, converging. One crowd has gathered for a funeral procession. The other crowd has gathered to follow Jesus. The cause of one crowd to gather is death. The cause of the other crowd to gather is Life. The disposition of the funeral crowd is weeping, mourning, and despair. The disposition of the crowd following Christ is that of hope and joy because "in His presence is the fullness of joy" (Ps. 16:11).

This scenario can also be seen as a picture of the two possible categories of spiritual condition into which each human fits. One category is the non-Christian category—following the ways of the world. The other category is being a follower of Jesus and thus a member of His church. With regards to morality, the world and the church are going in opposite directions. First John 2:16-17 says: "For all that is in the world—the lust of the flesh, the lust of the eyes, and the pride of life—is not of the Father but is of the world. And the world is passing away...." With respect to morality, the world is spiraling downward; it is "passing away." This reflects the law of entropy—that is, barring outside intervention, everything naturally moves from order to chaos. The law of entropy can be applied to the spiritual aspect of a person—one who has rejected Christ becomes more and more resistant to doing the will of God.[155] The church, conversely, is moving upward morally. Proverbs 15:24a says, "The way of life winds upward for the wise." The church is "being renewed day by day" (2 Cor. 4:16), is being conformed to the image of Jesus (Rom. 8:29), and is progressing "from faith to faith" (Rom. 1:17), "from strength to strength" (Ps. 84:7), and "from glory to glory" (2 Cor. 3:18)! Hallelujah! Is your spiritual journey indicative of such growth? Also, the world and the church are going in opposite directions eternally. Those who die without Christ go from earthly sorrow to infinitely multiplied sorrow as each will experience eternal torment in the lake of fire. Conversely, each member of Christ's church will one day receive a glorified body and live forever in the presence of God in heaven and in the New Jerusalem, where "there shall be no more death, nor sorrow, nor crying...no more pain" (Rev. 21:4). Heaven will include streets of gold, mansions in which to dwell, and varying degrees of treasure for those who served Jesus faithfully on earth.

The main figure of the funeral procession is a woman who had previously lost her husband and now has lost her only son. She is weeping, surely full of despair, and understandably so. The main Figure of the Jesus-following crowd is Jesus Himself, who is the "God of hope" who fills "you with all joy and peace in believing" (Rom. 15:13). When Jesus says to the grieving woman, "Do not weep," it is because He is about to replace her reason for sorrow with reason for great joy. She will soon be able to relate to the words of Psalm 30:11: "You have turned for me my mourning into dancing; you have put off my sackcloth and clothed me with gladness." (See also Isaiah 61:3.)

Verse 13 said that Jesus had compassion for the widow. After all, Jesus is love (1 Jn. 4:8). Because we Christians are called to imitate God (Eph. 5:1), love should be the motive of our hearts as we minister to others. First Corinthians 16:14 says: "Let all that you do be done with love."

Then Jesus, who is "the resurrection and the life" (Jn. 11:25), likely stuns the crowd with His next words: "Young man, I say to you, arise." Suddenly, the corpse comes alive, sits up, and speaks! Then Jesus presents the resurrected son to his mother. Similarly, in Mark 5:41-43, Jesus raises a daughter from the dead in the presence of her parents. In John 11, Jesus resurrects a brother, who had been dead four days, in the presence of his two sisters and many others. "For with God nothing will be impossible" (Lk. 1:37). Furthermore, Jesus is able to reconcile and restore any seemingly dead relationship that one may be experiencing.

As the world and the church are heading in opposite directions morally and eternally, the church should overcome any temptation to conform to the world. Rather the church should demonstrate to the world that the Lord Jesus Christ, who has been bodily raised from the dead, is able to meet every need. Second Corinthians 5:19 says, "God was in Christ reconciling the world to Himself, not imputing their trespasses to them, and has committed to us the word of reconciliation." God has called His church to be the agent of compassion, reconciliation, and healing in the world today.

Answering the Critics

Many people reject that healing is appropriated by faith in the atonement of Jesus. James Grant has responded in this way:

> The question is: What provision is there objectively for a Christian's faith to lay hold of? Such critics seems to be denying that there is any such provision, so that they seems to be leaving it on the basis of whatever will be will be. There must be a basis for faith? Faith has to be faith in something—a promise of God.

I assert that healing is a promise of God which is based on the atoning blood of Christ and is accessed by faith.

Luke 7:20-23 When the men had come to Him, they said, "John the Baptist has sent us to You, saying, 'Are You the Coming One, or do we look for another?'" (21) And that very hour He *cured* many of infirmities, afflictions, and evil spirits; and to many blind He gave sight. (22) Jesus answered and said to them, "Go and tell John the things you have seen and heard: that the blind see, the lame walk, the lepers are cleansed, the deaf hear, the dead are raised, the poor have the gospel preached to them. (23) And blessed is he who is not offended because of Me."

When John the Baptist was in prison, he sent men to Jesus to verify that Jesus was indeed the Messiah. Jesus' reply to John included His listing six results from His ministry, *five of which were specific types of healings* (verse 22). Notice that Jesus mentioned "the things you have seen" before He mentioned (the things you have) "heard," which again points to the fact that witnessing signs and wonders often opens one's heart to believe (Mk. 16:20). "The gospel preached" (verse 22) is the proclamation of the good news "that Christ died for our sins according to the Scriptures, and that He was buried, and that He arose again the third day according to the Scriptures" (1 Cor. 15:3-4); any person who believes in Him (and faith requires repentance) is forgiven and becomes indwelt by the Holy Spirit. "The poor" are specifically mentioned as recipients of the gospel. The poor are less likely to trust in money, their own accomplishments, etc.; thus they are more likely to trust in Christ. Nevertheless the gospel of Jesus Christ is available to all people—rich or poor—to whoever is willing to receive Him (Jn. 3:16).

Luke 8:1-2 Now it came to pass, afterward, that He went through every city and village, preaching and bringing the glad tidings of the kingdom of God. And the twelve were with Him. (2) And certain women who *had been healed* of evil spirits and infirmities—Mary called Magdalene, out of whom had come seven demons, (3) and Joanna the wife of Chuza, Herod's steward, and Susanna, and many others who provided for Him from their substance.

When Mary Magdalene met Jesus, she was possessed by seven demons. But Jesus delivered Mary Magdalene, and the passage implies that Joanna and Susanna had also been delivered of evil spirits and infirmities by Jesus. Then Mary and other women followed Jesus and helped fund His ministry. And God granted Mary the privilege of being the first person to see the resurrected Jesus. This should give hope to each person whose past has been marked by miserable failure—whether morally, spiritually, or in any other way—that through Christ's mercy and power anyone can become a new creation and be productive for the kingdom of God.

Answering the Critics

Some only pray for healing in this manner: "Lord, heal me (or this person) if it is your will." I have a problem with that type of prayer because the one praying has verbalized doubt and/or ignorance concerning God's will. That type of prayer can be a copout. Prayer should be an investment—we should pray in faith that what we are praying is in accordance with God's will (if indeed it is) because we believe we have rightly discerned God's will and so we pray to God boldly and affirmatively. We need to correctly interpret God's Word as well as seek to be led by the Holy Spirit in order to pray according to God's will.

Luke 8:26-39 Then they sailed to the country of the Gadarenes, which is opposite Galilee. (27) And when He stepped out on the land, there met Him a certain man from the city who had demons for a long time. And he wore no clothes, nor did he live in a house but in the tombs. (28) When he saw Jesus, he cried out, fell down before Him, and with a loud voice said, "What have I to do with You, Jesus, Son of the Most High God? I beg You, do not torment me!" (29) For He had commanded the unclean spirit to come out of the man. For it had often seized him, and he was kept under guard, bound with chains and shackles; and he broke the bonds and was driven by the demon into the wilderness. (30) Jesus asked him, saying, "What is your name?" And he said, "Legion," because many demons had entered him. (31) And they begged Him that He would not command them to go out into the abyss. (32) Now a herd of many swine was feeding there on the mountain. So they begged Him that He would permit them to enter them. And He permitted them. (33) Then the demons went out of the man and entered the swine, and the herd ran violently down the steep place into the lake and drowned. (34) When those who fed them saw what had happened, they fled and told it in the city and in the country. (35) Then they went out to see what had happened, and came to Jesus, and found the man from whom the demons had departed, sitting at the feet of Jesus, clothed and in his right mind. And they were afraid. (36) They also who had seen it told them by what means he who had been demon-possessed was healed. (37) Then the whole multitude of the surrounding region of the Gadarenes asked Him to depart from them, for they were seized with great fear. And He got into the boat and returned. (38) Now the man from whom the demons had departed begged Him that he might be with Him. But Jesus sent him away, saying, (39) "Return to your own house, and tell what great things God has done for you." And he went his way and proclaimed throughout the whole city what great things Jesus had done for him.

Jesus came face to face with a man plagued with monumental problems: he was homeless and lived in the tombs; he was naked, and he was socially isolated. But his greatest problem, which was the cause of his other problems, was spiritual—he was in bondage to sin and possessed by many demons. The demons often seized the man, likely triggering seizures and other harmful behavior. The demons gave the man supernatural strength, and this added to his isolation as he was dangerous to others as well as himself. Also, the demons drove the man into the wilderness, away from human contact. That demons "steal, kill, and destroy" (Jn. 10:10a) was evident in the miserable existence of this man.

Upon seeing Jesus, the demons confessed that Jesus is the "Son of the Most High God" (verse 28) and admitted that Jesus has the authority to send them into the abyss at that moment. Certainly, all demons will go to the abyss eventually, as Jesus spoke of an "everlasting fire prepared for the devil and his angels" (Mt. 25:41). But the demons, wanting to delay the execution of their judgment as long as possible and in the meantime wanting to inhabit some host, asked Jesus to let them enter the swine feeding nearby. Jesus permitted them, and they drove the swine into a lake where the swine drowned.

Hearing of the destruction of the swine, many people came out from the city and found the formerly demon-possessed man "sitting at the feet of Jesus, clothed and in his right mind" (verse 35). The people probably knew the severity of this demon-possession case (verse 29), and the eyewitnesses had reported to them the entire event (verse 36). If the Gadarene people were wise, they would have asked Jesus to remain with them and explain to them His ability to heal and cast out demons, and most importantly His identity. Instead, the Gadarenes asked Jesus to leave them; they wanted to maintain the lifestyle they already knew rather than repent and conform to the Lord's ways. This stands in contrast to the formerly demon-possessed man who expressed his desire to remain with Jesus. Therefore, despite this man's horrendous past, he was now in much better shape spiritually than the Gadarene citizens. Jesus sent the man home to testify of God's delivering power and mercy, and the man obeyed. As Jesus delivered this man of demons, thus allowing the man to pursue a productive life, Jesus is also able to deliver anyone today from demonic influence and illnesses.

Testimony—God Uses Evangelist Sumrall to Deliver a Woman from Demons!

In the 1950s, God called Lester and Louise Sumrall to Manila in the Philippines. In Manila there was a seventeen year old female inmate named Clarita Villaneuva who had been charged with vagrancy and was incarcerated in the Bilibid prison. Nightly she screamed saying two demons were attacking and biting her. Each incident might last for hours; she would sometimes foam at the mouth, and then she would lose consciousness. During the day, Clarita would speak sensibly and answer questions, but during the nightly attacks she became uncontrollable. The prison staff would enter her cell during these incidents and physically restrain her; nevertheless bite marks and welts would appear on her body, even in places where she could not possibly have bitten herself. The prison staff put Clarita under twenty-four hour surveillance, and her story received much media attention. Lester received permission from the mayor's office to go to the prison to pray for Clarita. His prayers for her took place over a two day period and occurred in the presence of prison staff and newspaper reporters. Initially, Clarita (or the demons in her) cursed him, God, and the blood of Jesus. But Lester continued to quote the Word of God and pray in Jesus' name for the demons to leave. The first day, Lester prayed for her from 9:00 a.m. until noon, and then left the prison to fast and pray. That night, Clarita was not attacked by the demons. Lester returned the next day and asked all the prison officials who were at her cell to kneel as he prayed, and they obliged him. Lester again commanded the demons to leave in Jesus' name, and within a few minutes, Clarita broke into a peaceful smile. He explained to Clarita that she had power through the blood of Jesus to submit to God, resist the devil herself, and then the devil would have to leave. (One account said the demons attacked her that night, but she commanded them to leave in Jesus' name. The demons left and never returned.) The prison doctor was amazed and admitted that had not believed in anything supernatural until he witnessed Clarita's deliverance. Soon thereafter, Clarita served out of prison, eventually got married, had children, and apparently lived a peaceful Christian life. The story of Clarita's deliverance received significant media attention which God used to open the hearts of the people of Manila to the gospel. Lester held revival services in Manila for six weeks. Nightly attendance reportedly swelled to 60,000, and in one night 5,000 people prayed to receive Christ! In those meetings a famous actor who had not been able to walk was healed. Also, a lawyer who walked with crutches for twelve years was healed—he walked out of the meeting holding his crutches. Those miracles boosted the media coverage of the Sumrall ministry even more. It is estimated that 150,000 souls were saved over those six weeks![156] So the healing of one opened the door for mass evangelism.

Luke 8:41–56 And behold, there came a man named Jairus, and he was a ruler of the synagogue. And he fell down at Jesus' feet and begged Him to come to his house, (42) for he had an only daughter about twelve years of age, and she was dying. But as He went, the multitudes thronged Him. (43) Now a woman, having a flow of blood for twelve years, who had spent all her livelihood on physicians and *could not be healed* by any, (44) came from behind and touched the border of His garment. And immediately her flow of blood stopped. (45) And Jesus said, "Who touched Me?" When all denied it, Peter and those with him said, "Master, the multitudes throng and press You, and You say, 'Who touched Me?'" (46) But Jesus said, "Somebody touched Me, for I perceived *power* going out from Me." (47) Now when the woman saw that she was not hidden, she came trembling; and falling down before Him, she declared to Him in the presence of all the people the reason she had touched Him and how she *was healed* immediately. (48) And He said to her, "Daughter, be of good cheer; *your faith has made you well.* Go in peace." (49) While He was still speaking, someone came from the ruler of the synagogue's house, saying to him, "Your daughter is dead. Do not trouble the Teacher." (50) But when Jesus heard it, He answered him, saying, "Do not be afraid; only believe, and she *will be made well.*" (51) When He came into the house, He permitted no one to go in except Peter, James, and John, and the father and mother of the girl. (52) Now all wept and mourned for her; but He said, "Do not weep; she is not dead, but sleeping." (53) And they ridiculed Him, knowing that she was dead. (54) But He put them all outside, took her by the hand and called, saying, "Little girl, arise." (55) Then her spirit returned, and she arose immediately. And He commanded that she be given something to eat. (56) And her parents were astonished, but He charged them to tell no one what had happened.

Jairus, ruler of the synagogue, was a man of prominence. Yet, Jairus set aside any pride stemming from his position and he humbled himself before Jesus ("he fell down at Jesus' feet"). He begged Jesus to come to his house because his daughter was dying. Jesus complied with Jairus' request, as Jesus healed everyone in the gospels who asked Him for healing.

Among the multitudes following Jesus was a woman who had "a flow of blood for twelve years." She had spent all her money on doctors with the hope of being healed. But the doctors failed her, so she turned to Jesus. Psalm 118:8 says, "It is better to trust in the LORD than to put confidence in man." (See also Ps. 60:11.)

This woman showed determination. She pressed through the crowd and touched the garment of Jesus despite her weakened physical condition, despite the presence of a crowd between her and Jesus, and despite the Levitical law that deemed her unclean and thus unfit to touch others (Lev. 15:25-31). Though many people were touching Jesus at that moment (verse 45), this woman's touch was distinguished from the rest. Her touch drew power from Jesus and into her body and captured His attention. Although the power of Jesus healed her, Jesus was not even aware of who had touched Him and received healing. In verse 47, when the healed woman fell down before Jesus (as Jairus had done) and testified to what had occurred, Jesus credited *her faith* as the reason she was healed. If she had no faith, she would have had a powerless touch like everyone else in the crowd who touched Jesus, and she would not have been healed.

As Jesus was speaking with the woman, a messenger from Jairus' house brought news to Jairus of his daughter's death. Then the messenger added his own opinion to the facts; he said, "Do not trouble the Teacher." Apparently, the messenger erroneously thought that resurrecting Jairus' daughter from the dead was beyond Jesus' ability. The messenger did not know that Jesus is Almighty God (Rev. 1:8). Nevertheless, Jesus countered the negative words by saying to Jairus, "Do not be afraid; only believe, and she will be made well." Jesus guaranteed Jairus that if he would have faith, then Jesus would raise Jairus' daughter from the dead. Jairus had a choice to make: to believe Jesus or not to believe Jesus. Faith is a revelatory gift from God (James 1:17). Nevertheless, we have the responsibility to participate with God in His redemptive work by choosing to believe His Word and demonstrating our faith through our actions.

In verse 51, Jesus placed restrictions on who could be in the room. He allowed his three closest disciples and the parents of the girl to be present. The text doesn't say why Jesus did this, but two reasons come to mind. One, putting the ridiculers and doubters outside would prevent an atmosphere of doubt. Two, Jesus wanted to keep the miracle of the girls' resurrection a secret, as verse 56 mentions, so that Jesus' popularity would not get out of hand and undermine His mission. But Jesus was willing to risk public awareness of the miracle because of His compassion for Jairus' family. In verse 54, Jesus took the girl by the hand

and commanded her to "arise." She "immediately" arose, just as the woman with the flow of blood was "immediately" healed! Hallelujah!

Part of the Meaning of "Salvation"

The Greek word for "save" is *sosei* (from *sozo*), which, according to the New Strong's Exhaustive Concordance, means "heal, preserve, save (self), do well, be (make) whole."[157] To increase our understanding of *sozo*, we can look at four instances of its use in Luke 8. *Sozo* first appears in Jesus' explanation of the parable of the sower. He says, "Those by the wayside are the ones who hear; then the devil comes and takes away the word out of their hearts, lest they should believe and be *saved*" (Lk. 8:12). Its second appearance is in the account of the exorcism of the Gadarene man who had been possessed by many demons. Verse 36 says: "They also who had seen it told them by what means he who had been demon-possessed was *healed*" (Lk. 8:36). Its third appearance is in the account of the woman with the issue of blood being healed. Jesus says to her, "Your faith has made you *well*" (Lk. 8:48). Its fourth appearance is when Jesus said to Jairus, "Only believe, and she will be made *well*" (Lk. 8:50). In the four accounts listed above, the italicized word is a form of *sozo*. So in Luke 8, we see that being saved includes: deliverance from demonic possession, divine healing, and resurrection from death. (You can learn more about salvation if you look at other places in the New Testament where *sozo* appears. It is used over ninety-five times.) Biblical salvation, which is holistic—benefitting spirit, soul, and body, can only come through faith in Jesus Christ. [Some form of the word "faith" (*pisteuo*) appears in three of the four passages: verse 12 "believe"; verse 48 "faith"; verse 50 "believe."] Salvation includes being delivered from sin and many of the negative effects of sin, including bondage or oppression of a physical, emotional, spiritual, or even financial nature. First Thessalonians 5:23b affirms this concept of holistic salvation: "and may your *whole spirit, soul, and body* be preserved blameless at the coming of our Lord Jesus Christ." (Third John 2 also supports this concept.) Our gracious God is concerned about our entire being.

Luke 9:1-2, 6, 10-11 Then He called His twelve disciples together and gave them power and authority over all demons, and to *cure* diseases. (2) He sent them to *preach* the kingdom of God and to *heal* the sick....(6) So they departed and went through the towns, *preaching* the gospel and

Jesus Heals Today!

healing everywhere.....(10) And the apostles, when they had returned, told Him all that they had done. Then He took them and went aside privately into a deserted place belonging to the city called Bethsaida. (11) But when the multitudes knew it, they followed Him; and He received them and spoke to them about the kingdom of God, and *healed* those who had need of *healing.*

Was this power (Gk.—*dunamin*) and authority (Gk.—*exusian*) over demons and disease available for the original disciples only, or is it available for all believers? The twelve did not have special access to the authority and benefits of Jesus that the rest of us Christians cannot have. We should not exalt the original disciples to a status of elitism.[158] Spiritually speaking, our power and authority does not come from our occupying a particular church office, such as being an apostle; our power and authority come from our union with Christ. In John 15:7, Jesus says, "If you abide in Me, and My words abide in you, you will ask what you will desire, and it shall be done for you." (See also Mark 16:17-18.)

Verses 2 and 6 support the proclamation-demonstration model of evangelism I described in Chapter 1. We also see that the disciples "went through the towns"—intentionally taking the message and power of the gospel to the people, where they were concentrated. When the apostles returned from "preaching the gospel and healing everywhere" (verse 6), they testified to Jesus and to one another of the many miracles they performed in His name (See John 14:12.). What an exciting and encouraging time that must have been. Then Jesus took the disciples to a deserted area, probably so they could rest. Nevertheless, the multitudes sought Him and found Him. And though Jesus probably preferred rest over ministry at that point, He set aside His desires and graciously received them and ministered to them. As Luke 5:15 and 6:17 say that great multitudes came to Jesus both to hear Him and to be healed by Him, here again Jesus spoke the Word of God to them and "healed those who had need of healing." (This last phrase indicates that Jesus healed *all* who were sick.)

Luke 9:38-43 Suddenly a man from the multitude cried out, saying, "Teacher, I implore You, look on my son, for he is my only child. (39) And behold, a spirit seizes him, and he suddenly cries out; it convulses him so that he foams at the mouth, and it departs from him with great difficulty, bruising him. (40) So I implored Your disciples to cast it out, but they could not." (41) Then Jesus answered and said, "O faithless and perverse generation, how long shall I be with you and bear with

❧ 247 ☙

you? Bring your son here." (42) And as he was still coming, the demon threw him down and convulsed him. Then Jesus rebuked the unclean spirit, *healed* the child, and gave him back to his father. (43) And they were all amazed at the majesty of God.

While sleeping at night, I had a dream of two huge water moccasins coming out of the water and wrapping around a man sitting nearby. I yelled to the man, "Don't you know those are poisonous snakes?" Then I awoke. I realized my wife, Kim, may have been under spiritual attack, as she was sleeping beside me. I quickly awakened Kim. She was thankful I did because she was having a horrible demonically-inspired dream. I prayed for her, and she slept fine.

We see the principle of asking and receiving and the principle of intercession (standing in the gap) as a man approached Jesus and asked Him to heal his son who was victimized by a demon. In verse 42, Jesus "rebuked the unclean spirit" and "healed the child." When we pray for someone to be healed, we should be mindful that a demon or demons may be causing or contributing to the infirmity; that may affect how we pray. Because of His disciples' failure to cast out the demon, Jesus referred to His disciples, and to the generation as a whole, as "faithless" and "perverse." Conversely, today's church needs to be faith-filled and holy. If a parent comes to our church requesting us cast the demon out of his or her child, through faith in Christ we should be able to do so.

Luke 10:1, 9, 17-19 After these things the Lord appointed seventy others also, and sent them two by two before His face into every city and place where He Himself was about to go. (2) Then He said to them, "...(9) And *heal* the sick there, and *say* to them, 'The kingdom of God has come near to you.'" (17) Then the seventy returned with joy, saying, "Lord, even the demons are subject to us in Your name." (18) And He said to them, "I saw Satan fall like lightning from heaven. (19) Behold, I give you the authority to trample on serpents and scorpions, and over all the power of the enemy, and nothing shall be any means hurt you."

Jesus commissions the seventy with instructions similar to those which He gave the twelve in Luke 9: to "say," or preach, "the kingdom of God has come near to you," and to "heal the sick there." So again, Jesus utilizes the proclamation-demonstration model of evangelism.

After the seventy had returned from their mission, Jesus spoke to them of the authority He was giving them from that moment forward. Authority is delegated power.[159] Jesus is the Power behind the believer's authority over demonic spirits and infirmities (see also Luke 9:1). If we abide in Jesus, then Jesus is backing us. In verse 19, Jesus did not say, "I gave you authority," but "I give you authority"—an ongoing authority. Jesus exhorted the seventy *to continue* exercising the authority that was theirs from that time forward. He placed no restrictions of time or place upon the authority and divine protection that He gave the believers. Therefore, we Christians can rightfully lay claim to Luke 10:19 today.[160]

Luke 10:19 is a virtual paraphrase of portions of Psalm 91. Psalm 91:10 says, "No evil shall be befall you, nor shall any plague come near your dwelling." This is similar to the latter portion of Luke 10:19—"nothing shall by any means hurt you." Psalm 91:13 says, "You shall tread upon the lion and the cobra, the young lion and the serpent you shall trample underfoot." This relates to having "*authority* to trample on serpents and scorpions, and over all the power of the enemy" (Lk. 10:19). Even in the Old Testament, believers had spiritual authority when certain conditions mentioned in Psalm 91 were met. Such conditions include: you must dwell "in the secret place of the Most High" (verse 1); you must make the LORD your refuge in whom you trust (verses 2, 9); you must "set...(your) love upon" the LORD (verse 14a); you must know the LORD's name (verse 14b).

Psalm 91 also speaks specifically of freedom from physical sickness. The derivative Hebrew word for pestilence used in verses 3 and 6—*deber*—means "that which destroys."[161] It appears in Deuteronomy 28:21, "The LORD will make the *plague* (KJV: pestilence) cling to you...." Deuteronomy 28:22 lists examples of the plague/pestilence (*deber*): consumption, fever, inflammation, severe burning fever, scorching, and mildew.[162] But "Christ has redeemed us from the curse of the law, having became a curse for us" (Gal. 3:13)! Christ has redeemed us from the curse of disease.

Luke 13:10-18 Now He was teaching in one of the synagogues on the Sabbath. (11) And behold, there was a woman who had a spirit of infirmity eighteen years, and was bent over and could in no way raise herself up.(12) But when Jesus saw her, He called her to Him and said to her, "Woman, you are loosed from your infirmity." (13) And He laid His hands on her, and immediately *she was made straight*, and glorified God. (14) But the ruler of the synagogue answered with indignation, because *Jesus had healed* on the Sabbath; and he said to the crowd, "There are six days on which men ought to work; therefore come and *be healed* on them, and not on the Sabbath day." (15) The Lord then answered him and said, "Hypocrite! Does not each one of you on the Sabbath loose his ox or donkey from the stall, and lead it away to water it? (16)

So ought not this woman, being a daughter of Abraham, whom Satan has bound—think of it—for eighteen years, be loosed from this bond on the Sabbath?" (17) And when He said these things, all His adversaries were put to shame; and all the multitude rejoiced for all the glorious things that were done by Him.

This woman's infirmity, which caused her to be continuously bent over for eighteen years, was caused by "a spirit of infirmity" (verse 11). A spirit of infirmity is a demonic spirit whose intent is to make one physically ill. Jesus affirmed that the spirit of infirmity was demonic in nature as He referenced Satan in verse 16 as the one behind the woman's bondage. This is another example of demons being linked to disease (Acts 10:38).

Jesus employed the laying on of hands method as well as the word of command to heal the woman. Her healing was immediate and complete, and it caused her to glorify God. Also, "all the multitude rejoiced" for this healing and the other miracles performed by Jesus (verse 17). Likewise, any blessing we receive from the Lord should cause us to rejoice and give Him praise and thanks.

However, the ruler of the synagogue did not rejoice nor display any amazement at this wonderful miracle. Perhaps he felt threatened by the power and popularity of Jesus. Religious leaders should be an example to the church and community of what it means to love and humbly serve God and others. However, sometimes an individual is put in a position of religious leadership due to certain natural abilities he has (or even for political reasons), and sufficient attention has not been given as to whether or not the individual humbly walks with Jesus and bears His fruit (Gal. 5:22-23). Others in religious leadership may have initially walked with God, but as time passed they allowed pride to come in. If such pride goes unchecked, the individual will experience some sort of fall, and consequently the organization he or she leads will also suffer loss (Prov. 16:18).

The synagogue ruler's misguided legalism hindered any compassion he should have had for the woman. Along with humility, a religious leader should be compassionate and merciful. Matthew 9:13 and Hosea 6:6 both say: "I desire mercy and not sacrifice." Due to the synagogue ruler's protest in verse 14, Jesus called him a hypocrite in front of the crowd. Jesus' reasoning was something like this: "You loose your animals from the stall to drink on the Sabbath, but you condemn Me because I loosed a daughter of Abraham from a demon of infirmity on the Sabbath!" Jesus' healing of the woman and His wise words caused his popularity to rise even more, while His opponents were publicly shamed, and thus angered even more.

Like this woman, maybe you have felt crippled, crooked, broken, or bound by the enemy. Maybe you have also been hurt by the hypocrisy of certain church leaders, and their pride has been a stumbling block to you. No matter what injuries have befallen you, please know that Jesus can touch you, loose you, heal you, causing the crooked places to become straight! Jesus has come to set the captives free! (Lk. 4:18).

Luke 14:1-6 Now it happened, as He went into the house of one of the rulers of the Pharisees to eat bread on the Sabbath, that they watched Him closely. (2) And behold, there was a certain man before Him who had dropsy. (3) And Jesus, answering, spoke to the lawyers and Pharisees, saying, "Is it lawful *to heal* on the Sabbath?" (4) But they kept silent. And He took him and *healed him*, and let him go. (5) Then He answered them, saying, "Which of you, having a donkey or an ox that has fallen into a pit, will not immediately pull him out on the Sabbath day? (6) And they could not answer Him regarding these things.

A man was present who had dropsy—a condition of swelling in the body due to excess water build-up. The Pharisees, who were hosting Jesus for a meal, would be critical of Jesus if He were to heal on the Sabbath. According to their man-made rules, healing on the Sabbath would be considered work and thus forbidden. When Jesus asked them if it was lawful to heal on the Sabbath, they remained silent. Jesus healed the man, affirming that it is lawful to heal on the Sabbath. Then Jesus pointed out their hypocrisy. They would save the life of one of their farm animals on the Sabbath, yet they criticized Jesus for healing a human being (made in the image of God, and much more valuable than any animal) on the Sabbath.

Based on these last two passages, Luke 13:10-18 and Luke 14:1-6, you should not be surprised if religious leaders criticize you for pursuing a healing ministry. Pursue it anyway.

Luke 17:11-19 Now it happened as He went to Jerusalem that He passed through the midst of Samaria and Galilee. (12) Then as He entered a certain village, there met Him ten men who were lepers, who stood afar off. (13) And they lifted up their voices and said, "Jesus, Master, have mercy on us!" (14) So when He saw them, He said to them, "Go, show yourselves to the priests." And so it was that as they went, *they were cleansed*. (15) And one of them, when he saw that *he was healed*, returned, and with a loud voice glorified God, (16) and fell down on his face at His feet, giving Him thanks. And he was a Samaritan. (17) So Jesus answered and said, "Were there not ten *cleansed*? But where are the nine? (18) Were there not any found who returned to give glory to God except this foreigner?" (19) And He said to him, "Arise, go your way. Your faith *has made you well.*"

The ten lepers employed the principle of asking and receiving (Mt. 7:7). They asked Jesus to show them mercy and heal them. Jesus instructed the lepers to go and show themselves to the priests in accordance with the Mosaic Law (Lev. 13; Deut. 24:8; Mt. 8:4). Their healings would serve as a testimony to the priests that Jesus is the ultimate High Priest (Heb. 9:11). The lepers' obedience to Jesus' instruction played a necessary role in their being healed—verse 14 says, "as they went, they were cleansed." The necessity of obedience in order to receive healing is also seen in the account of the healing of Namaan the Syrian who also had leprosy (2 Kings 5). As Namaan obeyed the Word of God through Elisha the prophet by dipping seven times in the Jordan River, he was instantly healed. Today's church should obey the word of God in James 5:14-16 and anoint the sick with oil and pray the prayer of faith.

All ten lepers were healed, but only one returned to worship and thank Jesus, and he was not an Israelite. Jesus expressed disappointment in the nine who did not return to give God glory, but He commended the one, saying, "Your faith has made you well." The healed man demonstrated faith in several ways: by *asking* Jesus to heal him, in his *obedience* to Jesus' command to go and show himself to the priests, and in his returning *to thank Jesus* and *to fall on his face at Jesus' feet* indicating his submission to Jesus' lordship. As the King James Version says of verse 19, "thy faith hath made thee *whole*," this pronouncement of wholeness, or wellness, by Jesus also included forgiveness of the man's sins. In verse 19, *well* (KJV—*whole*) comes from the Greek word *sozo*. For more on the meaning of *sozo*, see my commentary on Luke 8 found earlier in this chapter.

Luke 18:35-43 Then it happened, as He was coming near Jericho, that a certain blind man sat by the road begging. (36) And hearing a multitude passing by, he asked what it meant. (37) So they told him that Jesus of Nazareth was passing by. (38) And he cried out, saying, "Jesus, Son of David, have mercy on me!" (39) Then those who went before warned him that he should be quiet; but he cried out all the more, "Son of David, have mercy on me!" (40) So Jesus stood still and commanded him to be brought to Him. And when he had come near,

He asked him, (41) saying, "What do you want Me to do for you?" He said, "Lord, that I may receive my sight." (42) Then Jesus said to him, "Receive your sight; *your faith has made you well.*" (43) And immediately he received his sight, and followed Him, glorifying God. And all the people, when they saw it, gave praise to God.

This blind man had apparently heard about Jesus' amazing healing ministry, that He healed "every sickness and every disease among the people" (Mt. 9:35). Thus, when the blind man realized that Jesus was in the vicinity, he "cried out" to Jesus, asking for "mercy." And in accordance with the principle of asking and receiving, here again Jesus stops what He is doing to attend to the one requesting His help. Psalm 34:6 says, "This poor man cried out, and the LORD heard him, and saved him out of all his troubles." Similarly, we who are needy ought to cry out to our merciful Lord Jesus who is the gracious Supplier of all our needs (1 Sam. 1:10-11; Psalm 23:1; Phil. 4:19), for "He is not far from each one of us" (Acts 17:27).

A notable quality of the blind man was his determination. When others tried to prevent him from crying out to Jesus, he did not succumb to the peer pressure but he "cried out all the more." He refused to be deterred in his pursuit of Jesus' healing touch (see also Luke 18:1-8).

Though it was obvious that the man was blind and desired to see, still Jesus asked him, "What do you want me to do for you?" Jesus wanted the man to be specific in his request. Likewise, we should be specific in our prayer requests to God. For example, if the Lord leads you to pray for a wife, you could mention in your prayers certain qualities that you would like in a wife. You could specify each virtue spoken of in Proverbs 31:10-31 (the virtuous wife passage). You should also ask the Lord to make you a genuine man of God, one who will love his wife as Christ loved the church (Eph. 5:25).

Jesus healed the man's eyes. (In verse 42—"has made you well" is rendered by the KJV—"hath saved thee." These verbs come from Greek word *sozo*.) When the man was healed, he followed Jesus. Likely, this is because he correctly believed that everything else he would ever need, especially eternal life, would be supplied by Jesus (Phil 4:19). His following Jesus stands in contrast to nine of the ten lepers whom Jesus healed that did not return to thank Jesus. The healed man glorified God, and all the people who witnessed the miracle likewise joined in praise to God.

Luke 22:49-51 When those around Him saw what was going to happen, they said to Him, "Lord, shall we strike with the sword?" (50) And one of them struck the servant of the high priest and cut off his right ear. (51) But Jesus answered and said, "Permit even this." And He touched his ear and *healed* him.

The Lord Jesus displayed great mercy here as He healed a man who was among those arresting Him. This is along the lines of loving one's enemies (Mt. 5:44) and overcoming evil with good (Rom. 12:21), which Jesus commands each of us to do. Jesus perfectly modeled such love and mercy when He, from the cross, forgave those who were mocking and murdering Him.

Jesus employed the laying on of hands method of healing here. Perhaps he took the ear that had fallen to the ground and reattached it to its proper place and all of the blood vessels, nerves, and skin that had been severed also reattached and began working properly. This miracle must have amazed all who were present. Nevertheless, the guards went through with their arrest of Jesus, and perhaps some of them were even involved in His crucifixion. So we cannot say that people will always repent and believe the gospel just because they witness an undeniable miracle. Still, we are called to emulate the works of Jesus, which includes healing the sick in His name, for many *will* believe when they see (Jn. 4:48).

Chapter 13

The Baptism in the Holy Spirit

"...you shall be baptized with the Holy Spirit not many days from now." (spoken by Jesus, Acts 1:5b)

Testimony of My Reception of the Baptism in the Holy Spirit

In January 1993, I took a seminary course in American church history, which covered a period from 1865 to the present. When the professor reached the era of the Azuza Street Revival in Los Angeles (which began on April 14, 1906 and lasted about nine years) and the emergence of Pentecostalism, I felt a strong spiritual "stirring" inside of me. From this inner witness, I interpreted that the Pentecostal believers possessed something, or rather Someone, whom I had not yet fully experienced. A student in my class, Jeff, who was a minister at an Assemblies of God church in Louisville, encouraged me to pursue speaking in tongues. Because the New Testament advocates speaking in tongues (e.g., in 1 Corinthians 14:5a, Paul wrote, "I wish you all spoke with tongues"), and because it seemed logical that speaking in tongues would mean my having a deeper experience of God (which was what I wanted and for what I had earnestly prayed), I told Jeff I wanted to speak in tongues right away. Jeff asked me to read a particular book on speaking in tongues. I quickly read through some of the pages, and then I went to Jeff's room and said, "I'm ready; I don't want to wait any longer." Jeff told me that he would lay his hands on me and he would speak in tongues. He told me not to wait for an unusual feeling to come over me, but simply to speak. When I heard Jeff speaking in tongues, I instantly began speaking syllables which sounded similar to what he was saying. This went on for perhaps ten minutes, and during that time I did not feel anything unusual. But when I left Jeff's room and began walking down the hall, I became overwhelmed with the wonderful presence of the Lord—like a cloud of glory coming upon me! I was absolutely amazed at this intense manifestation of God—something I had never experienced before—and I spent much time in my room that night worshipping the King of the Universe who had enveloped me. After that evening, I would speak in tongues by myself but I did not feel the presence of God as I did that first time. Jeff left seminary shortly after that experience, so I quit speaking in tongues altogether. I should not have given up so easily. I should have continued to pray in tongues with others who were more experienced with that gift.

A few years later, a lady who attended a Louisville church, Eagle's Nest International, visited a home Bible Study that I attended. She invited my housemate, Scott, and me to Eagle's Nest to receive "the baptism in the Holy Spirit" and to speak in tongues. I was excited at the prospect of speaking in tongues again. Scott was open to speaking in tongues though he had never done so before. Our plan was that Scott would attend Eagle's Nest on Sunday night while I remained at our church, North 42nd Street Baptist Church, to teach the youth, and then I would go to Eagle's Nest on Wednesday night while Scott would teach the youth. That Sunday night, as I was wrapping up the youth service, the words "Holy Spirit" began to prominently flash over and over in my mind. The experience was much more than some fleeting thought; it was a revelation to me that Scott was encountering God in a dramatic way. When Scott returned home from Eagle's Nest, he said the Holy Spirit fell on him in a way more powerful than he had ever experienced. That night, Scott, in his zeal for God, threw all his secular CDs in the trash; he wanted to glorify God with his material possessions (1 Cor. 10:31). In subsequent worship services, Scott would raise his hands in praise (1 Tim. 2:8); I don't recall Scott doing that before. Scott was on-fire for the Lord, and I was thrilled to see him that way. On the following Wednesday (the day I was to visit Eagle's Nest), as I drove home from the seminary, once again the words "Holy Spirit" began to flash in my mind causing me to be filled with anticipation that God would also wonderfully visit me. That night at Eagle's Nest, it seemed that every worshipper (of the eighty or so people gathered there) were completely enthralled in the worship of God—raising their hands toward heaven with wholehearted zeal. I do not think I had ever seen such hunger and love for God displayed by a group of people. After the sermon, the preacher invited anyone who desired to be prayed for to come to the altar. I wanted to respond to this invitation, but the Lord did not release me to do so. While I was waiting upon the Lord, someone began singing a song, the words of which spoke of recommitting one's life to God. So I recommitted my life to God, and then I felt a release to go forward. I told a lady at the altar that I wanted to receive the baptism in the Holy Spirit and speak in tongues. The lady invited two other ladies to assist her in praying with me. They instructed me to step out and speak syllables given by the Holy Spirit, and that they would be doing the same, and I should not wait for a feeling to manifest before I begin speaking. The ladies laid hands on me and they began speaking in tongues. Immediately, I began emulating the sounds I heard from them. Initially, I felt nothing. But after about ninety seconds, my abdomen began to quiver. The quivering became intense. Suddenly, a mighty surge of power shot throughout my entire body, which I humbly describe as divine electricity—I was filled with the Holy Spirit! (Acts 2:4; Acts 9:17; Eph. 5:18). I was being visited by God in a way that was perhaps the most wonderful feeling I had ever had. (Certainly we are not saved by our feelings, but we are saved by the One whom we feel.) One preacher describes the baptism in the Holy Spirit as "liquid love." That is fitting because I uncharacteristically began hugging those around me though they were total strangers. The presence of God rested on me like a cloud all that night, and to a lesser degree for the next four or so days. I possessed an intense love and zeal for God, and wanted to share it with friends. At seminary, I began telling others about this tongues phenomenon and the baptism in the Holy Spirit, but most were leery of what I shared. I quickly learned to use discernment as to when to share about my Spirit baptism. One Baptist friend of mine, Ken, agreed to "check out" a Pentecostal service with me. During the altar time, as the minister laid hands on several people and they were being touched by God, Ken skeptically looked on from the pew. Then Ken read a verse that spoke to him—Mark 9:24b, "Lord, I believe; help my unbelief!" He approached the altar and said in the pastor's hearing, "Lord, I believe; help my unbelief." When the pastor laid hands on Ken, he was instantly filled with the Holy Spirit and began jumping up and down and praising God (very uncharacteristic of Ken). Later in that service, Ken testified to the church that the Christians he knew needed what this church had—Holy Spirit power! Acts 1:8 says, "But you shall receive *power* when the Holy Spirit has come upon you...." Also, 1 Corinthians 4:20 says, "For the kingdom of God is not in word but in *power.*"

After I received the baptism in the Holy Spirit, I was on-fire for the Lord (and I still am). The Word of God inside me had to come out. One day, I went to the Galleria Mall in downtown Louisville to preach the gospel outside the mall's entrance during peak hours. While preaching, a man stopped me and asked if I would talk to his friend standing nearby—a lady trying to cope with some personal struggles. I was able to share the Word of God with both of them. On another occasion when I preached at the mall, two homeless men stopped me and asked for money. I took them to a local restaurant, bought them a meal, and shared the Word of God with them. I was thankful that the Lord honored my willingness to publicly preach, and in both cases He opened the door for me to minister His Word on a more intimate level.

The Holy Spirit Upon and Within

Let's look at passages where the Holy Spirit comes *upon* various individuals in the Old Testament. Judges 14:6 says of Sampson: "And *the Spirit of the LORD came mightily upon him*, and he tore the lion apart as one would have torn apart a young goat...." Again, 1 Samuel 10:10 says of King Saul: "And when they came there to the hill, there was a group of prophets to meet him; and *the Spirit of God came upon him*, and he prophesied among them." Again, Ezekiel 11:5 says: "Then *the Spirit of the Lord fell upon me*, and said to me, 'Speak!...'" (See also Judg. 14:19, 15:13-15, 1 Sam. 19:20, 1 Kgs. 18:46, 2 Chr. 15:1-2, and

2 Chr. 24:20 for similar examples of the Spirit of God coming _upon_ people.) The Holy Spirit came _upon_ Old Testament saints to empower them to achieve God's purposes. For example, Sampson would become amazingly strong, King Saul and Ezekiel would prophesy, and Elisha would outrun Ahab's chariot.

The Holy Spirit could not come _within_ Old Testament saints in the same way that is expressed in the New Testament because old covenant believers could not be born again (spiritually regenerated) the way new covenant believers are. But the Holy Spirit can come _upon_ new covenant believers for power. For example, Acts 1:8 says, "But you shall receive power when the Holy Spirit has come _upon_ you; and you shall be witnesses to Me...." Also, concerning the Holy Spirit coming upon Jesus, we know that Jesus never had to be born again because He was never lost. Yet, Matthew 3:16 says of Jesus: "The heavens were opened to Him, and He saw the Spirit of God descending like a dove and alighting _upon_ Him." The Holy Spirit came _upon_ Jesus as an endowment of power, equipping Him at the very beginning of His public ministry which lasted three and one-half years.

Let's look at Scriptural references of the Holy Spirit being _in_ or _within_ the Christian? Prophesying of the new birth of the new covenant, Ezekiel writes: "I will give you a new heart and put a _new spirit within you_; I will take the heart of stone out of your flesh and give you a heart of flesh. I will put _My Spirit within_ you and cause you to walk in My statutes, and you will keep My judgments and do them" (Ez. 36:26-27). Again, 1 Corinthians 3:6 says: "Do you not know that you are the temple of God and that _the Spirit of God dwells in you._" Again, 1 Corinthians 6:19 says: "Or do you not know that your body is the temple of _the Holy Spirit who is in you,_ whom you have from God, and you are not your own?" Again, Colossians 1:27 says: "_Christ in you_, the hope of glory." Again, 1 John 4:4 says: "Greater is _He who is in you_ that he who is in the world." These verses indicate that the Holy Spirit comes _in_ or _within_ the new covenant believer, and this happens the moment one believes the gospel of Jesus Christ (and repentance is inherent to believing). One is not saved if one does not have the Holy Spirit residing _within_ (Rom. 8:9b).

We have seen two functions of the Holy Spirit mentioned in this section: 1) The Spirit coming _upon_ a person for power (This was available in the old covenant and is also available in the new covenant, but it is not required for salvation.); 2) the Spirit coming *within* or *in* the believer, which occurs at the moment one is born again (This is available for new covenant believers only.) Let me illustrate. If you drink a glass of water, then the water is *in* you. If you then jump in a swimming pool, the water is also *upon* you, or covering you. The water has not changed in essence; it simply has two different functions. Similarly, the Holy Spirit (who does not change) comes *in* at the moment of salvation, and the Holy Spirit may also come *upon* for power. These two functions may occur very closely together as at Cornelius' house (Acts 10:44-46), or there can be a significant span of time between the two occurrences (e.g. Jn. 20:22 and Acts 2:4; Acts 8:12 and Acts 8:17). Also, the believer may never receive the baptism in the Holy Spirit. Another illustration of these two functions of the Holy Spirit is that of a Christian worship service. All of the Christians in the worship service have the Holy Spirit *in* them. But as they wholeheartedly worship the Lord, they may experience the Holy Spirit descend *upon* them in a special way.

If I invite a friend named Scott to come to my house, and he comes, then all of Scott is in my house. Scott is a mechanic, but I do not invite him to work on my car. Scott is a cook, but I do not invite him into my kitchen to cook. Scott is a repair man, but I do not invite Scott to fix my table. All of Scott is in my house, but I do not take advantage of all of his abilities. Similarly, when one is born again—thus the Holy Spirit comes to reside within the believer, the believer does not receive only a portion of the Holy Spirit. The Holy Spirit cannot be divided; the entire Person of the Holy Spirit comes to live inside the believer at regeneration. The Holy Spirit has many gifts, one or more of which are for my use. Speaking in tongues is one of the gifts available for me (1 Cor. 14:5), but if I want to operate in tongues, I should invite the Holy Spirit to make this gift operational in me, and desire and pursue this gift (1 Cor. 14:1).

In John 4 and John 7, Jesus describes the Holy Spirit as living water. In John 4 He said, "Whoever drinks of this water will thirst again, but whoever drinks of the water that I shall give him (living water, verse 10) will never thirst. But the water that I shall give him will become in him a fountain of water springing up into everlasting life" (verses 13-14). In John 7, Jesus said, "'If anyone thirsts, let him come to Me and drink. He who believes in Me, as the Scripture has said, out of his heart will flow rivers of living water.'" But this He spoke concerning the Spirit, whom those believing in Him would receive; for the Holy Spirit was not yet given; because Jesus was not yet glorified" (verses 37-39). So the Holy Spirit, dwelling <u>within</u> the believer, may spring up and may flow out, filling the believer from head to toe, in order for the believer to be divinely empowered to be a witness for Christ.

When did the original disciples become born again and thus indwelt with the Holy Spirit? John 20:21-22 says: "So Jesus said to them again, 'Peace to you! As the Father has sent Me, I also send you.' And when He had said this, *He breathed on them*, and said to them, *'Receive the Holy Spirit.'*" It has been said that John Calvin, the Sixteenth Century theologian, interpreted John 20:22 in this way: the disciples received a smattering of the Holy Spirit in John 20:22, but the Holy Spirit came in full force in Acts 2. This would explain why in John 21 the disciples showed no signs of boldness; rather they went back to fishing. I interpret John 20:22 as the moment the disciples received the Holy Spirit <u>within</u> (the moment they became born again), which occurred on the same day that Jesus was raised from the dead (20:19 says: "the same day at evening"). This would be a logical time for the disciples to be born again because the death and resurrection of Jesus were now complete.

To further explain my interpretation, let's look at Acts 1:3-5:

> to whom he also presented Himself alive after His suffering by many infallible proofs, being seen by them during forty days and speaking of the things pertaining to the kingdom of God. (4) And being assembled together with them, He commanded them not to depart from Jerusalem, but to *wait for the Promise of the Father,* "which," He said, "you have heard from Me. (5) For John truly baptized with water, but you shall be *baptized with the Holy Spirit* not many days from now."

Jesus' command to His disciples to "wait for the Promise of the Father" most likely was given after He breathed the Holy Spirit into them in John 20:22. And in Acts 1:5, Jesus indicates that the baptism in the Holy Spirit had not yet come. So it is highly unlikely that the disciples received the baptism in the Holy Spirit in John 20:22. [Baptism means to be immersed. Baptism in water means to be immersed in water. (Sprinkling is not biblical baptism.) Baptism in (or with) the Holy Spirit means to be immersed, or covered, with the Holy Spirit.] The baptism in the Holy Spirit is described in Acts 1:8, which I consider to be the Great Commission verse as well as the theme verse of Acts. Acts 1:8 says: "But you shall receive power when the Holy Spirit has come *upon* you; and you shall be witnesses to Me in Jerusalem, and in all Judea and Samaria, and to the end of the earth." In short, the purpose of the baptism in the Holy Spirit is "power...(to) be witnesses."

Acts 2:1-4 is the account of the baptism in the Holy Spirit being poured out *upon* the church. It occurred on the Day of Pentecost.

Acts 2:1-4 When the day of Pentecost had fully come, they were all with one accord in one place. (2) And suddenly there came a sound from heaven, as of a rushing mighty wind, and it filled the whole house where they were sitting. (3) Then there appeared to them divided tongues, as of fire, and one sat *upon* each of them. (4) And they were **all** filled with the Holy Spirit and began to speak with other tongues, as the Spirit gave them utterance.

Around 120 believers were gathered together when "a rushing mighty wind...filled the whole house where they were sitting." Interestingly, the Greek word for wind, *pneuma*, is the same Greek word for spirit. So the Holy Spirit, who is illustrated by wind (see John 3:8), filled the house. Then "divided tongues, as of fire...sat *upon* each of them." John the Baptist had prophesied of this: "He (Jesus) will baptize you with the Holy Spirit and with fire" (Lk. 3:16). Fire can represent purification of the believer from sin. The body of Christ needs such purification in order to be ready for the coming of the Bridegroom. In verse 4, presumably all 120 believers spoke in tongues. (Some say speaking in tongues is not available for every believer. If that were true, then it is highly unlikely that all 120 would have spoken in tongues. But they did.) Initially these tongues could have been the tongues of angels (1 Cor. 13:1) or a private prayer language unto God "that no one understands" (1 Cor. 14:2). But at some point, the tongues were that of other human languages. This phenomenon became a sign to those in Jerusalem who had traveled from different regions where these languages were indigenous. They exclaimed, "We hear them speaking in our own tongues the wonderful works of God."

The Day of Pentecost in Acts 2 was the moment when the disciples received the baptism in the Holy Spirit—His coming *upon* them for power to be witnesses of the death and resurrection of Jesus Christ. Beginning then and continuing throughout Acts, signs and wonders such as healing the sick were frequently performed by God through the apostles and others, bringing confirmation of God's Word. No

Scriptural basis exists for believing that God has removed the gifts of tongues, signs, wonders, or healings from the church today.

[See Chapter 8 for my discussion of Acts 8:5-24 and its relation to the baptism in the Holy Spirit.]

Acts 10 contains another example of the Holy Spirit falling *upon* a group of people resulting in their speaking in tongues. It occurred as Peter preached the gospel at the house of Cornelius, a Gentile.

Acts 10:44-47 While Peter was still speaking these words, the Holy Spirit fell *upon* all those who heard the word. (45) And those of the circumcision who believed were astonished, as many as came with Peter, because the gift of the Holy Spirit had been *poured out on* the Gentiles also. (46) For they heard them speak with tongues and magnify God. Then Peter answered, (47) "Can anyone forbid water, that these should not be baptized who have received the Holy Spirit just as we have?"

It seems that at Cornelius' house, the Gentiles' reception of saving faith and the baptism in the Holy Spirit occurred closely together, perhaps simultaneously (as opposed to their occurring many days apart as we just saw in John 20:22 and Acts 2:1-4). And we see in verses 45b and 46 that speaking in tongues was a sign unto Peter and the other circumcised believers that the Gentiles had received the Holy Spirit: "the gift of the Holy Spirit had been *poured out on* the Gentiles also. For they heard them speak with tongues...." Later, when Peter recounts the events that occurred at Cornelius' house to Jews in Jerusalem, he says: "And as I began to speak, the Holy Spirit fell *upon* them, as *upon* us at the beginning. Then I remembered the word of the Lord, how He said, 'John indeed baptized with water, but you shall be *baptized with the Holy Spirit*'" (Acts 11:15-16). Therefore, I affirm that speaking in tongues is the initial physical evidence of one's having received the baptism in the Holy Spirit. (By evidence I mean an outward expression which is visible or audible and which testifies to an invisible, internal work. In Acts 2, the tongues spoken by the 120 believers was an outward evidence which men in Jerusalem, who were from every nation, were able to hear.

Acts 19 contains another example of the Holy Spirit coming *upon* a group of people and their speaking in tongues.

Acts 19:1-7 ...Paul...came to Ephesus. And finding some disciples (2) he said to them, "Did you receive the Holy Spirit when you believed?" So they said to him, "We have not so much as heard whether there is a Holy Spirit." (3) And he said to them, "Into what then were you baptized?" So they said, "Into John's baptism." (4) Then Paul said, "John indeed baptized with a baptism of repentance, saying to the people that they should believe on Him who would come after him, that is, on Christ Jesus." (5) When they heard this, they were baptized in the name of the Lord Jesus. (6) And when Paul had laid hands on them, the Holy Spirit came *upon* them, and they *spoke with tongues* and prophesied. (7) Now the men were about twelve in all.

Because the twelve men Paul found in Ephesus were called "disciples," I believe they were already saved (born again). Though they were indwelt by the Holy Spirit, they were ignorant of the title, doctrine, and workings of the Holy Spirit. As in the previous chapter where Priscilla and Aquila had explained to Apollos "the way of God more accurately" (verse 26), so Paul explained the full gospel message to these men. Paul articulated the requirement for being saved in verse 4: "believe...on Christ Jesus." He then "baptized (them) in the name of the Lord Jesus" (in water) in verse 5. (For one's water baptism to be effective, it must occur *after* one is born again.) In verse 6, subsequent to their born again experience, Paul "laid hands on them, the Holy Spirit came *upon* them, and they spoke with tongues and prophesied." Notice, *all* who were converted (all twelve) spoke in tongues, which is similar to the Day of Pentecost in that *all* 120 spoke in tongues. Also at Cornelius' house "the Holy Spirit fell upon *all* those who heard the word" and they spoke in tongues. Mark 16:17 says: "And these signs will follow those who believe: In My name...they will speak with new tongues...." It doesn't say "some" or "most" will speak with new tongues, but "they will speak with new tongues." First Corinthians 14:5a says, "I wish you *all* spoke in tongues..." (That was not just Paul's wish but God's wish, or God's will, for it is God's Word). If tongues were not available for every Christian then not all would have spoken in tongues on these different occasions.

In Acts 8 and Acts 19, the laying on of hands accompanied the reception of the baptism in the Holy Spirit. In Acts 2 and Acts 10, the baptism in the Holy Spirit came upon believers without the laying on of hands. I typically lay my hands on a person when I pray for him or her to receive the baptism in the Holy Spirit, and many have received. But laying on of hands is not required, for the Holy Spirit, who is likened to the wind (Jn. 3:8), is certainly not bound by any formula.

Note that in Acts 9, in Ananias' visit to Saul, the laying on of hands accompanied spiritual blessing. Acts 9:19 says: "laying his hands on him he said, 'Brother Saul, the Lord Jesus, who appeared to you on the road as you came, has sent me that you may receive your sight and be filled with the Holy Spirit.'" Maybe Saul spoke in tongues for the first time at that moment; we know he spoke in tongues frequently (1 Cor. 14:18). I cannot say for sure, but I imagine Saul did speak in tongues for the first time in Acts 9:18, for he was "filled with the Holy Spirit" and soon thereafter began preaching Christ in the synagogues (verse 20). Moreover, he "increased all the more in strength," confounded the Jews, and proved that Jesus is the Christ (verse 22). If indeed Saul received the baptism in the Holy Spirit in verse 18, then that reception was subsequent to his being born again which likely occurred in verse 5 when Saul received revelation that Jesus is Lord. That is why Ananias called him "Brother Saul" in verse 17.

If you desire to speak in tongues for the first time, I recommend that you meditate on verses that focus on speaking in tongues and being filled with the Spirit so that you may develop a desire and a faith for receiving the baptism in the Holy Spirit. Then invite one or more Spirit-filled believers to lay their hands on you and agree with you in prayer for you to receive the Holy Spirit's baptism, which is a free gift that one receives by faith (Gal. 3:5).

I want to share a few final thoughts on this topic: What if someone points out 1 Corinthians 12:30, which says "Do all speak with tongues?" and he says that tongues are not for all Christians because the Spirit distributes "to each one individually as He wills" (1 Cor. 12:11). I would reply that the "tongues" mentioned in 1 Corinthians 12 verse 10 and verse 30 are to be used in the public assembly of the church. For example, I have never felt led to publicly speak in tongues so that all would hear my tongues and wait for someone to interpret. But I believe others have that gift and should operate in it. However, I do speak in tongues regularly as my private prayer language. Tongues uttered in a public assembly must be interpreted; tongues spoken privately do not need to be interpreted.

Some say speaking in tongues only consists of speaking other human languages by the Holy Spirit, as we see in Acts 2 when Jewish Galileans were speaking the "wonderful works of God" in human languages they did not know. I agree that tongues can include that, but tongues can also include speaking in non-human languages. First Corinthians 14:2, 4a say: "For he who speaks in a tongue does not speak to men but to God,

for no one understands him; however, in the spirit he speaks mysteries...
He who speaks in a tongue edifies himself...." I would see the tongues
referred to here as the private prayer language—a non-human language,
for he "does not speak to men" and "no one understands him." As
verse 4 points out, I see one's private prayer language as a means of
edifying oneself—to build oneself up spiritually, like a battery charger
does for a battery. Jude 20 testifies of this: "But you, beloved, building
yourselves up on your most holy faith, praying in the Holy Spirit...."
First Corinthians 13:1 says, "Though I speak with the tongues of
men and of angels..."—denoting at least two types of tongues. (First
Corinthians 12:10, in speaking about the distribution of spiritual gifts
by the Spirit, carries the same idea: "...to another different kinds of
tongues....") I believe all Christians may speak in tongues as a private
prayer language. Only some Christians have the gift of tongues that is
to be spoken to a public assembly. And when that type of tongues is
spoken, it must be interpreted, so that the entire body will be edified.

Chapter 14

Confession

Hebrews 3:1b says: "Consider the Apostle and High Priest of our *confession*, Christ Jesus." Again, Hebrews 10:23 says: "Let us hold fast the *confession* of our hope without wavering, for He who promised is faithful." Many people fail to receive healing and fail to achieve victory in other areas because of their lack of biblical confession. In the Greek, "confession" is *homologea*. *Homo* means "the same; together"; *lego* means "speak to a conclusion." Confession means "to say the same thing."[163] We must say what God says in His Word. We must speak as of the oracles of God (1 Pet. 4:11). How can two walk together except they be in agreement? (Amos 3:3). How can we walk with God (Gal. 5:25) and have the mind of Christ (2 Cor. 2:16) if the content of our daily speech, confession, and conversation is incongruent with the Bible?

A word spoken in faith is powerful (Prov. 18:21), and its central role in the creation of the universe bears that out. Hebrews 11:3 says, "The worlds were framed by the word of God." Genesis 1:2 says: "The earth was without form, and void; and darkness was on the face of the deep. And the Spirit of God was hovering over the face of the waters." The Holy Spirit was poised, ready to create, but did not create until God spoke. "Then God *said*, 'Let there be light'; and there was light" (Gen.

1:3). So the Holy Spirit and the spoken Word of God worked together to create light, as well as the rest of the universe.

We also see the power of the spoken word in the ministry of Jesus. Jesus, who is the Word made flesh, healed the sick, cast out demons, raised the dead, and performed many other miracles through His spoken Word. The Word spoke the Word! The centurion recognized great authority in Jesus (who has all authority) and said to Him, "only *speak a word*, and my servant will be healed" (Mt. 8:8). Jesus spoke, and his servant was healed. This is in accordance with Psalm 107:20: "He sent His word and healed them, and delivered them from their destructions." Jesus said to the winds and the sea, "Peace, be still," and the storm abated (Mk. 4:39). Jesus said, "Go," and the demons went out of the men and entered the swine (Mt. 8:32). Jesus said, "Lazarus, come forth!" (Jn. 11:43), and Lazarus, who had been dead four days, rose from the dead.

The power of the spoken word is also seen in Jesus' confessions and proclamations of His own identity and deity. He said "I Am He" to the Roman soldiers, and they fell to the ground (Jn. 18:6). Jesus also proclaimed: "I am the Bread of Life" (Jn. 6:35); "Before Abraham was, I AM" (Jn. 8:58); "I am the light of the world" (Jn. 9:5); "I am the Good Shepherd" (Jn. 10:11); "I am the resurrection and the life" (Jn. 11:25); "I am the way, the truth, and the life" (Jn. 14:6); and "I am the Alpha and Omega, the Beginning and the End...who is and who was and who is to come, the Almighty" (Rev. 1:8). Jesus also confessed His perfect standing, or position, in the Father when He prayed, "You, Father, are in Me, and I in You...You loved me before the foundation of the world" (Jn. 17:21, 24). These confessions and proclamations by Jesus of His own identity, deity, and position in the Father serve several purposes: they stand as a vitally powerful testimony to humanity (imparting faith to many), they remind demonic principalities of His infinite power and authority over them, and they served as an encouragement to Himself, especially just before His trial and crucifixion.

We believers are to follow in Christ's steps (1 Pet. 2:21). Therefore, as the Father sent Christ into the world (Jn. 17:18, 20:21), Christ has also sent us into the world as ambassadors of His heavenly kingdom. Following Christ's example, we are to confess and proclaim who God is (that is, all three Persons of the triune God), as well as His redemptive work. Psalm 96:3 says, "*Declare* His glory among the nations"; verse 10 says, "*say* among the nations, 'The LORD reigns.'" Psalm 70:4

says, "Let those who love Your salvation *say continually,* 'Let God be magnified.'" We should daily preach the gospel—"*Proclaim* the good news of His salvation from day to day" (Ps. 96:2). We should remember God's benefits—Psalm 103:2 says, "Forget *not* all His benefits," foremost being "who forgives all your iniquities" (through faith in Christ) and "who heals all your diseases" (through faith in Christ). God says, "I will not remember your sins. Put Me in remembrance" (Isa. 43:25-26)—so we should respectfully remind God of His promises. We should also confess who we are in Christ [our legal standing before God as the righteousness of God in Christ (2 Cor. 5:21b)]—Psalm 107:2 says, "Let the redeemed of the LORD *say so.*" This would include that Christ dwells in us (1 Cor. 6:19; 1 Jn. 4:4b), and that "If God is for us, who can be against us?" (Rom. 8:31). Bosworth says: "Confession is simply believing with our hearts and repeating with our lips God's own declaration of what we are in Christ." This includes every phase of our salvation which we are to confess and believe throughout our entire Christian lives.[164]

Making such biblical confessions and proclamations in faith releases God's power. Such faith-filled confessions and proclamations of God's Word will drive out demons, disease, and doubt, and can inspire faith in others to receive Christ's grace and victory into their lives.

Two familiar verses which demonstrate the vital connection of one's confession to one's saving faith is Romans 10:9-10:

> That if you confess with your mouth the Lord Jesus and believe in your heart that God raised Him from the dead, you will be saved. For with the heart one believes unto righteousness, and with the mouth confession is made unto salvation.

As we saw in Genesis 1:1-3, here we see again that the spoken word, or one's confession, brings what is in the spiritual realm to be manifest into the natural realm. Proverbs 18:21 says, "Death and life are in the power of the tongue." So all of our confession, conversation, and spoken and written words are weighty. In fact, we will have to give an account to God for every idle word we speak (Mt. 12:36). Conversely, we will be rewarded for every godly word we speak in faith and love (2 Cor. 5:10)! In addition to our confession at conversion that Jesus is our Lord, the Bible tells us of our need for such confession any time we commit sin. First John 1:9 says, "If we *confess* our sins, He is faithful and just to forgive us our sins and to cleanse us from all unrighteousness." In confessing our sins, we should also forsake, or turn away, from them (Prov. 28:13). Bosworth said: "Some confess with their lips but deny in their hearts....The confession of your lips has no value as long as your heart repudiates it....Our confession of, and surrender to, Christ's Lordship is required."[165] We can also confess our sins to one another (James 5:16), for Christ our Forgiver and Healer dwells inside each Christian, and thus each Christian can stand with and encourage the one who is confessing to believe in God's forgiveness and healing. In Mark 11:23-24, we see the importance of faith-filled confession in the context of prayer. Jesus said:

> For assuredly, I say to you, whoever *says* to this mountain, "Be removed and be cast into the sea," and does not doubt in his heart, but believes that those things he *says* will be done, he will have whatever he *says*. Therefore I say to you, whatever things you *ask* when you pray, believe that you receive them, and you will have them.

This confession includes believing, and speaking in accordance with that belief, before seeing the answer to the prayer. God Himself models this for us: "God...*calls* those things which do not exist as though they did" (Rom. 4:17).

A Sampling of Positive Confessions

Many people do not have faith for healing and victorious living because they do not know who they are in Christ, and / or they do not regularly reflect on and confess who they are in Christ. Below is a list of some of the many confessions that we who are Christians can make, always in Jesus' name. We can claim these only because of what Christ has done for us. Our confidence that God will manifest these blessings in and through us will come as we allow His Word to richly abide in our hearts and be uttered through our speech.

- I am blessed in the city and blessed in the country (Deut. 28:3).
- The fruit of my body and the produce of my ground are blessed (Deut. 28:4).

- I am blessed when I come in and when I go out (Deut. 28:6). Also, Psalm 121:8 says, "The LORD shall preserve your going out and your coming in from this time forth, and even forevermore."
- As I submit to God and resist the devil, then in Jesus' name, any enemies (including demons, sickness, and disease) that try to rise against me must flee from me (James 4:7; Deut. 28:7).
- The LORD will command the blessing on my storehouses and in all to which I set my hand (Deut. 28:8).
- I am blessed to not have to borrow because God prospers me (Deut. 28:12; 3 Jn. 2).
- I am the head and not the tail, above only and not beneath (Deut. 28:13).
- Because of my faith in Christ, God is for me (Rom. 8:31), with me (Mt. 28:20), in me (1 Cor. 6:19; 1 Jn. 4:4b), and upon me (Acts 1:8).
- God speaks through me—"we are ambassadors for Christ, as though God were pleading through us, we implore you on Christ's behalf, be reconciled to God" (2 Cor. 5:20).
- I am redeemed, including from the curse of disease, for by His stripes I was healed and remain healed (Eph. 1:7-8; Gal. 3:13; 1 Pet. 2:24; Isa. 53:5).
- I am the righteousness of God in Christ (2 Cor. 5:21).
- I am complete in Christ (Col. 2:10).
- I am more than a conqueror through Christ who loves me and lives in me (Rom. 8:37; Col. 1:27).
- Because I am a new creation in Christ, I have legal use of the name of Jesus, which I am to use by faith and for His glory (Mk. 16:17; Acts 3:6, 3:16, 4:10, 4:12).
- Whatever I ask the Father in Jesus' name, if it is in accordance with His will and in faith, He gives me (Jn. 14:14; 1 Jn. 3:22; 1 Jn. 5:14-15; Mk. 11:23-24).
- No weapon formed against me shall prosper, including sickness and disease (Isa. 54:17).
- Satan's dominion over my life is broken through my faith in Christ (Lk. 10:19).

- Thanks be to God who always leads me in triumph in Christ (2 Cor. 2:14), who gives me the victory through my Lord Jesus Christ (1 Cor. 15:57).
- By faith in Jesus' name, I will cast out demons, speak with new tongues, and lay hands on the sick—they will recover (Mk. 16:17-18).
- I prosper in all things and have good health, as my souls prospers (3 Jn. 2; Ps. 1:3; Josh. 1:8).
- No evil shall befall me, nor shall any plague come near my dwelling (Ps. 91:10).
- Nothing shall by any means harm me (Lk. 10:19).
- I am blessed with length of days, long life, peace, and satisfaction (Prov. 3:3; Ps. 91:16).
- No grave trouble will overtake me (Prov. 12:21).
- I have the mind of Christ (1 Cor. 2:16). I cast down every vain imagination, every high thing that exalts itself against the knowledge of God, and I bring every thought into captivity to the obedience of Christ (2 Cor. 10:5).
- God grants me according to my heart's desire, and fulfills all my purpose (Ps. 20:4).
- "The LORD is my shepherd; I shall not want" (or lack; Ps. 23:1).
- "Goodness and mercy shall follow me all the days of my life; and I will dwell in the house of the LORD forever" (Ps. 23:6).
- The Lord has "turned for me my mourning into dancing"; He has "put off my sackcloth and clothed me with gladness" (Ps. 30:11).
- The Lord has "set my feet in a wide place" (Ps. 31:8).
- The Lord is "my hiding place"; He "shall preserve me from trouble"; He "shall surround me with songs of deliverance" (Ps. 32:7).
- As I trust in the Lord, mercy surrounds me (Ps. 32:10).
- God gives me drink from the river of His pleasures, and He continues His lovingkindness and righteousness to me (Ps. 36:8, 10).
- As the law of my God is in my heart, none of my steps shall slide (Ps. 37:31).

- The Lord shall never permit me to be moved, as I abide in Christ who is my righteousness (Ps 55:22).
- God "performs all things for me" (Ps. 57:2).
- God only is my rock and my salvation; He is my defense; I shall not be moved. In God is my salvation and my glory; the rock of my strength, and my refuge, is in God (Ps. 62:6-7).
- God is merciful to me and blesses me, and causes His face to shine upon me (Ps. 67:1).
- The Lord "daily loads" me with benefits (Ps. 68:19).
- No good thing does God withhold from me, if I walk uprightly (Ps. 84:11).
- The Lord's mercy is great toward me (Ps. 86:13).
- The Lord brings me out with silver and gold, and I am not feeble (Ps. 105:37).
- The Lord delivers me out of all my distresses (Ps. 107:6).
- As I fear the Lord and delight greatly in His commandments, wealth and riches shall be in my house, and my righteousness (through faith in Christ) endures forever (Ps. 112:1-3).
- As I love God's law, I have great peace and nothing causes me to stumble (Ps. 119:165).
- The LORD shall preserve me from all evil; He shall preserve my soul. The LORD shall preserve my going out and my coming in from this time forth, and even forevermore (Ps. 121:7-8).
- "The LORD will perfect that which concerns me" (Ps. 138:8).
- The Lord shall deal bountifully with me (Ps. 142:7).
- The Lord shall cause me to hear His lovingkindness in the morning, for in Him do I trust; the Lord will cause me to know the way in which I should walk, for I lift up my soul to Him (Ps. 143:8).
- God "is able to do exceedingly abundantly above all" that I ask or think, "according to the power that works in" me (Eph. 3:20).
- God works in me "both to will and to do for His good pleasure" (Phil. 2:13).
- "I can do all things through Christ who strengthens me" (Phil. 4:13).

- "He who is in me (the Holy Spirit) is greater than he (the devil) who is in the world" (1 Jn. 4:4).
- Sin shall not have dominion over me (Rom. 6:14).
- God is able to keep me from stumbling and to present me faultless before the presence of His glory with exceeding joy (Jude 24).

Here are a few worthy quotes from *The Power of Your Words*, by Don Gossett and E. W. Kenyon.

> We will never rise above our confession....Our faith or unbelief is determined by our confession. Confession is saying the same thing the Scripture says....It isn't confessing it once, but daily affirming your relationship to Him, confessing your Righteousness (in Christ), your ability to stand in His presence without the sense of guilt or inferiority....(For example) I confess that God laid that disease on Jesus and that Satan has no right to put it on me; that "by His stripes I am healed."...I hold fast to my confession that I am what the Word says I am. I refuse to be intimidated by sense evidences. I refuse to have my life governed by them....A doubting heart is a sense-ruled heart. A fearless confession comes from a Word-ruled heart.[166]

T. L. Osborn affirms this last point, saying, "Faith constantly ascribes everything to 'Thus saith the Word of God,' irrespective of pains, symptoms, or feelings."[167] Feelings fluctuate, but the Word of God is our trustworthy standard, our immoveable anchor.

In this chapter, I do not intend to imply that making continual positive confessions will ensure one of a life free from problems and suffering. Psalm 34:19 says, "Many are the afflictions of the righteous, but the LORD delivers him out of them all." (See also John 16:33.) Jesus said each of us has a daily cross to bear. Paul reiterated this, saying, "I die daily" (1 Cor. 15:31). We are to die to sin and be alive to God through Christ Jesus our Lord (Rom. 6:11). Furthermore, we "who are Christ's have crucified the flesh with its passions and desires," (Gal. 5:24) and we are to continue to crucify the flesh.

I also do not intend to imply that making positive confessions will always produce immediately happy results; nor do I intend to imply that making negative confessions will always produce immediately bad results. But the spiritual law of sowing and reaping (Gal. 6:7;

2 Cor. 9:6) is applicable to the words we speak. Kenyon said, "It is what we confess with our lips that really dominates our inner being."[168] If one speaks faithless, sinful words, he can be assured of a negative consequence. Proverbs 6:2 says, "You are ensnared by the words of your mouth." Hebrews 2:2 says, "every transgression and disobedience [including faithless, sinful words (my insertion)] received a just reward...." Conversely, Proverbs 25:11 says, "A word fitly spoken is like apples of gold in settings of silver." The words you speak affect the condition of your whole being. Your words can liberate you or ensnare you. Just because you do not yet see healing manifested, you should not undermine the prospect of your healing with confessions such as "I have an incurable disease" or "I cannot shake this sickness." You should not let persistent symptoms of illness cause you to speak doubt about the will of God to heal you, for God wills to heal all who are repentant and believe in Christ. You should not, by unbiblical confession, nullify the appropriation unto your body of such wonderful biblical promises as "(He) heals all your diseases" (Ps. 103:3), "He...bore our sicknesses" (Mt. 8:17), and "By whose stripes you were healed" (1 Pet. 2:24).

Lord, Help Me Tame My Tongue!

All of us have spoken words that we later came to regret. Perhaps we spoke words that were conducive to unbelief, or were overly critical, offensive, caused a fellow believer to stumble, or caused strife. Perhaps we gossiped about someone or slandered someone for whom Christ died. We should confess and turn away from such sins, and allow God's Word to dwell within our hearts richly. Meditation upon Scriptures that pertain to taming the tongue can instruct and inspire us to speak words that please God and impart healing and edification to others.

Proverbs 12:18 **"The tongue of the wise promotes health."** We can speak in a way that promotes healing of the spirit, soul, and body in others and in ourselves. Bosworth wrote: Our confession rules us.... The Word will heal you if you continually confess it (and believe)."[169] It is the wise who speak this way, so we should walk in wisdom, recognizing that Christ is the wisdom of God (1 Cor. 1:24; Prov. 8:12-36). Promoting health through our words is akin to speaking words of "necessary edification" and "grace" (Eph. 4:29). Such gracious, healthy speech stands in contrast to Proverbs 11:9: "The hypocrite with his mouth destroys his neighbor...."

Proverbs 15:4 **"A wholesome tongue is a tree of life, but perverseness in it breaks the spirit."**

As the tree of life (also mentioned in Genesis 2:9, 3:22, 3:24, and Revelation 22:2) bears good fruit every month of the year as well as bears leaves for the healing of the nations, a wholesome tongue also consistently speaks words indicative of the fruit of the Spirit as well as of healing. This verse also shows the converse: the perverse tongue breaks the spirit, which is indicative of death rather than life.

Proverbs 18:21 **"Death and life are in the power of the tongue, and those who love it will eat its fruit."**

What you say can bring death or life to you and your situation. You can sow to your own defeat through faithless, discouraging words such as "It's going to be a bad day," or "I'm going to get sick," or "I'm going to fail," or "I can't be a good husband and father." Proverbs 6:2 says, "You are snared by the words of your mouth...." Instead, sow life through speaking according to God's promises, such as, "I can do all things through Christ who strengthens me" (Phil. 4:13), "I will love my wife as Christ loved the church" (Eph. 5:25), "by His stripes I am healed" (Isa. 53:5), and "...my God shall supply all your need according to His riches in glory by Christ Jesus" (Phil. 4:19). Jesus said, "By your words you will be justified, and by your words you will be condemned" (Mt. 12:37).

Hebrews 13:15 **"Therefore, by Him let us continually offer the sacrifice of praise to God, that is, the fruit of our lips, giving thanks to His name."**

This is the New Testament version of Psalm 34:1: "I will bless the LORD at all times; His praise shall continually be in my mouth." Both of these verses exhort the believer to praise God unceasingly. Such continual praise of God by believers is an aspect of God's will being done on earth as it is in heaven, for in heaven the four living creatures "do not rest day or night, saying: 'Holy, holy, holy, Lord God Almighty, who was and is and is to come!'" (Rev. 4:8). Not only should we continually praise, thank, and bless God because He is worthy, but also because doing so will help us to keep our minds stayed upon Him, which is conducive to life and perfect peace (Isa. 26:3; Rom. 8:5-6;

Col. 3:2). "Sacrifice of praise" reminds us that we are to praise God even if we don't feel like doing so, just as we to obey God always even if we don't feel like doing so, just as we are to love our neighbor as ourselves even if we don't feel like doing so.

As God told Joshua, "This book of the law shall not depart from your mouth" (Josh. 1:8), so our speech and confessions should remain in harmony with the Word of God. Such godly confession will support the work of the Holy Spirit to provide continual healing and health to our bodies, and more importantly, faith, holiness, and love to our hearts.

Chapter 15

Christians in the New Testament Who Were Not Healed

John Wimber and Kevin Springer, in their book *Power Healing*, point out four instances in the New Testament where the sick were not healed:[170]

1) **Philippians 2:25-30** Yet I considered it necessary to send to you Epaphroditus, my brother, fellow worker, and fellow soldier, but your messenger and the one who ministered to my need; (26) since he was longing for you all, and was distressed because you had heard that *he was sick.* (27) For indeed *he was sick almost unto death*; but God had mercy on him, and not only on him but on me also, lest I should have sorrow upon sorrow. (28) Therefore I sent him the more eagerly, that when you see him again you may rejoice, and I may be less sorrowful. (29) Receive him therefore in the Lord with all gladness, and hold such men in esteem; (30) because for the work of Christ *he came close to death*, not regarding his life, to supply what was lacking in your service toward me.

There is no indication that Epaphroditus' sickness, which almost ended in death, was because of any particular sin in his life. Instead, verse 30 indicates that Epaphroditus was doing "the work of Christ" when he became sick. I do not know why he became sick. Maybe demonic forces brought great opposition to Epaphroditus. After all, he was away from the spiritual support found among the larger church family because he was on the mission field evangelizing new territory with Paul. Nevertheless, Epaphroditus was eventually healed because of God's mercy, and he continued to serve the Lord.

2) **1 Timothy 5:23** No longer drink only water, but use a little wine for your stomach's sake and *your frequent infirmities.*

First Timothy 5:23 advocates taking practical steps for the treatment of infirmity such as through the utilization of particular drink and diet. It should be noted that the amount of wine that Paul recommended was "little," and the reason for its use was for the improvement of Timothy's health. Paul certainly did not recommend wine for any fleshly pleasures of intoxication, since Paul condemned "drunkenness, revelries, and the like" in Galatians 5:21. Also Paul would not have advocated any practice that would go against Scripture, such as Proverbs 20:1, "Wine is a mocker, strong drink is a brawler, and whoever is led astray by it is not wise."

3) **2 Timothy 4:20** Erastus stayed in Corinth, but Trophimus I have left in Miletus *sick.*

Incidentally, Trophimus is also mentioned in Acts 20:4—Paul's traveling companion on his third missionary journey, and in Acts 21:27-29—during Paul's arrest in Jerusalem. Just because the prayers of Paul and Trophimus did not bring healing to Trophimus by the time Paul left Miletus does not mean that it was not God's will to heal Trophimus. Paul and Trophimus, though mighty men of God, were not perfect. As Christians, they were spiritually renewed, but they still had the flesh with which to contend. Paul explained this principle in Romans 7. Paul admitted that as a Christian he still had sin in his members causing him to do what he did not want to do (Rom. 7:17, 20, 23). This is not to say that Paul, Trophimus, Timothy, or Epaphroditus were guilty of excessive sin in the above accounts; nevertheless, these verses are reminders that they were human and residing in pre-glorified bodies. As I stated earlier, during their missionary endeavors, Paul, Trophimus, and others had to deal with severe spiritual warfare as Satan likely put up major opposition to the work of these ambassadors for Christ. Satan likely came at them often with attacks of sickness. The perfect Person, Jesus, would always overcome such attacks of Satan, but Paul and others might have suffered some setbacks, including sickness. How intense can spiritual warfare be? The angel that came to Daniel was delayed twenty-one days because he had to battle a demon—"the prince of the kingdom of Persia" (Dan. 10:13).

Concerning the accounts of New Testament believers being sick, we don't have the privilege of knowing all of the circumstances involved. But these men were mortal humans, not healing machines, and they likely became sick from time to time. Praise God that, despite our weaknesses and perhaps "frequent infirmities" (1 Tim. 5:23), God can still do great things through and for us.

4) **Galatians 4:13-14** You know that because of *physical infirmity* I preached the gospel to you at the first. (14) And my trial which was in my flesh you did not despise or reject, but you received me as an angel of God, even as Christ Jesus...For I bear you witness that, if possible, you would have plucked out your own eyes and given them to me.

God had used Paul to heal many people and had even raised the dead, but here Paul had a physical infirmity. Perhaps he had eye trouble; we are not sure. Paul categorized his physical infirmity as a "trial." God used Paul's trial of infirmity for good, for Paul said, "because of *physical infirmity* I preached the gospel to you at the first." As I shared earlier, when Christians are not healed, God can use those sicknesses and handicaps to bring glory to Himself. Preacher David Ring is a good example of a Christian with a handicap (cerebral palsy since his birth in 1953) that God has used to show that, in sickness as well as in health, Christians can live fruitful lives. If a person with a sickness loves God and is called by God, then God will use that person's sickness (and any other trial or tribulation he may experience) for God's glory. Romans 8:28 affirms this, saying, "And we know that all things work together for good to those who love God, to those who are called according to His purpose."

I discovered a fifth instance in the New Testament where people were not healed.

Mark 6:5-6 Now He *could do no* mighty work there, except that He laid His hands on a few sick people and healed them. (6) And He marveled because of *their unbelief.*

Jesus visited a particular town in His own country, and many of the sick people in that town were probably not healed. (Verse 5 reveals that Jesus did heal "a few.") This passage does not say "Jesus *would* do no mighty works there," but that "He *could* do no mighty works there." Verse 6 reveals that the residents of this particular town had *unbelief*, and likely a high degree of unbelief since Jesus marveled because of it. Their unbelief was the probable cause of Jesus not being able to heal many there, though He had healed at other places. Jesus often required faith on the part of the sick person or friend in order to heal. We see this in Mark 5:34: Jesus said, "Daughter, *your faith* has made you well." Indeed, "without faith it is impossible to please Him" (Heb. 11:6); but conversely, "all things are possible to him who believes" (Mk. 9:23).

Bosworth lists twenty-two reasons why people are not healed. I will share his list in its entirety and a fraction of his comments on each.

1) **Insufficient Instruction**: "Many have sought healing from Christ before they knew or heard enough of the Word of God....Multitudes today do not know that the perfect healing of their bodies is the fully revealed will of God in His written Word, the Bible....The early Church was in one accord in teaching this truth." Today, unbelief, opposition to a healing ministry, and lukewarmness often hinder the church from being united in prayer and in faith.

2) **Lack of United Prayer**: What is needed is a Spirit-filled and praying church which produces an atmosphere conducive for God to work.

3) **Community Unbelief**: There's a lack of teaching on divine healing today. Also, "the unspiritual condition" of so many churches hinders faith for healing.

4) **Traditions of Men**: Lie: "God is the author of disease and...He wills the sickness of some of His worshippers." Truth: "If sickness is the will of God for His true worshippers,...then every hospital is a house of rebellion." Lie: "We can glorify God more by remaining sick and exhibiting patience than we can by being divinely healed." Truth: If this is true, then Jesus robbed His Father of glory. Jesus healed all who appealed to Him, and "His Successor the Holy Spirit was sent down to augment what Christ began to do and to teach." Lie: "It is not God's will to heal all." Truth: If God only wills to heal some, "then none have any basis for faith until they shall have received a special revelation that they are among the favored ones." Then we must close our Bibles on

the issue. <u>Lie</u>: It is appropriate to say "If it be Thy will" when praying for healing. <u>Truth</u>: "If it be Thy will" is a "faith-destroying phrase."

5) **Breaking Natural Laws**: "Natural laws are God's laws." Some people suffer illness because of poor diet and neglect of their bodies. Repentance is needed.

6) **Unbelief of Elder or Minister Who Prays**. He cites Matthew 17:14-21.

7) **An Evil Spirit Must Be Cast Out**. He cites Matthew 17:14-21. I would also cite Matthew 9:32-33, Acts 10:38, and Luke 13:10-16.

8) **The Sick Person's Sin**: Some people do not get healed because they will not repent. "God has not promised to destroy the works of the devil in the body while we are clinging to the works of the devil in the soul."

9) **Lukewarmness of the Church**: "Lukewarmness is a much worse disease than cancer. God's higher priority is to move the church from lukewarmness to being on fire for Him.

10) **Unwillingness to Surrender to God.** When a man surrenders his will to God, then he is positioned to believe for healing.

11) **An Unforgiving Spirit**: How can God forgive and heal us when we won't forgive others? See Matthew 6:14-15.

12) **A Need to Seek Forgiveness**: "Wrongs that have not been made right hinder the faith of some to receive healing." See 2 Samuel 21, where seven sons of Saul were hanged to make restitution for Saul's sins against the Gibeonites. Verse 14 says, "And after that God heeded the prayer for the land," and the famine ceased.

13) **Lack of Diligence**: "God...is a rewarder of those who diligently seek Him" (Heb. 11:6).

14) **Seeking Miracles, Not Healing**: "Many fail to be healed because they endeavor to confine God to miracles. Because they are not made well and strong in an instant, these people cast away their confidence."

15) **Watching Symptoms**: Some people focus on their symptoms and feelings, thus making them the basis for faith instead of God's Word. "The things of God cannot be discerned, appropriated, and known by the natural senses….The healing of both our souls and bodies is based on the unchangeable truth of Christ's finished work, not on our feelings…."[171] When Peter, in faith, focused on the Word made flesh (Jesus), he victoriously walked on water. When he took he eyes off of Jesus and focused on the waves (which can represent what we see) and on the wind (which can represent what we feel), fear replaced faith in Peter, and he sank.

16) **Failure to Act on Faith**: We need faith with corresponding actions. Therefore those who are sick should call on the elders to anoint and pray. The friends of the paralytic demonstrated faith when they hoisted the paralytic onto the roof and then made a hole in the roof and lowered him into the presence of Jesus (Mk. 2:2-12). The woman with the issue of blood demonstrated faith when she pressed through the crowd and touched the hem of Jesus' garment. So we should think faith, speak faith, and act on faith.

17) **Lack of Confidence**: We need to hold the beginning of our confidence that Jesus is our Healer steadfast until the promise is fulfilled (Heb. 10:35). This applies to any promise of God.

18) **Not Receiving the Holy Spirit**: The Holy Spirit is the Carpenter (Rom. 8:11). We cannot limit the Carpenter to the outside of the house while asking Him to repair the inside. Paul said "The body…for the Lord" before he said "The Lord for the body" (1 Cor. 6:13).

19) **Lack of Faith**. Jesus often spoke of the need for faith: e.g., "According to your *faith*, let it be to you"; "Your *faith* has made you well" (Mt. 8:13, 9:29; Lk. 18:42).

20) **Failure to Receive God's Promises**: Some fail to receive the "written promise of God as His direct Word to them."

21) **Waiting for Healing to Believe**: "Some will not believe that their prayer for healing has been heard until they have experienced and seen the answer." In Mark 11:24, Jesus said "You will have them"

after He said "believe that you receive them." In John 11, Jesus prayed, "Father, "I thank You that You have heard Me," even though Lazarus was still dead.

22) **Focusing on Improvement rather than God's Promises**: "Some hinder God by basing their faith on their improvement after prayer rather than on His promise." If a farmer plants corn seed in good soil and waters it, he does not dig it up the next day to see how it is progressing. That would hinder its growth. Instead he believes the seed is producing even though its growth is invisible to him. Similarly, we should focus on God's promises, proclaiming "It is written," rather than focus on fluctuating symptoms and feelings. God wants us "to believe Him when everything we see, except His promise, is to the contrary."[172]

Paul's Thorn in the Flesh

Though Paul may have been ill from time to time, I doubt that the thorn in Paul's flesh, referred to in 2 Corinthians 12:7-11, was a sickness or disease. The reason is because of the Lord's response to Paul. The Lord did not say to Paul, "have more faith," or "fast and pray," or "repent and I will take away your thorn." Instead, the Lord said, "My grace is sufficient for you, for My strength is made perfect in weakness." For God to make that sort of statement about a physical infirmity would be inconsistent with the rest of Scripture. When did Jesus ever say to someone requesting Him to heal them, "No I won't heal you, because My grace is sufficient for you," or "I won't heal you; I want you to learn patience and gratitude in the midst of sickness"? Of course Jesus never made statements like these. On the contrary, Scripture reveals Jesus healing everyone who asked Him to heal.

Many people speculate about what Paul's thorn was. Some people reference Galatians 4:15 or 6:11 and say Paul had bad eye sight. Others say Paul had an unconverted wife. Again, that is speculation, for the Scripture does not specify what Paul's thorn was. Paul does use the word "infirmities" (verses 9-10) in referring to his thorn. Also, the Lord refers to the thorn as a "weakness" (verse 9). However, "infirmity" and "weakness" does not always mean physical in nature. Consider Romans 8:26: "Likewise the Spirit also helps in our "weaknesses." The King James Version translates this "infirmities." That may refer to being weak in spirit instead of weakness through disease.

The Case of Job

In all probability, the book of Job appears much later in the Bible than one would expect on the basis of the time frame of its events. As a primarily poetic book, it appears at the beginning of the poetic section of the canon, just before Psalms. However, Job likely lived during the patriarchal period narrated in Genesis, for the following reasons: 1) Job, like the patriarchs, offered his own sacrifices to God; 2) the Scripture states Job's wealth in terms of livestock and servants; and 3) Job's span of life—he lived 140 years from the end of his trial—was more nearly comparable to the longevity of the patriarchs than to the shorter life span characteristic of men of later times.

Since Job likely lived before the Exodus, he did not possess the wonderful covenantal promises on which later saints of God could stand. In Exodus 23:25, the LORD says, "I will take sickness away from the midst of you." Again, Psalm 121:7 states, "The LORD shall preserve you from all evil . . . ." (See also Psalm 91, where the LORD provides protection from the devil, disease, fear, and all evil for the man who by faith dwells in His secret place.) Again, Isaiah 59:19 states, "When the enemy comes in like a flood, the Spirit of the LORD will lift up a standard against him." Had Job lived during a later time and heard such Old Testament promises, he could have appropriated those promises by faith and successfully warded off the devil. T. L. Osborn said:

> You no longer take your place with Job of the Old Testament, thinking you must suffer sickness because Job suffered. Never! You have learned that you are living on *this side* of Calvary, under grace and truth that sets you free from the curse of the Law.[173]

Yet one can learn many valuable lessons by reflecting upon features of Job's experience such as the following: Job's amazing perseverance in the face of tribulation, the abundant mercy which God showed in prospering Job after his trial, and Job's realization that every fallen human being requires a Mediator who can rightfully come into God's holy presence on his behalf—a need whose divinely-supplied Answer one finds in Jesus Christ alone.[174]

Chapter 16

Miracles in the Old Testament

Biblical Evidence that Miracles Are Often a Catalyst for Faith in God's Word

Not only does the Bible contain the inerrant account of creation, sin, the history of Israel, the incarnation of Christ, redemption through faith in Christ, the Second Coming of Christ, and the new heavens and the new earth, among other things, but it also contains the accounts of numerous miracles. Miracles play a major role in God's plan of redemption. For example, we see the confirmation of Jesus as the Messiah through miracles in the following two verses: Acts 2:22 says: "Jesus of Nazareth, a Man attested by God to you by miracles, wonders, and signs which God did through Him in your midst..."; Hebrews 2:4 says: "God also bearing witness (to "so great a salvation") both with signs and wonders, with various miracles, and gifts of the Holy Spirit, according to His own will?" For this writing, a miracle is when God intervenes into the natural realm to do a work that supersedes natural laws. Many of the miracles of the Bible were irrefutable miracles—they were verifiable by sight, and any honest onlooker could have affirmed that a supernatural work occurred. God often performed such miracles to reveal His power, and to turn people's attention to the fact that He, the Almighty, was in their midst and that He required obedience to His Word. In other words, miracles motivated people to repent and believe. In the Old Testament, the people were to believe in God's Word through the prophets. In the New Testament, we are to believe in Jesus, who is the Son of God, and in His Word (the Bible). Thomas, one of the twelve, stubbornly said he would not believe unless he *could see* the resurrected Jesus and *could touch* the nail prints in His hands and side. Jesus graciously revealed Himself to Thomas and allowed Thomas to touch the holes in His hands and side. Jesus said, "Thomas, because you *have seen* Me, you have believed. Blessed are those who *have not seen* and yet have believed" (Jn. 20:29). Many people today are in the "Thomas Category"—they will believe only if they *see* a miracle. Jesus affirmed this truth when speaking to a nobleman whose son was at the point of death: "Unless you people *see* signs and wonders you will by no means believe" (Jn. 4:48). Jesus healed the boy, and the man's household believed in Jesus.

Since a vital component of the church's mission is evangelism—to go and preach the gospel to every creature so that as many people as possible will repent and believe, should not the church seek faith in Christ to perform miracles today in order to confirm His Word? For the sake of those in the Thomas Category, should not the church pursue the ministry of miracles, signs, wonders, and gifts of the Holy Spirit, so that in seeing many will drop their resistance to the gospel that they might believe when they hear the gospel? Should not the church even pursue irrefutable miracles—those verifiable by sight—in order to maximize the number of those who would believe? Emphatically yes!

This chapter summarizes many of the miracles, signs, and wonders found in the Old Testament. (Since much of this book focuses on the New Testament healing passages, I have not included New Testament miracles in this writing.) This chapter emphasizes the prominence of miracles in Old Testament times, and points to their indispensability to the overall redemptive plan of God.

Miracles in Genesis

In Chapter 7, due to the wickedness of mankind, God flooded the entire earth and destroyed all flesh, except Noah's family of eight. In

Chapter 11, God confused the human language at the tower of Babel, and scattered the people abroad over the face of the earth. In Chapter 12, God called Abram away from his father's house, and led him to the land of Canaan, promising to give that land to his descendants. Also in Chapter 12, God plagued Pharaoh and his house with great plagues because of Sarai, Abram's wife, for God's says, "Do not touch My anointed ones, and do My prophets no harm" (Ps. 105:15). In Chapter 19, God destroyed the wicked cities of Sodom and Gomorrah by raining down fire and brimstone from heaven. In Chapter 22, God caused Sarah to give birth to Isaac when she was ninety years old and had been barren (Abraham biologically fathered Isaac at the age of one hundred). In Chapter 24, God answered the prayer of Abraham's servant in selecting a wife (Rebecca) for Isaac. In Chapter 28, Jacob had a divinely inspired dream of a ladder reaching from earth to heaven, and angels were ascending and descending upon it. In Chapter 41, Joseph accurately interpreted Pharaoh's dreams (as he had done for the butler and baker); thus Joseph was promoted from being an inmate to being second-in-command in Egypt. The dreams foretold seven years of abundance in Egypt, followed by seven years of famine. Joseph stored much food during the years of abundance so that Egypt, and others including Jacob's family, were able to survive. Joseph's predictions of the dreams proved accurate.

In Genesis, we see that God intervened in time and space to direct history and to implement His plan of salvation for His elect by separating unto Himself the Jewish patriarchs.

Miracles in Exodus

In Chapter 3, God revealed Himself to Moses by speaking to him from a bush that was burning but not being consumed. In Chapter 4, God gave Moses two signs to confirm that He would use Moses to bring the Hebrews out of Egypt: 1) Moses' rod turned into a snake, then back into a rod; 2) When Moses put his hand in his bosom, it became leprous; then Moses' hand was restored when he put it back into his bosom. In Chapter 7, Aaron cast down his rod before Pharaoh and it became a serpent. Pharaoh's sorcerers did the same, but Aaron's rod swallowed their rods. In Chapter 7, Moses and Aaron struck the waters of the river in the sight of Pharaoh and his servants, and all the water in Egypt became *blood*. In Chapter 8, Moses warned Pharaoh that if he would not release the Hebrews, then God would strike the territory with *frogs*. Aaron stretched out his hand over the waters of Egypt, and frogs came up and covered the land. When Pharaoh hardened his heart, Aaron struck the dust, and all the dust of the land became *lice*. When the magicians could not bring forth lice, they said to Pharaoh, "This is the finger of God." But Pharaoh's heart grew hard again, which would occur after each of the first nine plagues. God willed this in order to multiply His signs and gain glory among the nations. Moses told Pharaoh that God would send *swarms of flies* to cover Egypt; and it was so. In Chapter 9, God struck the livestock of Egypt with a *very severe pestilence*. Also, Moses and Aaron threw handfuls of ashes from a furnace in the sight of Pharaoh; God turned the ashes into fine dust, causing *boils* to break out in sores on man and beast throughout Egypt. In Exodus 9:13-14, the LORD said to Moses, "Say to him (Pharaoh), 'Thus says the LORD God of the Hebrews: Let My people go, that they may serve Me, for at this time I will send all My plagues to your very heart, and on your servants and on your people, *that you may know* that there is none like Me in all the earth.'" Moses prophesied of hail to come the next day, and urged Pharaoh to get all servants and livestock indoors. The next day, *thunder, hail, and fire* darted to the ground and destroyed all who had stubbornly remained in the fields of Egypt. As a result, Pharaoh confessed, "I have sinned this time. The LORD is righteous, and my people and I are wicked" (9:27). God said, "I have hardened his heart...that I might show these signs of Mine...*that you may know* that I am the LORD" (10:1-2). Then God brought many locusts on the land so that no one could see the earth. Pharaoh again confessed, "I have sinned against the LORD your God and against you" (10:16). But when Pharaoh hardened his heart, God sent *three days of thick darkness* over all the land. Then God inclined the hearts of the Egyptians to give the Israelites clothing and articles of silver and gold. God instructed Israel to prepare the Passover, which included applying lamb's blood on the doorposts of their houses. God passed through all Egypt and killed the firstborn male of every household, of man and beast, wherever the blood of the lamb was not found on the doorposts of the houses. But where the blood of the lamb was found (foreshadowing the ultimate atonement through the blood of Jesus the Christ, the Lamb of God) on the doorposts, no death occurred. After this tenth plague of death of the firstborn, God caused the Israelites to depart from Egypt (after 430 years of slavery) in order that Israel might be set apart unto God, to know and obey Him. Concerning the ten plagues with which God struck Egypt, none of the plagues harmed the Israelites. Therefore, God made a distinction between the nation of Israel, whom He chose to favor, and Egypt, whom He opposed.

In Chapter 13, the LORD went before Israel "by day in a pillar of cloud to lead the way, and by night in a pillar of fire, to give them light. He did not take away the pillar of cloud by day or the pillar of fire by night from before the people" (verses 21-22). What a miraculous, irrefutable provision! At any given moment over a forty year period, any Israelite could look up and see the pillar of cloud or the pillar of fire, and not only know the route Israel was to take (as well as the time to camp or break camp), but also be reminded of God's faithfulness and nearness to His people. Another example of God's faithfulness is that none of their clothes wore out, nor did any of their feet swell during those forty years when God sustained them in the wilderness (Dt. 8:4).

Parting the Red Sea

The parting of the Red Sea is viewed as the premier miracle of the Old Testament, the one that, more than any other miracle, distinguished Israel as God's chosen people. As Israel approached the Red Sea, God showed Israel exactly where to camp. Then God hardened Pharaoh's heart so that he pursued Israel. God willed that Israel be trapped between the sea and Pharaoh's army so that Israel would come to know God as the ultimate deliverer. Because of God's deliverance, Israel should have learned to look to God to meet all their needs, and to realize that God is willing and able to intervene in whatever ways are necessary to save, bless, and prosper His people.

Moses said, "Do not be afraid. Stand still, and see the salvation of the LORD, which He will accomplish for you today....the LORD will fight for you..." (14:13-14). The Angel of God, who went before the camp of Israel, moved and went behind them; and the pillar of cloud went from before them and stood behind them. The cloud was darkness to the Egyptians but was light to the Israelites; the cloud kept the two apart. Chapter 14, verses 21-23 say:

The LORD caused the sea to go back by a strong east wind all that night, and made the sea into dry land, and the waters were divided. So the children of Israel went into the midst of the sea on dry ground, and the waters were a wall to them on their right hand and on their left.

Furthermore, "the LORD troubled the army of the Egyptians. And He took off their chariot wheels" (verses 24-25). When Israel crossed to the other side of the sea, Moses stretched out his hand over the sea, and the sea returned to its full depth and drowned all of Pharaoh's army. Verse 31 says: "Thus Israel *saw* the great work which the LORD had done in Egypt; so the people feared the LORD, *and believed* the LORD and His servant Moses."

Then Israel went three days into the wilderness and found no water, except for bitter water at Marah. When Moses cried out to the LORD, the LORD showed Moses a tree. When Moses cast the tree into the waters, the waters were made sweet. Here God revealed His name: *Jehovah-Rahpa*—"the LORD who heals you" (Ex. 15:26).

In Chapter 16, God began giving Israel manna from heaven ("angel's food"), which He did every morning for the next forty years, despite Israel's unfaithfulness and frequent complaining. Also, the LORD manifested His glory in the sight of the people: "the glory of the LORD appeared in the cloud" (verse 10). In Chapter 17, God brought water from a rock to quench the thirst of Israel. Then Israel faced their first military test—an attack of the Amalekites. As Moses' arms and hands were extended vertically (an act of intercession on behalf of the Israelite army), God empowered Israel to conquer their enemy. God's name, *Jehovah-Nissi*—The-LORD-Is-My-Banner, was revealed here (Ex. 17:15-16). In Chapter 19, at Mt. Sinai, God reminded Israel of what He had done for them: "You have *seen* what I did to the Egyptians, and how I bore you on eagles' wings and brought you to Myself" (verse 4). On the third day, the LORD descended upon Mt. Sinai "in the *sight* of all the people" (verse 11). Thundering and lightning occurred, and a thick cloud appeared on the mountain, which was completely in smoke, because the LORD descended upon it in fire. The mountain quaked greatly, and God answered Moses by voice. Then God wrote with His own finger the Ten Commandments. Chapter 20, verse 18 says, "Now all the people *witnessed* the thundering, the lightning flashes, the sound of the trumpet, and the mountain smoking; and when the people *saw* it, them trembled and stood afar off." The manifestation of God's power on the mountain caused a healthy fear to come into the Israelites, for "by the fear of the LORD one departs from evil" (Pr. 16:6b). Chapter 24:9-10 says:

> Then Moses went up, also Aaron, Nadab, and Abihu, and the seventy of the elders of Israel, and they *saw* the God of Israel. And there was under His feet as it were a paved work of sapphire stone, and it was like the very heavens in its clarity.

In Chapter 32, the Israelites made an idol, a golden calf, which was a great sin, violating the first two of the Ten Commandments which the LORD had just given them. Verse 35 says, "So the LORD plagued the people because of what they did with the calf which Aaron made." Chapter 33 says that whenever Moses went to the tabernacle of meeting, all the people rose and watched. They saw the pillar of cloud that descended and stood at the door of the tabernacle of meeting, and they worshipped, each man in his tent door. Also, at Moses' request, God hid Moses in a cleft in a rock, and God passed by in His goodness and glory, and He allowed Moses see the back side of His glory! In Chapter 34, Moses ascended again to the top of Mt. Sinai to receive two new tablets of the Ten Commandments, and "the LORD descended in the cloud and stood with him there, and proclaimed the name of the LORD" (verses 5-7. See also verse 10). When Moses descended down the mountain with the Ten Commandments, his face shone the glory of God so that he had to veil his face. In Chapter 40, once the tabernacle was erected:

> the cloud covered the tabernacle of meeting, and the glory of the LORD filled the tabernacle.... For the cloud of the LORD was above the tabernacle by day, and the fire was over it by night, in the sight of all the house of Israel, throughout all their journeys (verses 34, 38).

The number and magnitude of miracles, including the manifestations of God's presence and glory, in Exodus is astounding. God graciously revealed Himself so that Israel would have reason to trust and obey Him. Yet, most Israelites did not renew their minds with God's commandments, and they persisted in doubt, fleshly lusts, and rebellion.

Miracles in Leviticus

In Chapter 10, when Nadab and Abihu, the sons of the high priest, Aaron, "offered profane fire before the LORD…fire went out from the LORD and devoured them, and they died before the LORD" (verses 1-2). The LORD said, "By those who come near Me I must be regarded as holy" (verse 3a).

Miracles in Numbers

In Chapter 11, "when the people complained, it displeased the LORD….So the fire of the LORD burned among them, and consumed some in the outskirts of the camp" (verse 1). Also, the LORD took of the Spirit that was upon Moses and put the same upon seventy elders so that they could assist Moses in bearing the burden of the people. Verses 31 and 33 contain miraculous provision as well as divine judgment:

> A wind went out from the LORD, and it brought quail from the sea and left them fluttering near the camp…about two cubits above the surface of the ground….But while the meat was still between their teeth, before it was chewed…the LORD struck the people with a very great plague.

Because of their complaining about not having meat, God provided quail daily for one month.

In Chapter 12, Miriam and Aaron spoke against Moses because he had married an Ethiopian. God descended and spoke to all three, rebuking Miriam and Aaron. When God ascended, Miriam was immediately struck with leprosy as a judgment against her sin. But Moses, with a forgiving heart, prayed for Miriam to be healed, and presumably she was healed.

In chapters 13-14, the Israelites rejected the good report of Joshua and Caleb, two men of faith who spied out the Promise Land. Instead, they believed the bad report of the ten spies. Thus they rejected the Promise Land and God will for their lives, and they wanted to return to Egypt, which represented sin and bondage. Therefore, the LORD pronounced judgment against Israel so that the ten spies who brought the faithless report died immediately, and all Israelites twenty years and above (except Joshua and Caleb) were sentenced by the LORD to die in the wilderness where they would have to wander for the next forty years.

In Chapter 16, Korah and around 250 leaders rebelled against Moses and Aaron. Verse 19 says, "Then the glory of the LORD appeared to all the congregation," and the LORD told Moses to instruct Israel to get away from the tents of the rebels. Moses said:

> By this you shall know that the LORD has sent me to do all these works, for I have not done them of my own will. If these men die naturally like all men, or if they are visited by the common fate of all men, the LORD has not sent me. But if the LORD creates a new thing, and the earth opens its mouth and swallows them up with all that belongs to them, and they go down alive into the pit, then you will understand that these men have rejected the LORD (verses 28-30).

When Moses finished speaking, the ground split apart under the rebels, and the earth opened its mouth and swallowed them up, with their households. So the rebels "went down alive into the pit; the earth closed over them….And a fire came out from the LORD and consumed the two hundred and fifty men who were offering incense" (verses 33, 35). The next day, the entire congregation blamed Moses and Aaron for the deaths that occurred the previous day. Therefore, the LORD struck Israel with a great plague, so that 14,700 died. More would have died, but an atonement made by Aaron halted the plague.

In Chapter 17, Moses prepared twelve rods, one from each father's house, with each father's name written on his rod. Also, Aaron's name was written on the rod of Levi. Then Moses placed all the rods in the tabernacle of meeting before the Testimony, with the understanding that the rod that God would choose would blossom. The next day, the rod of Aaron had sprouted and put forth buds, had produced blossoms and yielded ripe almonds. The miraculous blossoming of Aaron's rod was a sign against the rebels, to silence their complaints lest they die.

In Chapter 20, when the children of Israel found no water, they again contended with Moses and Aaron. So the LORD told Moses to speak to the rock before the eyes of Israel, and the rock would yield water for them to drink. Instead, Moses struck the rock twice. Water came out abundantly, and the congregation drank. But the LORD was displeased that Moses, in striking the rock, did not hallow the LORD in the presence of Israel. Therefore, the LORD declared that Moses would not bring Israel into the Promise Land.

In Chapter 21, the children of Israel once again spoke against God and Moses, and even called God's provision of manna worthless. Therefore, God sent poisonous snakes against Israel, and many were bitten and died. The Israelites confessed their sin and asked Moses to intercede for them. When Moses did, God instructed him to fashion a bronze serpent on a pole so that anyone who was bitten could look at the bronze serpent and live. This type of atonement which provided healing foreshadowed the ultimate Atonement found in Christ who was lifted up on a cross so that all who would look unto Christ in faith would be saved. (Healing is included as a benefit of salvation.)

Also in Chapter 21, God gave the Israelites military victories over King Sihon and the Amorites and over King Og and the Bashanites. (The reports of what God did in the land of Egypt, especially the parting of the Red Sea, as well as the destruction of Sihon and Og were a testimony to the Canaanite nations of the power of the God of Israel. See Joshua 2:9-10.)

In Chapter 22, King Balak of Moab urged Balaam to speak a curse against Israel. Balaam displeased God by going with the princes of Balak. Therefore, an Angel of the LORD, who was invisible to Balaam but visible to his donkey, stood in a narrow path so that the donkey could not pass by. When Balaam struck his donkey three times, the Angel caused the donkey to speak human words. Then the Angel made Himself visible to Balaam and rebuked him. Thus, Balaam confessed his sin.

In Chapter 25, many Israelite men committed harlotry with the women of Moab, and they were joined to Baal of Peor. Thus they aroused the LORD's anger, and He commanded Moses to hang the offenders. Additionally, a plague came upon Israel so that 24,000 died. The plague ceased when Phinehas, in his zeal for God, made atonement for Israel.

In Chapter 31, God gave Israel a military victory over the Midianites.

Miracles in Joshua

In Chapter 3, when the Israelite priests carrying the ark of God stepped into the Jordan River, "the waters which came from upstream stood still, and rose in a heap very far away....Then the priests who bore the ark of the covenant of the LORD stood firm on dry ground in the midst of the Jordan; and all Israel crossed over on dry ground..." (3:16-17). In verse 10, Joshua told Israel, "By this you shall know that the living God is among you, and that He will without fail drive out from before you the Canaanites...."

In Chapter 6, at God's instruction, Israel marched around the walled city of Jericho once for six days. On the seventh day, Israel marched around Jericho seven times. Upon completion of the seventh lap, the priests blew their trumpets, the people shouted with a great shout, and the city wall fell down flat. Then Israel took the city.

In Chapter 10, the Israelite army fought the five kings of the Amorites and their armies who had attacked Gibeon, a nation with whom Israel had made a covenant of peace. Verses 10-14 say:

> The LORD routed them before Israel...the LORD cast down large hailstones from heaven....There were more who died from the hailstones than the children of Israel killed with the sword." Then Joshua spoke to the LORD in the day when the LORD delivered up the Amorites before the children of Israel, and he said in the sight of Israel: "Sun, stand still over Gibeon; And Moon, in the Valley of Aijalon." So the sun stood still, and the moon stopped, till the people had revenge upon their enemies....So the sun stood still in the midst of heaven, and did not hasten to go down for about a whole day. And there has been no day like that, before it or after it, that the LORD heeded the voice of a man; for the LORD fought for Israel.

Miracles in Judges

In Chapter 6, the Angel of the LORD appeared to Gideon, declaring that God would use Gideon to deliver Israel from the oppression of the Midianites. God confirmed this to Gideon through the sign of the fleece on two consecutive nights. In Chapter 7, "the LORD set every man's sword against his companion throughout the whole camp (of the Midianites); and the army fled....Gideon...routed the whole army" (7:22, 8:12).

In Chapter 13, the Angel of the LORD appeared to Manoah's wife, who was barren, and declared that she would bear a son who would begin to deliver Israel from the Philistines. On the second appearance of the Angel of the LORD to Manoah's wife (Manoah being with her this time), the Angel "did a wondrous thing while Manoah and his wife looked on—it happened as the flame went up toward heaven from the altar—the Angel of the LORD ascended in the flame of the altar!" (13:19-20).

In chapters 14-16, the Spirit of God came upon Sampson and he killed a lion with his hands (14:6), killed thirty Philistines (14:19), broke off the ropes by which he was bound and killed one thousand Philistines with the jawbone of a donkey (15:14-15). When Sampson cried out to God for water, "God split the hollow place...and water came out, and he drank" (15:19). Sampson also broke the seven bowstrings by which he was bound (16:9), and he broke ropes by which he was bound (16:12). Sampson's greatest feat was when he pushed down the pillars of the Philistine temple, killing about three thousand Philistines. He also died in the collapse of the temple.

Miracles in 1 Samuel

In Chapter 5, the Philistine god, Dagon, twice fell and broke in pieces while in the presence of the ark of God. Also, "the hand of the LORD was heavy on the people of Ashdod, and He ravaged them and struck them with tumors" (5:6). Thus the LORD did to all five Philistine cities where the ark of God was carried. After seven months, the Philistines returned the ark of God to Israel so that God would not kill them all. In Chapter 6, God "struck the men of Beth Shemesh because they had looked into the ark of the LORD. He struck fifty thousand and seventy men" (verse 19). In Chapter 7, in response to Samuel's prayer, "the LORD thundered with a loud thunder upon the Philistines that day, and so confused them that they were overcome before Israel" (verse 10). In Chapter 12, Samuel petitioned the LORD in the presence of Israel for thunder and rain as a sign unto Israel that their sin was great in asking for a human king. Verse 18 says, "So Samuel called to the LORD, and the LORD sent thunder and rain that day; and all the people greatly feared the LORD and Samuel." In Chapter 14, Jonathan and his armorbearer killed twenty Philistines in half an acre of land, for Jonathan, in faith, declared, "nothing restrains the LORD from saving by many or by few" (verse 6). Then God caused a severe trembling in the camp of the Philistines, "so that every man's sword was against his neighbor, and there was very great confusion.…. So the LORD saved Israel that day" (verses 20, 23). In Chapter 17, God guided a stone from the sling of young David, and it struck and killed the Philistine champion warrior, Goliath; this emboldened the previously fearful Israelites to defeat the Philistines that day.

Miracles in 2 Samuel

In Chapter 5, the LORD created a sound in the mulberry trees at Rephaim as a sign to King David to attack the Philistines. The LORD gave Israel victory. In Chapter 6, the LORD killed Uzzah for touching the ark of the LORD.

Miracles in 1 Kings

In Chapter 13, a man of God prophesied against an altar, saying that a future king, Josiah, would sacrifice the priests of the high places on that altar; a sign confirming the prophesy would be that the altar would split apart and its ashes would pour out. When wicked King Jeroboam heard the prophesy, he stretched out his hand, saying, "Arrest him." Suddenly, Jereboam's hand withered. Then the altar split apart, and the ashes poured out. At Jeroboam's request, the man of God prayed, and God graciously restored Jeroboam's hand. But the man of God ate and drank in that land, which God forbade him to do, so a prophet prophesied to him that he would die. Soon thereafter, a lion killed the man of God.

Chapters 17-19 contain several amazing miracles. In Chapter 17, the prophet Elijah pronounced to wicked King Ahab, "There shall not be dew nor rain these years, except at my word" (verse 1). Then God told Elijah to hide himself at the Brook Cherith, and God commanded ravens to bring Elijah bread and meat in the morning and in the evening. When the brook dried up, God told Elijah to go to Zarephath where God commanded a widow to provide for him. Though the widow and her son had only a little jar of oil and a handful of flour, God multiplied the oil and flour so that they did not deplete until rain came again. Then the widow's son died. Thus Elijah stretched himself out on the child three times, and prayed, and:

the LORD heard the voice of Elijah; and the soul of the child came back to him, and he revived....Then the woman said to Elijah, "Now by this I know that you are a man of God, and that the word of the LORD in your mouth is the truth" (verses 22, 24).

In Chapter 18, Elijah called for a contest on Mt. Carmel between the LORD (represented by Elijah) and Baal (represented by 450 prophets of Baal and 400 prophets of Asherah). King Ahab and all Israel were in attendance. Elijah proposed that two altars be built; he said, "the God who answers by fire, He is God" (verse 24). The prophets of Baal desperately petitioned their impotent god, Baal, all day, but no one answered. Then Elijah, after soaking his altar with water, petitioned the LORD. Suddenly,

the fire of the LORD fell and consumed the burnt sacrifice, and the wood and the stones and the dust, and it licked up the water that was in the trench. Now when all the people saw it, they fell on their faces; and they said, "The LORD, He is God! The LORD, He is God!"

At Elijah's command, all the prophets of Baal were executed. Elijah then prophesied to Ahab that rain would quickly come, ending the three and one-half year drought. Elijah prayed, and God caused a "heavy rain." When "the hand of the LORD came upon Elijah," he supernaturally outran Ahab's chariot.

In Chapter 19, when Elijah fled from Jezebel, an angel provided Elijah with a cake and water to sustain him for his long journey. When Elijah was in a cave at Mt. Horeb, the LORD passed by, and a great wind tore into the mountain; then an earthquake occurred; then a fire. The LORD's presence was not found in these events, but the LORD spoke in a still, small voice. He instructed Elijah to go and anoint three people, two to be kings and one to be the prophet who would replace him.

In Chapter 22, wicked King Ahab of Israel recruited King Jehoshaphat of Judah to help him fight the Syrians at Ramoth Gilead. The prophets, about 400 of them, were in unison to encourage the king to go and fight. But Jehoshaphat wanted to hear from a prophet of the LORD. So Micaiah, a prophet of the LORD, said:

I saw the LORD sitting on His throne, and all the host of heaven standing by, on His right hand and on His left. And the LORD said,

"Who will persuade Ahab to go up, that he may fall at Ramoth Gilead?"...a spirit came forward and stood before the LORD, and said, "I will persuade him...I will go out and be a lying spirit in the mouth of all his prophets." And the LORD said, "You shall persuade him, and also prevail. Go out and do so."

Thus, the king of Israel put Micaiah in prison. Then the two kings and their armies went to fight the Syrians in Ramoth Gilead. Verse 34 says, "Now a certain man drew a bow at random, and struck the king of Israel between the joints of his armor." So the king died, as Micaiah had prophesied.

Miracles in 2 Kings

In Chapter 1, on two occasions, Elijah called down fire from heaven to consume a captain and his fifty men.

In Chapter 2, Elijah struck the waters of the Jordan River, and "it was divided this way and that," so that Elijah and Elisha "crossed over on dry ground." Then "a chariot of fire appeared with horses of fire, and separated the two of them; and Elijah went up by a whirlwind into heaven." Then Elisha struck the water with Elijah's mantle, and said, "Where is the LORD God of Elijah?" Suddenly, the water "was divided this way at that." Then men informed Elisha that the water of the city was bad, and the ground was barren. Elisha told them to bring him a new bowl with salt in it. He cast the salt at the source of the water and said, "Thus says the LORD: 'I have healed this water; from it there shall be no more death or barrenness.'" The water was healed. Then some youths mocked Elisha. He pronounced a curse on them in the name of the LORD, and two bears mauled forty-two of the youths.

In Chapter 3, King Jehoshaphat and two other kings marched for seven days, but they found no water. They visited Elisha, and he requested the presence of a musician. When the musician played, "the hand of the LORD came upon" Elisha and he instructed them to make the valley full of ditches. He prophesied that there would be no rain, yet the LORD would fill the ditches with water. The LORD would also deliver the Moabites into their hands. In the morning, water filled the ditches; they also defeated the Moabites.

In Chapter 4, a widow of the wives of the sons of the prophets told Elisha that the creditor threatened to take her two sons to be slaves. All she owned was a jar of oil. Elisha told her to borrow many jars from neighbors, and then pour the oil into those jars. The LORD multiplied the oil so that when the last jar was full, the oil depleted. She sold the oil, payed the debt, and lived on the extra income.

Elisha prophesied to the Shunammite woman that in about a year, she would give birth to a son. So it happened. Some years later, the son died. Elisha prayed to the LORD, lay on the child twice, and the child rose from the dead!

A pot of stew was inedible. Elisha put flour in the pot, and thus nothing harmful was found in the pot.

When a visitor brought Elisha twenty loaves of barley bread and newly ripened grain, Elisha said to set the donated food before the 100 men that they may eat, and that there would be leftovers. The bread and grain multiplied so that they ate, and had leftovers.

In Chapter 5, Naaman the Syrian was healed of leprosy after he dipped seven times in the Jordan River at the word of Elisha. Naaman said, "Indeed, *now I know* that there is no God in all the earth, except in Israel" (verse 15). When Elisha's servant, Gehazi, greedily asked for and received gifts from Naaman, Elisha, by the Spirit of God, knew of this act of deceit and pronounced that leprosy would cling to Gehazi and his descendants forever. Immediately, Gehazi was struck with leprosy.

In Chapter 6, one of the sons of the prophets lost a borrowed ax head in the water. Elisha threw a stick in the water where the ax head fell in, and "he made the iron float."

The king of Syria repeatedly made war plans against Israel, yet each time Elisha supernaturally knew of the plans and warned the Israelite king so that he avoided being ambushed. So the king of Syria sent a great army, with horses and chariots, to surround Dothan where Elisha resided. When Elisha's servant saw the Syrian army, he was afraid. So Elisha prayed to the LORD to open the eyes of her servant, so "the LORD opened the eyes of the young man, and he saw. And behold, the mountain was full of horses and chariots of fire all around Elisha." At the request of Elisha, the LORD struck the Syrian army with blindness. Elisha led them to Samaria, where the Syrian army was fed, then sent home.

Then, Syria besieged Samaria, so there was a great famine in Samaria. The king of Israel blamed Elisha, and plotted to kill him. Elisha supernaturally knew of this plot. In Chapter 7, Elisha prophesied,

"Tomorrow about this time a seah of fine flour shall be sold for a shekel, and two seahs of barley for a shekel, at the gate of Samaria." An officer of the king expressed his doubt in Elisha's prophesy. Elisha replied, "In fact, you shall see it with your eyes, but you shall not eat of it." When four leprous Samarians went to surrender to the army of the Syrians, they found the Syrian camp abandoned, but their tents, with food and spoil, were left intact. The Lord had caused the Syrians to hear the noise of chariots and horses, and they assumed that Israel had hired other nations to help them. So the lepers notified the king of Israel. The Israelites went and plundered the tents of the Syrians, and "a seah of fine flour was sold for a shekel, and two seahs of barley for a shekel, according to the word of the LORD" (verse 16). The king's officer saw this miraculous turn of events with his eyes, but then he was trampled in the gate, in fulfillment of Elisha's prophesy.

In Chapter 8, Elisha prophesied to the Shunammite woman that the LORD had called for a famine in the land for seven years, and so she should stay elsewhere. His words came to pass. In Chapter 13, Elisha prophesied to King Joash of Israel about the victory they would have over the Syrians. Then, Elisha died and was buried. Sometime later, they put another dead man in the tomb of Elisha. When the dead man "touched the bones of Elisha, he revived and stood on his feet."

In Chapter 17:25, God sent lions into Samaria who killed some of the inhabitants because they had not feared the LORD. Chapters 18-19 contain the blasphemous words spoken by the Assyrian leaders against the LORD. Thus, in accordance with Isaiah's prophesy, an angel of the LORD killed 185,000 men in the camp of the Assyrians. Then Sennacherib was murdered by his own sons (Chapter 19).

In Chapter 20, Isaiah prophesied to King Hezekiah that God would heal him, giving him fifteen more years of life. A lump of figs was placed on Hezekiah's boil, and he recovered. Furthermore, Isaiah prophesied that God would deliver Hezekiah and that city from the hand of the king of Assyria. The sign that God would do these things was that the shadow on the sundial went backward ten degrees, as Hezekiah had requested.

Miracles in 2 Chronicles

In Chapter 14, a million man Ethiopian army came against Judah. Asa, Judah's God-fearing king, cried out to the LORD:

> LORD, it is nothing for You to help, whether with many or with those who have no power; help us, O LORD our God, for we rest on You, and in Your name we go against this multitude. O LORD, you are our God; do not let man prevail against You!" So the LORD struck the Ethiopians before Asa and Judah, and the Ethiopians fled.... So the Ethiopians were overthrown, and they could not recover, for they were broken before the LORD and His army" (verses 11-13)

In Chapter 20, three kings and their armies came against Judah. Note the response of Jehoshaphat, Judah's God-fearing king:

> (He) set himself to seek the LORD, and proclaimed a fast throughout all Judah. So Judah gathered together to ask help from the LORD; and from all the cities of Judah they came to seek the LORD.... (Jehoshaphat prayed) "O our God, will You not judge them? For we have no power against this great multitude that is coming against us; nor do we know what to do, but our eyes are upon You." ...Then the Spirit of the LORD came upon Jahaziel...and he said, "Thus says the LORD to you, 'Do not be afraid nor be dismayed because of this great multitude, for the battle is not yours, but God's....You will not need to fight this battle. Position yourselves, stand still and see the salvation of the LORD, who is with you....'" (verses 3-17)

The next day, when those who went before the Judean army began to sing to the LORD and praise Him, the LORD set ambushes against the enemies of Judah, and the enemies were defeated—they killed one another. The Judean army spend three days collecting all the spoil.

In Chapter 26, after many years of enjoying the LORD's favor and prosperity, Uzziah, King of Judah, became prideful. When he became angry with eighty-one priests, who were justly rebuking him, "leprosy broke out on his forehead...the LORD had struck him" (verses 19-20). He remained a leper until his death.

Miracles in Ezekiel

Ezekiel had amazing visions of the glory of God in chapters 1 and 8. Chapter 8, verse 3 says, "the Spirit lifted me up between earth and heaven, and brought me in visions of God to Jerusalem…" In Chapter 37, Ezekiel had a vision of a valley of dry bones being clothed in skin and coming back to life by the Spirit of God as Ezekiel prophesied. In Chapter 47, Ezekiel had a vision of a river of life flowing from the temple, imparting life to every living thing that it touched. Similar imagery is found in Revelation 22:1-2.

Miracles in Daniel

In Chapter 3, Nebuchadnezzar, king of Babylon, threw three Hebrew young men into a fiery furnace because they did not worship his idol. When Nebuchadnezzar looked into the furnace, he said:

> "I see four men loose, walking in the midst of the fire; and they are not hurt, and the form of the fourth is like the Son of God."…
> they saw these men on whose bodies the fire had no power; the hair of their head was not singed nor were their garments affected, and the smell of fire was not on them. Nebuchadnezzar spoke, saying, "Blessed be the God of Shadrach, Meshach, and Abed-Nego…there is no other God who can deliver like this." Then the king promoted Shadrach, Meshach, and Abed-Nego in the province of Babylon (verses 25-30).

In Chapter 6, when Daniel was cast into the lion's den "because he believed in his God" (verse 23) and thus refused to worship King Darius, God sent His angel and shut the mouths of the lions so that they did not hurt him.

Miracles in Jonah

When Jonah disobeyed God's command to go to Nineveh and preach His word to its citizens, God sent a storm to trouble the ship carrying Jonah. When Jonah was thrown overboard:

> the sea ceased from its raging. Then the men feared the LORD exceedingly, and offered a sacrifice to the LORD and took vows.

Now the LORD had prepared a great fish to swallow Jonah. And Jonah was in the belly of the fish three days and three nights (1:15-17)....So the LORD spoke to the fish, and it vomited Jonah onto dry land.

Conclusion

In reflecting upon the numerous and diverse miracles of the Old Testament, we see that God is not detached, uninvolved, or uncaring in regard to the world and its inhabitants whom He created. Instead, God is intricately involved, to the degree that "in Him we live and move and have our being" (Acts 17:28). God has manifested His power throughout history to reveal Himself, His holy ways, and His plan of redemption which ultimately is found through faith in Christ. May today's church meditate upon the miracles of the Bible, so that we will believe God to manifest His power through us, and make His gospel known, revered, and embraced in all the world.

My Parting Exhortation

A carpenter has a construction job to do. But his main tool, his hammer (a perfectly capable hammer), remains in his toolbox. He realizes that construction needs to take place—he has committed to do the job and others are relying on him, but his hammer does not do anything. It lies idly in the toolbox. Why? Because the carpenter has not picked up the hammer. Would it not be ridiculous for the carpenter to place the blame for the lack of construction on the hammer for its not taking initiative and doing the work? Obviously, only when the carpenter picks up the hammer and uses it correctly does construction occur.

The Word of God (the Bible) is like the carpenter's hammer. In Jeremiah 23:29, the LORD said to Jeremiah, "Is not My word like a...hammer that breaks the rock in pieces?" The Word of God is a divinely inspired instrument, a tool, intended for our constant use. But a Bible that remains on a shelf (rather than its contents being absorbed through our eyes and ears, residing in our hearts, and confessed by our mouths throughout the day) is like a hammer that remains in a toolbox—it is essentially idle and ineffective. Some people who need healing, strength, and blessing remain spiritually idle. They may say a prayer on occasion, they may read a few verses each day, but they spend the high majority of their time engaged in secular activities that produce no divine spiritual power or blessing. They may say they are waiting on God, but actually God is waiting on them. Believers should make full use of the Word of God; it is a priceless gift to us from our Lord. We must know the Word, obey the Word, speak the Word, sing hymns about the Word (Col. 3:16), meditate upon the Word day and night (Josh. 1:8, Ps. 1:2), praise the Word (Ps. 56:4, 10), memorize the Word, hide the Word in our hearts (Ps. 119:11), remind God of His Word (Is. 43:26), and share the Word with others (Mk. 16:15; Col. 3:16). We must make God's Word the basis for our thoughts and speech all the day (Ps. 119:97). If we truly love God, then we must love His Word, for He has magnified His Word above all His name (Ps. 138:2). Through the Lord Jesus Christ, who is the Word made flesh, God has made available all we need that pertains to life and godliness (2 Pet. 1:3). We, the church, need to abide in Jesus and thus bear His fruit, especially His love. And we, the church, need to wholeheartedly follow Jesus' evangelistic model—to proclaim and demonstrate with power the kingdom of God here on earth. God bless you!

Endnotes

Chapter 1—Proclamation and Demonstration

1   John Wimber with Kevin Springer, *Power Healing* (San Francisco: Harper & Row, 1987) 41.
2   John Wimber with Kevin Springer, *Power Evangelism* (Ventura, CA: Regal, 2009) 30.

Chapter 2—Divine Healing and Health in the Old Testament

3   F. F. Bosworth, *Christ the Healer.* (Fleming H. Revell., Grand Rapids, MI. 1924) 79-80.
4   *Webster's American Dictionary*, Second College Edition, (Random House, Inc. 2000) 186.
5   James Strong, LL.D., S.T.D. *The New Strongs' Exhaustive Concordance of the Bible. Machela* (Thomas Nelson Publishers, Nashville, 1984) 961, 64.
6   T. L. Osborn, *Healing the Sick* (Harrison House, Inc., Tulsa, OK, 1977) 81-82.
7   James Strong, LL.D., S.T.D. *The New Strongs' Exhaustive Concordance of the Bible. Rapha*
    480, 110.
8   James Grant, in conversation with me.
9   F. F. Bosworth, *Christ the Healer*, 92, 118-119.

Chapter 3—Healing throughout Church History

[10] Adoniram Judson Gordon, *The Ministry of Healing—Miracles of Cure in All Ages* (Forgotten Books, www.peterwade.com, 2006).

[11] Ibid., 59-60.

[12] Ibid., 61.

[13] Ibid., 62-63.

[14] Ibid., 69-70.

[15] Ibid., 72-73.

[16] Ibid., 79-80.

[17] Ibid., 80-84

[18] Ibid., 89-91.

[19] Ibid., 91.

[20] Ibid., 92.

[21] Ibid., 93-94.

[22] Ibid., 95.

[23] Ibid., 98-99.

[24] Ibid., 101-102.

[25] Ibid., 108.

[26] Ibid., 109-110.

[27] Ibid., 113-114.

[28] Ibid., 119.

[29] Ibid., 126.

[30] Ibid., 120.

[31] Ibid., 122.

[32] Ibid., 122-123.

[33] Ibid., 124-125.

[34] Ibid., 175-178.

[35] Ibid., 180-182.

[36] Ibid., 184-185.

[37] Ibid., 187-191.

[38] Reuben Archer Torrey, *Divine Healing: Does God Perform Miracles Today?* (Fleming H. Revell Co., 1924) 18-20.

[39] Adoniram Judson Gordon, *The Ministry of Healing—Miracles of Cure in All Ages*, 224-225.

Chapter 4—Atonement

[40] F. F. Bosworth, *Christ the Healer.*

41 Niels-erik A. Andreasen, "Atonement/Expiation in the Old Testament" in W. E. Mills (ed.), *Mercer Dictionary of the Bible* (Mercer University Press, 1990)

42 Kenneth D. Mulzac, "Atonement," *Eerdman's Dictionary of the Bible* (William B. Eerdman's Publishing Col, Grand Rapids, MI., Cambridge, U.K., 2000) 127-128.

43 James Grant, in conversation with me.

44 James Grant gave me this insight on the double cure in Exodus 24.

45 James Grand, in conversation with me.

46 Robin J. DeWitt Nkauth, "Jubilee, Year of," *Eerdman's Dictionary of the Bible*, 743.

47 James Strong, LL.D., S.T.D., "Griefs," *The New Strongs' Exhaustive Concordance of the Bible* (Thomas Nelson Publishers, Nashville, 1984) 436, 39.

48 The Assemblies of God General Presbytery, August 20, 1974. *Divine Healing, An Integral Part of the Gospel,* (Gospel Publishing House, Springfield, Missouri) 5.

49 James Strong, LL.D., S.T.D., "Sorrows," *The New Strongs' Exhaustive Concordance of the Bible*, 66, 997.

50 F. F. Bosworth, *Christ the Healer*, 37.

51 Ibid., 24-25, 27, 29, 35, 41-44.

52 Adapted from F.F. Bosworth's *Christ the Healer*, with some changes, deletions, and additions on my part. 41-44.

53 H. A. Maxwell Whyte *The Power of the Blood* 11-12.

54 Andrew Murray, *Divine Healing* (Whitaker House, 1982) 8, 9, 23, 24.

55 Ibid., 86-87.

56 Ibid., 87-88.

57 Norman Grubb, *Rees Howells Intercessor* (CLC Publications, 1952) 84-85.

58 Adoniram Judson. Gordon, *The Ministry of Healing*, from Chapter 2.

59 T. J. McCrossan, M.D., *Bodily Healing and the Atonement,* (First published in 1930. Reedited by
Roy Hicks, D.D., and Kenneth Hagin, D.D.; Rhema Bible Church, Tulsa, OK, 1982) 27-29.

60 *John G. Lake: His Life, His Sermons, His Boldness of Faith* (Kenneth Copeland Publications, Fort
Worth, Texas, 1994) 176.

61 E. W. Kenyon, *Jesus the Healer* (Kenyon's Gospel Publishing Society, 2010) 17.
62 T. L. Osborn, *Healing the Sick,* 62–64, 83.
63 F. F. Bosworth, *Christ the Healer,* 49–50, 87–88.
64 Ibid., 55.
65 T. L. Osborn, *Healing the Sick,* 34, 64–65.

Chapter 5—F. F. Bosworth, a Pioneer Healing Evangelist

66 Eunice M. Perkins, *Joybringer Bosworth: His Life's Story* (1921).
67 Roberts Liardon, *God's Generals: The Healing Evangelists* (Whitaker House, 2011).
68 Ibid., 7.
69 Ibid., 7.
70 Gordon P. Gardiner, *Out of Zion Into All the World* (Shippensburg, PA: Companion Press, 1990), 5–7, 334.
71 *Bosworth's Life Story: The Life Story of Evangelist F. F. Bosworth,* 3, 7–8.
72 Roberts Liardon, *God's Generals: The Healing Evangelists,* 110.
73 *Bosworth's Life Story: The Life Story of Evangelist F. F. Bosworth,* 10.
74 Ibid., 12–14.
75 Ibid., 3.
76 F. F. Bosworth, *Christ the Healer,*176–177.
77 Perkins, *Joybringer Bosworth,* 121–122.
78 Ibid., 124–129.
79 Ibid., 129–133.
80 Ibid., 154–171
81 F. F. Bosworth, *Christ the Healer,* 240.
82 Eunice M. Perkins, *Joybringer Bosworth: His Life's Story,* 240–242.
83 Ibid., 210–211.
84 Ibid., 173.
85 Ibid., 175–177.
86 Ibid., 178.
87 Ibid., 200–226.
88 Ibid., 226–227.
89 Roberts Liardon, *God's Generals: The Healing Evangelists,* 38–39.
90 "Christ the Healer," www.healingandrevival.com.
91 F. F. Bosworth, Wikipedia, and F. F. Bosworth, *Christ the Healer,* 245.
92 F. F. Bosworth, *Christ the Healer,* 245–246.

Chapter 6—Healings in Matthew's Gospel

93 F. F. Bosworth, *Christ the Healer*, 92-93.
94 Ibid., 50.
95 T. L. Osborn, *Healing the Sick*,67-69.
96 James Grant, in conversation with me.
97 Henry L. Carrigan, Jr., "Blasphemy," *Eerdman's Dictionary of the Bible*, 191.
98 Adoniram Judson Gordon, *The Ministry of Healing—Miracles of Cure in All Ages*, 23.
99 Pikeville Cut-Through, Wikipedia.

Chapter 7—Healing Evangelists and Testimonies—Part 1

100 George Stormont, *Smith Wigglesworth, A Man Who Walked with God*. (Harrison House, Tulsa, 2009); Julian Wilson, *Wigglesworth The Complete Story: A New Biography Of The 'Apostle Of Faith' Smith Wigglesworth* (Biblica, 2004) 82-83.
101 Stanley Howard Frodsham, *Smith Wigglesworth: Apostle of Faith* (1948) 44-45.
102 Don Stewart, *Only Believe: An Eyewitness Account of the Great Healing Revivals of the 20th Century*. (Revival Press, and Imprint of Destiny Image Publishers, 1999) 12-13.
103 Lester Sumrall, *The Life Story of Lester Sumrall* (Green Forest, AR: New Leaf Press, 1993) 28.
104 The information for this section came from: www. HealingandRevival.com. 2004; "John G. Lake," Wikipedia; *John G. Lake: His Life, His Sermons, His Boldness of Faith* (Kenneth Copeland Publications, Fort Worth, Tx., 1994) xiii-xxxi.
105 *John G. Lake: His Life, His Sermons, His Boldness of Faith*, xxi.
106 Gordon Lindsay, in collaboration with William Branham, *William Branham, A Man Sent From God* (Published by William Branham, Jeffersonville, Indiana) 94-96.
107 Ibid., 86-87.
108 D. J. Wilson, "Branham, William Marrion," *The New International Dictionary of Pentecostal and Charismatic Movements, Revised and Expanded Edition*, 440-441.
109 *William M. Branham*—Wikipedia
110 Don Stewart, *Only Believe*, 42.

111 *William M. Branham*—Wikipedia.

112 Ibid.

113 *Healer and Prophet,* www.healingandrevival.com.

114 *A. A. Allen,* Wikipedia.

115 *The Miracle Man,* www.healingandrevival.com.

116 Don Stewart, *Only Believe,* 75.

117 R. W. Schambach, *Miracles* (Destiny Image Publishers, 2009) 103-108.

118 Ibid., 94.

Chapter 8—The Healings of Acts

119 Timothy B. Cargal, "Proconsul," *Eerdman's Dictionary of the Bible,* 1085.

120 F. F. Bosworth, *Christ the Healer,* 67-68.

121 Ibid., 50-51.

122 Ibid., 51.

123 Bill Johnson and Randy Clark, *The Essential Guide to Healing: Equipping All Christians to Pray for the Sick* (Chosen Books, 2011) 21.

Chapter 9—Healing Evangelists and Testimonies—Part 2

124 Chappell, P. G., "Roberts, Granville Oral," *The New International Dictionary of Pentecostal and Charismatic Movements, Revised and Expanded Edition,* 1024-1025.

125 Oral Roberts, *Expect A Miracle: My Life and Ministry. An Autobiography* (Thomas Nelson Publishers, Nashville, 1995).

126 Chappell, P. G. "Roberts, Granville, Oral," *The New International Dictionary of Pentecostal and Charismatic Movements, Revised and Expanded Edition,*1024-1025.

127 Oral Roberts, *Expect A Miracle,* 113-118.

128 *I Believe in Miracles,* www.healingandrevival.com; Jamie Buckingham, *Daughter of Destiny: Kathryn Kuhlman.* (Bridge-Logos Publishers, 1999); *Kathryn Kuhlman,* Wikipedia.

129 Kathryn Kuhlman, *I Believe in Miracles,* 31-38.

130 Ibid., 11-22.

131 T. L. Osborn, *Healing the Sick.*

132 Ibid., 328-332.

133 Ibid., 393-395.

134 Jennifer Leclaire, "Evangelist R. W. Shambach Passes at 85," *CharismaNews.*

135 R. W. Schambach, *Miracles*; 149-151.

136 Ibid., 159-161.

Chapter 10—Scriptures Related to Healing in the Epistles

137 T. J. McCrossan, M.D., *Bodily Healing and the Atonement,* 35, 37

138 Perkins, *Joybringer Bosworth,* 202-206.

139 Ibid., 30-31.

140 F. F. Bosworth, *Christ the Healer,*40.

141 Eunice M. Perkins, *Joybringer Bosworth: His Life's Story* (1921), 209.

142 Adoniram Judson Gordon, *The Ministry of Healing—Miracles of Cure in All Ages,* 32.

143 F. F. Bosworth, *Christ the Healer,*133-137.

144 T. J. McCrossan, M.D., *Bodily Healing and the Atonement,* 33.

145 C. P. Wagner, "Wimber, John," *The New International Dictionary of Pentecostal and Charismatic Movements, Revised and Expanded Edition,* 1199-1200. Also, Wimber with Springer, *Power Healing,* xv-55.

146 John Wimber, *Power Evangelism,* 53-55.

147 Jack Deere, *Surprised by the Power of the Spirit* (Zondervan Publishing House, 1993) 33-41.

Chapter 11—Healing Evangelists and Testimonies—Part 3

148 Reinhard Bonnke, *Living a Life of Fire, an Autobiography* (Harvester Services Inc., 2010)
238-262.

149 Ibid., 262.

150 H. V. Synan, "Bonnke, Reinhard Willi Gottried," *The New International Dictionary of Pentecostal and Charismatic Movements, Revised and Expanded Edition,*438-439; Also *Reinhard Bonnke,* Wikipedia.

151 Reinhard Bonnke, *Living a Life of Fire,* 557-559.

152 G. W. Gohr, "Hinn, Benedictus," *The New International Dictionary of Pentecostal and Charismatic Movements, Revised and Expanded Edition,*713-714.

153 *God's Healing Touch* video (Benny Hinn Ministries, 2003).

154 T. L. Osborn, *Healing the Sick.* 83.

Chapter 12—The Healings of Luke's Gospel

155 James Grant helped me understand the spiritual application of the law of entropy.

156 Roberts Liardon, *God's Generals*, 116-118. Also Don Stewart, *Only Believe*, 94-98.

157 James Strong, LL.D., S.T.D. *The New Strongs' Exhaustive Concordance of the Bible.* "Save," 913.

158 James Grant, in conversation with me.

159 Kenneth E. Hagin, *The Believer's Authority.* (Kenneth Hagin Ministries, Tulsa, OK, 1985).

160 James Grant, in conversation with me.

161 James Strong, LL.D., S.T.D. *The New Strongs' Exhaustive Concordance of the Bible.* "pestilence,"
817, 29.

162 I credit James Grant with assisting me concerning some of the content of this section.

Chapter 13—The Baptism in the Holy Spirit

Chapter 14—Confession

163 HELPS Word-studies 1987, 2011 by Helps Ministries, Inc./ HelpsBible.com

164 F. F. Bosworth, *Christ the Healer*, 142.

165 Ibid., 145-150.

166 Don Gossett and E. W. Kenyon, *The Power of Your Words*, 28, 49, 50, 56.

167 T. L. Osborn, *Healing the Sick,* 54-57.

168 Don Gossett and E. W. Kenyon, *The Power of Your Words* (Whitaker House, New Kensington, PA and Kenyon Gospel Publishing Society, Lynnwood, Washington, 1977, 1981) 27.

169 F. F. Bosworth, *Christ the Healer*, 145-150.

Chapter 15—Christians in the New Testament Who Were Not Healed

170 John Wimber and Kevin Springer, *Power Healing,*149-152.

[171] F. F. Bosworth, *Christ the Healer*, 121, 124.

[172] Ibid., 166–191.

[173] T. L. Osborn, *Healing the Sick*. 63.

[174] I credit James Grant with contributing some of the content and writing of this chapter, especially "The Case of Job."

Appendix

AN OVERVIEW OF THE HEALING MINISTRY OF JESUS

Description	Matthew	Mark	Luke	John
1. Man with an unclean spirit		1:23-25	4:33-35	
2. Peter' mother-in-law	8:14-15	1:30-31	4:38-39	
3. Multitudes	8:16-17	1:32-34	4:40-41	
4. Many demons		1:39		
5. Leper	8:2-4	1:40-42	5:12-13	
6. Paralytic	9:2-8	2:3-5	5:17-25	
7. Man with withered hand	12:9-13	3:1-5	6:6-10	
8. Multitudes	12:15-16	3:10-11		
9. Gerasenes demoniac	8:28-32	5:1-13	8:26-33	

Description	Matthew	Mark	Luke	John
10. Jairus' daughter	9:18-19; 23-25	5:22-24; 35-43	8:41-42; 49-56	
11. Woman with issue of blood	9:20-22	5:25-34	8:43-48	
12. A few sick people	13:58	6:5-6		
13. Multitudes	14:34-36	6:55-56		
14. Syrophoehnician's daughter	15:22-28	7:24-30		
15. Deaf and dumb man		7:32-35		
16. Blind man		8:22-26		
17. Child with evil spirit	17:14-18	9:14-27	9:38-43	
18. Blind Bartimaeus	20:30-34	10:46-52	18:35-43	
19. Centurion's servant	8:5-13		7:2-10	
20. Two blind men	9:27-30			
21. Dumb demoniac	9:32-33			
22. Blind & dumb demoniac	12:22		11:14	
23. Multitudes	4:23-25		6:17-19	
24. Multitudes	9:35			

Description	Matthew	Mark	Luke	John
25. Multitudes	11:2-5		7:20-23	
26. Multitudes	14:14		9:11	6:02
27. Great Multitudes	15:30			
28. Great Multitudes	19:02			
29. Blind & Lame in Temple	21:14			
30. Widow's son			7:11-15	
31. Mary Magdalene & others			8:02	
32. Crippled woman			13:10-13	
33. Man with dropsy			14:1-4	
34. Ten lepers			17:11-19	
35. Servant's ear			22:49-51	
36. Multitudes			5:15	
37. Various persons			13:32	
38. Nobelman's son				4:46-53
39. Invalid				5:2-9

Description	Matthew	Mark	Luke	John
40. Man born blind				9:1-7
41. Lazarus				11:1-44
42. And Many More				John 21:25

Taken from Power Healing, by John Wimber and Kevin Springer. Appendix D. HarperSanFrancisco. 1987.

Printed in the United States
By Bookmasters